John Knox – Democrat

JOHN KNOX
DEMOCRAT

RODERICK GRAHAM

ROBERT HALE · LONDON

© Roderick Graham 2001
First published in Great Britain 2001

ISBN 0 7090 6984 7

Robert Hale Limited
Clerkenwell House
Clerkenwell Green
London EC1R 0HT

A catalogue record for this book is available from the British Library

2 4 6 8 10 9 7 5 3 1

Set in Sabon by
Derek Doyle & Associates, Liverpool.
Printed by
St Edmundsbury Press, Bury St Edmunds
and bound by
Woolnough Bookbinding Limited, Irthlingborough

To Fiona

Contents

Acknowledgements

The author would like to thank the staff at the following institutions:
Staff at the Edinburgh Room, Central Library, Edinburgh.
Staff at the Scottish Department, Central Library, Edinburgh.
Staff at the National Library of Scotland.
Staff at New College Library, University of Edinburgh.
Staff at Edinburgh University Main Library and Special Collections.
Staff at the Mackenzie Medical Centre, Edinburgh.
The Church of Scotland Information Office, George Street Edinburgh.
Dr Brian Hillyard of the National Library of Scotland for advising me on
    Latin translations.
Christine Gascoigne at Special Collections, St Andrews University Library.

Illustrations

Credits

The Scottish National Portrait Gallery: 1,4,7,10,11,16,17,18.
The National Library of Scotland: 20.

All other photographs are from the author's collection.

Prologue

On Monday, 31 May 1982, Pope John Paul II was in procession from Meadowbank Stadium to St Mary's Cathedral in Edinburgh when he made a significant detour. The cavalcade left Princes Street and wound its way up the Mound, which links the Old and New Towns of the city, to the twin towers of the Victorian building that, each year in May, houses the General Assembly of the Church of Scotland. This assembly meets under the chairmanship of the Moderator, appointed annually, who, in a strictly non-hierarchical organization, is the senior representative of the Church of Scotland. In the person of the Right Reverend Professor John McIntyre he was waiting on this evening to greet His Holiness the Pope. At 7 p.m. precisely, for the first time in history, the two heads of their respective churches met and exchanged what were referred to as courtesies. The Moderator then returned to the building behind him and The Pope continued to St Mary's Catholic Cathedral, where he performed the medieval task of presenting the Cathedral with a shoulder blade of St Andrew. The Cathedral of St Andrews had possessed an upper-arm bone, a tooth, several fingers and a knee-cap of the saint, but these relics had been lost during the Reformation. Although a subsequent Moderator visited the Vatican in 1993, the two churches have never again met so formally nor so publicly.

Dominating the courtyard where the two men met is a larger than life-size statue of John Knox, the reformer who was instrumental in founding the present Church of Scotland and ending the ecclesiastical dominion of Rome in Scotland. We can be sure that what he saw taking place beneath his feet, over 400 years after his death, would have horrified him. But there he stands, his left hand clutching a book, presumably the Bible, while his right is raised in mid peroration. Whether he is condemning some error or praising some revisionary effort is left to our imagination.

I like to think he was exhorting his fellow Scotsmen to make greater efforts toward democratic control of their lives.

However, a quick survey of contemporary Scotsmen's opinion of John Knox would give us a picture of a ranting, vain, dogmatic misogynist. All four accusations are totally untrue.

Knox in the pulpit himself criticized his own vehemence, and some thought he might strike the lectern to pieces. But in conversation or even debate, he preferred to use the logic in which he had been trained. It hardly needed a dogmatic tyrant to render Mary, Queen of Scots tearful.

Knox does seem to exhibit a remarkably low level of vanity in refusing a bishopric or advancement in the Church of England, being a reluctant pastor in Frankfurt, and grateful for his replacement as secretary to the Protestant Lords in revolt against the Queen Regent, Mary of Guise. He accepted the position of minister of St Giles in Edinburgh as the rightful place from which to lead the Reformation. There is no doubt that he argued to win, but this was from conviction not vanity. He often said that his greatest ambition was for the peaceful life of a scholar.

His dogma was simply to accept the Bible as literal truth, and to condemn anything man-made imposed on worship. Knox's precept was that a man, any man, should, and could, talk directly to Christ as his saviour, without intercession. This took reform to the gates of revolution and the paradox is that Knox as an older man preached reform to a much younger Establishment.

The accusation of misogyny is based on one (usually unread) tract alone in which he condemns Mary Tudor for replacing the established religion and giving equal power to her husband, a Spaniard. Personally he was thoughtful and understanding in his relationships with women, writing many letters of comfort to them. He married twice and fathered five children, and although we know little of these relationships, they were admired by colleagues. Moreover, he displays great sympathy and remorse for having given his first wife, instead of the calm routine of a peaceful ministry, a life that was often fraught with danger.

He was a self-admitted failure as a diplomat and lacked any sense of guile. His other noticeable lack was that of a sense of humour. When it does briefly appear it is of the bleakest sort and quickly becomes dark irony. Knox was not a clubbable man, nor an entertaining dinner companion. But great men driven to high achievements are frequently poor company.

He maintained that if rulers were unjust, the people had the right to remove them. It was this belief in the rights of the people that was at the root of his achievements, for what Knox did was to give modern Scotland three great foundation stones. They were the Church of Scotland, the acceptance of an obligation to care for the poor and infirm, and the Scottish system of education.

Knox also sowed the seeds for the emergence of a Scottish character that questioned, challenged and enquired. The idea that any Scot can achieve anything and is entitled to question the highest in the land is exemplified in his interviews with Mary, Queen of Scots. While fully aware of the power of his southern neighbour, Knox was very much a European – he lived abroad for over six years – as well as a Scot, but the Europe he lived in was very different from the one we know today.

1   A Pupil in His Place

There are many ways of describing the divisions that define 21st-century Europe. For example, Latin Europe or Northern Europe; inside the European Community or outside it; ex-Warsaw Pact or Nato member – the list of definitions is as long as one wishes it to be. But it can also be defined along religious lines, Protestant, Catholic, Orthodox, or Muslim, and we can quickly sketch the origins of most of these divisions.

Christianity travelled outwards from Jerusalem to be adopted by the Roman emperor Constantine at the start of the fourth century. It then divided into Greek and Latin Christianity when the Emperor Constantine moved his capital to Constantinople in 330. Apart from a brief exile to Ravenna a hundred years later, Rome remained the centre of Catholicism, while Eastern Europe embraced the Orthodox faith emanating from Constantinople. By 609 Islam had been founded and continued to nibble at Eastern Christianity until 1453, when Constantinople itself fell into Islamic hands. In the West, Muslim armies advanced as far as Poitiers in 732, when they were stopped by Charles Martel, falling back to establish a highly civilized and educated state in Spain until their expulsion by Ferdinand and Isabella in 1482.

Roman Catholic Europe then stretched from Lisbon to Warsaw and from Norway to Sicily. Great monarchies ruled Portugal, Spain, France and the Netherlands, England, and Scotland. The Italian Peninsula was a constant maelstrom of warring states, while Central Europe, east of the Rhine and west of the Vistula, was nominally under the overall rule of a Holy Roman Emperor. This empire, founded by Charlemagne in the ninth century, was a federation of Germanic states under the control of their elected emperor, who was, in turn, endorsed and crowned by the Pope. This line of rule was echoed elsewhere, as monarchs were crowned and anointed by bishops, who were the Pope's appointees. Thus in Western Europe secular rule was endorsed by Rome, from where spiritual rule came directly.

Such schools as existed were run by the Church; all Church services were in Latin, as were the first printed books, which did not appear until 1465. All access to God was controlled by the priesthood, who held the awful power of absolution, thus allowing progress from Purgatory to Heaven. Prayer often meant mumbled responses in a language few people understood. There was even a particular demon — Tutivillus — who collected such mumblings and carried them to Hell, where they were registered as a special sin. The laity could pray to saints, who were presumably multilingual, but basically education, civil behaviour and salvation were in the hands of the Roman clergy. And the lessons of scripture were whatever Rome chose to teach. Enquiring and lively minds went into the Church, if they were also docile or ambitious — and into a dungeon if they were neither. Unsurprisingly, obedience was a much valued virtue, since heterodoxy — being off-message — frequently meant torture followed by an agonizing death.

Although the Church was home to many devout and charitable men, as well as to many great scholars, such a narrow focus of power was bound to lead to abuse, and this demonstrated itself in many ways. The upper echelons of the Church often lived a life of luxury equal to that enjoyed by the aristocracy. At the absolute apex of the pyramid was the papacy, beneath which were the cardinals, or 'princes of the Church'. The pyramid widened towards the base with its surfeit of illiterate fat priests tending superstitious and hungry parishioners.

The Church collected tithes (tenths of the parishioner's income) in kind as often as in cash. Burials had to be paid for by even the poorest, while the rich listened uncomfortably to sermons about the camel's difficulty with the eye of the needle. Much of the glory of our medieval church architecture derives from the effect of those sermons, as the rich and powerful bought their way to paradise with chantry chapels and generous endowments. The power of excommunication could lead to earthly rejection of the cruellest kind and the certainty of suffering for eternity in the depths of Hell. Even the poorest churches would have a wall-painting showing the enthusiastic torture of the damned, while access to the delights of Heaven was strictly controlled by the priesthood. Questions by the laity were easily answered by explaining that it was all ordained by the mysterious will of God, as set down in the unreadable Bible.

By the end of the fourteenth century, however, the ice was starting to flex dangerously under this rigid structure. In mid century the outbreak of the Black Death carried off nearly a third of the population, a natural disaster unparalleled until the influenza epidemic of 1918 exceeded even the plague's numbers. Prayers of all sorts were offered to no avail. Extreme religious sects flourished, and Jews were blamed and persecuted, but the horror of the plague continued in spite of the Church's best efforts. Those who survived may have had their lives intact, but their faith in the Church was severely shaken. The prayers of the priesthood must have seemed totally ineffectual. God certainly knew about the suffering, since, after all, Christ was present when the wine changed into his blood during the Mass, and on receiving the host they had all experienced what has been called 'the dry taste of God in their mouths'. There was a mood of questioning and a desire to penetrate the mysteries of the Mass and the teachings of the Roman Church.

This Church itself was now physically divided by the 'Great Schism', in which two rival Popes were supported respectively by the secular powers of France in Avignon and their traditionalist enemies in Rome. Both Popes taught the exclusive truth and the absolute word of God in Latin, still understood only by the priesthood.

This cloud of Latin was about to be dispersed, in England at any rate, by John Wycliffe, described by the nineteenth-century historian Thomas Carlyle as 'the deep-lying tap-root of the whole tree', meaning the Reformation. Wycliffe provided a translation of the Bible into English and recommended a return to studying the scripture, rather than the countless commentaries that had been produced. He was, in fact, building on the foundations already begun by Bradwardine, the fourteenth-century archbishop of Canterbury, who himself had returned to the teachings of St Augustine and the need for grace as a prerequisite for salvation. Wycliffe asserted that it was the right of every man to read the Bible for himself and that wicked kings, popes, and priests should be stripped of power. This was a path that John Knox would later tread.

Wycliffe organized teams of friars that preached against the power of excommunication, the Church's monopoly on salvation and the miracle of bread and wine being turned into actual flesh and blood. This doctrine of transubstantiation asserted that during each celebration of the mass, a miracle took place in which the wine and bread being used by the celebrant actually changed into the blood and flesh of Christ. This miracle was witnessed by the congregation at a distance or from behind a screen. The Church of England would favour consubstantiation in which the wine and bread stood as symbols but no miracle occurred. In the Church of Scotland the congregation share the wine and bread with the minister as an act of fellowship and as a memory of Christ's fellowship with his twelve disciples. Wycliffe's questioning of the transubstantiation miracle was rank heresy. His followers – called Lollards, literally 'mumblers' – were falsely accused of fomenting the English Peasants' Revolt in 1381, but, thanks to protection in high places, he was allowed to die in comparative peace, still railing against the corruption of the papacy. But he had touched a chord and allowed the unthinkable to be debated.

Not so fortunate was Jan Hus in Bohemia, rector of the University of Prague. Though much influenced by Wycliffe, he rejected Wycliffe's denial of transubstantiation (the actual transformation of the wine into blood during the 'miracle' of the mass). Hus also developed the belief in individual salvation by virtue.

Summoned by the Council of Constance in 1415 (itself in existence to try to end the Papal Schism, unsuccessfully as it turned out) to explain himself, Hus was naturally wary about attending and obtained a safe conduct from the Emperor Sigismund. Armed with this guarantee of safety he answered the summons. The safe conduct did him no good at all since he was promptly arrested and burned to death. For good measure at this point the English dug up Wycliffe's bones and threw them into the River Avon. The local rhyme was,

> The Avon to the Severn runs,
> The Severn to the Sea,
> And Wycliffe's dust shall spread abroad
> Wide as the waters be.

Talk of reform was spreading like the waters, too, and by the turn of the fifteenth century a meeting took place in London between Thomas More, King Henry VIII's Catholic chancellor, and a visiting Dutch scholar who was convalescing after a bad bout of lumbago. He was Desiderius Erasmus, who cast the cloak of his humanism across all of Europe. He had studied at Montaigu in France with John Mair, (sometimes Maior or Major), who was to be Knox's teacher. John Mair was a distinguished scholar at the Collège Montaigu, the college pre-eminent in theology at the University of Paris.

The University, at that time, had three colleges, Sorbonne, Navarre and Montaigu. Mair had been a leading figure at the college of Montaigu, which stood near where the present day Pantheon stands. Erasmus had parted company with Mair, finding the academic scholasticism of Paris too narrow. The physical circumstances at Montaigu were severe, with scholars sleeping on the ground among lice and cockroaches. Erasmus is also reputed to have found the food inadequate. Studying and writing in London, Oxford, Paris and Cambridge, he decried some of the most fiercely held tenets of the Church, including selling indulgences (they claimed to guarantee a faster exit from Purgatory), praying to the saints for intercession, going on pilgrimages to venerate relics – he was horrified when shown Thomas Becket's hair shirt at Canterbury – and, obviously, he was opposed to fasting. A vivid demonstration of his liberalism comes when he left his accumulated wealth to the city of Basle to create a *Stiftung*, or charitable foundation, providing not only scholarships for boys, but in a markedly enlightened manner, marriage dowries for poor girls.

To aid study of proper texts he made a fresh translation of the Bible, though still into Latin – his preferred tongue, since few spoke his native Dutch – and used his wit and humour to attack the follies of his day. He wrote advice for young princes advocating moral responsibilities and a short satire, *Julius excluded from Heaven*, in which Pope Julius II himself is barred by St Peter. Even though Julius was dead Erasmus wisely published this anonymously. But totalitarians of all colours are notoriously short of a sense of humour, and eventually he had to flee to Basle, where he later died in July 1536 full of years and honours. There is much in Erasmus that many so-called democratic regimes of today would wish to suppress.

It was becoming more and more difficult for the papacy to keep reform at bay; the once seamless robe of the medieval Church was becoming seriously unstitched. One good tug should part it beyond repair, and Martin Luther gave it that tug.

Luther was a monk, indeed he was sub-prior, of the Augustinian monastery at Wittenberg. As a doctor of theology he lectured in the university and preached in the city church. He believed that man is justified by faith alone, and that grace is obtainable by humility, repentance, and freedom from sin, without the intercession of the Church. This he expounded in the city church in language as sympathetic to his lay listeners as he could muster. Simplicity, not obfuscation, was his aim.

All of this was dangerous enough, but there was not yet an issue that would bring matters to a head. This *casus belli* came from the particularly cynical sale of a special issue of indulgences to finance the rebuilding of St Peter's Basilica in Rome. The dispensation, or rather franchise, to sell these indulgences was bought, after fierce negotiations, by Albert, archbishop of Mainz, with finance provided by the banking house of the Fuggers of Augsburg. Half of the proceeds went to Rome and the other half was split between the archbishop and the Fuggers. It is interesting to note that a bull of Aeneas Sylvius, or Pius II, in 1460, allowed the archbishopric of St Andrews exclusive rights to sell indulgences for the financing of the building of St Salvator's college. The college got two thirds of the sale and one third went to Rome, nominally to finance a crusade against the infidels. In Mainz, however, with rather worse financial terms applying, the sales were made by Archbishop Albert's agent, one Tetzel, in his turn accompanied everywhere by an agent of the Fuggers, bankers who clearly trusted no one.

For Luther this was the straw that broke the camel's back and he drew up his ninety-five theses, or complaints, against the established Church and nailed them to the door of the castle church on 31 October 1517. Knox, three or four years old at this time, in a Scottish lowland farming community, had been conventionally baptized into the Church that Luther was attacking publicly. Nailing the theses to the church door was an accepted procedure for a public notice, and the fact that they were written in a level-headed non-hysterical Latin, not German, meant that they would only be read by churchmen. He pointed out that there was no such thing as a treasury of merit that could be sold off piecemeal by indulgences and that the grace of God was the sole repository of goodness. He also attacked Rome for using untruths to extract money from the poor and credulous, when the institution of the Church itself possessed untold wealth.

But for all his seeming reasonableness, Luther must have known that others had been condemned for attacking the sale of indulgences, and he cannot have been surprised that his theses were rapidly translated into German and circulated widely. Immediately accused of heresy, he published *Resolutions concerning the Virtue of Indulgences*, setting out his case formally, and appeared before the provincial chapter of his order in Heidelberg to make a vigorous defence of his case. He was then summoned to Rome, but managed to have the hearing transferred to Augsburg. Before attending, and perhaps sensing what the outcome might be, he published a *Sermon on the Validity of Excommunication*, arguing that a Christian can only be excommunicated by God. The stakes had risen.

Support for Luther was growing, as can be seen by the fact that his works were burned in Paris, and in Scotland their import was a criminal offence. By the time Knox arrived at St Andrews, some years later, they must have been available clandestinely, since such rigorous banning tends to increase popularity. Luther's circle now included Philip Melanchthon, a scholarly quiet contrast to Luther's sometimes coarse personality. Luther said, 'I am rough, boisterous, stormy and altogether warlike. I am born to fight innumerable monsters and devils, but Master Philip comes along softly and gently with joy, according to the gifts that God has abundantly bestowed upon him.'

In 1520 a papal bull giving notice of excommunication, *Exsurge Domine*, was issued and Luther publicly burnt it, referring now to the Pope as the Antichrist. Pamphlets and tracts poured forth from him as his thinking refined itself.

The Holy Roman Emperor, Charles V, was caught between papal demands from Rome for Luther's trial and his German princes' support for the new order, but in 1521 he listened to the demands from Rome and summoned Luther to be examined at a diet (or parliament) in Worms. Issued with safe conducts from all and sundry, but mindful of their lack of efficacy in the case of Jan Hus, he surrounded himself with supporters acting as bodyguards; so escorted, Luther was cheered along the route before appearing in front of the emperor and the archbishop of Trier. He was told that the Church's authority could not be questioned and therefore he had no option but to recant instantly.

He promised to recant only if his beliefs were disproved by scripture, otherwise he was immovable. '*Hier stehe ich. Ich kann nicht anders* (Here I stand, I can do nothing else)', he stated with startling simplicity. There being no further debate possible with such intransigence and invoking his safe conduct, Luther wisely left to go into hiding in the Wartburg forests. Wisely, since the wrong-footed Emperor Charles issued the Edict of Worms, excommunicating Luther in the strongest terms for heresy and disobedience to established political authority. Charles had unintentionally turned a religious reforming movement into a secular revolution. Nearly forty years later the Queen Regent of Scotland, Mary of Guise, would make the same mistake.

But all was not complete harmony among the reformers, for Erasmus, who 'laid the egg that Luther hatched', was beginning to diverge in view from Luther. Erasmus believed that man's intellect controlled his will, while Luther largely ignored man's will in favour of an all-controlling God. Knox, while not being in sympathy with all of Luther's opinions, would support this latter view in coming years.

Nor was Luther's cause helped when in June 1524 the underlying discontents of the peasantry started to erupt all over Germany. This culminated, in 1525, in a list of Twelve Articles spelling out their demands, and the German Peasants' War began.

Luther was now being tarred with the same brush as the peasants, despite having written *Against the Murdering Hordes of Peasants*, an extremely unpleasant work exhorting the princes to slaughter without mercy. In spite of moderating his views later, he believed the common people had misunderstood his teachings, and never quite trusted to popular support again.

But while unrest and the beginnings of reform were growing in southern Germany, across the border in Switzerland other events were taking place. In the canton of Zurich the Church's business was coming under the scrutiny of Ulrich Zwingli, a canon of the great minster. He had achieved his canonry in spite of preaching for large-scale reforms, mainly as Luther had demanded. Indeed, at this point the two men, who were almost the same age, largely coincided also in thought. Zwingli also held public disputations and by 1525 he was celebrating communion in fellowship with other worshippers in a much reformed Church.

Throughout Zurich walls were painted white, statues and decorations vanished, altars made way for communion tables, and music ceased. The Bible and catechism appeared in German and Church courts of morals were set up. Local congregations held sway over local matters and higher affairs were dealt with by an annual synod. By and large the hierarchy of the Roman Church was giving way to a more democratic Church that spread rapidly to other cantons, such as Basel, under the leadership of the splendidly named Johannes Oecolampadius.

A temporary guarantee of tolerance by the Emperor for the dissenting princes in Germany was withdrawn in April 1529. The princes, not unnaturally, protested and the movement got its name. It was now the Protestant movement. It was about this time in Scotland that Knox left school to start his university education.

It has been said that the purpose of school is to knock most of the nonsense out of someone and the purpose of university is to put some of that nonsense back. It is certainly true that schools do not encourage scepticism to any great extent, and if a delight in dispute has not been engendered by university, a huge opportunity will have been missed and will seldom be found in later life. Even today, when universities have often been forced to provide a more vocational training, the Latin root of 'education', as *ex ducere*, to lead out of, still can be faintly perceived. The two stages of school and university are the times when the seeds of future opinion or future belief will be planted. These seeds may only come to fruition much later. Although it is true that the straightforward experience of life can occasionally alone form the intellectual personality, for many it is the formal education process that provides the framework for the future. Students find themselves in an environment that encourages them to advance their minds beyond what is taught, or even to encourage rejection of the dogma of the day. So it was for John Knox, whose roots gave no clue to his subsequent status as a religious reformer and political democrat.

He was born in the East Lothians, a farming area to the east of Edinburgh. It was then, as it is now, pleasant, prosperous farming land lying between the gently sloping Lammermuir Hills and the waters of the Firth of Forth, with a soft climate only occasionally swept by an East wind that 'starts in Siberia, and the next thing it hits is East Lothian'. Little is known of Knox's parents except that they were probably of farming stock, living in, or near, Haddington, about seventeen miles from Edinburgh. Their house was in an area of the town called 'Giffordgate', which has given rise to the erroneous belief that Knox was born in Gifford, which is an attractive eighteenth-century village nearby. In fact the family home seemed to be in a suburb across the River Tyne from the church of St Mary's, and in a legal document of 1606 this area still had property bounded by 'Knox's Walls'.

In 1562, when Knox was in his late forties, he told the earl of Bothwell that he had 'borne a good mind to your house' and that both grandfathers and father had 'served your Lordship's predecessors and some of them have died under their standards.'

Protection of Haddington was pledged by the local keeper of Hailes Castle, who was, in fact, the earl of Bothwell, so we may presume that Knox's forebears did in fact come from Haddington and had given service to their local protector. But the earl of Bothwell was a Hepburn and Hepburn protection came at a price, being very often 'protection' in the Mafia sense rather than the more benevolent form we might expect. Haddington stood in the centre of the Lothians across the main access road to Edinburgh from England. Given this situation it was a favourite target for English invaders. A piece of seventeenth-century doggerel says:

> Next unto Berwick, Haddington faced all
> The greatest dangers and was Scotland's wall.

However, this was a prosperous, bustling market town with several ecclesiastical establishments, one of them the church of St Mary's, a building so magnificent that it became known as the 'Lamp of the Lothian'. When it was burnt by Edward III, John Mair felt that it may have been a just retribution for the Minor Friars to possess a building of such beauty. In the seventeenth century it was, 'a church excellently built of hewn stone, the ruins whereof do testify to its former splendour. In a Chapel belonging to this Church there is an excellent burial-place for the chiefs of the family Maitland.' The family Maitland's history would intertwine closely with that of John Knox. The present St Mary's is equally magnificent and its situation beside the River Tyne makes it today one of the most beautiful sights in all Scotland, a country otherwise poor in intact churches. Depredations to its buildings, either local or foreign, have been too common a feature in Scotland's turbulent history. Few churches have survived the effects of war, weather or bigotry. Later we shall look at the role John Knox played in this destruction.

The grammar school once attached to the church was reputed to have been attended by Duns Scotus, the thirteenth-century philosopher, and it seems possible that Knox followed in those distinguished footsteps. John Mair also had been a pupil there and had complained about the harshness of the regime imposed by the master George Litstar, to the point of fervently wishing to leave. Fortunately for sixteenth-century scholarship, Mair's mother insisted that he continued his education. Similarly, Knox's parents seemed to have been sufficiently ambitious for their son, and wealthy, to provide a similar education for him.

James IV had decreed that all burgesses and freeholders should send their eldest sons to a school until they had perfect Latin, an Act more often honoured in the breach than the observance, so that John Mair lamented that even the children of the nobility were largely uneducated. However, Knox would have received an education at the church school. His elder brother, William, also left home to establish himself as a merchant in nearby Prestonpans, and so we can presume that their father was rich enough not to need to follow the traditional pattern of keeping his sons with him. It argues strongly that he was more than just a simple farmer. There may even have been books in the house, and the family would undoubtedly have attended Mass on Sundays, possibly in the church in which Knox was baptized into the Catholic faith.

Given Knox's early employment as an ecclesiastical notary and tutor to the sons of the local lairdry he must have had some family connections in the area to give him access to such posts.

James Ker of Samuelston was a local landowner with whom Knox lodged around 1543, and for whom he conducted several legal affairs. Ker's mother shared her maiden name, Sinclair, with Knox's mother, so it does seem likely that at this time his future would have lain obscurely, but comfortably, among his lairdly relatives.

As we know, the outcome could hardly have been more different. The young John Knox was being prepared by his comparatively prosperous parents for a career that would take him much further than the farmlands of the Lothians. He must have wondered what this rare commodity, education, would do for him, apart from sparing him the back-breaking labour and urban squalor he could see all around. The field labourers lived in mud-and-wattle huts, without any facilities even of the meanest sort, often without windows, stinking in summer and freezing in winter when the east wind scoured the land. Their dwellings had the doubtful advantage that when the English tore them down, they were easy to rebuild, but John Knox must have known he would never live in one of them. The town dwellings would have been more substantial, but overcrowded and insanitary.

His education would have given him a freedom denied to these people, living under the subjection of the local landowners and in the fear of eternal damnation preventable only by total obedience to the Church. Although the affairs of continental Europe would have been unknown to him – while Luther was hammering his theses to the church door in Wittenberg, young Knox was rote-learning Latin declensions in his harsh school – it may indeed have been at this time that the iron of perceived injustice entered his soul.

He would have learned his Latin from the *Ars Minor*, the *grammaticalia* or elementary grammar book of Donatus, as well as logic, science and arithmetic. At first he would have been a *puer*, or boy, and his studies would have been *puerilia*, before he graduated to being an adolescent, or *iuvenus*. At the 'song' schools attached to church foundations, these divisions were determined by the boys' voices breaking. In many schools the entire education was conducted in Latin – even the old men in the almshouse in Haddington had to pray in Latin and were tested regularly on their competence. During his professional life Thomas More would have conversed in Latin as often as he ever spoke in English. International travel to places of learning throughout Europe was essential at a time when books were rare and expensive, and for a Dutchman such as Erasmus to be able to talk with a German-speaking Swiss like Zwingli or John Mair, a Scot, at the University of Paris, it was imperative to have a common language. Latin, of course, did not have any nationalist connotations, as has English today, and so the contemporary Tower of Babel of translators we find in Brussels and Strasburg was undreamed of. In Knox's day it was even more important than the ability to operate a word processor is today. It was, quite simply, the medieval equivalent of access to the internet.

Forty years after Knox, Latin still had a near magical aspect, for Horatio in Shakespeare's Hamlet is asked to speak to the Ghost of Hamlet's father. 'Thou art a scholar,' says Marcellus, implying that Horatio would speak Latin and could thus be understood by the Ghost – ghosts presumably only spoke Latin – but, fortunately for us Hamlet's father has not yet completed his descent into the underworld and the dialogue continues in English.

So Knox would have left school with fluent Latin and a basic knowledge of grammar, mathematics, logic and science. This was sufficient for university, and it was not until after his fortieth birthday that he attempted to learn Greek and Hebrew.

There is considerable debate as to where Knox received a university education and the facts are unclear. His name, 'Johanes Knox', is registered as a student of Glasgow University on 25 October 1522, when Knox would have been about eight years old. Although his name appears on the university register, it must be noted that during the sixteenth and seventeenth centuries forty Knoxes, eight of them Johns, were also registered. Similarly we have no guarantee that Geoffrey Chaucer, the courtier and government servant, whose sister-in-law was John of Gaunt's mistress, was, in fact, the same person as Geoffrey Chaucer, the poet. So a certain amount of caution must be exercised.

The principal of Glasgow University was John Mair, who had recently arrived from his successful career at the Univerity of Paris. Older than Knox by forty or so years he was one of the most eminent scholars of his day. He had studied first in Cambridge, at Godshouse, later renamed Christ's College, and then graduated in Paris in 1506, before returning in 1517 to take up his position at Glasgow, where he wrote his history of Greater Britain, *Historia Maioris Britanniae*. (In it he argues for a union between England and Scotland and an end to the Auld Alliance – an alliance that had brought Scotland into an unnecessary war with Henry VIII, culminating in the appalling slaughter of the greater part of the Scots army, ineptly gener-alled at Flodden in 1513, the probable year of Knox's birth.) John Mair's book was physically so large, however, that Scottish technology could not print it and he returned briefly to Paris for its publication in 1521. By 1522, when he was back in Glasgow, his works were already required read-ing in the great University of Salamanca and his reputation was established throughout Europe. But in 1531 Mair went to St Andrews University as a teacher of theology. Knox tells us that 'his word was then held as an oracle in matters of religion' and John Mair became a jewel in the institution's crown. This was in spite of a marginal note in Mair's own copy of *Quartus Sentenarium* – 'bad beer at St Andrews!'

Although contemporary records for admissions at St Andrews do not exist, having been either destroyed, lost, or never kept in the first place, it is probable that in the autumn of 1529 John Knox went there to study theology. There was logic to this, since Haddington lay in the diocese of St Andrews. However, he may have attended Glasgow first, since he wished to be taught by fellow Haddingtonian John Mair. The first biographical details of Knox's education come from the *Icones*, published in 1580, eight years after Knox's death. The book is a collection of sketches by Theodore de Beza, a minister in Geneva at the same time as Knox. De Beza became an amanuensis to John Calvin, eventually succeeded him, and must have met and spoken to Knox on many occasions. They corresponded in the 1560s when de Beza calls Knox 'my very dear brother'. De Beza tells us that 'Ioannes Cnoxus, Scotus, Giffordiensis' went to sit at the feet of John Mair, the most celebrated among the Sophists, for his education in the town of St Andrews. He also tells us that Knox was so celebrated a reformer that Cardinal Beaton sent assassins to Edinburgh to murder him. This is arrant nonsense, although de Beza does give us the dates of Knox's final days with total accuracy. This work was translated into French a year later by Simon Goulart as *Les Vrais Portraits des Hommes Illustres*, with the approval of de Beza. Goulart thanks God that Knox has made it possible that contemporary believers in Scotland are no longer mired in darkness and barbarity – '*n'est plus obscure ni sauvage.*' It is unlikely that de Beza's information was from Knox himself, but even if this version came from gossip, which seems doubtful when de Beza was writing about a former colleague, it is odd that it should contain such a simple inaccuracy as mistaking a university. We can, therefore, have some confidence that the foundations for Knox's thinking were laid on the north coast of Fife in the University of St Andrews.

In the special collections at St Andrews University library there does exist a copy of Augustine's *De Trinitate* with many marginal notes, some in a hand believed to be that of Knox. But however fascinating to scholars may be the search for proof of the geographic location of Knox's university education, it is finally only of passing academic interest compared to what he thought or achieved.

Perhaps equally of tangential interest, Goulart in his book did not use the engraving of Knox's portrait found in *Icones* but substituted another, which turns out, in fact, to be that of John Wycliffe. The engraving de Beza used in *Icones* appears elsewhere some seventy years later as that of de Beza himself! Since all further representations of Knox are based on this engraving, up to and including the giant statue in the quadrangle of New College, Edinburgh, we can have no clear idea of what Knox looked like. The exception, according to Thomas Carlyle in his *Portraits of John Knox*, is the 'Somerville' engraving where he is seen wearing a skullcap, with a sharply pointed beard and holding a copy of the folio edition of the 1562 Geneva Bible. But Carlyle does not offer very cogent evidence for its authenticity. The engraving in *Icones* is as accurate a portrait as exists.

The shape of his beard notwithstanding, and at the age of sixteen it cannot have been significant, Knox arrived in St Andrews. St Andrews in the sixteenth century was a small, grey town on the north Fifeshire coast dominated by the abbey church and the archbishop's castle, both forbiddingly set on the cliffs overlooking the North Sea. It was buffeted by chill winds from the East in winter and distinctly cool breezes in summer. By the middle of the century (1552) the game of golf would first be played on the grassy links beside the sea, but the only major influence on the town apart from the abbey and castle was the university. The University of St Andrews was brought into official being in 1414 when papal bulls were received from the schismatic Pope Benedict XIII; the college of St Salvator was later founded in 1450. It was dedicated to the Holy Saviour, or, in Scots, 'Sanct Salvatour', although it is now affectionately known as 'St Sally's'. The four universities of the day, St Andrews, Glasgow, and the King's and Marischal Colleges at Aberdeen, held among them far fewer students than any one of them does today – the faculty of St Salvator's numbered only thirteen, to echo the number of Christ's disciples. Knox would have arrived as a 'bejanus' (the word derives from *bec jaune*, or yellow beak, since first year students at the University of Paris wore such a brim to their caps) to rise through being a bachelor with the eventual aim of becoming a magistrand. The bejanus was counselled by a senior student, to whom he would have presented a pound of raisins at the end of his first term, in return for a receipt in ribald Latin. He would have lived with his fellow students in lodgings similar to those of monastic life. The shock would have been colossal for a country-born son of sparsely educated parents. There would have been no let-up in the scholarly atmosphere with all conversations in college precincts being carried on in Latin and the monastic aspect empha-sized within the all-male community. The college laundress was the only female allowed to enter and she had to be over fifty years of age.

Knox found himself thrust into an intellectual maelstrom altogether more vivid than the one he would have experienced in Glasgow or in Haddington. St Andrews was dominated, as has been said, by, on the one hand, the university, and, on the other by the castle and cathedral of the archbishop James Beaton. Beaton had been a regent during the infancy of James V and was a strict adherent to orthodoxy in all things, supporting the current conservatism of thought in banning the importation of works by Luther and others.

He had enthusiastically supervised the burning for heresy of Patrick Hamilton as well as at least three other alleged heretics. James Beaton would be succeeded in 1539 by his nephew David Beaton, who would become, not only cardinal archbishop, but *legatus a latere* as well – in other words, the Pope's personal representative in Scotland, who could act in most matters without further reference to Rome.

The life of luxury enjoyed by the senior clergy is illustrated by the fact that John Mair, not himself a particularly zealous reformer, stated that he felt bishops should have no more than twelve or fourteen servants. The luxury was not confined to fine wine, food, and furnishings, for the vows of chastity quickly went the way of the vows of poverty. Cardinal Beaton, rumoured to have been the lover of the Queen Regent, Mary of Guise, fathered ten illegitimate children, eight by his mistress Marion Ogilvie. Although the exact number of children is in some doubt and the rumour of his involvement with the Queen Regent is too obvious a slander to be entirely credible, a general picture does emerge. He was described as 'a prelate who did not adorn the spiritual estate'.

But the university was peopled by men who did adorn the intellectual estate and none more than John Mair. Mair was appointed provost of St Salvator's College in 1531, and it was in this capacity that Knox met him. John Mair was a colleague of Hector Boece, who was now teaching at Aberdeen. And Boece was a colleague of Erasmus, the leading humanist of the day. Mair had known Erasmus in Paris, at the college of Montaigu, but they had undoubtedly taken diverging paths since, for Mair was a strict adherent of traditional scholasticism, while Erasmus was a devoted humanist and liberal. In one passage describing the scholars of Montaigu, Erasmus uses the word *nihil* no less than eight times, 'in language no more than barbarous, in wit no more than stupid...' and so on. François Rabelais, another distinguished former pupil, has Ponocrates in his novel Gargantua describe the villainy and cruelty with which dissent was treated – 'worse than the Moors and Tartars'. But then Rabelais was no admirer of rigour.

Mair was a devout Catholic and adherent of medieval philosophic method, but he did have some extraordinary ideas for his time regarding the position of rulers. He believed they were supreme over each individual subject but subordinate to the whole people. In his *Historia* he emphasizes the rights of the people against unjust tyrannies. Astonishingly, he claims that it is the people who appoint the king, and the people who, therefore, may depose him. However, he defined the 'people' as the nobility who act for the commonality and not 'that many headed monster the unbridled populace'. Like all scholars he had a terror of the mob. He condemned the oppressions of Richard II but, at the same time, decried his deposition. 'Rather inconsistent, to say the least, on the part of the worthy St Andrews professor,' says Dr MacKinnon in his *History of Modern Liberty*. Dr MacKinnon goes on to point out that, although Mair seldom strayed from the orthodoxy of his academic chair, in an age when the penalty for unorthodoxy was often the stake, this was wholly understandable since there was 'little scope for the play of philosophy'. Knox absorbed these dangerous arguments and later would refine them into a democratic manifesto for individual liberty.

At St Andrews Knox would have also have heard lectures from the like of the Frenchman Jean Charpentier, who, among others, brought the views of the European reformers. Knox would have been immersed in Old Testament studies, and thus his constant references to these in later life are no more exceptional than an educated man in the eighteenth or nineteenth century habitually quoting from the Classics. Eusebius, the 'Father of Church History', was in the collection of books at St Leonard's College and would have been available to Knox, as would Josephus' *Histories*. Works by Philo would have led him to Plato and he would have read Aquinas's *Commentaries on Aristotle*. All this in addition to works by Cicero and, of course, the output of John Mair himself was easily available. Knox would certainly have read Augustine's *De Civitate Deo* and *De Trinitate*. Locally he would have found John Johnsone's *An Confortable Exhortation*, John Gow's *Richt way the Kingdom of Heaven* and the Wedderburns' *Gude and Godly Ballads*.

The new and dangerous writings by Luther, Melancthon and Erasmus may not have been available openly, but smuggled versions would certainly have found their way into universities. Students have always sought out the latest thinking, made all the more attractive if it is thought to be scandalous, as was seen with the popularity of Chairman Mao Zedong's *Thoughts*, the fashionable Little Red Book of the Sixties. The difference here was that, while possession by the student body of Mao's book earned only raised eyebrows from the establishment, in Knox's day possession of Luther's work would lead to banishment at best, after interrogation as to where and from whom the work had been acquired. The fact that there was a law forbidding their importation means that such felonies were taking place in spite of the danger. How potent their message must have been to a student from Haddington is impossible to quantify, but Knox would have imbibed their contents with urgent enthusiasm in spite of the ever-present danger.

And danger there certainly was, for very early in his *History of the Reformation* Knox tells us of the martyrdom of Patrick Hamilton in 1527. Since this had taken place at the door of St Salvator's College, a spot Knox would have visited frequently – now marked by the initials 'PH' set into the pavement – memories in the university would have been recent and vivid.

Knox tells us that the points for which Hamilton suffered were comparatively minor, a disbelief in purgatory, a condemnation of the efficacy of prayers to the saints, and so forth. He then praises him as 'a godly man, well learned in philosophy'. He describes Hamilton going to the stake and giving his outer garments to his servant, saying,

These will not profit in the fire, they will profit thee. After this, of me thou can receive no commodity, except in the manner of my death which, I pray thee, bear in mind; for albeit be bitter to the flesh, and fearful before men, yet it is the entrance unto eternal life, which none shall possess that denies Christ Jesus before this wicked generation.

Hamilton was then tied to a stake amidst coal and timber, with a trail of gunpowder which was set on fire. This exploded and had the effect of scorching his left hand and the side of his face, but failed to ignite the fire. While Hamilton stood in half-burned agony men were sent running to the castle – about half a mile distant – to fetch more powder. The fire was eventually lit, but it 'was slow and therefore was his torment the more'. Then showers of rain and a strong north wind conspired from time to time to put the fire out. During this six-hour horror, Hamilton was harangued by one Friar Alexander Campbell, crying, 'Convert, heretic!' Mercifully, 'after long sufferance' Hamilton died and Knox notes with satisfaction that a few days after, the friar, 'as one despaired', died of a stroke in Glasgow.

On 21 April 1528 the masters and professors of theology at the University of Louvain sent a letter of congratulation to 'his excellent virtue', the archbishop of Saint Andrews. John Mair, with more charity, described Hamilton as 'an unhappy follower of the Lutheran heresy'. Thus, speaking openly against the establishment, secular or spiritual, carried the most severe penalties.

It was in this atmosphere that Knox would have heard Mair advocating a return to the study of the scriptures, rather than a study of the commentators on them. He was internationally respected for his views on physics, mathematics, international law and political theory and was 'the most distinguished representative of the old learning'. He was also described as a cold commentator who was subject-centred, unlike Philip Melanchthon, who was student-orientated. A prayer by Mair demonstrates the depth of his faith:

we therefore beg of thee, O hope of the human race, Jesus Christ, God born of God, our refuge and our strength, our sole consolation, whom in the distance, like the star of the morning and the sun of justice, standing on the shore of our heavenly home, we long to see and yet can barely discern for the tears in our eyes. Govern our ship with your right hand, marked as it is with the nails of the cross, lest we perish in the waves. Grant us we beg, Lord Jesus,

to hold a mid-course between Scylla and Charybdis, so that, avoiding vice
and error and all dangers, we may, our ship and gear safe, securely come to
port at last.

In many ways John Mair was a complete renaissance Christian. Finding
no conflict between science, theology and the arts, he clung to the orthodox Roman faith with a breadth of knowledge that was exceptional.
Inevitably he passed on this openness of mind to his pupils, and Knox was
no exception.

The detail with which Knox recounts the sermons of William Airth indi-
cates that he was present at them as well as John Mair, who examined the
friar for heresy. Airth had condemned the clergy for misuse of their powers
of excommunication as well as avarice, lechery and ignorance. He was, in
spite of all, found to remain faithful to Rome at heart and no official action
was taken against him. His fellow Friars, however, had less confidence in
his safety and he was recommended to flee to England, where, ironically,
he was promptly arrested for papistry and thrown into prison.

Knox tells us that thanks to the atmosphere in St Andrews, and St
Leonard's College particularly, many began to call in doubt what they had
held before for an unquestioned certainty. 'They began to smell somewhat
of the verity, and to espy the vanity of the received superstition.' One John
Lindsay, whom Knox describes as 'a merry fellow', advises Archbishop
Beaton, 'My Lord, if you burn any more, except you follow my counsel, ye
will utterly destroy yourselves. If ye will burn them, let them be burnt in
secret cellars; for the reek of Master Hamilton has infected as many as it
blew upon.' In spite of this advice the archbishop did burn Henry Forrest
for no greater crime than the possession of a New Testament in English.

Knox tells us that Forrest had been long imprisoned in the sea tower of
the bishop's castle. This tower contains, apart from a more or less normal
cell, the notorious Bottle Dungeon, now a tourist sight, but once in regular use. It is about twenty feet deep, carved vertically into the solid rock
and in the shape of a bottle. The unfortunate prisoner would be lowered
down the neck of the bottle into the widening space at the foot where he
would be left in total darkness without light, food, water, or sanitation.
Madness would have brought a merciful release. Henry Forrest's release
was to be burnt alive.

It was in this atmosphere of risk and doubt that the seeds of Knox's later
defiance were planted. The clerical establishment, wielding arbitrary

punishments of the most cruel and sadistic kind, sought to control thought and dissent as rigorously as the Stalinist regimes of Eastern Europe. But in continental Europe the clouds were beginning to part and news of reform was in the air.

It was a world of rigid monarchies, exerting totalitarian rule over populations within which aspects of religious reform were coming to the surface in many different forms. And in many places there were fears that religious reform could spread, causing temporal repercussions. Any incursions into what could be seen as princely power would be crushed ruthlessly. So, while at the university Knox would have become very well aware of the political and religious situations existing, not only in Scotland, but throughout the entirety of Europe. In later life, Knox was often attacked for personal cowardice, but perhaps along with the seeds of defiance came a very realistic knowledge of martyrdom in its most vivid and horrifying forms. Dead men tell no tales and martyrs preach no more sermons. But student debate was, for the moment, unassailed and Knox would have been part of it. By 1536, however, Knox had left the comparative safety of university, without either patron or protection, to enter a Catholic Church that would soon be torn by dissent and reform.

2   Sir John Knox

ffairs in Europe had not been standing still. The Holy Roman
Emperor Charles V demanded that the Lutherans renounce their
reforms and return to Mother Church by 1531. This was regarded as an
ultimatum by the Protestant princes and together they formed the military
union of the Schmalkaldic League against the imperial edict. Their intent
was not reform but war. If the teaching of the Church could be rejected,
the power of the empire could be challenged – the dangerous realization
that intellectual freedom was indivisible from religious dissent was growing
apace.

The most direct threat was, of course, when the political status quo was
threatened, and one of the most potent growing threats came from a religious splinter group of reformers generally called the Anabaptists. Their
name derived from their practice of adult baptism, although if became a
blanket term to cover a wide range of sects that arose in this period, including, as a brief list, the Bloodfriends, the Dreamers, Cornelians, Gabrielites,
and Sabbatarians. Many were millenarians, foretelling the end of the present
world and the coming of the thousand years when Christ would rule the
world in person before Armageddon. They were seen as so extreme that
Luther himself declared that they were worthy of the death sentence, a
punishment he had previously reserved only for blasphemy and sedition. All
established churches found them blasphemous and the temporal powers had
no hesitation in pronouncing them seditious. Eventually the reputation of
their often misinterpreted beliefs was used as a stick to beat any reformers,
as Lollardry had been over a century earlier, and their name would even be
thrown, unjustly, at Knox at a later time. They were, in many respects, primitive democrats setting up communities of their own without regard to the
principality in which they existed. They refused to pay tithes and they

preached pacifism. This led to their being accused, unfairly, of instigating the Peasants' War, simply on the principle that 'if you are not for me, then you are against me'. Rumours of all sorts started to spread – they will slaughter all priests and nuns, polygamy will be enforced – in spite of a statement by the second-century Christian writer Tertullian that, 'Christians share everything except our wives'. Multiple executions became widespread, although the vigour with which they were pursued was greater in the staunchly Catholic areas. In Salzburg they were herded en masse into a church which was then burnt – 'they lived long and shrieked pitifully' – and in Haarlem, where an extreme commune had been set up, the community was destroyed and the followers were then tortured to death. In fact, torture flourished particularly in the extirpation of the Anabaptists. Michael Sattler had his tongue torn out before being flayed alive with red hot pincers; many were roasted to death over slow fires, and there were mass drownings. Between 1525 and 1539 there were upwards of 780 executions.

It is clear that their very existence produced a particular horror in the secular powers. Troubling though their spiritual reform of the Church might be, it was nothing to the fury inspired by their reforming of the social structure. It has been said of them that, 'With all their follies and shortcomings, they were in a sense the forerunners of Modern Socialism', and any weakening of the hierarchical structure of the time was therefore to be crushed utterly with all ferocity. Thus any reformer that strayed from theology was liable to be branded 'Anabaptist' and treated with extreme severity. In 1558 Knox would write a lengthy refutation of their denial of predestination.

Meanwhile, west of the Rhine, Francis I of France, one of the great princes of the Renaissance, was being forced to take notice of reform. On 17 March 1534 every public square in France received posters proclaiming *The True Articles upon the great Horrid and unbearable abuses of the Papal mass, devised contrary to the Holy Supper of Our Lord, the one mediator and only Saviour, Jesus Christ*. Presumed to be the work of Anabaptists, this struck home, especially since one had even been pinned to the door of the royal bedchamber at the palace of Amboise. Francis could not ignore this. Until now he had allowed a certain latitude among intellectuals regarding reform, in spite of pressure from the conservative theologians at the Sorbonne. His personal instincts were for splendour and innovation – his favourite palace at Chambord had a double helix staircase, reputedly designed by Leonardo da Vinci – and he had no interest in starting an internal rupture based on religion. But now, with little option, he was forced to let the religious conservatives of the Sorbonne have their head and 200-odd suspects were arrested, with twenty-four of them being publicly burnt. In January 1535 Francis clearly felt that events had gone far enough. He forbade the printing of any book whatsoever, heard Mass in Nôtre-Dame, burnt six heretics, had dinner and addressed the clergy and the university. He told them he wished to see the errors chased out of the kingdom, and added that if he himself had one of his arms infected by them he would cut it off. No appeal was to be allowed by anyone condemned of heresy and anyone sheltering heresy was to be treated as a heretic. This seems to have been an impetuously violent personal reaction, for by July most of this was repealed and Francis then declared the nation free of heresy.

Across the Channel, England was ruled by Henry VIII, who was using religious reform to give authority to his dynastic machinations, his need for an heir. Twelve years after Henry had succeeded to the throne he repudiated the works of Luther in his *Assertio Septem Sacramentorum*, duly presented to Pope Leo X in a gold cover, and was rewarded with the still held title of *Fidei Defensor*, a title still held by the sovereign. He indeed defended the faith, pursuing heresy with vigour, and on one day in 1535 he burned twenty-five Anabaptists – an event which must have come to Knox's ears. Nevertheless, in the previous year he had passed the Act of Supremacy, which can be seen as marking the beginning of the English Reformation. In this he was proclaimed head of the Church in England. But it must be noted that the Church remained the same, while Henry simply replaced the Pope as its head. Quite bluntly, this allowed him to act as he wished in religious matters without foreign intervention. The Roman Catholic rising in the North, the Pilgrimage of Grace, was put down with efficient ferocity and Henry's chancellor, Thomas Cromwell, had a free hand in the highly profitable dissolution of the monasteries.

Although Henry had repudiated the authority of the Pope in order to marry Anne Boleyn, the destruction of the monasteries was as much an economic as a theological action. In addition, the Pilgrimage of Grace, while rooted in conservative Catholicism, also had an underlying theme of the North opposing any arbitrary change imposed by southern England. In other words, the Act of Supremacy, the Pilgrimage of Grace, and the Dissolution of the Monasteries were all three essentially English events and finally more political than theological in origin. Henry's daughter, Elizabeth, would have a lifelong fear of being condemned to hellfire, albeit a Protestant hellfire, for her father's Godless sins.

In spite of this seeming laicization of religious topics, by the end of Henry's reign, devotional texts were being taught in English, and the Bible in English was circulating to an extent that caused Henry to comment that the Bible was being 'rhymed, sung and jangled in every ale-house and tavern'.

He made sure that his son Prince Edward was educated by reforming clergy and he even contemplated substituting Communion for the Mass. Luther had said, 'What squire Harry wills must be an article of faith for Englishmen, for life and death.' It must have been of little comfort to the martyrs of his reign that, as the fires were being lit around their feet, their real offence had not been against the religion of the state, but against the temporal power of Henry Tudor.

The conscience of the individual was never Henry VIII's concern and as his daughter later was to state, neither he nor she had any wish to 'make windows into men's souls'. The historian S.T. Bindoff says that he professed 'a faith which brought man and God into a communion where neither King nor priest might obtrude'. Whatever the motives, it was a true reformation and must have been the subject of many a debate amongst the scholars and students in St Andrews. The seventeenth century may have possessed no satellite uplinks or web sites, but the need for news was just as great and the interest probably greater.

In Scotland under James V, the established order of the Catholic faith still held an increasingly fragile grasp on affairs and the populace was not unaware of events either in England or in the Lutheran states of Northern Europe. James V had married Madeleine, daughter of Francis I, but she died after only two months in Scotland. On Francis's suggestion, he then swiftly married Mary of Guise, thus linking himself, and therefore Scotland, with one of the most powerful Catholic families in France, and sowing justified suspicion in the mind of his neighbour, Henry Tudor. However, before these suspicions were fully realized, two powder trails were about to be lit, one in Geneva and the other in Scotland.

In Geneva, the bishop of Savoy had oppressed the citizenry to such an extent that they had formed a resistance movement to confront him. These 'confederates', in German, *Eidgenossen*, or in French *Eiguenots*, later corrupted to 'Huguenots', combined with Protestant allies from Bern to overthrow the Catholic hierarchy. By August 1535 Geneva was a Protestant republic. In August 1536, a man from Picardy in the north of France was appointed as reader in holy scripture to the Church in Geneva. His name was Jean Cauvin, which he had adapted to John Calvin, and his was the first powder trail to ignite.

The second trail was that of John Knox, who left university for a career in the Catholic Church. His powder would take longer to burn.

Knox's first documented appearance as a priest in the Catholic Church coincides with the arrest of a friar, William Murdoch, in April 1604. Mysteriously, he was found to be carrying a paper recording: *Ionnes Knox fax Scotiae diaconus sabbatho in passione dni 1536 aprilis prima Presbiter in vigilia pasche 18 April eodem anno a Willelo Epo Dunblanensi.* Now, '*Sabatho in passione dni*' was April 1 and Holy Saturday '*in vigilia pasche*' was actually 15 April, not the 18th, but otherwise the paper states with absolute clarity that John Knox was ordained, first, deacon by William, Bishop of Dunblane on 1 April 1536 and then priest on the 15th.

A later symposium in *The Innes Review* (a learned historical journal) starts with doubt being cast on this paper, yet however many academic hairs are split – Was he merely a deacon in lower orders? Had he a licence to preach? Why was the Friar carrying this paper? – the fact remains that, as we shall see, he found that the first steps towards reformist thinking involved him in painful apostasy from his original ordination. The actual level of his ordination did not affect that.

We have no evidence of the actual date of his graduation from St Andrews but thereafter he is referred to as 'Sir' John Knox. This was not a chivalric title, but an indication that he was in holy orders as a priest, and had achieved the degree of Bachelor, and not the higher degree of Master. When Knox is referred to as 'Master' Knox the title is purely honorific, and denotes his probable employment as a tutor.

Perhaps it is also convenient at this time to point out that the pronunciation of his name was probably sounded with a hard letter 'K''. Since spelling in the sixteenth century was simply phonetic and since he was variously spelt as Knox, Knocks, Knokkes, or even Cnox the pronunciation seems clear. On one glorious occasion he was even referred to as 'Quenoques'. However, heavy-handed Latin puns were latterly made on 'nox' for night and 'noceus' a criminal, so doubt remains.

On 27 March 1543 he follows his signature as *Joannes Knox* with *sacri altaris minister Sanctiandrae dioceseos auctoritate appostolica notarius*. So Sir John Knox, priest, was launched on the world in 1536 and seven years later he had an appointment as a papal notary. He had also witnessed documents and appeared before the courts as a notary since 1540. However, under canon law no ordained priest was allowed to hold the office of notary, but since educated laymen were rare and unlikely to seek such humble employment, this was yet another law honoured more in the breach than in the observance. Indeed, the lack of educated churchmen had caused John Mair to remark that 'in Scotland canons who are graduates are as rare as snakes in Ireland or dormice in Glasgow'.

The state of learning and teaching by the church caused Alex Arbuthnot to comment,

> Religioun now is reknit as ane fabill
> All hope of hevin now is hauldin vanitie
> And Hellis paine is comptit poetrie.

But Knox was that rarity, an educated churchman, albeit one holding a lowly position in the clerical hierarchy. He was now working as tutor to William, son of Stephen Brounefield of Greenlaw, while he lived with Ker of Samuelston, for whom he acted legally. He may have acted as tutor to children of other gentry in the area and possibly conducted services in the chapel at Samuelston.

All of this is situated within a few miles of Haddington, so Knox had, to some extent, come home to a comparatively comfortable living as a man of learning and faith among the minor lairdry in the pleasant countryside of East Lothian. He probably held this not very onerous position between 1536 and 1543, and there he might have stayed, depending on preferment and the possible elevation of his patrons. Since we have no knowledge of the fate of his parents, we cannot know if he returned from university to the family home, but, as we have heard, his mother's Sinclair connections must have lifted him into the society of people such as Ker.

The tradition of the cleric who lived in the great house acting as tutor and private chaplain continues well into the nineteenth century, and Knox could have accepted the comfortable obscurity such a position offered with ease. The world would have heard no more of John Knox. But such comfortable clerics would have had no doubts about their faith or their Church, and Knox most certainly had. They may have been in his mind, hidden since St Andrews, but they surfaced in 1543 when the first shoots of his reforming spirit broke through. It is a little enough thing, merely a Latin subscription to his signature saying, '*Testis per Christum fidelis, cui gloria*' – 'a witness faithful through Christ, to whom the glory'.

This is the first written notice that Knox believed that faith came directly from Christ and that He alone was to be glorified for it. Behind this simple assertion was the dangerous assumption that faith in Christ alone was enough. It denied the power of the Church and threw the weight of redemption on to the shoulders of each individual, glorifying Christ. Now, when Knox was dying he was asked if would like some passage of Scripture to be read to him. He asked for St John, chapter 17, 'in which I first cast my anchor'. In this passage Christ talks to His Father of his followers:

> I pray for them, I pray not for the world, but for them whom thou has given me; for they are thine. And all mine are thine, and thine are mine; and I am glorified in them. [And later], Sanctify them through thy truth: thy word is truth.

Knox was saying that truth was to be found, not in studying the teachings of the Church, but in studying Christ's teachings in scripture. He alone was the interpreter of God's word, and all true believers followed Him alone. The affairs of men and the world are unimportant, but true Christians glorify Christ alone. Since current doctrine was that scripture should only be made available through the interpretation of the Church, that is, Rome, to advocate that the uninterpreted truth of the scripture be studied as the message of Christ was to deny one of the basic powers of the Church and would be seen immediately as darkest heresy. It also meant that eternal redemption was in the hands of Christ alone and did not depend entirely on the absolving power of the Church, nor could it be bought for money by acquiring indulgences. By accepting this Knox was already rejecting a basic tenet of the Church into which he had been ordained.

And he cannot have been unaware that reforming study groups, or 'privy Kirks', were being tolerated, or that James V was leaning towards an accommodation with Henry VIII. As we have heard, James V had married Mary, daughter of the immensely powerful house of Guise. Whether her devout Catholicism played any part is difficult to say, but unfortunately James lost his political nerve and failed to appear at a conference with the English at York. Henry VIII, who felt justifiably slighted, by way of retaliation routed a superior but totally inept Scottish army at the battle of Solway Moss in 1542.

James died less than three weeks later, 'of a lack of will to live', leaving the crown to the one-week-old infant Mary. Scotland was now ruled by a governor in the person of James Hamilton, Earl of Arran, who nailed his colours to the Protestant mast by appointing Thomas Gwilliam and Thomas Rough, two Protestant preachers whom we shall meet again, as his chaplains. This brief flirtation with Protestantism became known as his 'Godly fit'. He moved further by agreeing the Treaty of Greenwich in 1543, which provided for the marriage of Henry VIII's son, Prince Edward, later King Edward VI, to the infant Mary.

But Henry VIII distrusted the Franco-Scottish connections and insisted that Mary be sent immediately to England – Tudor high-handedness that drove Scottish opinion furiously in the other direction and into the Catholic arms of Mary of Guise and Cardinal Beaton.

Governor Hamilton promptly changed religion. In Knox's words, 'The Governor violated his faith, refused God and took absolution of the devil.' The persecution and arrests of Protestants began in earnest, and Knox met a man whose inspiration would lead him to the stake. His name was George Wishart, although J. Row, the seventeenth-century historian, perhaps prophetically, calls him Mr George Wiseheart. (Buchanan, in his *History of Scotland* of 1582, calls him 'Sophocardius' and the original family name was probably Guiscard.) His acquaintance with Knox would change the latter's life.

Martyrs feature largely in the early part of Knox's *History of the Reformation of Religion within the Realm of Scotland: containing the manner and by what persons the light of Christ's Evangel hath been manifested unto this realm after that horrible and universal defection from the truth which has come by the means of that Roman Antichrist*. Mercifully, it is usually referred to as Knox's *History of the Reformation*. Much of Book I is given over to accounts of the martyrs, starting with a dubious reference to an unnamed heretic, burnt in Glasgow in 1422. More than fifty pages pass before the name of George Wishart is mentioned. But it must be borne in mind that Knox is writing with hindsight from the point of view of self-justification; the book is a quasi-autobiography. The distinguished historian and editor Prof. W.C. Dickinson calls the book 'a piece of special pleading, a party pamphlet rather than a history . . . and, as such, one-sided in many of its statements. But its very bias can give us a useful insight into the mind of the propagandist.' Very few historians are without a personal point of view and even fewer – C.V. Wedgwood is a shining example of this – ever admit to a change of opinion, so I think we should not be too strident in our criticism of Knox. And as Wishart was the first martyr personally known to Knox, that early whiff of the stake must have had an inspiring effect on him.

Wishart was probably born in 1513, the same year as Knox, into a well-connected family. His father James Wishart had been clerk of justiciary and king's advocate under James IV. It seems likely that he was educated in Germany, then returned to Scotland and took a place as a teacher of Greek in Montrose. But, in 1538 he was reported to the bishop of Brechin for the heinous crime of distributing the Testament in Greek to his pupils and he fled to Cambridge. He was there at the invitation of a Dr. Barnes, whom he may have met in Wittenberg, where Barnes was a colleague of Luther himself. Now Barnes forged a further link in the reforming chain by introducing Wishart to Latimer, bishop of Worcester. Previously Latimer had been accused of heresy when preaching in Bristol, but there was now greater tolerance in the Church of England under the rule of Archbishop Cranmer at Canterbury, so Wishart was sent as a 'reader' to preach at Bristol.

But the Bristol clergy were forewarned of his views and Wishart was arrested for preaching dangerous doctrines condemned by the Church. Under rapid and sensible advice from Archbishop Cranmer, Wishart made a public retraction on 13 July 1539. This involved Wishart undertaking the arcane ritual of carrying a faggot, or the bundle of kindling symbolizing the fire in which he would have been burnt, to the Church of St Nicholas and then setting fire to the wood, before making his public retraction. The accusations levelled at Wishart are extremely confused and give the impression that the accusers had misunderstood Wishart's assertion that Christ and no other was our mediator and intercessor.

However, he returned to the Continent, probably to Switzerland, before coming back in 1542 to Cambridge to work as a tutor. But he brought back with him the *Helvetic Confession*, a doctrine of the reformed faith from Switzerland.

If any single document can be said to have encapsulated the future beliefs of the Protestant Church it is the *Helvetic Confession*. Its central beliefs remain with us today. It was written by a group of reformers in Basle in 1537, a year after Knox's ordination. One of this group was Heinrich Bullinger, who took the document to Wittenberg. Wishart may have encountered it there at first hand.

Or it may be that he was introduced to the *Confession* in Cambridge, but at any rate Wishart translated the document into English. Its main points are worth noting since they will recur in various forms.

Its first claim is that holy scripture is the word of God and is the most perfect and ancient science and doctrine of wisdom. 'It alone containeth consumately all Godliness', and its interpretation should be sought 'out of itself'. In other words everything necessary for truth can be found by the study of scripture without any priestly interpretations. 'The traditions of men that withdraweth us and stoppeth us from the Scripture are as of things hurtful and unprofitable.' It then quotes Matthew, chapter 15: 'They worship me in vain, teaching the doctrines of man.' Knox would find that the Mass was from the tradition of men, not from scripture, and so was unprofitable and idolatrous.

The *Confession* goes on to state that sin can be healed with the help of God alone. Therefore, one can presume, confession and the absolution given by a priesthood are valueless, for 'The principal office of the ministration is to preach repentance and remission of sin through Jesus Christ.' Now, medieval churches abounded in Judgement scenes in which Christ watched as the archangel Michael weighed the souls of the dead, and parcelled them up either to join the angels in Heaven, or go to colourful torture in Hell. St Peter held the keys to the kingdom of Heaven, and his ambassador was the Pope. But the *Confession* is saying that only Christ can grant absolution after due repentance and that the entire panoply of churchly power is a mockery. Christ himself is the sole head of the Church, and he alone can inspire teachers. In St Andrews Knox would follow this, claiming that no man can be head of the Church. Thus the *Confession* denies the authority of the papacy.

The *Confession* then turns to the vexed question of the sacraments, which it reduces to two. They are, firstly, baptism in which water is the sign, but 'the thing and verity is regeneration and adoption in the people of God'. And secondly, the communion of the body of our Lord, where 'the bread and the wine are the signs but the thing and verity is the communion and health and salvation found with the remission of our sins, the which are received by faith even as the signs and tokens are received by mouth.' This denies the concept of transubstantiation, and in case this was not immediately clear he hammers the point home.

Not so that the body and blood of the Lord are communed naturally to the bread and the wine, or lost in them as in one place; or put in them by any carnal or marvellous presence; but because the body and the blood are received verily of one faithful soul, and because the bread and the wine by the

institution of our Lord, are tokens by which the very communion or participation of the Lord's body and blood are exhibited of the Lord himself,
through the ministration of the Church, not to be a meat corruptible of the
body, but to be a nourishment and meat of eternal life.

This called for an entirely new order of service and entirely new thought.

The mystery of the priesthood was called severely into question, and the
spiritual power of the Church, from the archangel Michael to the poorest
parish priest, was declared void. This went far beyond the bounds of the
petty heresies that abounded: this was a call to revolution.

Whether Wishart would be allowed to utter that call was a matter of
some doubt. However, with the improved relations between Scotland and
England after the treaty of Greenwich, and Governor Arran's embracing of
Protestantism, Wishart felt it was safe to return north in July 1543.

But his ambition to act the evangelist in his homeland was thwarted by
the end of Governor Arran's 'Godly fit' and the start of the Protestant
persecution. However, an act of the Estates of 19 March 1543 had made it
legal for all men to read the Old and New Testaments in their mother
tongue. Knox said, 'Then might have been seen the Bible lying on every
gentleman's table. The New Testament was borne about in many hands.
Some that, perchance, had never read ten sentences in it had it most
common in their hand.'

But the Act was hedged about with conservative caution, punishing any
that preached contrary to the scripture with pain of death. What constituted contrariness was, naturally, a matter of Church opinion. Wishart
preached his exposition of the scriptures in Montrose and Dundee, only
seven miles from St Andrews, and this proximity proved too much for
Cardinal Beaton. He charged Wishart with 'convoking the liegemen without royal sanction' and sent a magistrate to call on him to desist. Wishart
fled south to Ayrshire, where he had an outstanding invitation to preach.
To prevent this the archbishop of Glasgow occupied the church in Ayr, but
Wishart preached out of doors to a crowd at the market cross, where, Knox
tells us, 'he made so notable a sermon that his enemies themselves were
confounded'. He continued to preach variously in those past centres of
Lollardry, and later of outdoor Covenanting, Ayrshire and Kyle – 'Christ
Jesus is as potent in the fields as in the kirk' – until news of an outbreak of
plague in Dundee drew him back north. There were the inevitable rumours
that the plague was a punishment for his original banishment from the area,

but whatever the cause, Wishart remained there preaching and comforting the plague victims.

At this time, an attempt was made on Wishart's life by John Wigton, a Dundonian priest, who, while carrying a hidden dagger, hid behind the pulpit from which Wishart was preaching. The sharp-eyed Wishart seized and disarmed the assassin, saving him from the immediate vengeance of the congregation and sending him on his way with forgiveness. Wigton was 'a desperate priest, corrupted by the Cardinal's money'. Whether the supremely political Beaton would have resorted to such a blatant piece of open violence is unlikely. Since the would-be assassin would almost certainly be seized even if he had been successful, and he seemed to be singularly inept, it seems that Wigton was more probably a lone operator, bigoted to the point of madness.

The accusation of the cardinal's involvement was as predictable as Hitler blaming the Reichstag fire on Communists, and just as incredible. But whatever the motivation, the result was that from then on, Wishart travelled with an armed escort, usually carrying a two-handed sword.

He then came south, first to Leith, having been warned that Edinburgh itself was unsafe for him. He was passed from safe house to safe house – now a hunted man without any formal charge but for the extreme displeasure of the Cardinal. At the house of Hugh Douglas of Longniddry, a village a few miles east of Edinburgh, he met Knox, who thereupon became his sword-bearer and escort in the Lothians. Here we begin to discern Knox having a reputation for dissent in his area, and given the close-knit society of local lairds, Knox may well have been summoned to meet Wishart, whose reputation would have marched before him.

At this point Knox had no public stature as a reformer, but locally he may well have been known for his dissenting views. He would have known of Wishart and been keen to meet him.

Wishart preached to large and enthusiastic assemblies in Tranent and then on 14 January 1546 came to Haddington. At his first appearance there was a considerable number in the church, with Knox the sword-bearer on duty at the foot of the pulpit stair, when Wishart saw two greyfriars whispering to the congregation as they entered.

Ironically, he called for people to stand aside and let the visitors enter, as the friars may have come to learn. When the friars clearly carried on disturbing the congregation, Wishart called out, 'O, sergeants of Satan, will ye neither hear God's truth nor suffer others to hear it?' At this point the observers, having heard enough, left and by that afternoon and on the next day, the attendance was sparse. Rumour had it that the entire operation was under close scrutiny and any supporters would be easily identified. Cardinal Beaton's net was closing.

The word was that the local landowner, Patrick Hepburn, earl of Bothwell, a friend of the cardinal, would not look kindly on his tenants listening to heresy. Wishart was, however, being sheltered by Sir Richard Maitland of Lethington, father of William, who in the future was to be the debating opponent of Knox – a fact, Carlyle says, that gives 'a pleasant little twinkle of interest to secular readers'. But here Wishart received letters telling him that his support was melting away. He said 'that he was weary of the world since men were weary of God', and next day he preached patience to the few people who had appeared. Knox says 'his auditure was small'. There was a glimmer of popular support when after the service, and before the congregation had left, Sir George Douglas, brother of the earl of Angus, publicly declared, 'I know my Lord Governor and the Cardinal will hear that I have been present at these services and I will make no denial, for I will fearlessly defend the preacher and uphold his doctrines'. The fact that Sir George escaped arrest owed in part to his position, and in part to the fact that the cardinal was busy with another scheme due to come to fruition in a few days. Wishart was due to go on to the house of John Cockburn at Ormiston, some six miles away, and Knox intended to accompany him; Wishart forbade him though and took the sword from Knox, saying, 'return to your bairns, and God bless you. One is sufficient for a sacrifice'. He then turned to walk to Ormiston, the roads being too frozen for horses. They never met again. The fact that Wishart was able to accept Knox as his sword-bearer and his virtual chaplain marks out our humble papal notary as a trusted member of such a reforming movement as there was. His doubts of three years previously seem to have turned into open apostasy. Indeed, Knox had to be dissuaded from accompanying Wishart to his almost inevitable arrest. Knox was to say of him that he was,

a man of such graces that before him were never heard within this realm. He was not only singularly learned as well in godly knowledge as in all honest humane science, but also he was so clearly illuminated with the spirit of prophecy.

Indeed later in the *History* Knox quotes Wishart's prophecy: 'my travail is near an end . . . God will send you comfort after me. This realm shall be illuminated with light of Christ's Evangel . . . the house of God shall be builded to it. It shall not lack the very cope-stone.' Knox does seem to be reporting, with advantages, his own future career.

On the night of 16 January, Wishart's host, Cockburn of Ormiston, and his guests, Wishart, John Sandilands and Crichton of Brunstone discussed the deaths of God's chosen servants and sang the metrical version of Psalm 51 together before retiring to bed. But at midnight they were disturbed by the noisy arrival of a detachment of armed and mounted men. These were Bothwell's men from his stronghold at Elphinstone Tower, where, unknown to the company, the cardinal himself was now lodged. It was clear that they had come for Wishart, but Bothwell assured him that he would be under his personal protection and that no harm would come to him.

Wishart said, 'I thank God that one so honourable as your lordship receives me this night, being assured that, having pledged your honour, you will preserve me from injury.'

Bothwell replied, 'In my keeping you shall be secure till I restore you to freedom or bring you again to this place.'

Lit by torches, in the freezing January night and surrounded by steel-helmeted retainers, Bothwell could, from his mounted position of power, offer anything in the knowledge that Ormiston, Wishart and the others could only agree. They were virtual prisoners.

Bothwell then assured Ormiston and his other guests that they had nothing whatsoever to fear. Realizing that any prevarication would result in instant bloodshed, Wishart said, 'Let the will of the Lord be done', and surrendered. He was immediately placed under close guard and Bothwell delivered him to the cardinal at Elphinstone Tower. Bothwell then returned to arrest Wishart's hosts with Hamilton, the governor of Edinburgh Castle. It was clearly all quite civilized, for we hear that while Hamilton was being entertained with wine, now at about 3 a.m., Crichton of Brunstone managed to escape. However Ormiston and Sandilands were summarily despatched to imprisonment at Edinburgh Castle. Bothwell's guarantees of safety, which in any case, no one had believed from the first, were seen to be as worthless as Jan Hus's safe conduct. Sandilands was able to buy his freedom, while Ormiston himself athletically escaped by climbing over the wall of the castle. Bothwell's rewards for this deceitful deed were gold from the cardinal, and a promise from the Queen to favour his lawful suits with women. Knox says that the earl was at that time in the 'glondours' with the Queen, presumably meaning he was in disgrace for non-lawful suits with women, always a weakness with Bothwell. In 1570 the chronicler Lindsay of Pitscottie tells us that from that time forth the Earl of Bothwell never thrived well, nor none of his affairs prospered with him. But Pitscottie was fond of finding divine retribution wherever he could, for soon after this he tells us,

> Also on 26th February, Arran, Beaton and the Earl of Argyle, as justice general, hanged four honest men for eating a goose in Lent, and drowned a young woman for not praying to Our Lady and other Saints during labour. But from that time forth, the Earl of Argyle to his dying day was ever diseased both in body and spirit

Had Knox been at Ormiston's house that night he too would have been carried into captivity as a man already marked by association. But even allowing for his escape, his life could now never be the same again. Wishart, however, was removed to the sea tower at Cardinal Beaton's castle at St Andrews.

Charles Rogers, in his *Life of George Wishart*, is definite that he was thrust into the horror of the Bottle dungeon, but the sea tower contains another, more salubrious cell, and it seems more likely that Wishart was kept there. Beaton applied to Governor Arran for authority to appoint a commission with a civil judge, but Arran drew back and asked that all proceedings be stopped. The balance of power between the cardinal and the governor is neatly demonstrated by the fact that Beaton simply ignored the governor's instructions and set about Wishart's trial, which convened in the cathedral on the morning of 28 February. This would have been a grand theatrical occasion with a specially constructed grandstand for the clergy in front of the chancel screen and the townsfolk filling the nave.

Knox tells us,

> My Lord Cardinal caused his servants to dress themselves in their most warlike array, with jack [quilted jacket], knapscall [helmet], splint [arm armour], spear and axe more seeming for war than for the preaching of God. Master George was conveyed unto the Abbey Church by the Captain of the Castle and the number of an hundred men, like a lamb to the sacrifice.

After a lengthy sermon by John Winram, the sub-prior, Wishart was put into the pulpit and charged by one John Lauder. As accuser, he would have, dramatically, been wearing a red hood to his gown. Knox goes on, one of the fed flock, a monster, full of cursings, threatenings, maledictions and words of devilish spite and malice, saying to the innocent Master George so many cruel and abominable words and hit him so spitefully with the Pope's thunder, that the ignorant people dreaded lest the earth would have swallowed him up quick. When that this fed sow had read all throughout his lying menacings, his face running down with sweat, and frothing at the mouth like a bear, he spat at Master George's face, saying, 'What answerest thou to these sayings, thou runagate, traitor, thief which we have duly proved by sufficient witness against thee?'

Wishart then prayed and started a defence of his actions, but as soon as he claimed that he had preached only scripture in the mother tongue, he was interrupted again by Lauder – with 'hoggish voice' – who appealed to the congregation of prelates. Knox then tells us that the prideful and scornful people that stood by would at that point have given sentence against Wishart, but certain men counselled the Cardinal to read the articles of accusation. There were eighteen of these and to them all Wishart gave 'Godly answers and true reasons', but was summarily condemned to be burnt as a heretic. Wishart was then allowed to pray to God to forgive his accusers and taken back to the castle, where two friars were later sent to hear his last confession. He sent them away and, oddly enough, insisted on confessing to Winram, lately one of the principal accusers.

Next morning, Beaton ordered all the castle guns to be trained on the stake that had been erected just beyond the castle grounds. The tower and the front windows of the castle were covered with silk hangings and tapestries, whence the cardinal and the bishops watched the events in cushioned splendour. Wishart was then led out, with his hands bound. He was taken to the stake where he prayed, claiming that he had no fear of the grim fire, and beseeched his hearers not to fear, 'them that slay the body, and afterwards have no power to slay the soul. For my faith is such, that my soul shall sup with my Saviour this night.' He forgave his executioner, and then, 'by and by, was put upon the gibbet and hanged, and there burnt to powder. And the people might not withhold from piteous mourning and complaining of the innocent lamb's slaughter.'

Wishart is also reputed to have caught the eye of the cardinal and prophesied, 'He who in such state, from that high place, feedeth his eyes with my torments, within a few days shall be hanged out at the same window, to be seen with as much ignominy, as he now leaneth there in pride.' Rogers asserts that he had been, 'hung about with bags of gunpowder and he was made fast to the stake while a heap of faggots was piled about his body. Fire being applied, the bags of gunpowder exploded and he ceased to live.' Pitscottie, naturally, gives us more dramatic detail with his obligatory thunderclaps.

> Two tormentors came to Master George, one with a coat of buckram and the other certain packets of powder. He was put on the scaffold and bound to it with iron chains, he prayed and they laid fire to him and gave him the first blast of powder which was very terrible and odious to see, for there came so great a thud of wind out of the sea and so great a cloud of rain out of the heavens that when the wind and wet met together, it had such noise and sound that all men were afraid that heard or saw it. It had such force and strength that it blew down the stone walls and the men that sat thereon to the number of two hundred persons, who fell in the bishop's yard. And so many of them fell therein that two of them drowned immediately and so there was sacrifice of fire and water. Master George said, 'God forgive that man that lies so glorious on that wall head, but within a few days he shall lie as shamefully as he is glorious now.' With that they pulled the tow [probably a strangling-cord] and built the great fire about him and when he was burnt all from the waist down they bade him remember on God and make a sign thereof; to that token he leapt up a foot of height in the fire, which was a great rejoicing.

From any version, we can see that the authorities at St Andrews had learnt a lot since the bungled death of Patrick Hamilton, with whose sad ghost the spirit of Wishart is still occasionally seen to walk the beach below the cliffs.

The fact that, in later days Knox knew, and questioned, Winram, Wishart's confessor who later converted to Protestantism, means that we must give a certain credence to his account of the trial. Rogers's authority is largely the first edition of the martyrologist Foxe's *Actes and Monumentes* published in 1563, seventeen years after the event. That narrative is itself based on an undated black-letter volume possibly prepared by Knox in 1547, the year after the execution, and it is this version we find in his *History*. But whatever the source a definite picture does emerge of Wishart's trial and execution as a great political event over which care had been taken.

Up until this point in his life Knox would have read the reforming works from Europe, have sat at the feet of free-minded teachers, and have come to believe personally that truth would only come from direct study of scripture. He also believed that the intercession of the Roman Church to ensure salvation was an unnecessary obstruction to Christ's promises, making the Pope an Anti-Christ and Rome itself an obscenity. But now he had seen and heard this truth being openly preached and had sheltered and admired a man who was prepared to die for these beliefs. He had watched him go willingly to meet a certain death.

If 'Luther hatched the egg Erasmus laid', then Wishart's effect on Knox and the entire Scottish Reformation is directly similar to Erasmus' egg: the results of his martyrdom cannot be overstated. It would not be until 1548, two years later, that Wishart's translation of the *Helvetic Confession* was published in England.

It is also interesting that with the arrival of Wishart in his *History*, Knox starts to tell us of his own part in the affairs of the time, albeit in the third person, for perhaps it was from here that Knox felt his mission started. His apostasy must have begun much earlier and it was with great spiritual distress that he rejected the Church into which he had been received, but Knox was now committed to the reforming faction.

His immediate concerns, however, were more worldly. He was the only guardian of the 'bairns' Wishart had recommended he return to, Francis and George Douglas and Alexander Cockburn. And he was fatally tainted in the sight of Beaton by his association with Wishart. In other words, it was certain he would have been hunted down and executed as a proponent of heresy, were it not that the cardinal himself was about to leave the stage in a most dramatic way.

Cardinal Beaton's enemies in this act of the drama were motivated not only by religious intolerance but also by temporal grievances, and it seems to have been a mixture of these that led to the events of 29 May 1546, just three months after the martyrdom of Wishart.

William Kirkcaldy, Norman Leslie, his uncle, John Leslie, James Melville and Peter Carmichael were all members of the junior lairdry, all were discontented with the cardinal's high-handed rule and all had lost out financially in some manner to him. They had lost enough, in fact, to let discontent grow to a determination for revenge.

The castle of St Andrews, impregnable except by what would be a foolhardy direct approach from the land, was being refortified and there was a confusing coming and going of masons and workmen early in that morning of 29 May. The drawbridge was down to allow this traffic and the five conspirators approached the porter to enquire, politely, if the lord cardinal was stirring. They would, in all likelihood, have seen Marion Ogilvie, Beaton's mistress, leaving earlier by a privy postern. Knox, with his tongue firmly in his cheek, says that the cardinal and Mistress Ogilvie had been all night 'busy at their accounts,' and 'a morning sleep was requisite for my Lord Beaton resting, after the rules of physic'. The porter took fright, but was silenced before he could raise the alarm and thrown into the moat, while approximately sixteen more armed insurgents arrived. The workmen and servants were driven out, and William Kirkcaldy was set to guard the gate against any further attempt to enter the castle, in which Beaton was now alone, except for his valet. Realizing that escape was out of the question, Beaton took his two-handed sword, hid a box of gold under the fire coals and with his valet tried to fortify the bedchamber by piling the bed, so recently vacated by Mistress Ogilvie, and other furniture against the door. Leslie threatened to set fire to the door and the cardinal, accepting the inevitable, opened it to admit Leslie, Carmichael and Melville. Beaton had sat down declaring that as a priest he should not be harmed, and Leslie and Carmichael struck out at him, but Melville held them back, asking that everything be done with gravity. Indeed, Knox called him 'most gentle and most modest!' This most gentle and modest man told Beaton to repent of his wickedness in burning Wishart and being an obstacle to Christ Jesus and his Holy Evangel and put the point of his sword to his breast. When Beaton hesitated to repent Melville then modestly and gently ran him through and the cardinal fell to the floor crying, 'I am a priest, I am a priest, fye, fye, all is gone,' before dying on the floor. What became of the gold and the valet we do not know.

The townspeople, realizing what was happening, came to the castle, and on being told that the cardinal had received his just reward and would trouble them no more demanded to see him. The assassins tied the body by a foot and a wrist and hung it out of a window for all to see. Ironically it was probably the window from which Beaton had watched Wishart burn. Again, never one to miss high drama, Pitscottie tells us that when Beaton was hanging on the wall, 'ane called Guthrie pisched in his mouth, that the people might see a part of George Wishart's prophecy fulfilled.'

However, the weather being warm, a rarity in St Andrews, even in late May, his body was salted and put into a lead coffin, which was then, with a fine sense of irony, lowered into the Bottle Dungeon.

He would eventually be clandestinely buried in the chapel of the Blackfriars in the town. The occupiers, now called the Castilians, settled down to withstand the inevitable siege.

The Castilians probably numbered about 150 and the siege, as with most things instigated by Governor Arran, was a fairly half-hearted affair coming to a temporary halt in December with an uneasy armistice, or 'appointment'. Arran may have been cautious about appearing overly severe towards the Castilians since his son, who had been an unofficial ward of the cardinal's, was in the rebels' hands. The Castilians were more or less free to come and go as they pleased in the town and mixed with the garrison. The garrison, for their part, made no attempt to enter the castle, apart from digging a huge tunnel under the fortifications. This attempt was thwarted by the Castilians, who dug their own counter-mine to meet it. The Queen Mother had asked for help from France and received only prevarication, while Kirkcaldy and his fellow Castilians sought help from Protestant England. All of this became doubly complicated, when in January of 1547 Henry VIII died, to be succeeded by his ten-year-old son Edward VI. England was now under the protectorship of the earl of Somerset, who promised the Castilians much but delivered little of practical value in fear of angering France, with whom England had an uneasy peace. The second complication arrived on 27 March when Francis I of France died, to be succeeded by his son Henry II.

Henry II believed, quite simply, that heresy was an infection of the lower classes and should be regarded as seditious treason. His queen was Catherine de Medici, loathed by the old aristocracy as merely an Italian banker's daughter who was reputed to dabble in witchcraft and arcane poisons. His mistress was Diane de Poitiers, a widow who habitually wore black and white as her mark of eternal mourning, but who at least provided some shafts of romance in a court otherwise gripped by the sordid machinations of a fading aristocracy led by the Guise faction, all of whom were related to the Queen Mother. This, then, was the end of the era in which Henry VIII and Francis I had vied with one another in magnificent displays of Renaissance hubris on the field of the cloth of gold.

All this while Knox, still acting as a tutor in the Lothians and daily expecting arrest by John Hamilton (about to be the new archbishop of St Andrews), thought of fleeing to Germany, but was persuaded by the fathers of his pupils to take them to St Andrews and join the Castilians during the truce.

And so in April he did just that, taking the three children with him. It is a mark of the respect in which Knox was already held that his charges' parents did not remove their children from his care and let him shift as best as he could on his own. They obviously felt that the 32-year-old Knox's views were preferable to the rigid Catholicism available elsewhere and that their children would prosper spiritually under his tutelage.

The Castilians' comparative freedom, thanks to the vagueness of Arran's 'appointment', had caused severe divisions in the town. The military were earning their inevitable reputation for pillage and plunder in the neighbourhood, while the more devout Castilians found opposition from the local clergy such as Dean John Annand, whom Knox, with customary candour, calls 'a rotten papist'. If he had ever posessed a dream of a quiet life it shattered forever as he entered the divided town with his pupils. The *Diurnal of Occurents* calls Knox a preacher and 'ane priest'.

Knox diligently instructed his charges in humane studies, grammar and the customary classical background, as well as teaching them a catechism that they delivered publicly in the parish church.

It was in this church that one John Rough was preaching. As we have heard, Rough had been chaplain to Governor Arran, during Arran's 'godly fit', and he had heard Knox lecture in the Castle Chapel on the testament of St John. ('In which he had first cast his anchor.') The parish church being also available to the cardinal's faction, Rough was under attack from Annand and called on Knox to preach with him. Knox refused, saying that 'he would not run where God had not called him'.

Now, this may mean that he felt he was officially unqualified, as he had not received a licence to preach when he was ordained – that is to say, he was only a deacon and not a fully ordained priest. But it is more likely this was the natural reticence of one who had, so far, not preached from the pulpit. There is no doubt that by now Knox had broken all ties with the Catholic Church and could have no qualms about breaking canon law. If he had been ordained priest, but had been harbouring doubts, his comparatively obscure position as a notary would have allowed him to keep them to himself. But now he was being called into the open arena. Wishart had conquered his doubts and embraced the new freedom, and Knox must have seen that he would soon have to make a similar move. He was in St Andrews with Protestant colleagues around him, and in a familiar town where the university continued to sit at the feet of John Mair, but still he prevaricated, perhaps until circumstances would make it impossible for him to refuse. These circumstances were supplied by John Rough, who, with Sir David Lyndsay of the Mount, already a known reformer, and Henry Balnaves, a highly placed civil servant who had joined the Castilians, conspired to make Knox's continuing refusal impossible. With Knox present in the church, Rough preached a sermon on the election of ministers, and the power of the congregation to appoint them, and then turned directly to Knox and entreated him to preach. For added drama he asked the congregation if that was indeed also their wish. They agreed that it was and echoed Rough's call on Knox to preach. He now had little option but to comply, but with 'most abundant tears' he fled from the church.

Knox realized that he was being asked to continue where Wishart had left off, and to enter into a debate that would probably last the rest of his life, if it did not cause him to lose that life altogether. Instead of his preaching giving him a reputation, his reputation was forcing him into a life in the pulpit, and after this there could be no turning back into an academic, or any other sort of life. His commitment would have to be total and he tells us, 'no man saw any sign of mirth of him . . . many days together'.

The gauntlet was thrown down a second time when Dean Annand, the 'rotten Papist', at a public debate, averred that the Church's authority damned all Lutherans and heretics, and, therefore, he needed no further disputation. The St Andrews public called out to Knox, 'we cannot all read your writings, but we may all hear you preach. Therefore we require you in the name of God, that you will let us hear a proof of what you have affirmed, for, if it be true, we have been miserably deceived.'

Knox then spoke:

We must discern the immaculate spouse of Jesus Christ, from the mother of confusion, spiritual Babylon, lest we embrace the harlot instead of the chaste spouse. I offer myself, by word or writ, to prove the Roman church this day further degenerate from the purity which was in the days of the apostles, than was the church of the Jews from the ordinance given by Moses, when they consented to the innocent death of Jesus Christ.

Unsurprisingly, this challenge was accepted and he committed himself to preach on the following Sunday.

His future was now determined, and he was in the spotlight to fight the championship bout without contesting any preliminaries, for he would be preaching not only to the people of the town as well as the garrison

SIR JOHN KNOX

soldiers, but also to the intellectual elite of St Andrews University, including John Winram, canons and friars of both orders, and, probably more important to Knox, to his old mentor John Mair.

He took his text from the seventh chapter of Daniel, in which Daniel dreams of the apocalyptic beasts, and in verses 24 and 25, in which a king arises who speaks against the most high and consumes the saints of the most high.

He started by confirming the love God has for His Church in granting foreknowledge to its members of disasters to come, then went on to give a summary of the history of the Babylonian, Persian and Greek empires. The Roman empire he maintained, had decayed, producing the last beast, which was the Roman Church, as all but the blind could clearly see. In the New Testament this beast, or king, was the Anti-Christ or the Whore of Babylon, and the name could apply also to a body or multitude, which would likewise be infected with the sin of the head. He analysed the lives of various popes and reached the crux of his argument that man is justified by faith alone. He continued, saying that 'the blood of Jesus Christ purges us from all sins,' so that the papist attribution of justification to laws of man's invention, pilgrimage, pardons and so on was repugnant to the laws of the Evangel. He then quoted the Revelation of St John the Divine, 'that the merchandise of that Babylonian harlot, amongst other things, shall be the bodies and souls of men', decrying the power of the Mass, before finally throwing down a challenge to the authorities to engage him in later debate when he would produce scriptural proofs for all that he had put forward, and prove that his interpretations were correct.

This sermon had no half-measures or prevarications, it was an absolute denial of the authority of Rome and the Catholic Church. Man's salvation was in his own hands, and by his faith and belief alone would he be saved. The intercessions of the priesthood and the obstacles they put in the way of the faithful were unnecessary and sinful. One can only imagine the suppressed fury and revulsion of some members of his audience. But the reaction of John Mair remains a mystery, since Knox, unsurprisingly, only reports favourable reactions. 'Others sned [cut] the branches of the Papistry, but he strikes at the root, to destroy the whole. . . . If the doctors defend not now the Pope and his authority . . . the Devil have my part of him and of his laws both.'

His listeners were aware of the potency of Knox's sermon, prophesying, 'Master Wishart spake never so plainly and yet he was burnt: even so will he be.' But John Hamilton, the archbishop-to-be, had different views and called on the sub-prior, John Winram, to oppose himself to this diatribe in answer to Knox's challenge. Winram duly called a convention in St Leonard's Yards with the friars of both orders (Knox calls them 'Grey friars and Black fiends'), as well as John Rough and Knox.

Nine Articles were read by Knox that conform with the *Helvetic Confession*, and since they are crucial as a basis for the Scottish Reformation, are worth quoting in full:

1. No mortal man can be head of the Church.
2. The Pope is an Antichrist and so is no part of Christ's mystical body.
3. Man may neither make nor devise a religion that is acceptable to God: but man is bound to observe and keep the religion that is from God received, without chopping and changing thereof.
4. The Sacraments of the New Testament ought to be administered as they were instituted by Christ Jesus, and practised by his apostles: nothing ought to be added to them; nothing ought to be diminished from them.
5. The Mass is abominable idolatry, blasphemous to the death of Christ, and a profanation of the Last Supper.
6. There is no Purgatory in which the souls of men can either be pined [punished] or purged after this life: but heaven rests to the faithful, and hell to the reprobate and unthankful.
7. Praying for the dead is vain, and to the dead is idolatry.
8. There are no bishops, except they preach even by themselves, without any substitute.
9. The teinds [tithes] by God's law do not appertain of necessity to the kirk-men.

Knox thanked Winram, whom Knox must have known agreed with most of these points, for so modest and quiet an 'auditure' and went on to answer the questions raised, somewhat softly, it must be said, by the same man. Arbuckle, a grey friar, then attempted to tackle Knox by logic and ended in such a tangle that 'few would have thought such a learned man would have given such a foolish answer'. This debate does, however, show that Knox was no mere ranter but could, on occasion, use calm logic and reason to support his arguments and defeat his opponents.

Since there was no possibility of defeating Knox in debate the next move by the authorities was to prevent him from Sunday preaching in the Church again. To this end Winram ruled that only preachers from the abbey or the university would address the Sunday services. Knox circumvented this petty decree by simply holding communion on weekdays, drawing a congregation not only from the Castilians but also the town.

There is no doubt that Knox had worked out in private the basis for his future beliefs before making these public statements, and while some authorities dispute that the roots of democratic faith were present here, it seems undeniable that the denial of the ceremony of the Mass, the disbelief in Purgatory, and the stress on individual salvation through faith put every individual man in charge of his own destiny in a manner that was inimical to the elaborate hierarchy of the established Church. His preaching style was vehement and he was accused of taking a bludgeon to the arguments of Rome, but he was preaching to the laity as much, or even more, than he was appealing to the sophisticated minds of the clerical intelligentsia. In any case, their minds would already be locked in unshakeable bigotry.

The 'appointment' between the Castilians and Governor Arran was always an uneasy peace and now was becoming more uneasy. Balnaves brought encouragement, but not much more, from England, as Protector Somerset found his hands full at home. Rough left St Andrews shortly after the St Leonard's debate, never to return. He married and had a parish in Hull, but to escape Mary Tudor's persecutions in England, he fled to Friesland where he earned a precarious living knitting caps and hose. Twelve years later, in 1557, he came to London on a wool-buying trip and was elected minister to a secret congregation there. He was betrayed, arrested in Islington, interrogated and taken to the scaffold in Smithfield. He beseeched the crowd to, 'look up with their eyes of hope, for redemption is not far off, but my wickedness hath devised that I shall not see it.' He was then burnt to death.

Knox, now sole spiritual leader of the garrison, preached against its libertine ways, but it might seem that God favoured the contrasting prayers of the Queen Mother and the French ambassador D'Oysel. Arran offered a papal absolution, remitting their sins, to the Castilians, but they, probably wisely distrusting him and certain that England would come to their aid, refused and kept up their watch for a relieving fleet to appear. But when, on 29 June, a fleet was sighted, it was flying a French standard. There were twenty-one war galleys under the command of Leo Strozzi, prior of Capua, admiral of the French galleys and cousin to Catherine de Medici.

The initial engagements went in favour of the Castilians and the French retired to Dundee to lick their wounds. But by mid July Arran's forces appeared on the landward side, artillery was mounted in the abbey and on the roof of St Salvator's that could fire directly into the court of the castle. Finally, on 29 July, a six-hour barrage shattered the outer walls.

Plague had broken out among the garrison, the French fleet cut off all hope of relief from the English, and further defiance was fruitless. William Kirkcaldy, who had guarded the outer gate during the murder of Cardinal Beaton, went to negotiate a peace with Strozzi, whose men occupied the castle.

Since the surrender had been made to the French and not to Arran's forces, the garrison was taken aboard the French ships. Had the landward forces taken the castle, then, in all probability, some of the prophesies made after Knox's sermon would have been carried out, so the fact that he fell into French hands probably saved him from the stake. He would certainly have been burnt and the original Castilians would have met a similarly final fate. More importantly to Arran probably, the treasure in the castle, including all of Beaton's wealth, would have fallen to him. Instead of which about £100,000 and 120 men fell into French hands, not as prisoners of war (there was nothing similar to the twentieth-century Geneva Convention), but merely as assets of the French crown to be used as economically as could be devised. This meant that they would go for the remainder of their lives into the French galleys as slaves. The Pope congratulated Henry II and Governor Arran on their actions to avenge the death of Beaton. Arran despatched a messenger to France asking, with the malevolent spirit of the triumphalist weak man in victory, that the prisoners be treated with particular severity. Knox notes with satisfaction that the messenger broke his neck at Dumbarton on the return journey.

But Knox was not to leave the French galleys for eighteen months and it must have seemed a particularly cruel stroke of fortune that so shortly after he had preached his first sermon, allying himself totally with the forces of reform, his mouth had been effectively stopped. His public debate had set out a manifesto for a reformed Church and had undoubtedly been noted by like-minded thinkers, but there was now no opportunity to spread his message further. Had he been taken by Arran's forces, his alliance with the Castilians meant that he would have been accused of treason as well as heresy and summarily executed. Instead he was to face undreamt-of horrors.

3   Prison and Peace

There was no real need for Arran to ask for particularly sharp handling of the prisoners, since the normal fate of the galley slaves was horrifying enough. Professor Hume Brown calls it 'a form of life which for unutterable horror is perhaps without a parallel in the history of humanity'.

The use of galleys by France was widespread in the Mediterranean, the North Sea, the English Channel, the Baltic and even in the Caribbean, not disappearing until the end of the eighteenth century. Most commonly they were 40 to 44 metres long with a low 2-metre freeboard, decked, about 6 metres wide, with usually two masts, but driven mainly by the oars. With twenty-four to thirty banks of oars and three or five men on each oar, the rowers at the inboard end of the oars had to stand most of the time, walking backwards and forwards with the stroke. The slaves were chained to the benches, under which they also slept. Food consisted of biscuit and a kind of porridge of maize or beans, with water or oil when it was available. The toilet arrangements can only be imagined. A sleeveless jerkin was provided, leaving the arms free for rowing, the speed of which was controlled by an officer who patrolled the 'coursier', a central gangway between the banks of oars. He was provided with only a whip, since the lash did not break bones that would have prevented the slave from rowing.

A galley could achieve a speed of three nautical miles in an hour, and would try to approach an enemy ship at right angles, having most of its armaments mounted on the bow, where there was often a boarding platform to be used after ramming. The crowded conditions and the power of the forward mounted cannons meant horrifying casualties. One Venetian seaman records forty instant deaths as a result of one salvo. In a battle, when two ships collided side on, as often happened, the snapping of the ten metre oars would crush with appalling ease the ribs and spines of the chained slaves in the confined space of the rowing deck. Constant replacements were needed, so criminals and heretics – Muslims seemed to acquire a fatalism that made them particularly useful – were automatically despatched to the galleys.

This was the fate awaiting Knox on 7 August 1547 when Strozzi led his fleet back to France. They arrived first at Fécamp, then going on up river to Rouen, where the prisoners with a claim to nobility were divided from the rest. Norman Leslie, James Kirkcaldy of Grange and David Moneypenny were sent first to Cherbourg, then transferred to the greater security of Mont Saint-Michel, the great cathedral standing on an island pinnacle off the northern shore of Normandy and reached only by a causeway at low tide. Vigorous efforts were made to convert them to Catholicism but they simply said that 'the Captain had commandment to keep their bodies, but he had no power to command their souls'.

They also threatened, in the most direct way, that if they were forced to attend Mass, they would disrupt the service. Henry Balnaves was held in the Castle of Rouen, where he was thought of as being especially learned, and so 'was most sharply assaulted of all' to convert, but managed to write a *Treatise of Justification by Faith*, which he passed to Knox for comments. Knox added a prefatory letter and had the documents, which in modern printed form run to well over a hundred pages, sent on to Scotland.

He summarizes it as being in three parts.

1. How man, being in trouble, should seek refuge in God alone.
2. How man is released of his troubles by faith and that faith alone justifieth before God.
3. The fruits of faith are good works which every man should work according to his own vocation and he ends his recommendation, 'The works before written, are they in which every Christian should be exercised, to the glory of God, and utility of his neighbour.'

Given this ringing endorsement of Balnaves' *Justification* we can assume that Knox was in total agreement with it. He says that there are two ways in which men can be called to preach: first, directly by God as the original prophets and apostles were; and secondly, when one man called another, as Paul called Timothy and Titus. Perhaps here Knox was mindful of his own experience of being called to preach by Rough and Balnaves himself. He continues by asking his brethren in Scotland to remember that 'it is no speculative Theologue which desireth to give you courage, but even your brother in affliction, which partly hath experience what Sathan's wrath may do against the chosen of God'. He endorses Balnaves's command to honour the king, and be obedient to him because it is the will of God, and to live with your neighbour at rest and quietness, everyone supporting others as members of one body and giving loyalty to the civil powers. If they are in error then they should be prayed for, not overthrown.

Later in life Knox would examine these thoughts closely, coming to an altogether different conclusion.

But he also finds that the truth of justification is 'to cleave fast unto God by Jesus Christ, and not by our self, nor yet by our works'. There is a great simplicity in the belief that salvation and justification comes directly from God through Jesus Christ without the intermediaries in a manmade Church, that is, Rome. Therefore, the laws, structures and ceremonies of Rome, which are entirely manmade are necessarily contrary to the teachings of the scriptures. They are then clearly blasphemous. Knox and Balnaves are of one mind and he commends the treatise to his fellows in Scotland.

Balnaves is specific in saying,

Therefore the godly men, in their troubles and afflictions take great consolation and comfort and anchor themselves upon God alone by faith. Take no care what the world judge of thee but to thine own conscience and the Scriptures of God. The Scripture teaches me, having no respect to man's opinion, that thereby we may have consolation through our mutual faith. Christ is our justice, our Saviour and Redeemer, satisfaction for our sins and consummation of the law, and hath freed us from the law, sin and death . . . why will we usurp his office to ourselves and spoil Christ of His glory? The blessed sacrament offered daily to this or that saint and called his 'mass' for doing of the which there is not a syllable in God's word for you, but the contrary expressly commanded. The said godly declarations made against the superstitious worshipping of the saints, pilgrimage, purgatory, hallowing of water, foundation of masses to public or private idolatry, offerings or sacrifices, choice of meats, abuse of the Christian religion by the shaven, oincted, or smeared priests, bishops, monks and friars having only their vocation of man, and by man. And the greatest punishment is sent by God, for doing of the most excellent work, after the judgement of man, because it was not commanded by God.

This passage carries the marginal note by Knox, 'Mark diligently.'

There is no doubt that the *Jusitification* embodied most of Knox's thinking at the time and that he was wholly in agreement with its thrust. We are told that the tract was revised by Knox before being sent on to Scotland, but to what extent we have no way of knowing. The document was not published until 1584, when it was accidentally discovered, long after the death of both Knox and Balnaves and as to whether or not it circulated in some 'zamisdat' form we can only guess. It does, however, demonstrate that Knox was not alone in his belief that only scripture and not Church would lead to salvation. It was necessary enough when existing under the imminent risk of arrest and death for a reformer to know that he had support and was not a lone voice crying in the wilderness. It must have been even greater solace in the circumstance in which Knox now found himself. However, all this presumes that paper and writing materials were made available to both Balnaves and Knox. The normal fate of galley slaves did not allow for the composing and editing of religious tracts, and it does seem, in spite of Arran's vengeful recommendation, that the Scots slaves were given some special treatment, although Knox said he was 'sore troubled by corporal infirmity'. Surprisingly, uncensored correspondence between the prisoners was also possible, since the Mont Saint-Michel prisoners wrote to Knox asking if they would damage their conscience by trying to escape. Knox told them that, provided they committed nothing against God's express commandment, they could take whatever opportunity God provided. Clearly one was provided, since they did escape in the best Colditz style, evaded search parties and after various adventures managed to get passage to England. The existence of colonies of Scots in Rouen and elsewhere, some of whom were already Protestant, meant that a fairly sophisticated system of smuggling and intelligence was in existence.

Also, quite obviously, the entire time of their enslavement was not spent on the galleys themselves, especially in the winter months, and shore barracks were used as landward prisons. These were called 'bagnes', since the first of them were established in Constantinople near the Imperial Baths, and it is probable that Knox was allowed a certain licence when ashore.

The spirit of resistance among all the Scots prisoners was indeed still strong, in that they refused to give reverence to the Mass, which was either celebrated by a priest in the galley, or, possibly too fastidious or fearful to come aboard, standing on the shore in sight of the ship. On Saturday nights, when *Salve Regina* was sung, the Scots would cover their heads with whatever they could find in defiance of the accepted custom. Knox gives us another extraordinary example of defiance. His ship had now gone to Nantes at the mouth of the Loire for winter quarters when a painting of the Virgin was brought aboard for veneration and offered to a Scot to be kissed. The Scot said, 'Trouble me not, such an idol is accursed, and therefore I will touch it not.' The *argousin*, or lieutenant of the galley, then thrust the image into his hands. The prisoner then, 'advisedly looking about', presumably to make sure that his actions would not go unnoticed, threw it into the Loire, saying, 'Let our Lady now save herself, she is light enough, let her learn to swim.' (Given that Knox referred to himself in the third person, it is possible that the prisoner was himself. In the sixteenth century the word 'light' was also taken, when used as a description of a woman, to mean immoral and sexually profligate.) This defiance, or blasphemy, in the face of people who thought nothing of flogging a man to death if his rowing was seen to be uneven, shows amazing courage, but 'after that was no Scottish man urged with that idolatry'. Knox calls this 'a merry fact'.

In 1548 Knox shared a galley, the Nostre Dame, with James Balfour, who, on one occasion, asked Knox if he thought they would ever be freed. Knox said he was certain that liberty would come, even, when, with the cruellest of ironies, his galley had returned to attack St Andrews, in support of Mary of Guise, who was in conflict with the English.

His fellow slave Balfour then asked him if he knew the place. Knox replied that he did for he saw the steeple of the place where 'God first in public opened his mouth to his glory', and that, 'I shall not depart this life until my tongue shall glorify his Godly name in the same place.' Some authorities have taken this remark as evidence that Knox was starting to see himself in the role of Old Testament prophet, but it seems much more likely that it was simply the remark of a prisoner longing for freedom. The sodium glow of London nightlife can be see from inside the walls of Wormwood Scrubs prison, and certainly most inmates will look at the light and vow to rejoin the life outside. But there are very few prophets in prison.

Undoubtedly the period caused Knox considerable mental and physical distress, and he says that he was so sick that few hoped for his life. The physical effects of his privations were to stay with him for the rest of his life.

But in the first few months of 1549 Knox's nightmare came to an end and he was freed from the galleys as a result of a changed balance of power. The English Protector, Somerset, had attempted to force the Scots into agreeing to the marriage between Edward VI and the infant Queen Mary by a direct military invasion. He crushed the Scots at the battle of Pinkie, seized Haddington and burnt everything in sight around Edinburgh. This 'rough wooing' had not persuaded either Governor Arran or Mary of Guise to further the marriage contract, but rather it strengthened their resolve that Scotland's hope for support lay with Henry II in France. A parliament was called in Haddington Abbey, under the mouths of Somerset's guns, at which it was agreed that the infant Queen Mary should be betrothed to Francis, the four-year-old dauphin of France. So in July 1548 the six-year-old Mary Stuart, Queen of Scotland, set sail for France.

Carlyle, a confirmed Mariolater, says, 'By about the end of 1548 this jewel of a child was safe in St Germain-en-Laye; the brightest and bonniest little maid in the world . . . setting out, alas, toward the blackest destiny.' In Scotland Governor Arran was rewarded for his compliance in the proposed marriage with the duchy of Chatelherault. France had declared war on England, a war which had resulted in Knox's galley sailing as part of a raiding fleet. Mary of Guise, the queen mother, became regent, but the country was in a state bordering on civil war with many Protestant lords 'assuring' the English of their support. This was especially true of the Lothians, where there was steadfast support for the marriage with Edward. It is one of history's ironies that this was an area that had suffered most in the rough wooing. As far as Knox and his fellow galley-slaves were concerned, Protector Somerset, bizarrely, claimed that the Scots prisoners were, in fact, English subjects and demanded their release. The French, unsurprisingly, refused and negotiations dragged on. One extremely suspect source claims that Knox's release came when his galley was seized in the English Channel, but it is more likely that improved relations with France since the infant Queen's betrothal had softened French attitudes to the Scottish prisoners. Also the final accession of the boy King Edward VI had resulted in improved ambassadorial exchanges between England and France and by 1550 the sabre rattling had ended.

But England was encircled, and was, after the Emperor Charles V's defeat of the Schmalkaldic League at the battle of Muhlberg in 1547, also the last redoubt of Protestantism in Europe. Clearly Knox would be less than welcome in Scotland, but Somerset realized that he had an asset to the reformed faith in his hands. However Professor W. Stanford Reid, in his excellent *Trumpeter of God*, points out that with a heavy lowland Scots accent Knox was of limited use in the South of England. In later life, Knox had obviously lost most of his accent and was accused of 'knapping sudron', in other words, speaking like a Southerner. He may well have acquired a Southern accent out of sheer expediency, since, as a preacher, communication skills were essential, even living in a time when regional accents were normal and the bland 'received pronunciation' of the twentieth century did not exist. But Berwick was as far north as the Protestant faith extended, although the congregation there lacked a preacher and as a preacher Knox had, as yet, a very limited experience. However, to Berwick he was sent.

His reputation was well established by his sermon and debate in St Andrews, so he was enough of a celebrity for Protector Somerset to single him out for special observation. Somerset had also allied himself strongly with the archbishop of Canterbury Thomas Cranmer, who was actively producing a *Book of Common Prayer* which would wipe away much of the ceremony, so detested by Knox, as well as ensuring that all services took place in English. None of this went as far as Knox would have liked – he was no gradualist – but, in England at any rate, events were moving in his direction. Personally, however, he was moving north towards an area still rejecting reform and a town in a desperate state. He had, however, been licensed to preach by the Privy Council on 7 April 1549, and this marked him as almost a missionary for Somerset's view of the Reformation in England. Henry VIII's reforms had legitimized the royal marriage, dissolved the wealth of the monasteries, crushed the Pilgrimage of Grace and allowed communion to be given to the laity, and *The First Book of Common Prayer* allowed for the Mass to be said in English, although the vexed question of the adoration of the Host was left unaddressed.

Even these minor changes were opposed by many, especially in the north, and particularly by Cuthbert Tunstall, Bishop of Durham, under whose aegis Knox's new parish came. Somerset and Cranmer were keen for further reform, and Knox was a potent weapon against such institutional reluctance. The bishop was 'dilatory and luke-warm' in bringing about changes. He was also a reluctant Protestant and dyed-in-the-wool conservative, as well as being a skilful politician. Politics and diplomacy were two skills that eluded Knox throughout his entire life, since the depths of his convictions led him to a simple directness that most people mistook for bigotry. It is inconceivable that Somerset did not know that Knox would set about ignoring the existing rubric and changing the order of service drastically. That is probably why he was sent.

Berwick was a border town and host to a large garrison, most of whose occupants had recently returned from the siege of Haddington, which had hardly endeared them to the Scots. There were other garrisons nearby at Norham, Wark and Holy Island and all these places were full of mercenaries from Germany, Albania, Italy, and even renegade Scots, some of whom were lacking pay, and so depending on theft for existence. The streets were filthy and the sick died where they lay. Among the parish were many Scottish Protestant refugees, so that, for by no means the last time, Knox would be preaching to religious exiles. He was also in a permanent position, possessed of a stipend (£5 was paid on 7 April) and bound to make public in his preaching what, up until now, had been secret in the galleys. For the first time it was possible to acquire books and to indulge in study, while giving his body time to recover from the physical privations he had endured for the last fifteen months. A considerable amount of travelling would be needed, and Knox's physical health was still not good: 'the pain of my head and stomach troubles me greatly, daily I find my body decay, but the providence of my God shall not be frustrated'. Like everything Knox undertook, he gave a total commitment. He was now, however, able to set aside a day a week for study and prayer, even, at one point being caught still in bed when a messenger arrived. But with an anti-Scots garrison and a civilian congregation more used to the old ways it was not going to be a rest cure. A contemporary said, 'It will require a stern disciplinarian in the pulpit as well as a stirring preacher, to work out a moral and social reform.' But Somerset had chosen a preacher who had defied the worst conditions and the most repressive regime in Europe, and for Knox, his time in the Northeast of England was the most peaceful he ever experienced. Certainly, later he would tell Mary, Queen of Scots, 'God so blessed my weak labours that in Berwick (where commonly before there used to be slaughter by reason of quarrels that used to arise amongst soldiers), there was as great a quietness all the time that I remained there as there is this day in Edinburgh.' He even managed to include some of the garrison in his congregation, a congregation that admired his preaching so much that, in one case at least, the admiration grew to marriage. We are told that his congregation included the soldiers of Edward VI in the white and green livery of the Tudors, who came to listen to a warrior 'clothed in the full armour of God, who loved the language and metaphors of soldiership and battle'. This is not that Knox was embroidering his message to suit his audience, but rather that his fondness for the more vivid sections of the Old Testament suited his military hearers.

He felt himself enough at ease to devise his own order of service centred on the sermon, where he felt the greatest responsibility of the preacher lay in teaching, guiding and explaining scripture to his 'little flock'. He would begin the service by giving a discourse on a text from scripture, expounding the meaning of the text and ending with an explanation of how all the foregoing might apply to contemporary life. He would then offer a prayer for faith to be strengthened, and a call for sinners to repent. The promise of forgiveness would come from scripture and he would then share bread and wine, 'to be received with faith, and not with mouth, nor yet by transfusion of substance, for in the sacrament we receive Jesus Christ spiritually. In the supper of the Lord all were equally participant'. The sacrament was also for 'certifying the consciences of such as shall use the Lord's Table without superstition'.

By 1550 he gave a more detailed description:

And as concerning these words, *Hoc est Corpus meum* [incidentally, the origin of the contemporary phrase 'hocus-pocus'], on which the papists depend so much . . . if we should believe that His very natural body both flesh and blood, were naturally in the bread and wine, that should not save us, seeing many believe that, yet receive it to their damnation. For it is not His presence in the bread that can save us, but His presence in our hearts through faith . . .

The exhortation ended the minister comes down from the pulpit and sits at the table, every man and woman in like wise taking their place as occasion best serves; then he takes bread and gives thanks . . . this done he breaks the bread and delivers it to the people, who distribute and divide the same amongst themselves, according to our Saviour Christ's commandment, and in like wise gives the cup.

Knox continued in this form of the sacrament to the end of his days and cannot have created it simply on a whim, but rather as a result of study and a deep-rooted belief in the equality of all before God. This form had no connection whatsoever with the exclusivity of the priesthood of the

Catholic Church as seen in the Mass, but rather puts forward the democratic course of worship – 'equally participant' – as he beseeched the congregation directly to receive salvation through faith alone: mankind, responsible for its own actions, and face to face individually with its saviour.

Since his congregation was growing and no divine thunderbolts from above were arriving, Bishop Tunstall felt he had to act, so Knox was summoned to Newcastle to explain his deviation from *The Book of Common Prayer*. This he did at St Nicholas's Church on 4 April 1550 before the bishop and the Council of the North, a body with several Catholic members. 'The Fourth of April in the year 1550 was appointed to John Knox, Preacher of the Holy Evangel of Jesus Christ to give his confession why he affirmed the Mass idolatry.'

Knox knew that, as never before, he was in the public eye and whatever he said would be so widely reported that his licence to preach would be in jeopardy. Indeed he regarded this event so seriously that, in what was a very rare action for him, he printed his sermon afterwards. In it his position was unchanged. True Christianity arose only from the scriptures, and he started in full medieval logic with two syllogisms.

> All worshipping, honouring, or service invented by the brain of man in the religion of God, without His express commandment, is idolatry:
>
> The Mass is invented by the brain of man, without any commandment of God: therefore it is idolatry. All honouring or service of God, whereto is added a wicked opinion, is abomination. Unto the Mass is added a wicked opinion. Therefore it is an abomination.

John Mair would have been proud of him.

He then went on to provide examples and illustrations from scripture – some later shown to be of dubious logic – with his usual vehemence. But it must be said that with his compendious knowledge of the Bible, it would have been possible to prove almost anything, and his devotional energy easily outstripped the critical faculties of his audience. He gained an added celebrity with this sermon, especially in the north, which added to his popularity as a minister. His services were not only admired by reforming minds but also by the ordinary parishioners of Berwick, since he taught them that their sins could be forgiven by faith alone without the sacrifices required by the Catholic Church.

His clear message and vigorous physical style – 'I pray you pardon me, beloved brethren . . . vehemency of spirit compelleth me' – made him an especial favourite with the ladies in his parish, who, as is still often the case with charismatic preachers today, provided the backbone of his congregation. And none more so than Mrs Elizabeth Bowes of Aske. She was the daughter of Sir Roger Aske of Aske in Yorkshire and wife of Richard Bowes, the captain of Norham Castle, to whom she had given some fifteen children, of whom a daughter, Marjory, and eldest son, George, were still living with him.

It appears that the males of the family were more inclined towards traditional Catholicism and disapproved of Knox. Since one of the leaders of the Pilgrimage of Grace was from a branch of the Aske family this is hardly surprising. But Elizabeth and Marjory were enthusiastic followers of reform. In Knox's numerous letters to Elizabeth and Marjory we see a gentler side of the man who is usually portrayed as the Trumpeter of God, spewing fire and brimstone in all directions.

Elizabeth Bowes, rather than her daughter Marjory, seemed haunted by the fear of losing her faith and so falling into sin. Knox's replies to her many letters show her to have had a morbid depression that needed constant reassurance. He delivers a mixture of logic – 'if you fear damnation, then you must fear God, therefore your faith is as strong as ever' – and reassurance – 'Satan never tempts those he has already won'; 'You are sick, sister, but you shall not die. Your faith is weak and sore troubled, but you are not unfaithful, nor yet shall your infirmity be impute unto you.' He also confesses to his own feelings of spiritual inadequacy, saying that although no adulterer, his heart is infected with 'foul lusts'. He goes on to list the commandments he feels he himself breaks, even if only in his mind, in spite of which lapses he is compelled to thunder out the threatenings of God against obstinate rebels, and blow his master's trumpet.

In a letter of February 1552 there comes a celebrated passage which has been the subject of much debate. 'Call to your mind what I did when standing in the cupboard at Alnwick, in very deed I thought that no creature had been as tempted as I was.' In this instance he was writing to Elizabeth and not to her daughter Marjory, who would, in time, become his wife, and he signs the letter, as he often did, 'in great haste'. The temptation, given the location, could have ranged from stealing a piece of cheese, to a snatched kiss with his future bride or even his future mother-in-law. And Knox admits only to the temptation to which he appears not to have submitted.

But he goes on, 'But when I heard proceed from your mouth the very same words that he troubles me with, I did wonder . . . knowing in myself the dolour thereof.' Now for a spiritual mentor to confess that he, also, has doubts is just permissible, but to admit that he has as deep a trouble as his supplicant is probably too confidence-sapping for the supplicant, and I feel that the temptation he referred to was probably that he himself felt his faith slip from time to time, and at that particular moment, he was tempted to declare the anguish of his doubts when continually tested by God. All genuine reformers have doubts – Martin Luther threw ink pots at the Devil – and if Knox was tempted to confess his we cannot be surprised. In later times he writes of his despair and despondency, both wrought from what must have been near total exhaustion.

These letters to a troubled parishioner add much to the human dimension of Knox and endorse Thomas Carlyle's view that 'They go far wrong who think this Knox was a gloomy, spasmodic, shrieking fanatic. Not at all, he is one of the solidest of men, a most shrewd, observing, quietly discerning man; an honest-hearted, brotherly man – brother to the high, brother also to the low, sincere in his sympathy with both'. Indeed his sincerity in that sympathy for what must have been the occasionally tiresome doubts of Elizabeth Bowes comes clearly through.

One authority is of the opinion that the relationship with Elizabeth 'served to cultivate and bring out the softer elements of his richly-endowed nature and to provide a needful counterpoise of humility and sympathy to his heroic strength'.

There is also much in these letters of the normality of his life, his tiredness in travelling about his parish and his inability to sleep with the pain of 'gravel'. (This resulted from concretions of uric acid forming a stone or 'calculus' either in the kidney or the bladder, and passing down the urinary tract as small, but extremely painful particles. The cause is not known, but was probably dietary and dated from his time in the French galleys.) He also reports an encounter with his brother William, who was now a merchant settled in Prestonpans, on the south coast of the Firth of Forth not far from Haddington, but at this time proceeding up the coast back to Scotland on commercial business. He goes on to ask Elizabeth if there is anything she would like fetched back. This was a period in Knox's life when he could, for the first time, enjoy a settled existence. His position with Ker of Samuelston was above that of servant but in line with that of a Victorian governess, so he was of the household but not of the family. At St Andrews he was thrust into a military operation and his vocation was found at the very moment when his liberty was torn away. When he was freed from the galleys he would have possessed only the clothes he had worn in the galleys. In Berwick he could acquire books and even furniture; he could establish a routine for study and rest, to be combined with his pastoral duties. And these duties involved social contact of a benign form. At the same time he was undertaking reform of the order of service of the most radical sort. But his time of peace and calm was, as it would always be, severely limited.

The fame of his sermon had obviously spread south and he was swiftly moved from Berwick to St Nicholas's Church in Newcastle, where he had delivered it. William Purye, the current incumbent, disappeared gently from history. Knox still travelled back and forwards to Berwick, but the eyes of London were now on him. His patron, the Protector Somerset, however, had overreached himself and been replaced by the earl of Northumberland. Knox spoke out with his usual vehemence against this, even blaming an outbreak of the 'sweating sickness' on it. Somerset was arrested on 16 October 1551 and the sickness struck Newcastle on the 31st. 'Let Newcastle witness!'

But in spite of his public condemnation of the earl of Northumberland's actions Knox was given a high office in the Church of England. In December it was decided to appoint six 'chaplains in ordinary', who should not only wait upon the king, but be 'itineraries' and preach the Gospel across the nation. There can be no doubt that Knox was one of these chaplains, since in October 1552 the Privy Chamber is instructed to pay to 'Mr. Knokes, preacher in the North, the sum of forty pounds', presumably in arrears. In January 1553, when he quit the office, he writes to Mrs Bowes that either the Queen's Majesty or some treasurer will be £40 richer. In modern terms Knox, having been head-hunted, was now being fast tracked, since half his fellow chaplains went on to wear the bishop's mitre.

A prelate who was ambitious for his own advancement would have taken this appointment as a golden opportunity to further his career. But Knox was interested only in furthering the teachings of Jesus Christ, and continued to preach without any seeming reference to *The Book of Common Prayer*.

He may well have known that a revised version was in preparation, and at any rate he must have known that schism was appearing in the Church of England, with Archbishop Cranmer inclining towards the views of Knox and Geneva, while others were giving support to the Lutheran ideas of consubstantiation.

Rome taught that during the Mass the bread and wine actually changed into the flesh of Christ, a miracle adored by the kneeling congregation, and experienced only by the officiating priest. This was 'transubstantiation', described by Knox as 'the bread the devil hatched . . . fostered and nourished by all his children, priests, friars, monks and other [of] his conjured and sworn soldiers . . . chiefly by Stephen Gardiner and his black brood in England.' Gardiner was the deposed bishop of Winchester. Knox displays his earthy common sense later when he says, 'Concerning the natural body and blood of our saviour Christ, they are in Heaven and not here. For it is against the truth of Christ's natural body to be in more places than in one at one time.' Luther believed that in the Mass the bread and wine became infused with the spirit of Christ: 'consubstantiation'. Knox and Geneva rejected the Mass totally as idolatry of the worst sort, but taught that the bread and wine were shared by the minister and the congregation in memory of Christ's fellowship with his disciples at the Last Supper. Cranmer's new *Book of Common Prayer* would have to land on one side or other of the fence and whatever he decided was bound to cause contention even among the committed Anglicans, to say nothing of the still existing traditionalists. This diversity was increasing because England was also receiving religious refugees of all sorts from Continental Europe. For example, a body of Walloon weavers (French-speaking Netherlanders) were allowed to settle in Glastonbury, under their leader Valerian Poullain, using a much simplified prayer book based on the Genevan mode.

Northumberland, now a duke and warden general of the Northern Marches, came to Newcastle and must have heard Knox preach on many occasions. In spite of Knox having severe reservations about Northumberland's sincerity (rightly as it turned out) he acceded to the duke' requests to accompany him to London. Once again Knox was being thrust into the spotlight.

Knox was well aware that in the revised prayer book under preparation there was to be a direct ruling requiring the congregation to kneel during the elevation of the Host at the Lord's Supper. To this he took extreme objection, voicing his objections publicly before the King at Windsor towards the end of September. Knox claimed that kneeling implied adoration, and therefore idolatry. John Utenhovius, an elder at the Protestant Church of Foreigners in London, heard the objection raised by 'a good man, a Scotsman by nation,' and hoped that some good to the Church would arise from it. It certainly caused the archepiscopal temperature to rise, for the new prayer book was already at the printers and Cranmer was not at all keen to have it altered. In a rather waspish letter he said that there was no direct instruction in scripture as to the posture required, and if the custom prevalent in Biblical times is to be followed, Communion would be celebrated 'as the Tartars and Turks use yet at this day to eat their meat lying upon the ground.' However, the Privy Council did what bureaucrats have always done, so they set up a committee, including Knox, to arbitrate. His arguments against kneeling were, as we have seen, that kneeling implied adoration and therefore idolatry, while sitting could be seen as a sign of joy in the equality of the ceremony. Later in life, Knox would say 'that we will neither worship the signs, in place of that which is signified by them; neither yet do we despise and interpret them as unprofitable and vain.'

This entire episode should not be seen simply as a piece of liturgical sophistry. Knox's objection made it quite impossible to receive communion in the Church of England. A declaration on 27 October endorsed Knox's view and a fresh page, known as 'the Black Rubric', was inserted into the prayer book which came into use on 1 November 1552. The Rubrics, or instructions to the congregation, were printed in red, but in this instance Knox's insertion was printed with black ink.

Kneeling was now allowed but was not obligatory, and could be seen as a mark of respect to the minister, not to any idolatrous ceremony or any adoration of the bread or wine. Of course, if you wished to adore the miracle you were in a position to do so, but if you believed there was no miracle and merely an infusion of the spirit you were similarly well placed. If you believed neither of what Knox regarded as heresies, you could simply feel you were giving due respect to the celebrant. The Church of England was demonstrating its breadth admirably. This was a major compromise from a man not often given credit for compromise. Elizabeth I was more all-inclusive in her views on the Church and had the declaration withdrawn. It was reinserted in 1662 as opinion swung towards the Puritans.

Northumberland, as Knox's patron, was well aware of the controversy raised by his protégé, and on 28 October he suggested, strongly, that 'Mr Knocks' might be appointed to the vacant bishopric of Rochester. It may seem strange that such intransigence should be rewarded, but Northumberland's reasons were, as ever, purely practical and political.

First, Knox's presence in Kent would sharpen the archbishop of Canterbury, especially with regard to the recent incursions of foreign Anabaptists; secondly, his ministry in the North would have to come to an end; and so thirdly, he would cease to act as a magnet for Scots coming south to hear him preach in Newcastle. Knox visited the duke at his London house, turned the offer down unconditionally and returned to Newcastle. Not for the last time, Knox had bitten the hand that fed him. Northumberland, feeling understandably slighted, wrote to Cecil, 'I love not to have to do with men which be neither grateful nor pleasable. I assure you I mind to have no more to do with him, but to wish him well.' This appears to have been a temporary fit of pique, since he later referred to 'poor Knoxe . . . you may perceive what perplexity the poor soul remains in at present.'

By Christmas 1552 the poor soul was issuing stern warnings about the increasing support for Catholicism, as he, along with the sentient majority, knew that the young King Edward VI was dying. It followed, therefore, that the King's openly Catholic sister, Princess Mary, would gain the throne before long. Knox was accused of exceeding his authority by local unreformed Catholics but was given protection by Northumberland, who clearly was not holding any grudges against Knox for his rejection of the bishopric. He certainly raised no objection to Knox being offered the vicarage of All Hallows, Bread Street, in London. This would deliberately place Knox under the ever-watchful eye of Nicholas Ridley, bishop of London. Equally deliberately Knox rejected the offer. Freedom to preach his message was far more valuable to him than advancement.

It was also about this time that Marjory Bowes became more than the daughter of a distressed parishioner. His letters carry dates that were, unfortunately, added long after they were written and are at best random, but he does change his form of address to Elizabeth from, 'Dear beloved Sister,' to 'Dearly beloved Mother,' so we can presume that some form of betrothal had taken place, most likely only an exchange of vows before witnesses.

Marjory was probably about twenty years Knox's junior, and really all we know of her is that, in spite of considerable opposition from her family, she remained steadfastly loyal to her itinerant, often hunted and penniless husband. If a sixteenth-century wife committed no improprieties and carried out her duties uncomplainingly she would not be thought worthy of mention.

But in early April he was back in London to preach his last sermon before the young King, who was now clearly dying of pulmonary tuberculosis.

Knox preached on the deceit shown to David and Hezekiah by the treacherous advisors Achitophel and Shebna. No one could be in any doubt that he was condemning the current counsellors to the king. This had gone well beyond scripture and was openly political. He was now, if not yet a liability, then at least an embarrassment to a church and political establishment that was holding its breath until the royal succession was settled – in all likelihood a Catholic restoration – and Knox was promptly despatched to Amersham in Buckinghamshire. This pleasant small town, in rich countryside, was remote enough from London for a discreet silence, and yet near enough for a swift recall should that need eventually arise. Discreet silence was not in Knox's nature, and he must have known that his sermons would be closely monitored. On 16 April Knox preached a sermon that would haunt him in later days. King Edward had died and Mary Tudor had become Queen. He attacked Mary for embracing the Catholic faith, and denounced the Emperor Charles V as 'no less enemy to Christ than was Nero'. Since there were strong rumours that Queen Mary would shortly become espoused to Charles V's son, Philip II of Spain, this was a direct challenge to the Queen, an insult to her prospective father-in-law and the most powerful monarch in Europe, as well as to his son. Knox must have known it could not go unpunished.

Knox was thereafter, to all intents and purposes, on the run as more and more magnates allied themselves with Mary. First in Kent, and then, as the old religion was being re-established around his head, in mid December, he travelled north, 'with less money than ten groats and not in good case to have travelled being sore troubled in the gravel'. The Mass had been restored and Mary Tudor was officially to be married to His Most Catholic Majesty Philip II of Spain. Knox was in Newcastle on 22 November and hoped to visit Berwick in order to see his mother-in-law and betrothed, but he was persuaded that such a meeting was far too dangerous for all concerned. With a heavy heart he landed in Dieppe some time in February 1554. It is difficult for us to realize that his existence now was that of a desperate exile. While in a quasi-Protestant state he was comparatively safe, provided he caused no major disturbance to the civil power. In Catholic France he could be arrested at any time, with no possibility this time of outside help. England would be glad to see him executed, Scotland never wanted to hear from him again, and so his death, while not being actively sought, would be welcome. Naturally, before being executed he would be interrogated as to who had given him shelter, provided him with food or transport, and his interrogators would not be satisfied until he gave them some names. His experiences in the galleys would have let him see the extent of human savagery that few scholars of his time witnessed. Such an existence had the effect of hardening his opinions and moving his thoughts towards rejecting the blind obedience to rulers that had been unquestioned up to this time. Even those things which had been Caesar's were about to be called into question.

4   Troubles in Frankfurt

It must have been almost beyond human power for Knox to hold any glimmer of optimism at this moment. He was in his mid forties, almost penniless and in dangerous exile, cut off from his friends, his betrothed, Marjory, and her mother, Mrs Bowes. He can be excused a feeling of failure at a time in his life when his major achievements should have been behind him. Instead of which he was a former galley slave of the country in which he now found himself, separated from his family and ousted from his parish just at a time when his reforms were beginning to gain support.

In France, Henry II had recently created a subdivision of the *parlement* in the form of the *chambre ardente*, a vigorous French extension of the Spanish Inquisition, which itself was feared to be soon arriving in England, with Mary Tudor's proposed marriage to Philip of Spain. Scotland was firmly under the Catholic thumb of Mary of Guise, and the Protestantism tolerated in Germany was for Knox dangerously close to Rome. The armies of France were en route for confrontation with Charles V's strength in the Netherlands and Knox's temporary refuge in Dieppe was perilously near to the line of march. Three years previously Mary of Guise had been told that there was not a single Protestant in the town, but since she was, in fact, passing through the town at the time, this can be taken with the same confidence as a statement from a holiday courier that the current torrential rain is a bizarre anomaly and will vanish tomorrow. However, it does demonstrate that Knox was in great danger of arrest and probable death. Toleration of those few enclaves of dissent that existed was fickle in the extreme.

Knox's understandable depression was exacerbated by his feelings for those he had left behind. Indeed he has been accused of deserting his charges, but, as we shall see, his reasons for choosing exile were quite valid, and his spiritual guidance continued in five 'admonitions' or 'epistles' in that year. They were in fact written sermons in which Knox started to codify his religious thoughts and began to debate the political implications of his beliefs.

But before writing even these he sent *An Exposition on the Sixth Psalm of David* to Elizabeth Bowes, now firmly addressed as 'beloved Mother'. He asks the question, 'Why did I flee?' and answers, 'Assuredly I cannot tell; but of one thing I am sure, the fear of death was not the chief cause.' And he longs for the time when he may come to battle before the end of the conflict, even if it is in the very hour of death. He tells her that he refused high office from the foresight of trouble to come. He then reassures her, once again, that doubts, and even a feeling that God had become an enemy, are not uncommon among the elect, but that God is not offended by what are only 'voices of the flesh'. He ends the first part by telling her that they shall meet again, 'if not in this wretched and miserable life, yet in that estate where death may not dissever us'. This can hardly be said to express wild optimism about his future. Then, oddly, he says that he had never believed that any nation could displace Scotland in being first in his affections, but that 'the troubles present – and appearing to be [that is, yet to come] in the Realm of England are more dolorous to my heart than ever were the troubles of Scotland'. This part of the letter is dated 6 January and was probably written before leaving for France.

However, part two seems to have been written later and is dated 28 February 'upon the very point of my journey'. In this letter he reassures her that doubts and sins were felt by David, but forgiven by God, and exhorts her to hold fast to the reformed faith, even though he has,

> In the beginning of this battle, appeared to play the faint hearted and feeble soldier, yet my prayer is that I may be restored to the battle again. Mother, let no fear enter into your heart, as that I, escaping the furious rage of these ravening wolves (that for our unthankfulness are lately loosed from their bands), do repent any thing of my former fervency.'

It seems that the departure he refers to is the start of his journey to Geneva, but dated on the same day is his *Admonition or warning that the faithful Christians in London, Berwick, and others may avoid God's vengeance*, 'from a sore troubled heart upon my departure from Dieppe, 1553 [New Style 1554] whither God knoweth'.

Undoubtedly, he knew very well that his destination was Geneva, but how he was to get there, with no money and as a known heretic, indeed only God knew. However, the *Admonition* was the first of his major sermons. The title page of the first edition carries a woodcut of 'Truth' in the stocks held with a rope round his neck by 'Tyranny', while 'Cruelty' prepares to flog him. The second edition in July carries the bleak joke that it was printed in Rome before the Castel St Angelo, the Pope's fortified residence. In it Knox assures the faithful that the 'corporal commodities' are worthless beside the 'comfort and joy of the soul'. Later he would discover what happened to reform when it touched people's pockets. He was obviously aware of the accusations that he was no more than a ranting bigot who had cast himself in the role of an Old Testament prophet. And although he stresses that the arrival of the 'sweating sickness' in Newcastle might be seen as divine retribution for the arrest of the Protector Somerset, he comforts his readers with the statement that his 'assurances are not the Marvels of Merlin, nor yet the dark sentences of profane prophecies, but the plain truth of God's word'. Later he was accused of necromancy, and since the reformers regarded Rome as the Antichrist and embodiment of the Whore of Babylon, the established Church and its adherents saw reform as equally the work of the Devil. Hyperbole of exchanged insults was the order of the day. Once again Knox inveighs against the idolatry of the Mass:

and therefore avoid it, as that ye will be partakers with Christ with whom ye have sworn to die and to live in baptism and in his Holy Supper. Shame it were to break promise to men, but is it not more shame to break it unto God? Avoid all idolatry and all participation thereof. Fly from idolatry and stand with Christ Jesus in this day of his battle which shall be short and the victory everlasting.

Knox had realized that preaching this message in England was a direct challenge to the authorities, which became more Catholic by the day, and would have inevitably resulted in his capture. Elizabeth and Marjory Bowes would be under immediate suspicion and it would also have resulted in the pursuit, capture, and probable death of those who sheltered him, as well as the brutal interrogation of those who might be presumed able to reveal his whereabouts. Exile left him comparatively free to preach and publish from across the Channel, provided he caused no unnecessary trouble to his hosts.

But he had preached disobedience by the individual to a secular power, if that power imposed a faith that was repugnant. This was a first step away from the blind duty to authority preached by John Mair. What was the line between this and treason? And was action against a sinful ruler also sinful? In the *Admonition* he comes to the brink of these questions but draws back without either posing or answering them. For that he needed a higher authority. This authority he would find in John Calvin in Geneva. Calvin had arrived twenty-two years earlier in July 1536. He had been educated, as had been many reformers, at Montaigu in Paris, where he was remembered for hard work and diligence. But at his father's behest, he changed his course of study from theology and took a degree in law at Bourges.

Then in 1532 his father died. Calvin rejoined the Church, but was soon dissatisfied,

> as if by a sudden ray of light I now recognized in what an abyss of errors, in what a profundity of filth, I had hitherto been plunged. Now, therefore, O Lord, I did what was my duty, and fearlessly, condemning with tears my earlier life, I followed in thy footsteps.

However in 1534 Calvin was forced, as a result of Francis I's persecutions, to flee France to Strasburg where, at the age of twenty-six, he wrote *Institutio Religionis Christianae*, endorsing Protestantism. It was published in Basel in 1536, and, astonishingly, was dedicated to Francis I! Although he considered returning to France, he was persuaded against this folly by his fellow Frenchman and Protestant leader in Geneva, Guillaume Farel, so he settled in that city of some twelve or thirteen thousand souls, as a preacher at the Cathedral of St Pierre.

Knox called the Genevan Church 'the best school for a Christian which has ever existed on earth since the days of the Apostles'. He heartily approved of the reverence shown for the teachings of Christ propounded by Calvin, who said, 'It would be better for heaven and earth to be thrown into the abyss together than that the honour which Christ has been given by God his father should be diminished.' Calvin became overtly political when he said 'Not only princes but all magistrates were not rightly inaugurated in their duties unless they consecrate themselves to God and reverence his majesty.' Knox would want to examine this closely.

The rigidity of Calvin's preaching had a direct effect in Geneva, at least, as we can deduce from William Monton's useful *Historical and*

Demographic Study of 16th Century Geneva. Calvin preached his disapproval of the use of 'superstitious' (i.e. secular) names in baptism and between 1550 and 1558 over 80 per cent of children had names from the Old or New Testaments. Calvin instituted a form of self-examination for the secular Council, exhorting them to meet once a month (at 6 a.m.) for a session of self-accusation with charitable and brotherly remonstration among themselves, so that 'the Lord may make it redound to the profit of us all'. This system was adopted and the pastors of the various churches undertook this self-criticism on a weekly basis. In 1546 Calvin forbade all non-religious festivals and replaced the taverns with State eating-houses, equipped with Bibles. Calvin's rigidity of thought allowed little room for argument, and when Michel Servetus denied the existence of the Holy Trinity and the divinity of Christ, Calvin promptly had him burned at the stake. Calvin was also training apostate French priests. They were returning to France to preach with such effectiveness that Catherine de Medici wrote personally asking him to stop. In spite of the seeming inflexibility of this theocracy, or perhaps because of it, since it did at least allow expression of reformed thought, Geneva became a place of refuge for religious dissidents. For example, on 14 October 1557 alone, 200 French, fifty English, twenty-five Italians and four Spaniards took citizenship. And between 1555 and 1585, 800 refugees became citizens, eventually reaching such numbers that Calvin could count on them to turn a public vote in his favour. Given the probable population comparable to contemporary Elgin or Ripon, the number of dissidents there now transferred the centre of gravity of the Protestant movement from Wittenberg and Zurich to Geneva.

It was therefore obvious that it would be to Geneva that Knox would go. He travelled on borrowed horseback for well over 300 miles, avoiding towns where persecutions were likely to be taking place. Dependent only on rumour for safety and charity for food, he had from time to time to find shelter from the worst weather of the year. The warm fire and restful study of his lodgings in Newcastle were for Knox a thing of the past. Possessing now only as many books as he could carry in his saddlebags, he must have cut a sorry figure. Riding alone and wetly wrapped against the winter, the privations of the galleys would have returned to haunt him a hundredfold throughout the short days and freezing nights.

But Knox's determination drove him on not, oddly enough, as a fugitive but as an intellectual pioneer with four questions to ask – questions whose

answers might provide a validation for his future actions. In these circumstances, to believe in a future at all needed more determination than most
people are capable of imagining, far less possessing.

Knox finally arrived in Geneva in March and was received by Calvin.
Knox put his four very formal questions to him, about which he had obviously thought long and hard. Lonely rides on bad roads had given him the
chance to prepare his ground carefully, as today a television interviewer
would prepare before interviewing a particularly influential head of state.
Like such a head of state, Calvin knew that Knox would make his replies
public and the subjects were indeed, controversial. Having been the centre
of enough controversy in Geneva for the severity of his rule (adultery was
punished by decapitation for men and drowning for women) he gave Knox
answers in private and then passed him on to Lausanne, where one Viret
rapidly passed him on in turn to Heinrich Bullinger in Zurich. Bullinger was
the son of a priest and was married to a former nun. He had also been a co-
author of the *Helvetic Confession*. Fifty years of age, he had succeeded
Zwingli as the leader of reform in Zurich.

The first question Knox asked him was

> Whether the son of a King, upon his father's death, though unable by reason
> of his tender age to conduct the government of the kingdom, is nevertheless
> by right of inheritance to be regarded as a lawful magistrate, and, as such to
> be obeyed as of divine right?

It was obvious that Knox was talking about Edward VI and Bullinger
assured him that he was, in all forms, a lawful sovereign to be obeyed.
Clearly Bullinger approved of Edward's Protestantism and declared that 'he
ruled the kingdom after a more godly manner than the three most wise and
prosperous kings who immediately preceded him.' (Henry VIII, Henry VII,
Richard III; in this instance Edward V can be ignored as never having
ruled). This answer was predictable and safe.

With the second question the ice under Bullinger was getting thinner.

> Whether a female can preside over, and rule a kingdom by divine right, and
> so transfer the right of sovereignty to her husband?

Obviously Knox was now asking for validation of Mary Tudor's proposed
act of transferring her sovereignty to Philip of Spain. Bullinger started off

confidently enough. 'The law of God ordains the woman to be in subjection and not to rule.' But qualifications then came thick and fast – for example, if she holds the reins of government, 'it is a hazardous thing for godly persons to set themselves in opposition to political regulations'. But if the sovereign is an ungodly and tyrannical ruler, different rules apply and the Lord will in his own time destroy unjust governments. Feeling, perhaps, that the ice was beginning to crack beneath him, Bullinger then pulled back. 'With respect to her transferring power to her husband, those persons who are acquainted with the laws and customs of the realm can furnish the proper answer.'

The third question was now extremely dangerous.

Whether obedience is to be rendered to a magistrate who enforces idolatry and condemns true religion; and whether those authorities who are still in occupation of towns and fortresses, are permitted to repel this ungodly violence from themselves and their friends?

Once again Bullinger started off with great confidence and vigour. 'We must not obey the king or magistrate when their commands are opposed to God and his lawful worship,' and he backed up his arguments with scriptural precedents. But he felt that the current times were too full of danger, and thus accurate knowledge of particular instances would be essential. So not possessing such knowledge, it would be foolish to recommend anything specific. He ends the answer by stressing the need for much prayer and much wisdom, 'lest by precipitancy we occasion mischief to many worthy persons'. In other words, 'In order to respond to your question, I would have to know the answer.' Medieval logic was seldom so well chopped. But, at least, he ended by telling Knox that death is preferable to the admission of idolatry.

Finally Knox wanted to know to which party must godly persons attach themselves in the case of a religious nobility resisting an idolatrous sovereign. Bullinger ducks this question completely, advising leaving a decision to the judgement of godly persons. He ends with, 'Let us lift up our eyes to Him, waiting for his deliverance, abstaining in the meantime from all superstition and idolatry, and doing what he reveals to us in his word.'

Whatever Knox thought of these responses, they were immediately communicated to Calvin, who endorsed them. Calvin was now able to say that while he did not object to the views stated by Bullinger, he personally had never uttered them. If Knox had hoped for a rallying call to arms, and that perhaps not entirely metaphorically, he received instead an elegant lesson in diplomacy, and diplomacy was never Knox's strong suit. He retraced his weary steps to Dieppe, which was probably the nearest point to England that he had any hope of reaching, and was, at least, comparatively safe. In any case, to cross the Channel would have been far too dangerous. Ridley, Latimer and Cranmer were all in prison and Mary's religion was attracting more and more of the nobility, since secular advancement was impossible without attachment to the crown and therefore to Rome. Knox's late patron, Northumberland, had tried to alter the rules of succession to allow the crown to pass to Lady Jane Grey, the late King's cousin and Northumberland's hastily married daughter-in-law. This had led to a panicky open revolt, with the unfortunate Jane proclaimed Queen but under no circumstances did Northumberland have the power base to carry the revolt to a conclusion. A fortnight after the king's death, Northumberland, his sons, and Lady Jane Grey, the innocent pawn in a great magnate's desperate bid for power, were all behind bars, awaiting the inevitable rendezvous with the axe.

The sixteenth-century French historian, Mezeray, hints that Northumberland was suspected of poisoning Edward VI, a deed for which there is not the slightest shred of evidence. However, Knox's mistrust of Northumberland was thoroughly justified when, astonishingly, on the scaffold he claimed he had always been a Catholic in secret. This last-minute apostasy rang somewhat false and he was swiftly parted from his head. There were some residual mutterings against Queen Mary's marriage to Philip – the English did not take easily to the prospect of being ruled by a Spaniard. Sir Thomas Wyatt led a brief and abortive rising against the impending marriage, but it was quickly crushed, and he too went to the scaffold. Mary's net had drawn tight and no dissent was now possible. Even the Princess Elizabeth went to the Tower, on the evidence of trumped-up servants' gossip, but her sister drew back from executing her.

All this left a legacy of fourteen fresh gallows in London, while a month later Mary Tudor was married to Philip II of Spain, albeit by proxy, since Philip did not arrive in England until July.

There were underground Protestant services, some led by Knox's old fellow Castilian Thomas Rough as we have seen, at the cost of his life. But the grip of Mary Tudor was firm. Two devoutly Catholic Marys were in power in England and Scotland, while the legitimate ruler of Scotland was a twelve-year-old girl living in the court of France. France itself was ruled by the Catholic king Henri II with Catherine de Medici and Diane de Poitiers breathing down his neck. So Bullinger's opening answer to Knox's second question must have seemed highly relevant. 'It is a hazardous thing for godly persons to set themselves in opposition to political regulations.'

Yet Knox was not to sit idly by grieving in Dieppe, for, if he could not cross the Channel, at least his letters could, and on 10 and 31 May he completed two epistles to his *Afflicted Brethren in England*. He gives them hope by pointing out that the Church in the past was 'wondrously preserved' in the face of 'cruel, tyrannous and ungodly magistrates'. He echoes the prayer of Jeremiah: 'Let me see thy vengeance taken upon thy enemies, O Lord!'

And he tells them that, 'I have travelled through all the congregations of Helvetia, and have reasoned with all the Pastors and many other excellently learned men.' He goes on, with a degree of self-contradiction, to say he has discussed 'such matters as now I cannot commit to writing: gladly I would by tongue or by pen utter the same to God's Glory'. However, he is unequivocal:

> If I thought I might have your presence, I would jeopardise my own life to let men see what may be done with a safe conscience in these dolorous and dangerous days. But seeing that it cannot be done instantly without danger to others than to me, I will abide the time that God will appoint. But hereof be assured, that all is not lawful nor just that is statute by civil law, nor yet is everything sin before God which ungodly persons allege to be treason.

He was starting to nudge open the door to justified opposition.

In his second letter he repeats the invocation to find comfort and hope in the history of early persecutions and to look forward to a certain deliverance. He also launches personal attacks on Bishop Tunstall of Durham, 'murderer and thief' and Gardner, bishop of Winchester, telling them to 'drink the blood of God's Saints till they be drunk and their bellies burst, yet shall they never prevail'. All of this is comparatively calm, and even if read by Knox's opponents in England, as is likely, it would have been regarded as no more than the vituperation of an exiled dissident. However, in the words of an as-yet-unborn poet, he seems to have been 'nursing his wrath to keep it warm'.

On 20 July he tells Marjory Bowes that he has written a letter 'in great anguish of heart'. It was the *Faithful Admonition to the Professors of God's Truth in England*. It comes with a commendatory prologue by 'a banished man out of Leicestershire, one time preacher of God's word there'. He was probably a colleague of Knox's in Dieppe and certainly of a like mind, as he tells the reader to keep the work in safeguard, 'wherein you shall find much comfort'.

Knox starts off on familiar enough ground with the story of Christ walking on the water and Peter failing to do so from a lack of faith. He then berates himself for lack of zeal and blames the 'blind love I had for this wicked carcass [which] was the chief cause that I did not fervent enough in that behalf, for I had no will to provoke the hatred of all men against me'. It is difficult to say what more Knox could have done apart from embracing martyrdom.

He reviews the path of reform to date, including the courageous feat of Cranmer to refute the doctrine of transubstantiation, but also 'the knots of devilish sophistry, linked and knit by the Devil's Gardener and his blind buzzards'. A scarcely concealed attack on Bishop Gardner. Once the gateway to personal attack was opened, Knox launches on an attack on Sir William Paulet, now marquess of Winchester and lord treasurer under both Edward VI and Mary, and a noted turncoat. He quotes Paulet as having said, 'Bastard, bastard, incestuous bastard, Mary shall never reign over us. She is an errant Papist: she will subvert the true religion and will bring in strangers.' And yet Gardner in front of Mary 'croucheth and kneeleth'. He tells us that the Bishops are the obedient servants of the Devil – 'wily Winchester, dreaming Durham and bloody Bonner, with the rest of their bloody, butcherly brood: they cannot cease or assuage their furious fumes, for the Devil, their sire, stirreth, moveth and carrieth them even at his will.' But still he promises his readers that salvation shall come in 'the fourth watch, when they looked not for him'. However, the pinnacle of his mounting venom is now reached when he turns his pen on Mary herself. He compares her, unfavourably, with the celebrated villainesses of scripture: Athalia, Salome, her 'hoorish' mother Herodias, and finally, Jezebel, who murdered Naboth, but never erected half so many gallows as 'mischievous Mary'.

And now, does she not manifestly show herself to be an open traitress to the Imperial Crown of England, contrary to the just laws of the Kingdom, to bring in a stranger, and make a proud Spaniard king . . . to the slavery of the communality, to the overthrow of Christianity and God's true religion, and finally, to the utter subversion of the whole public estate and commonwealth of England?

He pleads to Winchester ('more cruel than any tiger. O thou son of Satan!') for the lives of Latimer and Ridley, who had previously befriended Winchester. He then seems to pause for breath in order to regain some control of his pen and ends by reassuring his brethren that one day shall 'be the song of God's elect in the Realm of England, after that God hath poured forth his vengeance upon those inobedient and blood-thirsty tyrants, which now triumpheth in all abominations, and, therefore, yet again, beloved in the Lord, abide patiently the Lord's deliverance'.

It is impossible to read the *Admonition* without seeing a division into three parts, with the first and the third being a conventional, if passionate, sermon on a text from St Matthew's gospel and, in the central part, an amazing interpolation of personal attack. Indeed some scholars are of the opinion that the central portion is a later addition. But wherever the truth of this lies it is a powerful piece of personal invective. Professor Hume Brown in his biography of Knox wisely reminds us that 'In reading the controversial literature of the sixteenth century it has never to be forgotten that modern [Hume Brown was writing in 1895] canons of good taste were then equally unknown to theologians and scholars.' But whereas such vehemence nowadays might at worst bring you face to face with a libel suit, in the sixteenth century you were more likely to meet an executioner. Some historians, and even his contemporary exiles, have blamed Knox's vitriol for fuelling the ferocity of Mary's persecutions. Certainly his imprecations cannot have pleased her, but it is difficult to lay the entire blame at Knox's door.

Without doubt it made any return to England impossible while Mary Tudor reigned, but the *Admonition* would have given heart to the reformers and been read with a certain grim satisfaction by Knox's opponents. Here was not only scriptural difference, to be interpreted as heresy of the deepest sort, but open treason. If he fell into their hands, he had already hanged himself with his pen.

True, there was no overt call to arms, and his statements in Berwick had counselled tolerance inside an errant Church while avoiding the sin of compliance. But all of that had referred purely to religious matters, while now he had called the Queen a traitress, acting contrary to the laws of the state. He had also by implication accused her husband Philip II of Spain and her father-in-law the Emperor Charles V of heresy. He had crossed the limits of tolerance, making even Dieppe no longer a safe haven. Thus at the beginning of August 1554 he wearily set out again for Geneva where, among other activities he hoped at last to study Greek and Hebrew. This intention was not simply for self-improvement; a mastery of these languages would allow Knox access to the original versions of the Bible. Until it were possible to return either to Scotland or England, Knox would spend his time in quiet reflection.

It is not difficult to see that in middle life, having been chained to a galley oar and preached reformation, been co-author of the *Second Book of Common Prayer* and betrothed, been offered and refused a bishopric and cast into religious exile, that the calm life of a scholar, able at last to call his family to his side, would hold considerable appeal. And all this could happen in a city where Protestantism was the rule and Knox need no longer keep watch for summary arrest, but could hold out hope for a parish, possibly among like minds working openly towards the same ends. Not just a dream, for by this stage in his life Knox had long since bidden farewell to fanciful expectations, but a probability. But it was not to be, for as so often happened in John Knox's life, events were taking place that would thrust him into the maelstrom of controversy once more.

That the Marian persecutions were now in full swing in England was evidenced by the steady stream of religious exiles arriving in Europe, with the existing Protestant communities of Germany and Switzerland as their destinations. So great was the influx of exiles that they imposed their own characteristics on their refuges, and we are told that of these communities, Emden was the richest, Wesel the shortest-lived, Strasburg the least disturbed by controversies (a rare attribute), Zurich the most scholarly, while Frankfurt enjoyed the greatest privileges.

The Frankfurt Protestant foundation was now French- and German-speaking, since, as we have heard, under Edward VI a congregation of already exiled Walloons, led by Valerian Poullain, had found refuge at Glastonbury, but being forced to flee again at the accession of Mary, had, after some further travelling, found themselves in Frankfurt. The leading magistrate of the town, Johann von Glauburg, accommodated them in the Weissfrauenkirche (the Church of the White Ladies). Frankfurt was already an international crossroads for intellectual thought, as witnessed even then by the flourishing Frankfurt Book Fair, which had established the city as a centre for international scholarship as well as trade, helped more than a little by its geographical position in the centre of Western Europe.

By April 1554 the Walloons had established their church under their pastor Poullain; the services took place in French. Then English exiles appeared in the city and were welcomed at the church by Poullain, who may well have been expecting them. In the best traditions of the English abroad, none of the new exiles spoke a word of French, so von Glauberg allowed them the use of the French Church to hold their services in English; but on certain conditions. They would have access to the church on alternate days to Poullain, and the two communities could arrange the hours of services on Sundays among themselves. A more severe condition was that the newcomers accepted the *French Confession of Faith* as practised by Poullain, even though it would be expressed in English, which meant abandoning much of *The Book of Common Prayer* and moving nearer to the Genevan Order of Service. The responses, the litany and the wearing of a surplice were all disallowed, while metrical psalms were sung. Indeed, one of their number, William Whittingham, had been a pupil of Calvin's in Geneva and he may have found much of this familiar. But while some of the exiles were happy to change, many were not.

Since it had been their adherence to *The Book of Common Prayer* that caused their exile in the first place one can sympathize with them, but a confrontation of rival Protestants seemed inevitable. If all of this seems unreservedly petty to contemporary ears, we must realize that we are dealing with the creation of a new form of worship that was replacing one with an immensely long history and passionately held traditions. Symbols are of the greatest importance to emerging beliefs, as are the uniforms and rituals of the protagonists. Clerical vestments fall into the same category and in 1550 when John Hooper, a friend of Bullinger, was being consecrated as bishop of Gloucester, he refused to wear the traditional vestments, to the point of imprisonment. Eventually he agreed that he would wear a surplice, but by choice, not by obligation. (Such compromise did him no good, however, since he was burned for heresy in February 1553.)

In the reformed Church the priest was a teacher, a spiritual leader, and *primus inter pares* in his congregation. Any suggestion that he was possessed of supernatural powers, or led his congregation in formal ritual, was anathema and the rankest heresy. The two greatest supporters of this view among the exiles were Knox and Whittingham.

We are told of what happened next in *A Brief Discourse of the Troubles begun at Frankfurt in the year 1554*, which was most probably written by Whittingham. Having failed to find a minister from Strasburg or from Zurich who could negotiate a compromise between the English and the Walloons, a letter was sent to Knox on 24 September, signed by twenty-one of the congregation, setting out their case. 'We have received letters from our brethren of Strasburg, but not in such sort and ample wise as we looked for.' Their request for a pastor had been turned down. 'Whereupon we assembled in the Holy Ghost, we hope, and have with one voice and consent chosen you so particularly to be one of the ministers of our congregation here, to preach unto us the most lively word of God, according to the gift that God hath given you. . . . We mistrust not but that you will joyfully accept this calling.' An offer which made up in vehemence and sincerity what it may have lacked in tact. Now it was undoubtedly flattering that his fame as a preacher made him attractive, even although he was obviously not the first choice. After all, he had argued against much of the existing *Book of Common Prayer* to the point of gaining the inclusion of the Black Rubric. This had alienated the conservative wing of the church. Also he was seen as being so inflexible in his views that he had turned down a bishopric. And it must have been clear to Knox that the controversy he would be asked to resolve would require diplomacy and tact, two qualities of which he was fully aware he lacked. But while in the past he had been reluctant to 'go where God had not called' him, here was a congregation asking for his preaching. Knox took his reluctance to Calvin, for if he refused he would still have to depend, as did everyone in Geneva, on Calvin's good offices. It seems that he was further persuaded by Calvin, and so Knox accepted the offer and reluctantly was appointed pastor of the English Church in Frankfurt by November. 'Mr Knox's reputed merit did naturalise him, though a foreigner, for any Protestant congregation.' So to Frankfurt Knox went.

This was a bustling commercial centre with a population of about 20,000 (present-day Dumfries or Stratford-upon-Avon) with high gabled multi-storied houses crowded under the shadow of the medieval Church of St Bartholomew and all clustered against the east bank of the River Main. But speaking only Scots, English, French and Latin, Knox would have been cut off from much of the daily life of the city, and confined to the somewhat quarrelsome company of his congregation.

Delegations from Strasburg, where a form of *The Book of Common Prayer* was in use, came to and went from Frankfurt in an attempt to achieve unity. The idea of unity among the exiles was of great importance, since everyone, including Knox, believed in their eventual return to England and earnestly hoped that they would return with a reformed religion devoid of schism. It was obvious to Knox and Whittingham that anything in the order of service not provided for in scripture was manmade idolatry.

But Knox was clearly dedicated to finding an effective compromise, even although compromise was not his favourite course of action. The Strasburg suggestions were collated and read to the congregation in Frankfurt but finally were rejected by them. 'This order was very well liked by many, but such as were bent to the Book of England could not abide it.' He even suggested that he might simply preach, while some other person administered the sacraments. This was the first sign that Knox, extraordinarily for him, was considering a liturgical compromise. 'But to that the congregation would in no wise consent.' Then, in a move of devious diplomacy, it was decided to put the matter to the arbitration of Calvin himself. 'Knox, Whittingham and others, perceiving that these beginnings would grow somewhat, if were not stayed in time, drew forth a platt [descriptive summary] of the whole Book of England into the Latin tongue.' Clearly Calvin spoke no English. The author of the *Brief Discourse* tells us that, 'This description is very favourably put down,' but it is, in fact, an extremely biased version that Calvin would be bound to reject. It stressed the kneeling and rising of the priest, the spoken responses of the congregation, formal responses for sick visits, purification of women in childbed, and so on. All of which Knox and Whittingham must have known would be repugnant to Calvin. Knox also wrote to Calvin's colleagues in Geneva asking them to sound out Calvin as to whether he thought Knox's continued presence in Frankfurt was increasing the schisms, and if he felt Knox ought to leave. Knox would have been happy to have washed his hands of the quarrel and returned to his studies, but having had Calvin's encouragement to accept the position, he would be extremely unwise to relinquish it without a similar endorsement.

Interestingly, he seems to have signed this letter with a form of 'Sinclair', his mother's maiden name. This was a mark of the danger which even anyone carrying correspondence by Knox might find himself falling into, albeit in these comparatively tolerant parts. Calvin never replied to this plea, but did respond to the description of the order of service. His reply in January 1555 was exactly as expected. He was much grieved to find contention among brethren, especially in exile, and advised, somewhat uselessly, that they would be better off finding themselves a Church that 'should receive and nourish you in her motherly lap'. He avowed that he was 'gentle and tractable in mean things (as external ceremonies)' – he seems, conveniently, to have forgotten decapitation and drowning – and finds that the order of service, as sent to him, contained 'many tolerable foolish things, and that there was not that purity which was to be desired.' There is talk of Popish dregs, and the expected rejection was then read to the Frankfurt congregation. After a histrionic debate that included much kneeling, weeping, and hopes for hands to be struck off if that would bring unity, the difficulty was resolved by setting up a drafting committee of four, including Knox, who said, 'For so much as I perceive that no end of contention is to be hoped for, unless the one part something relent, this will I do for my part, that quietness may issue.' This was not a typical statement for Knox, relenting for a quiet life. It cannot be that his faith was wavering, but he was in a position he had not chosen, and his task was to arbitrate not to impose. Also, we must ask, was he tiring? Given the activities that lay ahead of him, he clearly had huge reserves of energy still untapped, but he could be excused for seeking a momentary pause from conflict.

For whatever reason, an order of service was eventually agreed on, to be used until the end of April, with an arbitration committee of five in case of dispute in the meantime. This sounded a rational and civilized way of maintaining peace. That peace would last until 13 March.

On that date Dr Richard Cox arrived from Strasburg with some other Protestant exiles intent on joining the Frankfurt congregation. Dr Cox was no ordinary exile. He had been a headmaster of Eton, renowned for his floggings, a tutor to Edward VI, as well as chancellor of Oxford University, where his manner of riding roughshod over all opposition had earned him the nickname of 'Canceller' Cox. Cox was a shining example of the highly political clerical apparatchik of whom Knox had only very limited experience and possessed no skill in handling. The new arrival would have known of Knox, and the two men may even have met during the drafting of *The Book of Common Prayer*. Cox and his fellow exiles immediately showed their mettle by ignoring all the carefully negotiated agreements in place, giving formal spoken responses during the service. On the following Sunday, one of Cox's party, whom Knox claimed had recently attended Mass in England, actually climbed into the pulpit at the morning service and read the litany, including all the responses objected to. Modern football supporters have shown greater respect for the customs of their foreign hosts. Knox himself was scheduled to preach that afternoon and seized the opportunity for rebuttal with such vigour that Professor Hume Brown tells us, 'when he left the pulpit a scene ensued which did not increase the chances of a reconciliation'. Knox had affirmed in his sermon that among many things that provoke God's anger against England, slackness to reform religion was one. He praised Hooper for his stand against vestments, and attacked the holding of multiple benefices. Since some of Cox's faction had become rich through the holding of such multiple livings Knox was sharply reproved as soon as he came out of the pulpit.

But reconciliation was tried on the Tuesday when a meeting was called to smooth the ruffled feathers. Since Cox's faction were not yet technically members of the congregation many were against allowing them to take part in the debate; but Knox, still looking for some form of rapprochement, himself championed the admittance of the newcomers, and they were accepted. But this now meant that their numbers swelled the existing minority who opposed Knox into a majority, and ironically he was then forbidden to 'meddle any more'! So much for his attempts at reconciliation and diplomacy.

Whittingham went to visit the magistrate von Glauberg, who, getting understandably angry with his squabbling guests, forbade any services that did not accord with Pullain's original formula – 'as he opened the Church door to them, so would he shut it again'. But Cox and his supporters had no intention of reaching any sort of compromise, and took direct action to oust Knox from Frankfurt. Knox was secretly visited at home by Edward Isaac, one of Cox's faction, who pointed out that if Knox did not agree immediately with the newcomers, an occurrence Isaac knew to be impossible, the preacher would be cast into prison, and 'he knew well I should not escape'. As might be expected, Knox did not immediately bow to this open threat, whereupon several of Cox's allies, including Knox's nocturnal visitor, denounced him before the Frankfurt magistrates. They accused him of nine articles of high treason against Charles V, Philip II and Mary Tudor. Certainly his remarks in the *Faithful Admonition* referred to above and his sermon in Amersham in 1553 left no doubt that he had accused them of heresy, and that he had called the Emperor Charles V 'no less enemy to Christ than was Nero'. But Charles V was now nearby at Augsburg with a large army and the good magistrates of Frankfurt were above all realists as far as the safety of their city was concerned.

Von Glauburg had one last attempt at reconciliation, which broke up in disorder. 'Then began the tragedy, and our consultation ended'.

Finally Cox promised von Glauberg that he would be happy to accept the French Order of Service as practised by Poullain and that it was acceptable in all points. It was a promise he had not the slightest intention of keeping.

Knox would have to go, thereby leaving Cox triumphant. Cox had also spread the old accusation that the Marian persecutions were a result of Knox's pamphleteering, an accusation that, as we shall see, he would repeat to Calvin. But in any circumstances Cox would have been hostile to Knox since, as a fellow drafter of *The Book of Common Prayer*, they would have been in disagreement over the Black Rubric which Knox had insisted was inserted. Cox was also a skilled politician and such people tend to dislike honest conviction, especially when firmly held with the fervency of Knox. First he isolated Knox, then he denounced him. Knox rather ruefully said, 'If I had been a man pleaser, men would not have persecuted me.' Later Calvin would say, 'Master Knox was neither godly nor brotherly dealt withall.' Throughout this unhappy episode Knox had attempted to bend with the majority without sacrificing his principles and had been instrumental in giving support to Whittingham and the other English exiles. During his time in England he had gone as far as he could in freeing *The Book of Common Prayer* from what he saw as unnecessary ceremonial and allowing freedom for extempore worship by the congregation. He had preached against the book's shortcomings in Newcastle and continued his opposition to much of it in Frankfurt. All this he had maintained simply out of faith, but Dr Cox was *The Book of Common Prayer*'s supporter from the position of one immersed in the politics of power, and used his advocacy of it for his own aggrandisement. Knox could never understand this.

Knox's preaching in Frankfurt and his support for Whittingham had, however, undoubted effects on the eventual Puritan movement in England. Indeed, it is not too difficult to discern Knox's influence still at work, given the breadth of the contemporary Church of England.

On the day before his enforced departure, Knox made 'a most comfortable sermon at his lodgings to about fifty persons'. He preached of the joy that was prepared for those that suffer trouble and persecution for the testimony of his blessed name. The next day he set out for Geneva, being seen off by his followers, 'with great heaviness of heart and plenty of tears'.

Whittingham had written to Calvin that Knox had been unjustly charged, with the regret of all good men, even including the civil magistrate. Interestingly, the victorious Cox also wrote to Calvin on 5 April, justifying his order of service and stressing that he had excised what was impure and papistical. Nowhere in the letter does he mention Knox. In Calvin's reply at the end of May, however, he makes only slight comment on the revised liturgy but reprimands Cox and his allies:

> it had been better for them to have tarried still in their own land, than unjustly to have brought into far countries the firebrand of cruelty, to set on fire those that would not be kindled. Notwithstanding, because it grieveth me to speak slightly of these evils, the remembrance whereof I would wish to be buried in perpetual forgetfulness.

Calvin was not allowed perpetual forgetfulness, for he received yet another letter from the minister and other members of the church in Frankfurt. It reads, however, as pure Cox. He points out that Knox's pamphlet and Amersham sermon 'added much oil to the flame of persecution'. He goes on, extravagantly, to assert that it was with the publication of the *Admonition to the Faithful* that the Marian persecutions began.

While it might be possible to admit the coincidence of timing, it is outrageous to lay the blame for the entire policy of Protestant extirpation at Knox's door.

Yet another chapter in Knox's life had ended in exile. This time he was being exiled by fellow Protestants with whom he had tried compromise so that 'quietness may issue', and the compromise had developed into a trap that closed around him. Knox had shown marked reluctance during this episode to try to change the minds of his fellow exiles. Perhaps because they were just that, and they were all bound by a common rejection of Rome. It is highly probable that the original dispute could have been solved and a compromise patched up if the vehemence of Knox had been moderated by the reasonableness of Whittingham. But the arrival of Cox changed the game irrevocably. Knox played for what he saw as the truth, while Cox simply played to win. It was inconceivable to Knox that in the face of bitter and widespread persecution personal power battles could be fought. To Cox such seeking after power was a way of life. But the episode is not one of complete gloom for Knox, since for the first time he had found himself with like-minded colleagues in the persons of Whittingham and a fellow preacher, Christopher Goodman. These were not parishioners like the

Askes, nor noblemen of the sort of Somerset or Northumberland, but open reformers and clerics, not under threat as had been the case with Rough and Balnaves. These were men with whom Knox could socialize, talk, and debate. His exile in Frankfurt may not have been so lonely.

5   A Perfect School of Christ

By April 1555, Knox was back in Geneva. Apart from one short break, it was to be his home for the next four years, providing the backdrop for what was his most peaceful and happiest period. Calvin had won elections in February that gave him and the Company of Pastors, which he dominated, almost total power to establish a theocracy. He also made it possible for 'strangers' to gain citizenship, thereby opening the door to religious exiles. This happened in spite of some local resistance, principally on the night of 16 May, when an event known as the *prise d'armes du 16 Mai* took place. More like a large drunken brawl followed by summary executions than a serious uprising, it was not reported by Knox until three years later, but it ruffled the calm waters of Lake Geneva and resulted in an increase in Calvin's power.

Knox was not alone in Geneva for long, since on 10 June a group of English exiles, now led by William Whittingham, finally driven out of Frankfurt by Cox, applied for leave to worship. Calvin arranged that a church, the Temple de Notre Dame la Neuve, be put at their disposal. Knox took the office of their fellow minister with Christopher Goodman, also driven into exile. But by the end of August he was on the move again, this time to Scotland.

He had received a clear summons from Elizabeth Bowes, his fiancée's mother, and against his better judgement had returned to Scotland in response. 'You alone, God made the instrument to draw me from the den of my own ease, you alone did draw me from the rest of quiet study,' he wrote. This alone tells us that he had found some calm and was comfortably established in Geneva. He had arrived at the start of April and in just over five months had achieved a 'den of my own ease'. To find the peace necessary to pursue scholarship was one of his most deeply held ambitions.

It must be remembered that he had been in exile of one sort or another since the fall of St Andrews castle, eight years previously, but he still held to the ambition of preaching again in Scotland. He had said as much to his fellow slave in the galley off St Andrews, and recently he had stated that Scotland and its troubles would always be first in his affections. But clearly, he knew that with Mary of Guise firmly established as Queen Regent, his scope for proselytizing would be severely limited.

Of the manner of his journey we know nothing, but he would have had to avoid England, taking ship from France direct to Scotland, a voyage fraught with danger and great expense, but he felt that Mrs Bowes's cry for help was too desperate to be ignored. The gulf between Elizabeth Bowes and her husband had widened to an intolerable degree and she must now have felt that exile as the mother-in-law of a reforming minister was preferable to life in the England of Mary Tudor. To this end she had written to Knox to return to Scotland while she and her daughter awaited rescue in the comparative safety of Berwick. On 4 November he wrote from Edinburgh, beseeching her to 'patiently bear [to wait] although I spend here yet some days, for depart I cannot, until such time as God quench their thirst a little'. This sounds as if Knox had expected merely to use Scotland as a convenient port of entry from which he would leave as soon as possible, but was now assailed by demands on his ministry from all sides. For all his lack of diplomatic skill, Knox was not disingenuous and he must have known that his time would be immediately occupied. His response to Marjory and Elizabeth sounds more like 'the soft answer that turneth away wrath'. At any rate it seems to have worked.

The Scotland that Knox found under the regency of Mary of Guise was in danger of becoming no more than a province of France, but the marriage of Mary Tudor to Philip II of Spain meant that France itself felt threatened. Henry II could not risk Scottish antagonism and so an uneasy tolerance to popular local reform existed in Scotland. At any rate, Mary of Guise showed none of the fervency for creating martyrs shown by her southern namesake. Knox, needless to say, moved only among the Protestant faction, whose, 'fervency here doth far exceed all others that I have seen'. His fame also attracted a significant number of ladies, and Elizabeth Adamson brought her troubled conscience to him. As wife to James Barron, the dean of Guild, she was a leading figure among the ladies of Edinburgh society, but her faith was so strengthened by this meeting and their subsequent correspondence that when she was offered extreme unction on her death bed, she said to the attending priests, 'Depart from me, you sergeants of Satan, for I have refused and in your presence do refuse all your abominations.' We are told, 'they departed, alleging that she raved'. Under the patronage of James Syme in Edinburgh Knox preached to any who chose to attend.

He also became a celebrity to the point of being the guest of one Erskine of Dun at a supper party. There he debated scripture with, surprisingly, William Maitland of Lethington, who presumably attended more out of intellectual curiosity than the need for spiritual reinforcement. Lethington's father, Richard, had been one of the lairds who sheltered Wishart. It was William's first debate with Knox but by no means his last. For Lethington, with his aristocratic background, this was his first brush with the new thoughts of men like Knox and Erskine. These men would never have met Knox previously, despite his much vaunted reputation, and they debated whether it was possible to attend Mass at the same time as professing the reformed faith. It may be that, for Lethington at least, they were testing the rigour of his thought.

Knox argued with his usual vehemence against what he saw as the unacceptable hypocrisy and apostasy put forward by Lethington. Lethington, who was 'a man of good learning and of sharp wit and reasoning', said, 'I see perfectly that our shifts will serve nothing before God, seeing they stand us in so small stead before man.' In other words, he acknowledged himself out-debated by Knox. At least on this occasion.

Hume Brown maintains that it was at this supper party that the keynote of the Scottish Reformation was struck. Certainly Lethington would have been given a healthy dose of the sort of debate he could expect from Knox, and would have realized that on spiritual ground he had little chance of winning any points or of shaking Knox's conviction. But politics seem not to have been mentioned, and the Scottish Reformation had a crucially political element. Erskine then invited Knox to preach at his country estates in Forfar, for although he was steadfastly in favour of reform his huge wealth meant that he was highly regarded by both sides. Money and position can nearly always buy safety.

In fact, many of the nobility favoured change and Knox spent this time going from one to another, always as a badly kept secret and taking care that no disturbance took place that might force the Queen Regent into taking action against him. It was at this time that Knox met Lord James Stewart, Queen Mary's half-brother, as an illegitimate son of James V, and also prior of Mâcon in France. In France Lord James was called 'Jacques, Bâtard d'Ecosse' ('Bastard of Scotland').

Knox tells us of a comet appearing in the winter of 1555. He calls it 'a fiery besom', which came as an omen of the death of King Christian III of Denmark. In reality the comet appeared in 1558 and Christian died in 1559, but Knox found it difficult to resist instances of divine intervention in human life.

However, the Church could not turn a completely blind eye to the rebel in their midst and finally Knox was summoned to appear at the Blackfriars Church in Edinburgh on 15 May to give a defence of his actions. On the specified day he appeared in the capital attended by Erskine and 'diverse other gentlemen'. Although we have no evidence of it, the 'other gentlemen' were presumably armed, and with the prospect of widespread bloodshed in the streets of Edinburgh looming, the confrontation never took place. In his *History* Knox says, 'but that diet held not, for whether that the bishops perceived informality in their own proceedings, or if they feared danger to ensue from their extremity, it was unknown to us'. However, Knox now moved into the palace of the bishop of Dunkeld in the High Street and there preached to a huge congregation.

He continued this preaching and his stock rose to a point when the earls of Marischal and Glencairn suggested he write to the Queen Regent herself, and this he did in May 1556. His letter was duly presented to her by Glencairn, and having read it, she passed the letter to James Beaton, Archbishop of Glasgow, saying, 'Please you, my Lord to read a pasquill.' (The derivation of this odd word is interesting. A piece of broken classical statuary named after Pasquino was disinterred in Rome and set up in the Piazza Navona. Annually, on St Mark's Day, it became the custom to dress the statue and pin lampoons or scurrilous poems to it. Thus lampoons posted in a public place became known as 'Pasquins' or 'Pasquills'.) In fact, the letter was comparatively innocuous, containing a warning to the Queen not to listen to rumour – 'if all reports were true, I were unworthy to live on the earth'. He goes on to thank her for her protection, since he may have believed that she had intervened with the bishops to prevent his examination. But then, with great circumspection, he writes 'I am not ignorant how dangerous a thing it appeareth to the natural man, to innovate any thing in matters of religion.' He urges her to abandon idolatry and embrace the true faith, 'to enter into a strange and grievous battle' before it is too late. He then prays for her illumination.

However, three years later, after an attack by the Scottish bishops, he would write again, clearly now having heard of Mary's high-handed slight, in an entirely different tone. Knox was stung by her proud and haughty remark, which, if true, was merely confirmation for him that if you offered the hand of conciliation to idolators it was liable to get bitten. He had already had this experience with Dr Cox in Frankfurt.

It would now have been possible for Knox to remain in Scotland and continue his ministry, albeit in a more or less underground fashion, but he received a letter from his congregation in Geneva, 'commanding him in God's name, as he was their chosen pastor, to repair unto them, for their comfort'. He could not ignore this call and he prepared to depart again, after taking care of a piece of business that, to modern attitudes, would have been of supreme importance, but that Knox lets us only guess at. In fact, if his principal reason for return had been to rescue Marjory and Elizabeth, he mentions only his spiritual mission in his *History*, so he must have used her plea as the necessity for the journey. Having arrived, however, he found the opportunity to preach impossible to resist. He obviously felt that as his marriage did not affect the progress of the Reformation it was therefore unimportant. He tells us, 'He sent before him to Dieppe, his mother-in-law Elizabeth Bowes and his wife Marjory, with no small dolour to their hearts, and unto many of us.' In other words, Knox had now moved from a betrothal and an 'understanding' to the full formality of marriage. His summons by Elizabeth Bowes had been to endorse her leaving her husband on the grounds of incompatibility of religion, and obviously Knox and Marjory felt that their future life in Geneva would be easier inside the formality of marriage.

The ink of many speculative academics has been spilt on the subject of Knox's sexuality. Robert Louis Stevenson, in his essay *John Knox and his Women*, with a true romantic's heart, feels that since Knox wrote caring letters to a Mrs Anna Lock, she was the only woman he really loved. Knox had met Mrs Lock in London in 1551 and she remained a firm friend. She had none of the gnawing doubt of Elizabeth Bowes and his letters to her are much more in the realms of spiritual debate. The fact that he wrote affectionately to Mrs Lock tells us nothing of the terms of affection he used privately to his wife. Unrequitable love may be an attractive scenario, but Stevenson confuses concern for her faith with physical and emotional attraction. Knox was in his fifties, of medium height and well built – his time in the galleys would have given him powerful shoulders – and he was undoubtedly the most charismatic preacher of his day. One has only to look, for example, at the female following of American evangelists today to see that he would have been an object of great attraction for many women admirers. But unlike many American evangelists there is not a scrap of evidence that he ever took advantage of this position. Rather it seems likely that all of his energy went into his mission, and like many driven men, politicians, captains of industry, scientists, or artists, for instance, his sexuality was sublimated in his work. The loving partnership sought after in the twentieth century was a great rarity in the sixteenth and we must not judge Knox if he seems almost dismissive about Marjory. She took only a tangential part in the Reformation in Scotland and Knox's letters, principally to her mother, show more pastoral care than personal affection. Carlyle summarizes his attitude as, 'Withal Knox was no despiser of women; far the reverse in fact: his behaviour to good and pious women is full of respect, and his tenderness, his patient helpfulness in their sufferings and infirmities are beautifully conspicuous'. Since Marjory is seldom mentioned we can presume that she caused him no distress; therefore this part of his life was not worthy of mention.

By 13 September Knox was back in Geneva, with his wife and mother-in-law, as well as a servant, James Young, and Patrick, described as a pupil.

As soon as he had left Scotland, and as a farewell gesture, the bishops summoned him again for non-appearance, and then, when he failed to appear for a second time, burnt him in effigy at the Mercat Cross in Edinburgh. It was a last petulant action by an increasingly impotent opposition.

The English congregation in Geneva, however, with Whittingham and Christopher Goodman at the helm, had flourished in Knox's absence, and for the next two years he found the calm haven that so far had eluded him. At least there was a family surrounding him now, even if his mother-in-law probably continued in her ferment of doubt. He writes to Anna Lock in London that he 'is now burdened with double cares'; in other words, he now has a wife and mother-in-law to support, 'a domestic charge wherewith before I have not been accustomed, and therefore are the more fearful.' He beseeches her to join the exiles in Geneva, 'where I neither fear nor shame to say is the most perfect school of Christ that ever was on the earth since the days of the apostles'. (Mrs Lock did go to Geneva with her son, daughter and maid in May 1557, but sadly her daughter died four days after their arrival.) However Knox's domestic life cannot have been entirely burdened with cares, since the church's register of baptisms for 23 May 1557 records 'Nathaniel, son of John Knox,' with Whittingham as godfather. Knox, now safe in Geneva, could at last start to relax into domesticity.

He presumably lived in what is now the old town, perched high above Lake Geneva with pleasant views of the distant Alps. His work in Geneva was arduous, with at least three sermons a week. Moreover he was still technically a foreigner, who was allowed three days' grace on his arrival before being required to report personally to the authorities. Knox had then to swear allegiance to the Republic of Geneva and pay a small fee, whereupon he would have been rewarded with a *lettre d'habitation*. This required the holder to be attached to a congregation, so that the pastors could report formally on the propriety of one's behaviour. All of this may have been a formality given his friendship with Calvin and his position as a minister, but it served to emphasize the fragility of his situation as a foreigner. If proof of this were needed it was found when the Italian congregation that shared the church was accused of heretical practices and told to recant or leave Geneva. In the event the Italians did both. But before the birth of his second son, Eleazar, Knox and Goodman had, on 21 June 1558 taken full citizenship. The fee for this would have been waived, because they were pastors. Goodman said, 'I do not repent of having stood forth and laboured with others in that cause which has been the chief agreement and solid peace which, by the great blessing of God, we enjoy in this place.'

The Peace of Augsburg was designed to bring an end to the various quarrels that had been spluttering across Europe often disguised as religious struggles. Largely they were, in fact, frontier disputes over possession of land. The treaty aimed to consolidate the existing boundaries and established the principle of *cuius regio, cuius religio* giving individual princes the authority to settle the religious belief in his province, either Catholic or Lutheran. It did not, however, recognize the reformed Protestantism of Zurich and Geneva.

Geneva was, as we have seen, a rigid theocracy with a strictly enforced code of behaviour, but inside the English-speaking colony, numbering 212 people, there was a feeling of security after many troubles. A contemporary tells us, 'Let other men feign miracles, but Geneva seemeth to me the wonderful miracle of the world, so many from all countries come thither as it were a sanctuary, not to gain riches but to live in poverty.' And without fear of persecution, he might have added. With the country outside in turmoil and Geneva itself beset by armed enemies it must have felt like being in a stout, warm house on a stormy night. The exiles were well aware of the storms outside. It could have been dangerous for some people even to be known to receive letters from Knox, so that in letters to individuals he still occasionally signed himself 'John Sinclair'.

But in Geneva, Knox, Whittingham and Goodman were like-minded scholars in whose congregation we find the roots of Puritanism. Their order of service had been drawn up by Knox, with Whittingham and three others before his departure for Scotland, and would be accepted by the Church of Scotland nine years later.

The Bible was translated into English, and this Geneva Bible became a standard text for over a hundred years, although Knox, with his little Greek and less Hebrew, can only have had a supervisory role. During this time Knox also made himself available to his co-religionists in Scotland, having gained a greater awareness of their plight during his visit.

We are told that 'the course they took in these sad times, was the same which the primitive Christians did when they were under their persecutions, namely prayers and tears'.

Knox certainly advised prayer in his *Letter of Wholesome Counsel* of 1556 as well as worship in the secrecy of private homes, and his 'good hope is that ye shall walk as the sons of light in the middle of this wicked generation'. Furthermore, with daily worship, 'ye shall be of the number of prudent virgins, daily renewing your lamps with oil'. Lairds and householders were to hold daily Bible readings and discuss with their servants and tenants the significance of the scriptures. It must have come as something of a surprise to some lairds that they should allow their servants to dispute with them, but since Knox firmly believed in the validity of faith, over and above all questions of class, his view was that one man's opinion was as valid as any other. He gave copious private advice to individuals, even putting idolatry ahead of adultery as a grievous sin.

In one unexpected burst of alliteration he found it difficult to respond to a question on the apparel of women, 'lest in so doing we either restrain Christian liberty, or else let loose the bridle too far to the foolish fantasy of facile flesh'. But ruling in favour of the status quo, he added 'the garments of women do declare their weakness and inability to execute the office of men'. On one occasion he wrote, 'Albeit I have no great matter to write unto you . . .' but goes on to assure his correspondent, a Mrs Guthrie of Edinburgh, that he prays for her, tells her that her doubts are understandable, makes no apology for fear causing him to flee, but prays that one day he may end his battle among his own people.

Knox's next opportunity to put this ambition into action came soon enough, for in May 1557 James Syme, his erstwhile host in Edinburgh, accompanied by James Barron, whose wife Knox had counselled, arrived in Geneva with a letter signed by the Lords Glencairn, Lorne, Erskine, and James Stewart. Therein they begged him to return to Scotland, where 'ye shall find all faithful that ye left behind you, not only glad to hear your doctrine, but ready to jeopard lives and goods in the forward setting of the glory of God'. At most times in his life Knox would have jumped at this opportunity, but at this point his first child, Nathaniel, had just been born, and his friend Mrs Lock had arrived in Geneva, in considerable distress at the loss of her daughter. He was established as pastor to a trouble-free flock, living at last among his immediate family. He was not being given hospitality in secret, like some escaped felon. He also had had time to study among some of the greatest minds in the reforming movement. But having consulted Calvin and 'other Godly ministers' about his requested departure, they with one consent told him 'that he could not refuse the vocation, unless he would declare himself rebellious unto his God, and unmerciful to his country'.

He told Syme and Barron that he would return with 'reasonable expedition, as soon as he might put order to the dear flock that was committed to his charge'. Clearly this would take some time and he did not arrive in Dieppe until 24 October, having left his comfortable life and new family in Geneva.

Once again, the journey cannot have been easy. France was still at war with Spain and Le Havre and Dieppe were filling with invasion fleets destined for England.

The Pope had authorized the setting-up of a formal inquisition in France, and Charles, cardinal of Lorraine, the Queen Regent's brother, had been appointed chief inquisitor. Then, Henry II had issued the Edict of Compiègne, providing for further extirpation of heresy.

In Paris a mob attacked a house in the Rue Saint-Jacques, where a Huguenot assembly had been secretly celebrating the Lord's Supper. In the ensuing riot the men, who had arms, managed to force a way through the mob, hoping by their flight to draw off the mob and ensure the safety of women and children who were still barricaded in the house. Their ploy failed, however, and about 120 women and children were arrested and confined in the Châtelet prison, where they were abused and subjected to great privations. By 11 October five had gone to the stake in the Place du Grève, although thanks to foreign interventions the remainder was eventually released.

So having traversed the undoubted perils of France Knox arrived in Dieppe: 'Of full mind, with the first ships to have visited you.' He wrote to 'some of the nobility in Scotland' just four days after his arrival, saying that he had received , 'two letters, not very pleasing to the flesh,' which told him that new consultations were taking place and that he should stay in Dieppe until they were completed. Apparently even those that seemed most 'frack [resolute] and fervent' were now lacking the boldness needed for such an enterprise. He went on to wonder how he could explain this apparent volte-face to those he had left behind in Geneva. He was quite understandably furious, his heart 'pierced with sorrow'. He attacks the nobility for having betrayed their realm to the slavery of strangers and asks them to consider their own miserable estate. He reminds them that they receive honour and tribute, not by reason of their birth, but by reason of their office and duty to deliver their subjects and brethren from all violence and oppression, to the utmost of their power. This could be seen as an opening shot in a campaign to define the duties of 'magistrates', or those with secular power over their fellows.

In spite of the repression, there was a reformed church, the Church of the Madeleine, in Dieppe. There Knox became co-pastor to a M. Delaporte, who also served Rouen. Dr McCrie tells us that 'a surprising change was soon observed on the morals of the inhabitants, which had formerly been very dissolute'. By 1 December he was less angry in a letter to his *Brethren in Scotland*' followed by another on 17 December to the '*Lords and other professing the truth in Scotland*'. The first is a long – even Knox admits it is 'mair ample' – restatement of faith and exhortation to continue in the face of hardship. After what has been rightly called a prolix start to the second letter he moves from the purely religious to the edge of secular theorizing. He hears that contradiction is being voiced and rebellion mounted against the secular authority and he explicitly commands that no one suddenly disobeys the established authority in things lawful, but rather seeks its favour. If, however, this cannot be obtained, then the extremity may be attempted, so that true preaching and correct administration of the sacraments may be achieved. He then has a thinly veiled side-swipe at his old adversary Arran, now Duke of Chatelherault, for which he feels he will be thought sharp. He is always careful to command that no disobedience be shown to 'things lawful', but he does not define 'lawful' nor yet advise what should be done if the matter is not lawful. This would come later.

Writing twenty-two years later in 1599, Shakespeare in *Henry V*, on the night before Agincourt, has the boy Michael Williams say to the King, 'if his cause be not good, the King himself hath a heavy reckoning to make . . . it will be a black matter for the king that led them to it'. While theologically Knox always felt on safe ground, he was extremely careful, almost to the point of timidity, to make sure that his political cause was good and not a 'black matter'.

A vindication of the Huguenot prisoners in Paris had been published in French and Knox brought out a translation with a preface and additions. He condemns these 'slaves of Satan the doctors of the Sorbonne'; later they are merely 'hell-hounds'. He quotes Tertullian's defence of the Christians, and goes on to say that, 'if a law be unrighteous, of very right it ought to be done away'. He writes that princes are blinded into persecuting their true subjects, who in fact maintain the honour of those very princes. In other words the Huguenots were quite strictly observing civil obedience, but at the same time committing what was seen as heresy. But it must be remembered that Henry II thought heresy and treason were the same thing. However, Knox claims that 'the chief cause why the Pope and his kingdom do hate and persecute us is that we affirm that no power on earth is above the power of the civil ruler'. He warns princes to take heed and not to tempt the long patience of the Almighty, who may easily eject them from glory, power and authority. 'The regiment of princes is come this day to such a heap of iniquity, that no godly man can brook office or authority under them.' He was warming to his theme that temporal power is conditional on a variety of factors, and that princes may be answerable for their actions to more than just their consciences.

Knox made his return to Geneva by an extremely roundabout way, visiting La Rochelle on the west coast of France, perhaps to avoid military centres or areas of known persecution. La Rochelle was, anyway, one of the centres of Protestantism and Knox may have been invited to preach there. Indeed in the town, according to John Row, quoting eye-witnesses some eighty years later, 'a noble woman came to hear him preach, and see him baptise a bairn who was carried many miles for that purpose'. Knox also claimed to the congregation there that 'within two or three years he hoped to preach the Gospel publicly in St Giles Kirk in Edinburgh'. So his dream was still alive and his prediction was accurate. He returned to Geneva via Lyons, where he wrote to Janet Adamson, back in Edinburgh. In this letter is one of his very rare clues to an improving situation: he beseeches God to 'make me mindful of his ample benefits, which he most plentifully pourest upon me . . . both in spiritual and temporal things'. Lyons had been, since the twelfth century, a centre of reform, first with Peter Waldo, who founded the Waldensian sect there. It then became a centre for various trades revolts and, at the time of Knox's visit, a heartland of Huguenot dissent. His route from La Rochelle would have swung south-east through Poitou, where dissent was also rife. This dissent had developed there to include the bourgeoisie and some of the petty nobility.

But by March 1558 he was back with his family and congregation in Geneva and able to resume his pastoral duties. Doubts still lingered as to whether he should not simply have ignored the procrastinating advice and returned to Scotland. Most importantly, on 16 April he wrote to Scotland a letter which is worth quoting at some length:

> and of very purpose to have visited you did I leave this congregation here, and also the family committed to my charge; but the cause of my stop I do not to this day understand. Shall Christ, the author of peace, concord and quietness be preached where war is proclaimed, sedition engendered, and tumults appear to rise? Shall not his Evangel be accused as the cause of all calamity which is like to follow? God hath most justly permitted Satan to put into my mind such cogitations. I grant that none of these dangers which are before expressed are any sufficient cause or excuse why I should not hazard all for the manifestation of Christ's Glory: for if the Apostles had looked to any of these, they would never have preached Christ; for all such troubles, and also more grievous did ensue [from] the publication of his Gospel . . . but therefore must not the messengers of God desist from their office . . . But Alas! as the wounded man, be he never so expert in physic or surgery, cannot suddenly mitigate his own pain and dolour, no more can I the fear and grief of my heart, although I am not altogether ignorant [of] what is to be done.

Hume Brown comments that 'no man could thus lay bare the secret motions of his heart, save one whose single purpose was to grapple with baser desires and fashion his life according to his deepest thought'. This letter quite clearly marks Knox as no driven zealot. The accusation that he saw himself as a reincarnation of the prophets of the Old Testament falls away as valueless, and reinforces the view that his courage was not only physical but also intellectual. True courage comes from the conquest of fear and Knox had fears that his efforts might cause war, sedition and tumult. He also had doubts that his faith might eventually be found to be lacking, but continued none the less. He felt it was quite right that his resolution should be tested in this way by God allowing Satan to try his faith. This should not be seen as a devious piece of reasoning by one trained in the medieval schools, but it does show that Knox was intellectually in control, even though his faith was God-given, and the effects of his teaching were deeply considered.

While in Dieppe he had started work on a pamphlet that he now completed. This was probably his most famous work, *The First Blast of the Trumpet against the Monstrous Regiment of Women*. Seldom read, but famous none the less, most probably for the magnificent sound of its much misunderstood title, which should, however, now be read as *The First Blast of the Trumpet against the Improper Reigning of Women*. It was indeed a time when a comparatively large number of women were in positions of power. In his native Scotland, Mary of Guise was Queen Regent for the sixteen-year-old Mary of Scotland, who, in April 1558, had finally married Francis, the dauphin of France. The huge cannon, Mons Meg, in Edinburgh Castle was fired to celebrate the fact of her marriage. Her father-in-law Henri II's court in France was dominated by two extremely assertive women, his wife Catherine de Medici and his mistress Diane de Poitiers. But undoubtedly looming largest in Knox's mind was Mary Tudor, whose persecutions of the English Protestants had driven him into exile.

And so it was exclusively against Mary Tudor that Knox focused his arguments, once again casting her in the role of Jezebel. He finds it extraordinary that a country with so much wit as England should tolerate such a rule, but that, since it does, it deserves the 'confusion and bondage of strangers'. This is an undisguised reference to her husband Philip II, now King of Spain, and is a little unfair. Discovering Mary's barrenness and knowing that his father was about to die, Philip had in fact left England two years previously. He would only make a brief return to attempt to raise troops for an action in the Netherlands, but Mary had little in the way of concrete help to give him. Philip had, however, wholeheartedly endorsed Mary's devout Catholicism and violent persecutions. This was more than enough for Knox, who, although no xenophobe, could become incandescent with fury at attempts by foreigners to influence domestic religion. He repeats his certainty that 'it is more than a monster in nature that a woman shall reign and have empire above man'. He is very well aware of the danger in pointing to established situations and calling them sinful, but since he believes he is preaching God's truth, he has no alternative but to speak.

However, he tells us that he intends three blasts of the trumpet, the first two of which will be anonymous, but the last will be signed by him so that no one else shall be blamed for it. What follows is a long justification of his stand, quoting Aristotle, Tertullian and Augustine, among others, and bringing forth a whirlwind of biblical precedents of female perfidy. Jezebel, who worshipped Baal, and took power on the death of her husband Ahab; and Athaliah, Ahab's daughter, who kept power by murdering all but one of her grandchildren, and ruling for six years until murdered in turn by the grandchild she had failed to kill. He remembers the 'insolent joy' when Mary, 'that cursed Jezebel', was proclaimed Queen. He admonishes the populace who were 'become so blind that, knowing the pit, they headlong cast themselves into the same . . . and are now compelled to bow their necks under the yoke of Satan and of his proud ministers, pestilent Papists and proud Spaniards'. As biblical precedent of a female ruler, he excuses Deborah from his reproof since she had said she attributed her authority to God and, therefore, 'did usurp no such power or authority as our queens do this day claim'. Women, he allows, may inherit office, but should not then betray that power to strangers. Once again, he quotes Mary's marriage to Philip II and how Scotland, 'by the practises of a crafty dame, [is] resigned likewise under title of marriage into the power of France'. The crafty dame being the Queen Regent, Mary of Guise.

Lastly he calls on the realm and estates, presumably of England, to 'refuse to be her officers because she is a traitress and rebel against God'. They finally must study to repress her inordinate pride and tyranny to the utmost of their power. They ought to remove from honour and authority that 'monster in nature', and 'if any seek to defend that impiety they ought not fear first to pronounce and then after to execute against them the sentence of death'. He promises to tell us more of his thinking on this in the second blast, and warns Mary Tudor that the day of vengeance is already appointed in the counsel of the eternal. He ends, 'therefore let all man be advertised, for the trumpet hath once blown'.

The pamphlet has unfairly gained notoriety as a misogynist tract, whereas in fact it is highly political, questioning the absolute right of monarchs, especially female monarchs, and particularly Mary Tudor, and advocating a power struggle against sinful rule even to the point of death. His authority for this stance is taken almost entirely from the Bible, as was the prevalent manner of argument in his day, when total familiarity with both Testaments was presumed among the educated, and the Old Testament was taken as a literal and factually accurate history. Knox had obviously been considering this question of woman's temporal authority since he sent his questions to Bullinger some years before, and he was doing no more than stating in print what was received opinion at the time. It is true that someone with a greater sense of diplomacy might have found a way to put the case with less vehemence; but some eighteen years later, Knox's view would still be the received wisdom.

In 1576, after Knox's death, the French political philosopher Jean Bodin published his *Six Books of the Commonwealth*, in which he states quite categorically that 'women ought to be removed as far as possible from the majesty of government. As often as the Almighty declares [that] He is about to take bitter revenge on the enemies of his name He [then] threatens to subject them to the sway and laws of women.' Bodin reaches his conclusion by an examination of political theory. Although his book was highly popular in the latter part of the seventeenth century, today even its contemporary translator calls its style 'laborious' and the work itself 'repellent to all but the most determined reader'.

Calvin and the Protestant community in Strasburg dissociated themselves from Knox's *Blast*. Eventually a reply was produced by John Aylmer called, rather ponderously, *A Harbour for Faithful and True Subjects against the late blown Blast, concerning the government of women: wherin are confuted all such reasons a stranger of late hath made in that behalf, with a brief exhortation to obedience*. By the time this was published Elizabeth I was on the throne. Aylmer's line was that Knox was attacking Mary in particular, so if God gave a king no male heir then he clearly intended that a woman should rule and that subjects should not criticise the will of God. The will of God and Elizabeth were carried out and Aylmer became bishop of London, his diplomacy towards Elizabeth in this case having done his chances of elevation no harm.

But as we have already seen, diplomacy was never Knox's strong suit. Indeed, in a letter to Foxe, the martyrologist, on 18 May 1558 he apologizes for 'my rude vehemency and inconsidered affirmations, which may appear rather to proceed from choler than of zeal and reason'. However, he was clearly feeling at this time that his so far suppressed views on a variety of topics should be aired, and he followed the *First Blast* with three more tracts of increasing controversy. They were the tracts in which the bases for all his future actions were set out.

6   Letters Home

After the *First Blast*, Knox's next tract is known as a *Letter to the Queen Regent*, although he calls her 'Lady Mary Regent of Scotland' and on another occasion 'the excellent Lady Mary, Dowager Regent of Scotland'. It is a reiteration of the earlier letter, 'augmented and explained'. Knox had now certainly heard of her 'pasquil' dismissal of his earlier letter, two years previously, and had been stung by it. Not only were his powers of diplomacy weak, he could never resist the temptation to rise to the bait of a slighting remark.

Knox starts this letter by declaring his lack of fear for the tyrannical and blasphemous bishops who burned him in effigy, having failed to bring him to public trial. Then addressing Mary directly, he in effect lays the sins of all, dating back to Cain and Abel, upon the heads of the Catholic faithful today. 'And herein ought you, Madam, be circumspect and careful, if that you have any hope of the life to come.' Even though he is living abroad, he is well aware of her avarice and cruelty, 'for fame carries the voices of the poor' (afflicted by intolerable taxes). He points out that her power is only borrowed and she holds it by the permission of others, and that 'seldom do women reign long with felicity and joy'. He then mentions her loss of her sons and her husband and bids her beware that she provoke not further the eyes of God's majesty, 'for it will not be in the haughty looks of the proud, the strength of your friends, nor the multitude of men, that can justify your cause in His presence'. Finally he refers directly to her 'pasquil' remark, telling her that God may send messengers, 'with whom you shall not be able on that matter to jest' and he ends with a quotation from Revelations:

I am the beginning and the end. I will give to him that is athirst of the well of the water of life freely. He that overcometh shall inherit all things and I will be his God and he shall be my son. But the fearful and unbelieving, and the abominable and murderers, and whore-mongers and sorcerers, and idolators and all liars, shall have their part in the lake which burneth with fire and brimstone which is the second death.

This was much more unequivocal than the first letter and formed a direct attack on Mary in person. Coupled with the *First Blast*, it confirmed his implacable opposition to her rule. It remained to be seen if he would preach a popular rising against what he regarded as her idolatrous tyranny.

His next tract starts with an '*Appelation from the cruel and most unjust sentence pronounced against him by the false bishops and clergy of Scotland, with his supplication and exhortation to the nobility, estates and commonalty of the same realm.*' In other words he was appealing to the entire government of Scotland, with the obvious exception of the clergy. He had already set out his case to the sovereign, but now turned his attention to the remainder of the laity, starting with the nobility and estates.

First, somewhat pedantically, he refutes the charges laid against him by the bishops on the grounds that it is quite lawful for God's messengers to appeal against unjust sentences, quoting the Biblical instances of Jeremiah and Paul. In case any should think him arrogant to place himself beside these figures, he points out that the grounds of the case itself should be considered and not the person. He claims first that he could not be summoned by the bishops since he was living and preaching outside their jurisdiction, that is, in Geneva; secondly, that he was never shown a copy of their summons; thirdly, that he had been exiled by their 'unjust tyranny'; and lastly, that since he had accused them of crimes in his letter to the Queen Regent, they could not make counter-accusations until this had been answered.

But this is all by way of preamble, for now he exhorts the nobility directly to control the 'whole rabble of your bishops'. He asks assurance that,

I may have free access to my native country which I never offended . . . and also that you, by your authority, which ye have of God, compel such as of long time have blinded and deceived both yourselves and the people to answer to such things as shall be laid to their charge. In conscience you are bound to punish malefactors and to defend innocents imploring your help . . . God requireth of you to provide that your subjects be rightly instructed in his true religion.

He points out that Moses, as a temporal leader, was right in punishing Aaron the priest for his idolatry. The 'precept requireth not only that the king himself should fear God . . . but that he, as chief ruler should provide that God's true religion should be kept inviolated of the people and flock which by God was committed to his charge'. Then he comes to the crux of his argument:

> the common song of all men is, 'we must obey our kings be they good or be they bad, for God hath so commanded.' True it is, God hath commanded kings to be obeyed, but like true it is that in things which they commit against his glory . . . he hath commanded no obedience, but rather he hath approved, yea, and greatly rewarded, such as have opposed themselves to their ungodly commandments and blind rage.

This is, at last, a definite cry for open opposition. But he goes on,

> Hereof your Honours may easily espy that none provoking the people to idolatry ought to be exempted from the punishment of death. The punishment of such crimes as idolatry, blasphemy and others that touch the majesty of God doth not appertain to kings and rulers only, but also to the whole body of the people.

He allows that the struggle will not be easy, but draws their attention to the plight of the English, who

> hate the bondage of strangers, the pride of priests and the monstriferous empire of a wicked woman, yet they are compelled to bow their necks to the yoke of the devil, to obey whatever the proud Spaniards and wicked Jezebel list to command. Your bishops, accompanied with the swarm of papistical vermin, shall cry, 'A damned heretic ought not to be heard'.

But he ends by proclaiming his innocence and exhorting the nobility to follow his teaching. Since every proposition is backed by rigorous biblical case history it is a lengthy document but in it is a clear statement of his central belief: that the Catholic Church of Rome, by constructing the man-made Mass as intercession and requiring the further intercession of a priesthood between man and his God, to say nothing of the adoration of Saints and relics, is idolatrous and, as such, may be put down by whatever means, and those supporting it are guilty of blasphemy. This is simply a restatement of the *Helvetic Confession*. But he has moved from simply advocating reform to proposing revolution. Laws that impose idolatrous practices are unjust. If a ruler or magistrate is imposing unjust laws, it is the duty of the nobility to replace those magistrates, by force if necessary.

Knox was, however, well aware that there still stood a gulf between the nobility, or magistrates, and the common people. For them the risk of rising against the civil power was much greater, and he set out their freedoms as he saw them in his third letter *to his Beloved Brethren the Commonalty of Scotland*, also published in Geneva in 1558. He points out that what he has asked of the Queen Regent, the nobility and the estates, he must require of the commonalty, for,

> that religion is as the stomach to the body, which, if it be corrupted, doth infect the whole. For albeit God hath put and ordained distinction and differ-ence between the king and his subjects, between the rulers and the common people, yet in the hope of the life to come he hath made all equal. For as your bodies cannot escape corporal death if with your princes ye eat or drink deadly poison, so ye shall not escape the death everlasting if with them ye profess a corrupt religion.

He then goes on, in his usual manner, to prove the existence of this equality from the time of Moses. He offers, with 'diverse other godly and learned men . . . to jeopard our lives for the salvation of your souls'. Here was a restatement of one of his basic tenets: 'He hath made all men equal.' He accepts that there is a difference in the estate of nobles and commoners – he could hardly do anything else – but in the importance of eternal life there is no difference. Although he had not yet asked for a popular rising, he realized that in such a rising the commonalty could easily be crushed with military force, while the nobility could find some safeguards.

Taken together, the letters to the Regent, the nobility and the common-alty display the start of a change in his preaching. Clearly he still maintains that the Church of Rome is an Antichrist and the Mass is idolatrous. Since they rely on the creations of man, as opposed to the teachings of Christ as found in scripture, and involve human arbitration in the absolution of sin, they come between man and his saviour. The celebration of community that he feels should exist in the Lord's Supper is at odds with the Catholic adora-tion of a spiritual presence in the Host.

But now he proposes a community in which all are made equal, with that very equality overriding the status of birth, with each citizen possessing the God-given power to remove the unjust, no matter who they may be. At least, if they could not achieve the actual removal and replacement with more just rulers then, at least, they could withhold their tithes and clerical levies.

Knox was at this point clearly thinking about a return to Scotland, his appetite for preaching there having been sharpened by the depth of support he had found two years previously. He also set out ideas that would not become concrete until much later when he said that 'most justly ye may provide true teachers for yourselves, be it in your cities, towns, or villages . . . ye may moreover withhold the fruits and profits which your false bishops and clergy most injustly receive of you'.

At the same time he published a digest of what would be contained in the *Second Blast of the Trumpet*. First: 'it is not birth only nor propinquity of blood that maketh a king lawfully to reign'. Second: 'no manifest idolator nor notorious transgressor of God's holy precepts ought to be promoted to any public regiment'. Third: 'neither can oath nor promise bind any such people to obey and maintain tyrants against God'. Finally, 'that if rashly they have promoted any manifest wicked person . . . most justly may the same men depose and punish him'.

There are, in fact, no detailed references to female rule, and the promised Third Blast never appeared. It may be that Knox moved on to more general applications of his ideas, or simply that his chief target, Mary Tudor, died in November 1558.

However, the three pamphlets mentioned in the last chapter were enough for Professor J.W. Allen to say, 'he cannot but be regarded as one of the chief personal factors in the history of political thought in the sixteenth century'. In his invaluable work *A History of Political Thought in the 16th Century*, Professor Allen delineates three distinct phases. First, the Lutheran acceptance of non-resistance to constituted authority; second, the Genevan ideal of Calvin, that no matter what the circumstances, there must be no attempt to set up the kingdom of heaven by force. This doctrine sat firmly on the fence between compliance and revolt. In other words if the revolution has no hope of success it should not be attempted, but if government will change without the use of force then revolution is acceptable. In northern Germany, for instance, the secular power was already Protestant, so it was easy to preach non-resistance. Elsewhere, however, the arguments for the third phase, that of physical resistance, were brought into sharp focus by Knox.

The seeds for this course of action were already known to Knox. A pamphlet, known as the *Bekenntis of Magdeburg*, had been published in April 1550. It states that passive resistance is not enough and that subjects must defend true belief 'mit Leib und Leben' ('with life and limb'). Since God gives authority for justice then what is unjust is ungodly, and there is a duty to resist, by arms if necessary. Knox had undoubtedly read the work that he calls the *Apology of Magdeburg*, but he had his own agenda based on the Genevan ideal, coupled with his democratically based belief that all men are equal, including rulers, who hold their power as a trust. 'I find no privilege granted unto kings by God, more than unto the people.' In this he parts company with the *Apology of Magdeburg*.

In 1556 the exiled bishop John Ponet had published *A Short Treatise of Politic Power*, which Strype in his *Ecclesiastic Memorials* said was, 'not over favourable to princes'. Ponet asserted that 'all politic power and authority cometh . . . from God . . . and was ordained, that is, to maintain justice. Let every soul be subject to the powers that rule for there is no power but of God.' As to kings, they must obey the Ten Commandments, (committing adultery becomes 'hoormongering') and,

> neither pope, emperor nor king may do any thing to the hurt of his people without their consent. Is any man so unreasonable to deny that . . . those who have appointed an office upon trust, have not authority upon just occasion (as the abuse of it) to take away what they gave? And men ought to have more respect to their country, than to their prince, to the commonwealth, than to any one person. For the country and the commonwealth is a degree above the king.

Ponet then deals largely with economic ills arising from unjust rule, such as forced loans and debased coinage, and the necessity for a parliament to represent the common people. But he approaches the solution as to how to deal with an unjust tyrant with, one feels, considerable reluctance. He spells out a list of solutions, starting with self-reform by the ruler, then proceeding through similar action from the nobility and parliament, from Church ministers and the (undefined) people in general. Finally, although it cannot be maintained by God's word that any private man may kill except where execution of just punishment upon tyrants, idolators and traitrous governors is either by the whole state utterly neglected, or the prince with the council conspire the subversion or alteration of their country and people; any private man have from special inward commandment or surely proved motion of God; as Moses was commanded to kill the Egyptians, with such like; or be otherwise commanded or permitted by common authority upon just occasion and common necessity to kill.

This is hardly a call to man the barricades and gather round the guillotine, but then Ponet lacked the vehement conviction of Knox. However, his statement that the commonwealth was a degree above the king would have come easily from the mouths of the parliamentarian judges of Charles I; and his reluctant authority for violent action was such a leap into what could be seen as a justification for treason, that it none the less stands, for its time, as a great revolutionary statement.

Two years later Christopher Goodman was writing in Geneva. He was, as we have seen, a close colleague of Knox, his co-pastor, and had stood in for Knox during his visit to Scotland. Many authorities believe that the two may well have collaborated on Goodman's tract, *How Superior Powers Ought to be Obeyed*, which carries the subtitle '*and wherein they may lawfully by God's word be disobeyed and resisted. Wherein also is declared the cause of all this present miserie in England, and the only way to remedy the same.*' Large passages of it are, indeed, very Knoxian in tone: 'To understand that the papists were cruel butchers and insatiable bloodsuckers . . .' for example. But even before we have read a word of the tract itself, it has parted company with Calvin, although it carries an introduction by William Whittingham, another member of the English Church in Geneva. Goodman's work starts with a preface stressing the gravity of disobedience and goes on for two chapters to describe the persecution of the early Christians, telling how they could not resist but rather had to lay down their heads – in a marginal note he calls this 'a dangerous doctrine'. He declares that to obey is good, 'but to obey whom, wherein, and how far ought to be considered,' or else people are 'as men disguised upon a stage, who have turned their nobility to open shame amongst all nations, which now behold their folly'. This is counter to Calvin's philosophy of passive resistance, and the work, along with *The First Blast*, was banned in Geneva.

Goodman goes on to condemn the rule of women, 'saying expressly, from the middle of thy brethren shalt thou choose thee a king, and not amongst thy sisters'. Since Goodman published his tract in January, preceding *The First Blast*, which was published much later and anonymously, many people took Goodman for its author. But Knox had been working on *The First Blast* during his stay in Dieppe, and the confusion merely exemplifies the similarity in the thinking of the two men. Goodman goes on to tell us that it is not enough merely to condemn godless laws, people must go further and resist them. Thus all English are condemned: 'they are no Daniels'. They should not consider their worldly losses when they will 'have the reward of righteousness at the hands of God'. If not, 'will God then spare England alone?' The sins of Mary Tudor and her Spanish marriage are enumerated, as are the horrors that will befall when the wrath of God is let loose. The first section finishes with a call for repentance and a return to the true faith. Goodman now becomes more directly political, saying that obedience is only due to 'such as God has appointed to rule over us in his fear, for our profit and preservation of the commonwealth'. As to unjust rulers,

if without fear they transgress God's laws themselves and command others to do the like, then have they lost that honour and obedience which otherwise their subjects did owe unto them and ought no more to be taken for magistrates, but punished as private transgressors, as after I have promised to prove.

Not only rulers and magistrates must be a party to reform, but the common people cannot excuse themselves on the grounds of ignorance or powerlessness. He laments that the people of England 'defend the devilish Mass, and all the puddles of Popery with the caterpillars and rabble of all unclean spirits'. The only solution can be total rejection, even within the closest family members,

of provocation to idolatry, to serve strange Gods . . . [and] . . . thy hand shall first be upon such a one to kill him, and then the hands of all the people. No person is exempted by any law of God from this punishment, be he king, queen, or emperor, that is either openly or privately known to be an idolator, be he never so dear to us, he must die the death.

Puzzlingly, he then says that this is no doctrine of rebellion, clearly having realized that it is just that; he justifies the statement by asserting that replacing tyranny with the justice of God is not rebellious. Such actions, he accepts, may lead to martyrdoms, but 'these lessons are hard to the flesh but easy to the spirit'. Knox agreed with these sentiments and thus at times his faith did lead him to extreme positions but he could never realize that other people might not be as vehemently driven as he was.

The ideas in these tracts were still current seven years later in 1565, when a book of thirty-six wood engravings carried a drawing of two enthroned queens being harangued by two men carrying trumpets. Books were emblazoned on their hangings and a caption appended: 'No queen in her kingdom can or ought to sit fast, if Knox or Goodman's books blow any true blast.' Goodman was going further than Ponet, but was very specific in addressing the English, while Knox, although appealing to his brethren in Scotland, was advocating more general liberties. Ponet talked of equality and only reluctantly of action, while Goodman advocated physical action as obligatory. Knox synthesized the two and added his own thoughts in these three tracts. Later, even after political dilution, they are one of the foundations of the Scottish Reformation.

One last pamphlet emerges from this period, and although not directly concerned with democratic belief, it does lie at the heart of Knox's theology.

A certain Englishman had written a tract denying predestination and the English Church in Geneva was asked to refute it. Knox wholeheartedly followed Calvin in his belief in predestination. In his *Institutes* Calvin had stated,

> We call predestination God's eternal decree, by which he determined with himself what he willed to become of each man. For all are not created in equal condition; rather eternal life is foreordained for some, eternal damnation to others. Therefore, as any man has been created to one or the other of these ends, we speak of him as predestined to life or death.

He argued closely that throughout life men should strive to justify the possibility of being among the elect and should hope that even those predestined to damnation might obtain mercy. However, Calvin does admit that the subject is complex and much of God's purpose is hidden from us. This doctrine, embodying the belief in an original sin with which mankind has been burdened since the fall of Adam, and its redemption through the intercession of Christ, was crucial to Protestantism, although debate over its precise meaning still continues. Knox called the treatise *'The Confutation of the Errors of the Careless by Necessity'*, and thought it 'detestable, blasphemous and odious'. Although there is no trace of the original work, some authorities have found clues that lead us to the English Anabaptist Robert Cooke as its author. But Knox is quite unequivocal:

> the doctrine of God's eternal Predestination is so necessary to the Church of God, that, without the same, can faith neither be truly taught, neither surely established . . . And therefore we fear not to affirm, that so necessary as it is that true faith be established in our heart, that we be brought to infeigned humility, and that we be moved to praise Him for his free graces received; so necessary also is the doctrine of God's eternal Predestination.

With his customary vehemence he continues to demolish Anabaptist arguments, using scripture and logic, in a document that in David Laing's 1844 edition of the works runs to over 400 pages. Though probably written in 1558 it was not until November 1559, a year after Knox's departure from Geneva, that permission to print it was given and even then, not with Geneva as its place of imprint. Calvin saw no need to bring more trouble on his head than was strictly necessary.

Two events occurred in November 1558 that concerned Knox. As we have heard, his second son, Eleazar, was born and was christened on the 29th, the godfather this time being Miles Coverdale, the translator of the Bible. Typically, Eleazar Knox appears on the baptismal registry and promptly vanishes into the silence of Knox's private life.

But twelve days earlier Mary Tudor had died. Abandoned as barren and childless by Philip of Spain, loathed for her repressions by the majority of her subjects and given the sobriquet 'Bloody' by posterity, she cannot have had a happy reign. Her end, reputed to have been in the agony of untreated uterine cancer, was probably worse. By contrast, when the news of her death was brought to her half-sister Elizabeth, in de facto house arrest at Hatfield, it is said that she threw her hat over a giant oak tree with joy. Gullible tourists are still shown the tree. The accession of Elizabeth, however, might have been thought to change everything, since there could be no doubt of her Protestantism. The legitimizing of Henry VIII's marriage to her mother Anne Boleyn had started Henry VIII's rift with Rome and led eventually to the English Reformation. But Elizabeth had spent her life until now in the dark world of political expediency and personal survival. She had known her mother and step-mother go to the headsman's block, had been a prisoner in the Tower, her servants had been tortured to try to implicate her in the abortive Thomas Wyatt revolt, and she had narrowly avoided execution herself. She therefore took a coolly pragmatic view of all forms of religious belief, with the liberal intent not, as we have said, 'to make windows into men's souls'. Also she well knew that excessive zeal, political or religious, soon could lead to passion and passion to violence. Violence meant revolt and possibly war, all of which was expensive, both directly and indirectly. Since the treasury was all but empty she would practice a lesson she had learnt in vicissitude, that of offending no one – until she could afford to, or until necessity drove her. For all that she is remembered as Gloriana, bejewelled from head to toe, she privately clung to a very middle-class parsimony.

However, hope among the exiles in Europe was high for a restoration of Protestantism and they hastily printed part of the book of Psalms, translated into prose, along with a table of psalms in alphabetical order. The whole formed a type of concordance, complete with a congratulatory preface. This was sent to Elizabeth on 10 February 1559. Previously, in an attempt to unify the exiles, on 15 December the English Church in Geneva sent William Keith, a Scotsman, to present a letter to the churches at Aarau, Basel, Strasburg, Worms and Frankfurt. The letter was signed by Knox, Goodman, Whittingham and others, offering to put past quarrels behind them. Keith had little success, as the exiled churches were already in a high state of preparation for departure. Indeed, two old adversaries of Knox from Frankfurt had visited the Genevan church with generous gifts and only one survivor of the Troubles of 1555 was left. Even in Geneva it was time for the exiles to go, and the church sought permission from the City Council on 24 January for its members to depart, thanking them for their hospitality. They were provided with letters of quittance, and an emigration of nearly 200 people was set in motion.

The idea that religious freedom was now complete and idolatry on the run in England was so firmly held that it was even incorporated into an imaginary dialogue in a children's schoolbook by one Mathurin Cordier. In Geneva no more marriages or baptisms of strangers were recorded and soon only those exiles concerned with finalizing the translation of the Bible and seeing it through to printing were left.

Knox left his mother-in-law Elizabeth, his wife Marjory, and his children in Geneva to arrive in Dieppe on 19 February 1559. He was not alone, for the local Protestants welcomed a number of other eminent local converts, and Knox's old colleague, the Sieur de la Porte, took Knox as his co-pastor. Knox preached in Dieppe in the spring of 1559, presumably in French. His congregation would have been a mix of local Dieppois and the Scots merchants who had established a presence in the town. He was still risking arrest and death, but as tolerance, which relied entirely on the whim of the powerful, grew greater, he even preached in public. A contemporary witness reproted, 'he was audacious and learned, factious and so eloquent that he managed men's souls as he wished, [and] having preached at Dieppe for six or seven weeks [he] made such progress and increased the number of converts daily that they had the hardihood to go to sermon in full day'. Indeed, a month after his departure, his legacy of fervour was so great that on 26 May from 600 to 800 celebrated the Lord's Supper in public. By 1562 there were twelve Protestant pastors in Dieppe. In the summer of 1559 the First National Synod of the French Reformed Church was held in the Rue Visconti in Paris. This is in the heart of the Latin Quarter, that is, the area where the concentration of foreign students at the Sorbonne made Latin the common language. In Knox's time it was nicknamed 'little Geneva'.

Still in Dieppe he wrote to Mrs Lock:

> Touching my negligence in writing to you, at other times I fear it will be little amended . . . for oft to write where few messengers can be found is foolishness. Of nature I am churlish, and in conditions different from many: yet one thing I ashame not to affirm, that familiarity once thoroughly contracted was never yet broken on my default. The cause may be that I have need of all [more] than that any have of me.

Apart from giving us a glimpse of the physical difficulties of carrying out a protracted correspondence when in his dangerous circumstances – although there was considerable intercourse between Geneva and Dieppe at this time – there is a tinge of lonely self-accusation in this passage. One may presume that he had been criticized by Mrs Lock, and perhaps she had accused him of wishing to cease the correspondence. Knox assures her that this is not so but then admits to his need for friends – a need which, when filled, makes it all but impossible for him not to respond to.

This is typical of exiles, and we often see in expatriate communities today relationships of almost fevered closeness. New additions to these communities are frequently welcomed with smothering hospitality, and Mrs Lock had joined the Genevan exiles only recently (in May 1557) at Knox's behest. Later in the letter, however, his old confidence returns, and he sets about *The Book of Common Prayer* with great vigour.

> A portion of the mark of the beast are all the dregs of papistry which were left in your Great Book of England wherof I will never counsel any man to use . . . no man will I salute in commendation especially, although I bear good will to all that profess Christ Jesus; for to me it is written that my First Blast hath blown from me all my friends in England. The Second Blast I fear shall sound somewhat sharp, except men be more moderate than I hear they are.
>
> My book, I hear, is written against . . . Let no man be deceived, as that the quality of this time shall affray [frighten] me to answer, although corporal death should be my reward . . . and yet have I been a secret and assured friend to thee, O England . . . thus with sorrowful heart . . .'

The compromises of Frankfurt are gone and he realizes that the *First Blast of the Trumpet* has done him harm. As we have heard the Second was only sketched and the Third never appeared. But his resolve is certain, no matter what. He presumably intended his comments to be reported back to England by Mrs Lock.

But his immediate goal was Scotland. He had twice written that he longed to return and he had undoubtedly enjoyed his reception in 1556. The most obvious route was to pass through England, so he wrote to William Cecil, Elizabeth's secretary of state, for permission to undertake the journey. He already knew Cecil, who had served under both Edward and Mary without any difficulty of conscience. He was Elizabeth's most trusted servant, would become Lord Burghley and serve Elizabeth for the rest of his long life. His elegant diplomatic mind and her bourgeois common sense, combined with an unswerving devotion to her country, made them the most effective political combination in Europe. It was to this brilliant and intellectually rigorous man that he addressed himself for permission to pass through England.

Under the reign of Edward VI Knox had had a flourishing career in England, but his contacts with the English Church in exile had soured that memory and many of the enemies he had made in Frankfurt were now in positions of power. For instance, his arch-enemy Dr Cox would preach the sermon at Elizabeth's coronation, and Knox himself said that his *First Blast* had blown away all the friends he had in England. Also the Tudor that sat on the throne might nominally be a Protestant, but she was a woman who took less than kindly to criticism. In fact after the *First Blast* Elizabeth regarded him 'as the incarnation of everything in religion and politics her soul most loathed'. He was a zealot and zealotry could be troublesome. So Knox received two rejections to his request – Elizabeth regarded him as too dangerous to set foot on English soil. With typical tenacity he wrote again to Cecil. This letter is a mixture of arrogance and naiveté. He starts disastrously by reminding Cecil of his 'most horrible defection from the truth' and that since 'he was worthy of hell and God has allowed him to rise in the world' he should not stand in the way of Knox's teaching. He goes on to complain that his request to travel through England had been rejected and his agents all but imprisoned. On 10 April he comes directly to the point:

> I have written (say you) a treasonable book against the Regiment and Empire of Women; if that be any offence, the poor flock is innocent . . . I require that the blame may be upon me alone. The writing of that book I will not deny, but to prove it treasonable I think it shall be hard . . . I dare not promise silence in so weighty a business, lest that, in so doing, I shall appear to betray the verity which is not subject to the mutability of time. Yet if any think me enemy to the person, nor yet to the regiment of her whom God hath now promoted, they are utterly deceived in me.

He also pleads that no fault should fall on the people of Scotland, who beg for his return, and that if Elizabeth openly confesses that only an extraordinary dispensation of God's mercy makes her rule lawful, then 'shall none in England be more willing to maintain her lawful authority than I'. He promises not to frequent the court, to pass through as quickly as possible and 'to offer God's favours to any Northcountrymen who feel guilt'. He ends by reminding Cecil of his personal duty to God.

Receiving no answer, the letter was sent again on the 22nd and clearly displays Knox's complete lack of diplomacy and his arrogantly held belief that since he is the teacher of the true gospel, all things will be made easy for him. But in his History he tells us, 'To this letter was no answer made,' and one can hardly be surprised. Whether Cecil read it with incandescent fury or growing hilarity we do not know, nor do we know if he ever showed it to his sovereign. Since Tudor tempers were short, he was probably too wise to anger her without cause.

IOANNES CNOXVS.

John Knox after Adrian Vanson. This wood engraving of 1580 was used in the first biography of Knox, the *Icones* by Theodore de Beza. It is probably the best likeness of the reformer existing

St Mary's Church, Haddington. Knox was born a few yards from here and attended the school attached to this church

The north wing of Holyrood Palace. Knox met Mary in her apartments which were on the middle floor

MARIE

Mary, Queen of Scots after François Clouet. Twenty-one years old, she returned to Scotland in 1561, already a widow and Queen Dowager of France. She was unprepared for the in-fighting among the Scottish nobility but was determined to continue her mother's policies. Neither Knox nor she ever convinced the other in debate

The Market (Mercat) Cross in Edinburgh. Knox attended many of the proclamations made from here. This is a Victorian reconstruction

The Tolbooth, Edinburgh. Knox addressed the General Assembly here when it met in Parliament's room on the first floor

Mary of Guise by Corneille de Lyon. Daughter of the Duke of Lorraine, she was already a widow and niece to the most powerful family in France when she was married to James V of Scotland. James died soon after Mary had given birth to the future Mary, Queen of Scots and she became Queen Regent. Knox bitterly opposed what he saw as her Catholic French hauteur

James Mossman's house in the High Street, Edinburgh, where Knox spent his last days. It is now called 'John Knox's House'

St Giles' Cathedral, Edinburgh. Knox, who was minister here would now recognize only the tower and crown

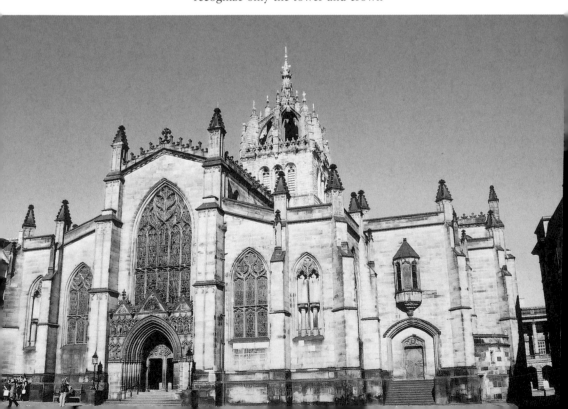

Henry Stuart, Lord Darnley, by an unknown artist. Father of James VI, he was handsome, insolent and vicious. His weakness and arrogance antagonized the Scottish nobility and eventually alienated the Queen. He was horrified by a sermon which Knox preached to him in St Giles' in 1565. He was assassinated in 1567

James Hepburn, 4th Earl of Bothwell by an unknown artist. 'A glorious, rash and hazardous young man'. His first recourse was to the sword and he plotted the assassination of Darnley before marrying Mary, Queen of Scots. Surprisingly, Knox patched up some of his more extravagant quarrels. After Mary's defeat at Carberry Hill he fled to Denmark where he died a hideous death

Edinburgh Castle.
James VI was born in
the room with the
small window, high on
the left

St Salvator's Chapel, St Andrews, where Knox worshipped as a student.
Patrick Hamilton was burnt in front of the gateway to the left

John Knox was now forty-six years old, and a married man with two children. He had had a reasonably secure position in the Republic of Geneva – although the exile population had markedly shrunk – where he could have continued preaching and pursuing scholarship in safety from persecution. There would have been an income, housing, and agreeable friends in an atmosphere of mutual support. And yet in spite of occasional doubt as to his fitness to undertake such a mission, he chose to answer the call of his native Scotland to return and preach reform in a nominally Catholic country. It was a call that he himself felt wavered in intensity, perhaps as God allowed Satan to plant doubt in his mind. His supporters in Scotland had drawn him into one dangerously unnecessary journey already, but perhaps Knox felt that he could steady the faith of his countrymen. However, his experiences in England and, more pertinently, in Europe, meant that the simple message of Christ's Evangel was now the core of a faith that was expanding into political sedition. What he had regarded as religious and political betrayal on the part of Mary Tudor had led him to Bullinger with his four questions. But behind them was the simple dilemma of whether or not it was just to remove the unjust ruler. This led inexorably to the questions: from where sprang the authority of the ruler; was that authority immutable; and was it all-encompassing? The responsibilities of the ruler vis-à-vis the people had to be redefined, and the rights of the people had to be established. Knox, like many before him, had allowed his examination of faith to extend to questioning the purely secular power of the ruler.

So far, to recap, in his *Letter to the Queen Regent* he accused Mary of Guise of unjust tyranny, in that she had imposed on her people a religion which was idolatrous and contrary to the true faith as laid down in sripture. In his *Supplication and Exhortation to the Nobility* he had demanded free access to Scotland as an innocent citizen and urged the nobility to punish the malefactors and defend the innocent. He reminded them that God greatly rewarded those who opposed ungodly commandments. Then, in his letter to his *Beloved Brethren the Commonalty of Scotland* he had stated, quite categorically, that God made all men equal. However, realizing that the common people can be easily crushed, he drew back from a call to arms, but suggested that a refusal to pay tithes and other impositions of the Church might be possible. Later he would find, to his own cost, that any policy that damaged individual pockets would come under immediate close scrutiny.

Knox also had read the *Apology of Magdeburg* (he would later cite it in an argument in 1564), urging resistance to unjust rulers with life and limb, as well as John Ponet's *Short Treatise of Politic Power* with its contention that no ruler may do 'any thing to the hurt of his people without their consent' and that there might be 'common authority upon just occasion and common necessity to kill'. Finally there was *How Superior Powers Ought to be Obeyed* by Knox's Genevan colleague Christopher Goodman, which Knox most probably co-authored. In this the final nail in the coffin of 'the divine right of kings' was firmly hammered home. Perhaps Knox had remembered John Mair's contention that it is the people who appoint the king, and the people who, therefore, may depose him. Idolatry and the worship of 'strange' gods should be punished by the hands of all the people, and whoever the idolator may be, ' be he never so near to us, he must die the death'. Considering all this in isolation, it would be an understandable mistake to feel that Knox was simply removing one tyranny to establish another, and that these policies would replace the Marian persecution of the Protestants with a Knoxian persecution of the Catholics. This view would be mistaken in the sense that Knox accorded the power, not to any ruler, but to the people. Now, his ability to sway his listeners from the pulpit was undisputed. A witness to his preaching in Dieppe believed that he was 'so eloquent that he managed men's souls as he wished'. But thanks to his recent experiences of the current situation in Scotland he knew that Protestantism was a viable belief. With greater access to the pulpits of Scotland, he felt sure that he could unite the nobility and commonalty. There would have been little point in his attempting the conversion of the Queen Regent herself, so he would have seen his task as giving the power of rejection or acceptance to the people and firing the nobility to support this appeal. Like George Wishart before him, he was bringing some dangerously explosive material to Scotland as part of his baggage.

At any rate, at the end of April Knox abandoned the idea of passing through England, took ship for Leith directly and landed in Scotland on 3 May 1559 to start his major work. In the five years since he left his church in Newcastle he had travelled over most of western Europe, with journeys totalling over 4,500 miles – this being the distance of reasonably direct routes, except that usually these routes were barred to him by reason of the danger of arrest. These journeys had often been made in all weathers, from time to time assailed by doubts, and in conditions of poverty that made him dependent on the charity of others. He had been an exile from Scotland for twelve years, but through his correspondence and pamphleteering had laid a foundation for total change in the authority of the civil government and for the foundation of a new Church. This was a considerable feat, but all this represented only a beginning. Knox's greatest work was just about to start.

7 Homecoming

It would be convenient if we could say that the Scottish Reformation started on the day Knox returned to Scotland from France. However, history is never so neat and we must look at the events occurring since his last visit to see the state of the growing tide to which he added a final impetus.

He had left Scotland in the summer of 1556 and the three intervening years had been tempestuous enough. The Franco–Scottish alliance was becoming more and more unpopular, so that when Mary, the Queen Regent, attempted an invasion of England, as we have heard, she got no further than Maxwellcleugh near Kelso when her Scots forces refused to go any further.

Knox tells us: 'after consultation amongst themselves [the Scots nobility] passed to the pavilion of Monsieur d'Oysel [the French Ambassador and now leader of the Queen Regent's military forces] and in his own face declared that in no wise would they invade England'. The French had been defeated by Spanish imperial forces at Saint-Quentin in August 1557, and with the Anglo-Spanish axis surrounding him, Henry II was desperate for allies. To strengthen his links with Scotland he asked for a mission to visit France with a view to completing the marriage of his son, the dauphin, to Mary Stuart, Queen of Scots, a marriage that had been agreed under the English guns at Haddington. To this end eight commissioners from the three estates of the Scottish Parliament left Edinburgh in December, including Lord James Stewart and Erskine of Dun. Lord James was, of course, the future Mary, Queen of Scots' half brother, but more significantly both he and Erskine were Protestants and had entertained Knox during his past visit to Scotland. The Queen Regent was giving a sop to parliament as well as showing her lack of hostility towards the reformers, since it was essential to her that this betrothal should pass without discord at home. However, all went well in Paris and on 19th April 1558 the formalities were concluded. That night Mary danced with her husband-to-be. They must have made an odd sight amid the splendour of the Louvre and under the watchful eyes of Catherine de Medici. Mary was beautiful, tall (some say almost six feet in height), elegant and a skilful and enthusiastic dancer. Her prince was stunted and under-developed in every way, and had a tendency to dribble. It is unlikely that he ever achieved puberty, and it seems probable that, beyond diplomacy, his relationship with Mary was only one of childish friendship. The marriage treaty, one of whose witnesses was Diane de Poitiers, was satisfactory to the Scots commissioners, confirming Mary of Guise's regency, while Mary agreed to observe all the ancient liberties of Scotland. Francis would be King of Scotland on Mary's accession, with France and Scotland to be united under one crown. Antoinette de Bourbon, Mary's grandmother, signed in place of the Queen Regent.

However, a secret treaty unknown to the commissioners had been signed a fortnight previously at Fontainebleau by Mary, advised by her Guise uncles. Its terms were much more severe. It also reveals that the French were doubtful as to the Dauphin's ability to breed. First: if Mary died without children, she gave to France 'a pure and free donation of the kingdom of Scotland' as well as her rights to the English throne, while Scotland would fall under the French king's power until the (unspecified) costs of defending Scotland against England were met. Also Scotland would be liable for the costs of her maintenance and education up to the point of her death. There was no precise machinery for calculating these costs and it would be very much in France's interest to ensure that they would be as crippling as the finest French fiscal brains could make them. An initial figure of one million pieces of gold, 'or some other sum to the entire satisfaction and recompense for the maintenance of the kingdom of Scotland' is mentioned. Finally this treaty carried a disclaimer to all other treaties, either in the past or in the future, regarding Mary's inheritance. After counsel from her uncles the cardinal of Lorraine and the duke of Guise Mary signed this treaty personally. She had willed the country of her birth to Catholic France. It shows clearly that Mary regarded herself as French by adoption and education, and, at fifteen, would agree to whatever was proposed by her Guise uncles.

No wonder Catherine de Medici was smiling when the bells of Paris rang out and she led Mary Stuart into the cathedral of Notre Dame to become

Marie de Valois. In the cathedral Mary was supported on her right by Henry II and on her left by the duke of Lorraine.

The wedding Mass was lavish, even by the luxurious standards of France, as were the balls and pageants that followed – all, as rumour had it, arranged by Monseigneur de Guise, Mary's uncle and the Queen Regent's brother. At the nuptial ball Mary spared her husband embarrassment and danced with the princess Elizabeth, Henry's daughter and her new sister-in-law.

Four days later the Scots commissioners took oaths of allegiance on behalf of the Estates to the dauphin and dauphiness as their future rulers. This oath, combined with the secret treaty, mapped out Scotland's future as a French vassal. But even beyond this, there was a final demand that stuck in the throats of the commissioners. They were asked to send the Scottish crown to Paris, so that the dauphin might be crowned with it – presumably by a Guise cardinal. Like good diplomats they replied that this was beyond their power to negotiate but that they would refer the matter to their masters in Edinburgh. So their duty done, they duly left for Scotland.

Four of the commissioners, the bishop of Orkney, the earls of Rothes and Cassilis, and Lord Fleming, died mysteriously on their way back to Scotland from France, and the immediate presumption was that they had been poisoned as revenge for not immediately agreeing to send the Scottish crown. Even allowing for the fact that Catherine de Medici was a notorious adept at arcane poisons and that the historian Mezeray believed that the de Guise faction had a hand in their deaths, it would have been an uncharacteristically clumsy step. It did however strengthen a belief that Henry II, with the connivance of the Queen Regent, was slowly pulling Scotland into his power like a hooked and impotently flapping fish. By June 1558 the citizens of Scotland were declared naturalized Frenchmen.

The surviving commissioners reported the results of their negotiations to the Estates at the end of November, and, as promised, submitted the French request for the crown. With French military power backing the Queen Regent in many strongholds of the country, and many nobles enjoying lavish pensions from France, the request was agreed.

Knox describes the situation in Scotland:

The glister of the profit that was judged hereof to have ensued to Scottishmen blinded many eyes. But a small wind caused that mist suddenly to vanish away; for the greatest offices and benefices within the realm were appointed for Frenchmen . . . to bring this head to pass, to wit, to get the Matrimonial Crown, the Queen Regent left no point of the compass unsailed . . .'

Knox then quotes the Queen Regent:

But will you be favourable to me in this suit of the Matrimonial Crown to be granted to my daughter's husband, then shall you see how I shall handle these heretic and traitors or it be long.

One cannot help feeling that here Knox is putting inflammatory words into the Queen Regent's mouth, since she usually behaved with greater discretion. Because Knox was not present he reports Mary with a vehemence that would have come more easily from himself than from her.

All Frenchmen were granted naturalization in Scotland and Lord James Stewart was appointed, with the earl of Argyle, to carry out the mission of taking the crown to France. Both men were Protestant and opposed to the increasing French influence. Lord James, of course, had had recent experience of the French, so there may have been a last flicker of pride in sending these particular men on this shameful journey. In fact, the mission never took place.

In the annals of Scottish independence this was an undoubted low point, with a French Queen Regent for an absentee princess who had given away her inheritance – much to the disquiet of the ever wavering former governor Hamilton, now duke of Chatelherault – and the likelihood of a Frenchman being crowned King of Scotland. The temporal fears that Scotland would become simply the northernmost province of France were well founded. The reformed Protestant religion was being tolerated, wisely, by the Queen Regent, but the greater part of the country was still nominally Catholic, with reform strongest among the nobility and lairdry. In part this was a selfish adherence, since many in the nobility feared a loss of power and revenue should Scotland fall totally under the French heel. The wider growth of Protestantism could signal a renaissance of nationalism, but the likely leader of such a Reformation was still in exile and able to communicate only by letter. However, Knox's letters had obviously taken some effect, at least with some of the nobility, for in the previous year, while kicking his heels in Dieppe, he had written to remind the nobility of their duty, not by reason of your birth and progeny (as the most part of false men do suppose), but by reason of your office and duty, which is to vindicate and deliver your subjects and brethren from all violence and oppression, to the uttermost of your power . . . for your conscience will one day be compelled to acknowledge that the Reformation of religion, and of public enormities doth appertain to more than the clergy or chief rulers called kings.

Knox then takes the credit for inspiring the creation of a document that set out the aspirations of the Protestant faction in Scotland. At one point the so-called Band of Congregation stated:

We do promise before the majesty of God, and his congregation, that we by His grace, shall, with all diligence, continually apply our whole power, substance, and our very lives, to maintain, set forward, and establish the most blessed word of God and His congregation; and shall labour at our possibility to have faithful ministers, truly and purely to minister Christ's Gospel and Sacraments to his people . . .

This crucial document was signed on 3 December 1557 by the earls of Argyle, Glencairn and Morton, Lord Lorne, and John Erskine of Dun, who were now referred to as the Lords of the Congregation. In effect they were declaring themselves as an alternative government executive.

The existing machinery of government was built around the sovereign, or, in this case, her regent. Dependent on her, and appointed by her or her advisers, were the Privy Council, which prepared legislation for consideration by the parliament. This body was made up of the three estates. First of these was the clergy, that is, bishops, abbots and priors, including the laymen who held church preferments. Then came the aristocracy, although their representation became restricted to the lords of parliament, that is, those with executive parliamentary powers and excluding the 'smaller barons' and lairds, although their membership had been guaranteed by James I. The third estate comprised the burgesses elected by local councils to represent the communities with burgh status.

Parliament, sometimes called a general council or convention, elected the Lords of the Articles to deal with the recommendations of the Privy Council. In practice, parliament accepted the decisions of the Lords of the Articles with a minimum of debate. Professor J.S Rait, in his admirably lucid *Parliaments of Scotland*, says,

Up to the Reformation . . . the Parliament of the Three Estates cannot be said to have exercised any decisive, or even any influential, voice upon the determination of National policy. It existed, normally, to ratify what had been done or was about to be done by the sovereign or those who exercised power over the sovereign.

The contemporary idea of Her Majesty's opposition simply did not exist, and the Lords of the Congregation were, in fact, a rival government. Five signatures may not seem like a torrent of protest, but the fact that such eminent members of the nobility were prepared to face royal conflict gave a focus for others. In further councils they deemed it expedient that the Common Prayers, from *The Book of Common Prayer* of Edward VI, should be said on Sundays and festival days in the parish kirks, with lessons read from the Old and New Testaments, either by the 'curates' or those most qualified.

However, in the April of 1558, four days after Mary's marriage to the dauphin, an exceptionally savage act took place that could only add fuel to the fire of reform. Walter Mill (or Myln), 'a man of decrepit age' – he was over eighty when he was arrested – who had been a Catholic, then converted to Protestantism in Germany, returned to Scotland, and setting aside all 'compelled' chastity, married. He thus exposed himself to being suspected of heresy. He was arrested in Dysart in Fife, where Pitscottie tells us, he was 'in ane poor wife's house, teaching her the commandments of God, and learning her how she should instruct her bairns'. He was brought to St Andrews for trial and after threats of torture he was put in the pulpit of the town church. He was so weak that he needed help to climb into the pulpit. But Sir Andrew Oliphant peremptorily told him to leave off praying, answer his accusers and not to 'hold my lords here over long'. Among the lords were five bishops and four abbots. The old man's inquisition was predictable, leading inevitably, since he stoutly maintained his Protestant faith throughout, to a sentence of death. All of this would have been savage if unsurprising; but what was surprising was that the provost of St Andrews then refused to carry out his temporal duties and burn the old heretic – he offered instead to give him a 'fair assize of temporal men'. Nor, thanks to civil disobedience, could the ropes and tar needed for the fire be purchased anywhere in the town. After a day's delay, Oliphant and a servant of the bishops', one Alexander Somerville, had to make all the preparations themselves, and Mill insisted that Oliphant himself help him climb to the stake.

This done, Oliphant forbade him to speak but the townspeople insisted that Mill be heard. He beseeched them not to be 'seduced by the lies of priests, monks, friars, priors, abbots, bishops and the rest of the set of Antichrist, but depend only upon Jesus Christ and his mercy'. He was then burned to death. The site of his martyrdom was marked, in spite of attempts by the church to prevent it, by a cairn of stones. Protest was becoming more open.

The Queen Regent herself was sensible enough to take regard of the growing toleration for Protestantism, but with the marriage of her daughter confirming the readiness of France to support her she felt in a strong enough position to condemn this heretical mood publicly. To this end she summoned the Protestant preachers to Edinburgh in July. But the preachers did not come alone, but as Knox did when summoned before the Edinburgh bishops. They came 'attended'.

The Edinburgh authorities, quite reasonably, could see trouble brewing, and rather than have their city drowned in riot, they ordered the preachers to serve a fifteen-day exile in the border country. It even caused the bishop of Galloway to burst into bad rhyme,

> Because they are come without order
> I red ye [counsel you] send them to the Border

If the authorities thought they had defused the situation they were sadly mistaken, for by an unfortunate coincidence, a company who had been serving on the border arrived in Edinburgh on the day of the preachers' departure. Inflamed by what they saw as gross mistreatment of their fellows they forced their way into a private meeting of the Queen Regent and her bishops. They complained about this 'strange internment' seeing that they were 'in faithful obedience in all things lawful'. Mary clearly prevaricated, but 'a zealous and bold man, James Chalmers' accused the clergy, threatening to 'make a day of it'. The accusation was that the clergy oppressed the common people to feed themselves, 'they trouble our preachers and would murder them and us: shall we suffer this any longer? No Madam: it shall not be'. And then, in a phrase of Knox's that still chills the blood, 'Therewith, every man present put on his steel bonnet.' Mary wisely forbade the bishops ever to trouble them or their preachers again. 'With these and the like fair words she kept the bishops from buffets at that time.' But it was clear to all that buffets remained a potent and ever-present threat.

However the bishops still clung to the enactment of old traditions and the feast of St Giles on 1 September was approaching. (St Giles is a slightly shadowy hermit of seventh-century Provence. As a patron he was kept busy tending cripples, lepers and nursing mothers as well as looking after blacksmiths.) During this feast, the image of the saint would be taken from St Giles and paraded through the city. Unfortunately the image in question had already been taken out of the church and first 'drowned in the North Loch' – where today the main east–west railway line runs – and then burnt – 'which raised no small trouble in the town'. The town council refused to pay for another, the archbishop of St Andrews cursed the city authorities to no effect and he then 'caused his curate Tod to curse them black as coal'. Finally a little idol of St Giles was borrowed from the Greyfriars Church, against a deposit of a silver piece. Knox calls this idol a 'marmoset', but rather than believing that it was a small, long-tailed, monkey-like creature, we must presume that Knox merely found the whole idea grotesque. It was covered in a golden coat, then secured to a frame and carried in procession by the assembled clerics with 'tabors and trumpets, banners and bagpipes, and who was there to lead the ring, but the Queen Regent herself, with all her shavelings, for honour of that feast'.

The procession went down the High Street to the Canongate and then towards Holyrood Palace, but the Queen left the parade in order to lunch with one Sandy Carpenter, whose house stood on the route. Immediately, it seems, some men offered to help carry the image and took the framework on their shoulders, but shook it violently hoping to dislodge it. This failed and the whole structure was thrown down, the image being smashed by the heels on to the roadway so that its head came off.

Knox reports all this with great gusto:

> down goes the crosses, off goes the surplice, round caps [priests' skull caps] corner with the crowns. The Grey Friars gaped, the Black Friars blew, the priests panted and fled; and happy was he that first got the house; for such a fray came never among the generation of Antichrist . . . The Queen Regent laid up this amongst her mementoes till she might have seen the time proper to have revenged it. Search was made for the doers, but not could be deprehended; for the brethren assembled themselves in such sort, in companies, singing psalms, and praising God, that the proudest of the enemies were astonished.

The citizens of Edinburgh were as volatile as any, and swung backwards and forwards throughout the entire Reformation struggle. Mob violence was always popular and attempts to enforce any rule not of their making would be dealt with arbitrarily. Within the next three years they would pack St Giles to hear Knox preach, vow to support Catholicism – as late as 1560 the Kirk of St Giles still possessed an arm of the saint – loot and despoil friaries and cheer the return of the Catholic Mary, Queen of Scots. 'Was ever feather so lightly blown to and fro as is this multitude?'

The congregation had been petitioning the Queen Regent for freedom from persecution, and now made a formal protestation, which they wanted to have registered in Parliament. Knox reports the Regent as saying, 'Me shall remember what is protested, and me shall put good order after this to all things that now be in controversy.' (Knox, oddly, always reported the Regent's speech as if she had less command of English than was probably true.) While the Regent seemed to prevaricate, control of events moved to the populace when on 1 January 1559 a document was nailed to the doors of all religious buildings across the country. These were 'tickets of warning'.

> The blind, crooked, lame, widows, orphans, and all other poor visited by the hand of God, as may not work, to the flocks of all friars within this realm, we wish restitution of wrongs past, and reformation in times coming, salutation . . . we have thought good, therefore, to warn you in the name of the great God, by this public writing affixed to your gates where ye now dwell, that ye remove forth of our said hospitals betwixt this and the feast of Whitsuntide . . . if you fail, we will at the said term . . . enter and take possession of our said patrimony, and eject you utterly forth of the same. Let him therefore, that hath stolen, steal no more; but rather let him work with his hands, that he may be helpful to the poor. From all cities towns and villages of Scotland, the first of January.

It has come down through history as the 'Beggar's Summons'. It is extraordinary that there is no evidence of the organization behind this document, which appeared to come spontaneously out of the empty air. No action was taken as a result of the summons and it stands alone as a symptom, perhaps, of reform being also a secular demand of more people than just the Lords of the Congregation. At any rate the Queen Regent, acting with the true arrogance of the Guises, ignored this plea from the commonalty and continued with her Frenchification. She gave the livings of the abbeys of Kelso and Melrose to her brother, the cardinal of Lorraine, an action taken by all Scots as a further sign of French annexation, especially given that the dauphin of France would be the next king of Scotland. Then on 9 February came an edict making any interference with the Roman Church or breaking the Lenten fast capital offences. Perhaps she thought the proper time had come to avenge the insults of St Giles's day. She did summon a provincial council of the clergy to Edinburgh on 1 March that attempted to deal with some of the scandals surrounding the Church, but the central precepts were, as expected, immovable. Its reforms were published as the 'Twopenny Faith' and it was the last such council of the Catholic Church to assemble in Scotland. Knox tells us that 'there was much ado for caps, shaven crowns, tippets, long gowns and such other trifles.'

Appeals by the reformers were given short shrift: 'Despite of you and your ministers both, they shall be banished out of Scotland, albeit they preached as truly as did Saint Paul.' The Queen Regent clearly had no intention to give any ground, for when Glencairn and Campbell of Loudun went to remonstrate with this threat, they were told, 'it became not subjects to burden Princes with promises, further than it pleaseth them to keep the same'. The Queen Regent must by now have been feeling more confident than she had been for some time, since two events had occurred to ease the political pressure on her native France.

As we have seen, in November 1558 Mary Tudor had died and with her died the Anglo-Spanish alliance. She had been replaced by her younger sister Elizabeth, a 25-year-old as yet untried on the international stage. She was known to be Protestant in religion, but although the Mass was no longer to be said in the Church of England, as yet she had set about no persecutions or incursions across her northern border. The second event was the signing in April 1559 by Henry II of the treaty of Cateau-Cambrésis, bringing to an end over forty years of French conflict with Spain and England. France had pursued claims against Spanish power in Piedmont and Savoy while England made incursions into Picardy and the Pas de Calais. Henry's defeat by Spanish forces at Saint-Quentin had made the treaty more or less inevitable, but he had at least gained Calais, so the English left France after 200 years of varying levels of military occupancy. France was now at peace, with secure frontiers, and the Queen Regent had reason to believe that she could call on French support. But in Scotland defiance to the Queen Regent was spreading and the reformers were now occasionally called 'the Faithful'. In Perth, Dundee and Montrose reform was being openly preached and her attempts to have preachers arrested had been unsuccessful, so she called the reformers to appear in Stirling on 10 May. This showed a lack of understanding of the depth of feeling against her, since the reformers were now a formidable force, concentrated on Dundee. To arrive in Stirling they would have to pass through Perth, whose provost had already told her that 'he could make their bodies to come to her Grace, and to prostrate themselves before her, till she was satiate of their blood, but to do anything against their conscience, he could not undertake.' She thought this answer 'too malapert', but untypically of one so shrewd, she had made a grave political mistake. Unwittingly she had concentrated the Protestant leaders in one area and now risked military confrontation. There was no doubt that the Queen Regent could win any battle if she was prepared to commit the French troops at her command, but that could precipitate a civil war, especially if the Lords of the Congregation found a leader.

On 1 May there was an interruption to a council meeting in the Blackfriars in Edinburgh when,

> one ran in and assured them that John Knox [who] was new come out of France, had been all night in the town; at which news, they, being all aston-ished, leaving the council, rose suddenly from the board where they sat, and passing forth to the yard, altogether abashed, fearing the thing which came suddenly to pass . . . they sent incontinent a post to Glasgow to the Queen, acquainting her of the matter, who caused him to be blown loud to the horn the third day after.

The leader had been found and, 'put to the horn', that is to say outlawed, or not, was making with all speed to join the congregation.

The Reformation had found a head who would provide the spiritual focus for the often quarrelling lords. A unifying political focus was provided by the Queen Regent. Mary of Guise was believed to be passing the control of Scotland into the hands of the French. Their soldiers abounded, earning the usual complaints; Hamilton, the ineffectual earl of Arran, had been bought off with the dukedom of Chatelherault; and the continuation of the Catholic faith meant many decisions were still made under the eye of Rome. Mary may have felt secure, but in fact she had little choice in her policy. Her daughter was married to the heir to the French throne; her son by her first husband, Louis of Orléans, was now in atten-dance at the French court; she was alone in a country filled with a rebellious and self-seeking nobility and was professing a faith that was more and more being seen by them as foreign. Hers was an unshakeable faith, with her grandmother having been in a convent for some years, and a brother under the tasselled hat of a cardinal. Her nearest neighbour, Elizabeth, had started busily dismantling the Catholic structures of her dead sister, Mary Tudor. The Queen Regent was forty-four years old and very tired, suffering from a fatty degeneration of the heart that would shortly kill her. And the Lords of the Congregation were implacably opposed to her both on the grounds of nationality and religion. Their religious grievance, however, had lacked the spiritual head that John Knox would provide. Professor Hume Brown declares, 'It was by his living voice and presence that Knox was to play the part in the crisis of his country's destinies which has given him his place as the most strenuous figure in the national history.'

Knox had written to Mrs Anna Lock,

> I am uncertain yet what God shall further work in this country, except that I see the battle shall be great, for Satan rageth even unto the uttermost, and I am come, I praise my God, in the brunt of the battle . . . Assist me, sister, with your prayers, that now I shrink not when the battle approacheth.

The Queen Regent lost no time in declaring the recalcitrant Protestants outlaws and had them 'put to the horn'. Erskine of Dun laid the grievances before her and she declared that the summons to Stirling was now unnecessary, since the congregation were outlaws. Outlaws they may have been, but they were now established in Perth, Scotland's only walled town – it was then called Saint Johnston, a name that today lives on only in the local football team – and they were gaining support daily. It would only take a spark for the violence, so far avoided, to erupt. And erupt it did on 11 May, when Knox preached in the parish church, the Holy Cross of St John the Baptist. Inevitably his themes were denunciation of the Mass as an abomination and condemnation of idolatry. After he had finished a priest, unbelievably, began to celebrate Mass, opening 'a glorious tabernacle'. A young boy shouted out, 'This is intolerable, that when God by his word hath plainly damned idolatry, we shall stand and see it used in despite.' The priest then struck the boy 'a great blow', and the boy, in turn, threw a stone at the priest, but missed and hit the tabernacle instead.

The rioting now began in earnest, but Knox is at pains to point out that it was confined to the 'rascal multitude' and not the gentlemen or earnest professors. Indeed, we must remember that to Knox the adoration of the host in the Mass was idolatry enough, but that praying to saints for intercession was also idolatrous. Therefore he could conclude that the riot and its attendant destruction was a result of a natural revulsion against idolatry, sparked entirely by the violent reaction of the priest.

This is somewhat specious, however, since he is presuming that such nice distinctions would be made by his listeners. Certainly neither Knox nor the reformers ever openly called for despoliation of clerical property, but they were comparatively silent in condemning the actions of the mob. In Perth the populace quickly became aware of what had taken place in the Church of St John, but the walls were already bare. He tells us that they found nothing in the Church of St John but went to the grey and black friars, where, 'the first invasion was upon the idolatry; and thereafter the common people began to seek some spoil.' Better linen and napery than that of any earl was found, eight puncheons of salt beef (an amazing amount of winter provender for late spring) for only the same number of nuns. This was distributed among the poor and the mob moved on to the charterhouse. The prior had summoned support in the form of Highlanders from Atholl, who demanded his best wine and were disappointed to receive only salt salmon and 'thin' drink. However, they were clearly no match for the mob, who, after allowing the prior to take away what gold and silver he could carry, set about total destruction. After two days, only the walls of the three establishments remained. It is an interesting coincidence, but no more, that all this despoliation took place four days before that threatened in the 'Beggar's Summons'. Knox tells us that no honest man was enriched by the value of a groat, but it is tempting to accept this truth with a similar quantity of salt.

The Queen Regent's first reaction to the rioting was to call for the total destruction of 'Saint Johnston, man, woman, and child, and to consume the same by fire, and thereafter to salt it, in a sign of perpetual desolation.' This was no more than royal pique, covered by the weak excuse that the charterhouse had been the tomb of James I, but it served to polarize the views of the two camps, with Mary and Knox as the principal protagonists. The immediate result was the writing and distribution of three letters to the Queen Regent, to D'Oysel and the French soldiery, and to the Scottish nobility. Though signed on 22 May by the congregation, they all have the touch, now hardening, of Knox himself. In the first, after promising all humble duty and obedience he goes on:

... with most dolorous minds we are constrained, by unjust tyranny proposed against us, to declare unto your Grace, that except this cruelty be stayed by your wisdom, we shall be compelled to take the sword of just defence against all that shall pursue us for the matter of religion, and for our conscience sake ... We signify moreover unto your Grace, that if by rigour we be compelled to seek the extreme defence, that we will not only notify our innocence and petitions to the King of France, to our Mistress and her husband, but also to the Princes and Council of every Christian Realm, declaring unto them, that this cruel, unjust, and most tyrannical murder, intended against towns and multitudes, was, and is, the only cause of revolt from our accustomed obedience, which, in God's presence, we faithfully promise to our Sovereign Mistress, to her husband and to your Grace Regent ...'

This was a direct threat and a stern reminder that Mary of Guise was only a Queen Regent and that the rightful Queen of Scots was still possessed of power, albeit at some distance. The letters were as widely distributed as was possible, with the Queen Regent's laid on the cushion of her stall in the Chapel Royal at Stirling. This ease of access to the royal chapel and the Queen's stall itself seems to signify that there were Protestant sympathizers even in the royal household. Knox says that she 'looked upon it and put in the pocket of her gown'. D'Oysel and his French officers were given their copies by their own men, some of whom seem to have been sympathetic, even, we may presume, Huguenots, for the letters caused the soldiery to 'rive their own beards'.

The appeal to the nobility was a call to join the congregation and Knox followed this with a much more direct threat to the clergy: '... shall we, with all force and power, which God shall grant unto us, execute just vengeance and punishment upon you ... Take this for advertisement and be not deceived.' The trumpeter of God was here in full blast and without any equivocation; there was to be no turning of the other cheek, but a full-blown Old Testament challenge to conform or be destroyed. This makes any claim that the congregation was only seeking tolerance of its own practices seem a little hollow, and they now appear to be setting about extirpating Catholicism in totality. Since Knox considered the Church of Rome as the Antichrist and Mary of Guise as an unjust ruler this is hardly surprising. At any rate fear was beginning to spread, and Sir James Croft, captain of Berwick and a principal source of information in Cecil's highly efficient spy service, told the English privy council, 'the Abbot of Cupar has put on secular weed.' In Ayrshire, the earl of Glencairn 'in zeal' declared,

> Let every man serve his conscience. I will, by God's grace, see my brethren in
> St Johnston; yea albeit no man should accompany me, I will go, if it were but
> with a pick upon my shoulder, for I had rather die with that company, than
> live after them.

This started a popular rally, despite a warning by the Lyon Herald, in his full heraldic power with tabard and trumpets, that they were guilty of treason. All went forward to join the congregation forces.

Mary appeared to go some way towards meeting Knox, by asking for the evacuation of Perth in return for toleration of Protestantism and an assurance that no French troops would be billeted on the populace. These terms were delivered by the earl of Argyle and Lord James Stewart, and Knox thanked God that there was to be no effusion of blood. The reformers withdrew towards St Andrews, and D'Oysel with the Queen entered Perth, immediately billeting 400 soldiers, who were Scots, as she had promised, but in fact being paid by France as mercenaries. The congregation were well aware of this duplicity, which they attributed to the inherent guile of the Guises. She heard Mass 'upon tables that had previously served drunkards, dicers and card-players, the altars having been profaned, but holy enough tables for the priest and his pageant' and condoned a drunken foray in which a child was shot. Mary is reputed to have said, 'It is a pity it chanced on the son, and not on the father, but seeing that so it is chanced, me cannot be against fortune.' When questioned about her breaking of the agreement, she said that she was not bound to keep promises to heretics, and that, anyway, princes must not be bound to keep promises. Argyle and Lord James promptly left to join Knox. It is difficult, even allowing for Knox's biased reporting, to account for Mary's seemingly self-destructive hauteur, except to seek the cause in the arrogance of the de Guise family.

At any rate, the result was a strengthening of the congregation, and the men of Fife, Angus, the Mearns and Strathearn were called on to meet in St Andrews. Mary, with D'Oysel and Chatelherault, had reached Falkland Palace, in which her husband James V had died. Meanwhile Knox, despite a threat from Archbishop Hamilton that he would be greeted by a salute of a dozen culverins most of which would land on his nose, fulfilled his promise, given over ten years previously in the galleys, and preached in the town church of St Andrews on 10 or 11 June 1559.

His subject was the ejection of the money-changers from the temple, and he compared the removal of this corruption to that of the papistry from the Church in Scotland. The provost and the civic powers were so taken with this that they stripped the churches of St Andrews of all 'monuments of idolatry', which they burned on the site of the aged Walter Mill's martyr-dom.

There is no evidence that anything other than the ornaments of the churches was destroyed, and we shall hear how Knox and the leaders of the congregation did try to prevent any wanton destruction. However, the plate and treasures of the cathedral were taken, including the relics of St Andrew and St Margaret, the silver spear of Alexander I, and the crystal cross that had been carried at Bannockburn. Lord James Stewart is accused of profit-ing from the sale of the metal from the bells and roofing, but the fabric of the great church remained sufficiently intact that Knox and his family could stay there twelve years later. However, as so often happened, with the desanctification of the building, it became no more than a quarry for the local people. Even today there are farm buildings in Northumbria built with stone from Hadrian's Wall. The archbishop fled to Falkland, where the Queen Regent did so 'kindle her choler' that she decided to take St Andrews by force. To forestall this manoeuvre Argyle and Lord James Stewart occupied Cupar, some ten miles to the west, with over 3,000 men – 'it appeared as if men rained from the clouds'. In the Regent's camp one Gavin Hamilton, who hoped for the Archbishopric, vowed that he would bring the traitors to her living or dead. The Queen Regent's forces moved their artillery forward during cover of darkness and drew up the infantry by 3 a.m. The aim of the congregation forces was purely defensive, with ordnance dominating the Queen Regent's forces, 'till we had come to hand strokes'. Ruthven so disposed the cavalry that their numbers could not be seen, and by a gloomy dawn, at about 5 a.m., the two sides stood, shrouded by mist, about a mile apart across the River Eden. But when, at about noon, the morning mists had cleared and D'Oysel and Chatelherault saw the numbers opposing them, emissaries were sent to agree terms. They agreed a truce for eight days during which time the Queen's soldiers, French and local, would leave Fife, and the Regent herself would withdraw to Falkland. Sir James Croft, Cecil's political adviser, or more truthfully, spy, in the north, wrote to England with a rumour about the reformers. 'It is not doubted that the Duke [Chatelherault] will join them and they are devising how to get his son home from Geneva. He is very well bent in religion and they are like to motion a marriage "you know where" '.

Chatelherault's son had acceded to his father's old title of the earl of Arran and did eventually suggest marriage to Elizabeth. During this truce the abbey of Lindores, a 'place of black monks', was reformed and many of the canonry of St Andrews joined the Protestant cause. Also in this breathing space the two sides started to call on support from abroad, D'Oysel writing to the French ambassador in London to ask for fresh troops from France, while the congregation approached Elizabeth for help against their Catholic regent. Finally a call went out for Protestant forces to convene at Perth on 24 June. In the two-and-a-half months since his return from France Knox had been spiritual mentor, preacher, general, and, as far as his personality allowed, diplomat, since he was now acting as secretary to the Lords of the Congregation.

Given the detail with which he reports the military dispositions at Cupar, he was clearly a close observer, and while not actually carrying a sword and wearing helmet and breastplate, he was militarily involved. After all, he had carried a two-handed sword for George Wishart, and had observed action in the galleys, so his thundering was not confined to the pulpit. However, in a long letter to Mrs Lock he says he had dreaded the extremity of battle:

not that we intended to pursue [it] but only to stand in camp . . . for defence of ourselves . . . The long thirst of my wretched heart is satisfied in abundance . . . for now, forty days and more, hath God used my tongue in my native country . . . The thirst of the poor people, as well of the nobility here is wondrous great which putteth me in comfort that Christ Jesus shall triumph for a space here, in the north and extreme parts of the earth. We fear that the tyranny of France shall, under the cloak of religion, seek a plain conquest of us.

He hopes soon to see Christopher Goodman, his colleague from Frankfurt and Geneva, saying, oddly, 'whose presence I more thirst than she that is my own flesh,' and gives a list of trusted colleagues who would give him accommodation on his arrival. He then asks Mrs Lock to urge his wife and mother-in-law to 'make the expedition' to visit him or at least to come to the North of England. Presumably he felt that whatever the danger

Goodman might experience it would be too great for his family. But why did he not write to them directly? He ends by commending his messenger, a poor man and clearly trading as a pedlar, and then asks Mrs Lock to show him favour 'touching his merchandise'.

The siege of Perth was soon over, but the Dundonians, wrongly believing that Patrick Hepburn, bishop of Moray, had been responsible for the burning of Walter Mill, set out to wreak vengeance on his palace and abbey at Scone. Argyle and Lord James Stewart managed, with Knox, to halt the despoliation overnight, with Knox personally guarding the granary. The French ambassador found it inhuman that the fruit trees and gardens were damaged. But the next morning the poor, 'in hope of spoil', attacked the abbey again. One of the Bishop's sons stabbed a Dundonian, and 'so was the Abbey and Palace appointed to sackage'. An unnamed old lady, who lived near the abbey, said,

> Since my remembrance, this place hath been nothing else but a den of whore-mongers. It is incredible to believe how many wives hath been adulterated, and virgins deflowered, by the filthy beasts which hath been fostered in this den. But especially by that wicked man who is called the Bishop.

Knox, however, is quite clear that 'if the labours or travail of any man could have saved that place, it had not been at that time destroyed; for men of the greatest estimation laboured with all diligence for the safety of it.' As we have seen earlier there is abundant evidence that Knox did all he could to preserve the fabric of the buildings – they would, after all, be needed as places of worship for the Reformed Church – but it has been all too easy for posterity to brand Knox as a church burner and random iconoclast. All the evidence points in the other direction, with the caveat that he was probably naive in thinking that the 'rascal multitude' could be prevented from looting by rhetoric and reason. However, it must be remembered that his condemnation of mob rule, unlike Luther's, which was direct and immediate, is largely contained in his *History*, which was not published until after Knox's death. On 28 June he wrote to William Cecil that the Reformation is somewhat violent, but assured him, for onward transmission to Elizabeth, that there was no intent to usurp the lawful authority.

> By narration of many, I understand that I am become so odious to the Queen's grace and her Council, that the mention of my name is unpleasing to their

ears; but yet I will not cease to offer myself, requiring you in God's name to present to the Queen's grace this letter, smelling nothing of flattery . . . My eye hath long looked to a perpetual concord betwixt these two realms, the occasion whereof is now present.

In a postscript he apologizes that he has had no time to write to the Queen directly, since the messenger had to depart, but hopes, rather like a repentant schoolboy, that Cecil will reassure her that 'willingly I never offended her Grace, and therefore she ought not [to] repute me an enemy.'

He was understandably keen that England understood the purposes of the congregation, and to this end he wrote to Sir Henry Percy, lord lieutenant of the North of England:

persuade yourself and assure others we mean neither sedition nor rebellion against lawful authority, but only to advance Christ's religion and the liberty of this poor realm. If we have the one with the other it will be better for England, which if we lack 'although we mourn and smart first' ye will not escape worse trouble in the end. But this I would rather communicate face to face than with pen and ink.

This qualification was duly reported to King Henry in Paris, with the added opinion that if this were the only aim of the congregation, the majority of the people would support them. In London Cecil was only too keen to be abreast of affairs on Elizabeth's northern frontier and to keep Knox as calm as possible. He wrote again to Percy:

Forbear not to write all your intelligence, though you may think it is already known to us . . . All must be circumspectly considered and prudently foreseen. Yet not altogether to waste time . . . ye may assure him that rather than see an ancient nation oppressed by a foreign power when her nobles seek to maintain the Christian religion, England would adventure aid against such invasion [by the French] and I dare affirm would be as sorry as if against ourselves.

Knox's apology clearly had little effect on Elizabeth, for Cecil commented that 'for his learning, as matters now be, he has no small credit, nevertheless his name here is not plausible'. In fact, Cecil would have cared little for Knox's standing with his sovereign, but the prospect of a Protestant

Scotland was very appealing indeed. With war coming to an end in main-
land Europe after the peace of Cateau-Cambrésis, France and Spain were
becoming worringly friendly towards each other, and England was
surrounded by Catholic powers. The removal of a Catholic threat on its
northern frontier was therefore highly attractive, although Cecil had the
twin problems of a lack of cash and a Queen who avoided war at all costs
for the same reason. But Cecil was expert at making a little go a long way
and he wrote to Sir James Croft, asking him to help the congregation with
promises; then, only if absolutely necessary, with money; and finally, only
in extremis, with arms.

Meanwhile, Argyle and Lord James heard that the Regent meant to seize
the bridges over the River Forth and set off to prevent this. Among their
troops were 300 staunch townsmen of Perth, or St Johnston, who came to
join the march on Stirling. Thomas Carlyle tells us,

The three hundred ranked themselves accordingly on one of the last nights of
June 1559, and so fierce was their humour, they had each, instead of the scarf
or riband which soldiers then wore round their neck, tied an effective measure
of rope, mutely intimating, 'If I flinch or falter, let me straitway die the death
of a dog.' They neither flinched nor faltered, but henceforth to deserve hanging was to deserve a 'St Johnston's riband'.

On 23 June Kirkaldy of Grange told Cecil, 'the Queen's craft is to bring
in the French. If you suffer this you will prepare a way for your own
destruction. It will be well that your Queen's marriage be not hasty. I beg
your speedy answer, for if this occasion is lost, you may seek for and not
find another.'

The Regent wisely withdrew from Stirling and Edinburgh to a safer
haven at Dunbar to the east, and the forces of the congregation entered
Edinburgh. Croft wrote to Cecil, 'The Protestants are in Edinburgh in great
number . . . the Queen Regent is at Dunbar in great fear.' However, de
Noailles, the French ambassador in London, was told that the Queen
Regent, lacking the forces to resist, had acted with great prudence.

The Edinburgh mob had taken advantage of their coming, and the
congregation found that the establishments of the grey and black friars had
been looted to such an extent that not a door or window remained. An
alternative view of this ransacking is that 'the Friars, hearing of the
approach of the congregation, began to dispose among their acquaintances

the best of their goods which were left at that time. Which thing the rascal people perceiving went in, finding the yetts [gates] open and suddenly fell to work and sacked all.' The first casualty of war is truth.

By midsummer there were 6,000 men in the forces of the congregation, Glencairn and his men from Ayrshire having arrived, and the pulpit of St Giles was open to Knox. He tells Mrs Lock in a few words scribbled as he came from St Giles that the professors are in Edinburgh. (By this he means, not the learned occupants of university chairs, but the professors of the Protestant faith.) He concludes, 'we mean no tumult, no alteration of authority, but only the reformation of religion and suppression of idolatry'. In an echo of Knox's letter to Cecil, Kirkaldy of Grange wrote to Sir Henry Percy endorsing Knox's views, and setting out the purely religious aims of the congregation, including the use of Edward VI's prayer book and the redistribution of the fruits of the abbeys to the rightful ministers. He also wrote to Cecil warning of possible defections:

> The Queen Regent already suspects some intelligence with England . . . some of us are poor and fear corruption by money, yet if these [people] were removed we would not be much the weaker: for all hearts both barons and commonality are so bent and inflamed against France, that if any of the nobility should decline . . . neither their friends nor servants would withdraw from professing Christ and liberty.

This profession of support in depth was echoed in letters on 19 July to Cecil and Elizabeth, signed by Argyll, Lord James, Glencairn and Ruthven. The letters, however, are in Knox's hand and he clearly was taking a political as well as a spiritual role at this point. It was always essential for the Scottish nobility to have a leader without a personal axe to grind, thus allowing them to focus unreservedly on the issue at hand. Since, at this moment at least, Knox's ambitions were for ecclesiastical reform, they would not threaten any temporal power. He was a safe focus for their discontent.

While Knox was writing to Cecil and Elizabeth, Mary and Francis were not sitting idle in Paris. Their first appeal for help went to the Pope himself. They point out that a severe Reformation is taking place, that the Queen Regent is waging war against England with little money, her patrimony having been spent to enrich the churches of Scotland. They beg for notable teachers, armed with gifts and 'grosse sommes de deniers' to defend Rome against the new sects arising by reason of the changed Church in neighbouring England. They blame the negligence of priests in the past for allowing theses doctrines to spread. The temporal lords are pressurizing the Queen Regent to allow the establishment of the new religion, and are preaching openly in town and country. The depradations at Scone are reported, even detailing the destruction of the abbey orchards and gardens, and more destruction was to be expected. They warn that the fire so lit may extinguish for ever the Roman Church in Scotland. Funds and a punitive inquisition are urgently needed to restore the Church to its former pristine glory. The letter was clearly based on very doubtful intelligence from the Queen Regent and is as heartfelt as Knox's warnings to Cecil, but it achieved no intervention from Rome.

D'Oysel himself had fears that if Knox continued to stress only religious reform the people would rally to him, so the ever fickle populace were being fed constant rumours by himself and Chatelherault that the congregation was about to set up a new regime, possibly with Lord James Stewart as king. Some fuel was added to the fire by King Francis and Queen Mary writing from France and asking the heralds to declare the Lords of Congregation guilty of treason and to command them to leave Edinburgh. In effect, the situation was a stalemate. Edinburgh Castle had not fallen and its governor, Lord Erskine, was still loyal to the Regent.

Knox had been appointed minister of St Giles Kirk on 7 July 1559, a position he would hold until his death in 1572, but the reformers' military support was leaking away and by mid July numbered only about 1,500. So far there had been much skirmishing and shouting, but no formal battles or sieges had taken place. The Lords of Congregation had been served by levies owing them allegiance and by townspeople inspired by Knox. The Queen Regent had an army of French mercenaries who were loyal while the money lasted. It would last longer than the reformers' loyalty. All the Queen Regent had to do was wait for events to unfold. The first event was a considerable shock.

8   War Leader

On 30 June 1559 in France King Henry II was indulging his favourite pastime of jousting. At the end of the session, against all advice, he challenged the count of Montgomery, colonel of the archers, to break a final lance with him. Henry was resplendent in black and white, the colours of his mistress Diane de Poitiers, and, to show his bravery, he charged with his visor open. The result was a disaster. Montgomery's lance shattered, as would have been normal, but two splinters pierced the King's head, one entering his right eye, the other piercing his throat. He was thrown to the ground, unconscious, and he remained semi-conscious for nine more days until on 10 July he died of what appears to have been septicaemia. His son, the fifteen-year-old Francis, became Francis II of France, and, more importantly for events in Scotland, his sixteen-year-old wife, Marie de Valois, née Stuart, now became, not only Queen of Scotland, but also Queen of France. (She had already quartered her arms with those of England, thereby, to the everlasting fury of her cousin Elizabeth, announcing her claim to that crown).

A contemporary French comment was that this coronation was the eve of the feast of the three kings, Francis of Valois, Charles of Lorraine, and Francis of Guise – the latter two being brothers of Mary of Guise, Queen Regent, and now mother to the Queen of France and Scotland. No wonder she could afford French mercenaries, while the Lords of the Congregation were rapidly running out of support.

But these events had no immediate impact on the conflict between the loyalist lords and those of the congregation, who by now had lost the impetus of St Andrews and Perth, and sent mediators unsatisfactorily back and forth to Dunbar. Croft warned Cecil that 'unless the French king's death delay preparations the Protestants are in great peril'. But cautious delay was not a Guise virtue and on 23 July the Queen Regent's forces set out for Leith, the way having been eased by the sudden desertion of Sir Robert Logan, the laird of Restalrig. His land lay more or less equidistant between Edinburgh and Leith and he had already received £3,000 as an earnest of the Queen Regent's goodwill. Knox describes the enmity that lay between Edinburgh and Leith, with Leith always feeling neglected, as its inland neighbour looked down at it over its aristocratic nose. With Leith as the bustling and sometimes rowdy port and centre for international trade, and Edinburgh as the presumably more sophisticated centre for law and govern-ment, the feeling of resentment is understandable, and indeed continues today, even allowing for the current gentrification and rising fashionability of Leith. The Queen Regent was able to play on this attitude by offering Leith free royal burgh status. Although this promise was never kept, Knox comments, 'the first fruits of their liberty they now eat with bitterness, to wit, that strangers shall possess their town. This is her just title which her daughter and she may claim to that town'. The congregation forces occu-pied positions on the Calton Hill, then on the northern edge of Edinburgh, but dominating Leith. They, in turn, were overshadowed by the giant bastion of Edinburgh Castle, whose commander sent to say that if the congregation made any resistance to the French soldiers entering the city, he would turn his guns on, not only the Protestant forces, but the city itself. Knox concludes that, ' we could not fight nor stop the enemy, but under the mercy of the Castle and the whole ordnance thereof'. The result was the inevitable treaty, or Appointment of Leith, signed on 24 July 1559.

The first proposal was that the congregation would be unmolested, idol-atry would not be re-established where it had been suppressed, the preachers of reform were to be unmolested, there would be no soldiers garrisoned in Edinburgh, and that the French would be expelled at some future time. This was proclaimed, 'by voice of trumpet at the Market Cross'.

The reality was somewhat different, with the congregation bound to leave Edinburgh before noon on 25 July, refraining from any further 'cleansing' of churches; meanwhile the preachers and lords of the congre-gation were guaranteed their peace, and Edinburgh was to be allowed freedom of religious conscience. The Queen also went a long way towards solving the garrisoning problem, either French or Scots. Later the Queen Regent would claim that under the marriage treaty of her daughter, now Queen, all Scotsmen were naturalized French and vice versa, so that there were no foreign troops on Scots soil. No one believed this.

The lords agreed the new terms, but defiantly broadcast their original claims again at the market cross before leaving for Stirling. Knox might have been left in Edinburgh as minister of St Giles, and he would have had great personal advantage by this. The city council would have housed him and provided a stipend, while he could continue the message of reform from his pulpit.

But clearly the Lords of the Congregation felt he would be of more value accompanying them as secretary: 'The which he so gladly consented, that it might evidently appear that he preferred the comfort of his own brethren, and the continuance of the Kirk there, to his own life.' To prevent the revival of the Mass, which was greatly feared, John Willock was requested as a worthy substitute in Edinburgh. Knox says that 'for his faithful labours and bold courage in battle, [he] deserves immortal praise,' and, of course, Willock's presence was far less controversial.

The situation in Edinburgh was very finely balanced with French troops in the Canongate being less than a mile distant. But as Knox's whole life to this point has shown, he could never back away from proclaiming his truth to the most influential ears available to him. So now he was in the thick of politics and diplomacy. He had already written to Cecil and to Sir Henry Percy assuring them of his friendship, and on 19 July had written to Elizabeth herself pledging to undertake whatever she might ask for the perpetual amity between the two realms. He is, between slabs of heavy flattery, merely forewarning Elizabeth of dangers to come and the letter is signed by six of the lords, including Argyle and Glencairn. It is significant in that Knox is now dealing with purely secular matters and has obviously accepted that he is more than just a spiritual adviser to the congregation. Knox wrote to Cecil pointing out that a refutation of *The First Blast* had just appeared (which he had not read) and that whoever the author was, was seeking worldly advancement, 'somewhat beside the glory of God and her Grace's advancement'. (Since this tract was probably *A Harbour for true and faithful Subjects* by John Aylmer, who was now bishop of London, his campaign for advancement had been successful.) In the same letter Knox once again stresses that a preacher of reform in the northern counties 'cannot but greatly advance this cause'.

The very next day he wrote to Elizabeth in person and could not prevent his diplomatic ineptitude from taking over. Bearing *The First Blast* in mind, and assuring her that he finds her reign just and that she cannot be accused of betraying her realm to a foreign husband, he castigates her for her flirtation with Rome under her sister and asks her to reflect on how she has been raised from 'the ports of death, to rule above his people for the comfort of his Kirk'.

Knox flatters Elizabeth that she might be regarded as a second Deborah, and, had he stopped there he might just have avoided Tudor wrath, but he cannot resist a warning. He tells her that if she rides roughshod over her own laws, then 'flatter who you list, your felicity shall be short'. Then, almost casually, he points out that he has written often asking for a licence to visit her realm and that, unless she grants this licence, he must remit his cause to God. Since Cecil was a tactful secretary to the council it is very likely that this letter never reached Elizabeth.

Cecil had, however, agreed to meet Knox in his role as a principal amongst the lords at his house in Stamford, Yorkshire, but the meeting was cancelled due to the Regent's actions at Leith. Knox was then equipped with instructions to agree a treaty of support from England by the end of July and set out, via Holy Island, to the horror of Henry Percy, 'in such unsecret sort.' to meet with Sir James Croft, who, hopefully had power to deal in money and matériel. Knox also wanted to assure the English that there would be a legal administration of Protestants with whom Cecil could deal and that the earl of Arran, Chatelherault's son, should be sent for. (One of Cecil's delaying tactics had been to assert that since the Scottish lords were in revolt against their lawful sovereign and therefore not a legal government he could not openly support them.)

Having delivered the message and having failed either to travel further into England or to meet Cecil face to face, Knox thankfully returned to Stirling with a letter from Cecil in which, with consummate skill, he promised everything and nothing.

It is perfectly clear that the lords were breaking at least the spirit of the Appointment of Leith in negotiating hard for English support. But their efforts had results, for in August Elizabeth had sent one Ralph Sadler north as a special envoy, which was, at least, an earnest of good faith. Cecil's instructions to Sadler had been:

Item. To nourish the faction against the French.
Item. To procure the Duke [Chatelherault] to oppose any governance except by the blood of Scotland.
Item. The nobility may require the Queen [Mary] to make peace and object to her false claim on the crown of England.

Item. The Duke may as well arrest D'Oysel and other Frenchmen as counters
   to Arran and Lord David [Arran's younger brother, also in exile].

Knox wrote to Sadler that if the congregation had 1,500 arquebusiers
and 300 horsemen, then 'France shall understand their minds'. Sadler
thought that two or three thousand crowns would be well employed for
this purpose. He also looked forward to the arrival of Arran, 'who should
have more estimation than his father'.

Mary, however, had some of her French soldiers billeted in Edinburgh's
Canongate and was still trying to persuade the population of Edinburgh to
allow the Mass to be said in St Giles. Chatelherault, as usual attempting to
ride two horses simultaneously, had attended the Protestant services being
held in St Giles by John Willock and was under heavy criticism for it, but
the congregation of St Giles held to the non-molestation clauses of the
Appointment of Leith. This was in spite of Knox's accusation that French
soldiers strolled about in the church, chattering during the service and
inciting the congregation to a violence that would have shattered the
already fragile peace. He prayed to be rid of such locusts. Minor violence
became commonplace and Lord Seton, a Regent's man, unprovokedly
broke a chair over one Alexander Whitelaw and, presuming him to be John
Knox, chased him for some miles.

Whitelaw, in fact an agent of Knox's, was accompanying Knox's brother
William, so the mistake is understandable. (William's life, as a merchant, is
shadowy and he eventually became a minister in the Church of Scotland at
Cockpen. It is difficult to imagine why Lord Seton was carrying a chair as
a weapon of assault and then pursuing his victim for three miles, but the
story has the unlikeliness of fact carelessly reported.)

The Regent kept up a campaign of leaflets against the congregation
while openly importing over a thousand French troops into Leith, 'sent for
the utter extermination of all them that would not profess the Papistical
religion in all points.' These men came fully armed, and with wives as well
as children, apparently to settle, once a complete French subjugation of
Scotland had taken place.

Direct threats were made to various members of the congregation,
including letters to Lord James from Queen Mary in Paris. King Francis
promised to 'spend the crown of France' to be revenged on such seditious
persons, while Mary threatened 'such punishment as you shall ever remember'. Lord James wrote back to King Francis, via the Queen Regent,

reasserting his loyalty to the crown but stressing his unswerving adherence to the reformed faith and praying for Francis's conversion. The Queen Regent thought 'that so proud an answer was never given to King, Prince, or Princess'. Knox is surprisingly liberal in commenting, 'Princes must be pardoned to speak what they please'. The duke of Chatelherault was, unsurpisingly, wavering in his loyalty – a loyalty, however, guaranteed by his son Arran, a Huguenot convert, still being held prisoner in France. It is ironic that the boy in question had been a possible reason for his father's half-heartedness in pursuing the siege of St Andrews Castle twelve years previously, and now was binding the vacillating duke to the Regent.

But in September 1559 the youthful earl of Arran escaped from France with help from England, and his father confirmed the rumours of that May by joining the congregation. The Regent sent ambassadors to lure him back when she would be 'gracious enough'. They were unsuccessful and received an unequivocal answer:

> No honest men durst commit themselves to the mercy of such throat-cutters as she had about her; whom, if she would remove, and join to her a Council of Natural Scotsmen, permitting the religion to have free passage, then none in Scotland be more willing to serve her Grace than should the Lords and Brethren of the Congregation be.

But in spite of this seemingly mollifying statement the stalemate continued, with the Regent daily gathering strength from France and the congregation praying to God to be 'our comfort and our protector against the fury and rage of the tyrants of this world; and especially from the insatiable covetousness of the Guisian's generation.' The voice does seem to be Knox's. As the Regent gained support Knox's fears of desertion by the supporters of the congregation increased. After apologizing for his non-appearance at Stamford, he spells out to Cecil the lords' financial dilemma, in a letter of 15 August:

> That unless without delay money be furnished to pay their soldiers (who in number are now but 500) for their service bypast, and to retain another thousand footmen, with three hundred horsemen for a time, they will be compelled every man to seek the next way for his own safety . . .
>
> To aid us so liberally as we require, to some of you will seem excessive, and to displease France, to many will appear dangerous. But, sir, I hope that you

consider that our destruction were your greatest loss, and that when France shall be our masters (which God avert) they will be slender friends to you . . . and therefore, in the bowels of Christ, I require you, sir, to make plain answer what they [the Lords of the Congregation] may trust to, and at what time their support shall be in readiness (how dangerous is the drift of time, in such matters you are not ignorant).

As so often, he started with a warning and ended with a peremptory demand. His work load was now formidable as a spiritual leader – he was still in correspondence with Calvin on such matters – as well as being the political secretary to the congregation. He was also attempting to persuade Sir James Croft to facilitate the passage of his wife, Marjory, since 'my wicked carcass, now presently labouring in the fever, needeth her service'. He also, writing as John Sinclair, asked for a licence for his mother-in-law – 'her conscience cannot be quiet without God's word truly preached, and his sacraments truly delivered.' Sadler passed the request to Cecil on 20 October. Knox writes to Mrs Lock from St Andrews that he has been travelling around the country 'blowing with trumpets' in spite of being vexed with fevers, but cheered by the spreading of reform as far as Jedburgh and Kelso. His appeals to Croft evidently had a beneficial effect, for Marjory and the rest of his family were granted licence to pass through England in the company of Christopher Goodman. Marjory arrived first at the end of September and by the end of October Knox was united with his family in St Andrews.

Edinburgh was still a city on a war footing under the shadow of the guns in the castle, and by way of retaliation, on 4 October seven great and three lesser cannon were hauled up to the roof of St Giles. The eight workmen were paid ten shillings and eightpence for the task.

Balnaves reported that, 'the enterprise of Leith has inflamed the hearts of our people to a wonderful hatred and despite of France, wherefore I think there shall follow a plain defection from France for ever'. The congregation was still desperately short of money and Knox wrote to Sadler for direct help from Lords Glencairn and Ormiston, Kirkaldy of Grange and Alexander Whitelaw. Sadler recommended this appeal to Cecil.

On 12 October Sadler and Croft had given Cecil a further report on feelings and events in Scotland.

'the Lords answered . . . that so long as a French soldier remained or the fortification of Leith continued they would not take her as the mother of the commonwealth. Lord Erskine has promised to keep the castle and it is thought he will remain neuter for a time. For all our persuasions the Protestants will not come forward sooner than appointed. They have lost much time which the French have gained. But the extreme and foul weather in the west and the north, keeping their harvests far behind may be the cause. The bruit of their musters is great, and also the courage and forwardness of Arran, who rides 'to and fro' . . . with 700 and 800 horse, 300 of them Hamiltons. The Regent said lately . . . that the congregation first rose for religion, but now she sees that they shout at another mark – the Duke and his son meaning to usurp the crown . . . but in defence of her daughter's right she fortifies Leith. She is in great perplexity, very weak and sickly and some think cannot long continue.

This is the first mention of the dropsy that would shortly signal the Queen Regent's death. On 5th October Overton, who was clerk of the musters, was sent north with £3,000. Sadler was told that Overton did not know what he was carrying, and that the delay had been caused in currency transactions. Should Overton be captured and the money found, it was in French crowns, making its source doubtful. This precaution was later to provide the cruellest of ironies.

The congregation had decided to break the logjam before the Regent imported even greater strength. A summons went out for their supporters to assemble at Stirling on 15 October to march on Edinburgh. This was achieved easily enough but counted for very little, since the Regent still occupied Leith and her French strength was in no way threatened. She also reminded the congregation that she had no intention, or indeed need, of conquering Scotland on behalf of France, since it was already promised to France by marriage. However, at a council in Edinburgh attended by Knox and Willock, the nettle was grasped. It was proclaimed that Mary's regency was at an end, and in the name of Queen Mary and Francis II she was proclaimed by the lords of the congregation to have been deposed.

Willock had made the principal accusations: first, that magistrates have their power from God; secondly, that subjects are commanded to obey the magistrates, while magistrates must give some duty to their subjects; and, thirdly, that although God has appointed magistrates, he never established any that might not be deprived; fourthly, since the Queen Regent had denied her chief duty to her subjects he could see no reason why the councillors, nobility and barons of the realm might not justly deprive her of 'all regiment and authority amongst them'.

Knox then echoed all of this, as particularly against the Queen Regent, while still maintaining the subject's obligation of loyalty. The proviso was that the deposition arose not from personal malice and could be repealed in the (extremely unlikely) event of her conversion to the commonwealth and submission to the nobility. The entire assembly then voted for her to be deposed.

This debate provided an interesting opportunity for Knox, since here was the practical example of an unjust ruler being ordered to go. Willock had agreed that magistrates are commanded to give duty to their subjects and that the Queen Regent 'denied her chief duty to the subjects of this realm, which was to administer justice to them . . . and to preserve their liberties from the invasion of strangers'. Knox again stressed the obedience a subject owed to a sovereign, even one as iniquitous as the Queen Regent, and warned that the people would be punished for deposing her out of malice and private envy. Finally he said that if she openly repented, 'regress should be granted to the same honours, from the which, for just causes, she justly might be deprived'. While hardly a call to arms, he was giving assent to secular action, but was clearly finding the jump from pamphleteer and agitator to political activist bigger than he had thought. His responses also show, not the raging demagogue of ill-deserved legend, but rather the philosophical politician. Knox certainly lacked diplomatic skills, but his grasp of politics was shrewd. The fact that there is little mention of religion was entirely consistent with the views of many who were unhappy at the growth of French power in Scotland, but were not yet ready to accept the new religion. However, the document, an Act of Suspension, was signed by, 'us the Nobility and Commons of the Protestants of the Church of Scotland', proclaimed at the market cross, and sent to Mary by the Lyon King of Arms, demanding her evacuation of Leith within twelve hours. Hereafter she was referred to as the Queen Dowager. The congregation had finally declared themselves the rightful government, which went some way to answering one of Cecil's prevarications that he could not, as an English diplomat, deal with anything less than a lawfully established government.

The Protestant council as declared here consisted of the duke of Chatelherault, the earls of Arran, Argyll and Glencairn, Lord James Stewart, Lord Ruthven and the master of Maxwell, the barons of Tullibardine, Dun and Pittarrow. The Third Estate was represented solely by the provost of Dundee. In October they would declare the offences against them by the Regent's establishment in an open manifesto to Christian princes. The council told Sadler that they were now a lawful government.

This political action did not, however, go any distance to achieving a military defeat of the Dowager's forces, who were openly preparing for a siege. So, too, was the congregation, constructing ladders in St Giles and so on, to the neglect of preaching. The congregation ranks were riddled with the Dowager's spies and their forces were mutinying for lack of pay, declaring that, 'They would serve any man to suppress the congregation, and set up the Mass again.' Presumably, if well enough paid. This situation was exacerbated when on 31 October, £1,000 of the £3,000 sent by England, was seized by James Hepburn, earl of Bothwell. This James Hepburn was the son of Patrick Hepburn who had connived at the arrest of Wishart. He promptly turned his spoils over to the Queen Dowager. It had been carried by Cockburn of Ormiston, a friend of Knox's, and Bothwell 'hurt the Lord upon the face with a sword sore'. Not only was this a bitter blow to the finances of the congregation, but the Queen Dowager now had solid proof of Elizabeth's support, thus breaking the Appointment of Leith. When Cecil heard of the loss he decided not to tell his sovereign for the moment. From London, de Noailles warned the Queen Dowager that Elizabeth was undoubtedly helping the congregation, while at the same time vigorously denying it.

This theft also gave rise to some attitudinizing and swaggering, as Arran accused Bothwell of a grossly dishonourable act. Bothwell reacted typically on hearing his honour so impugned and promptly challenged Arran to a duel. Arran responded that he was simply doing his duty by pointing out Bothwell's villainy and so would not answer his challenge. He warned Bothwell to take greater care in future.

This exchange had all the weight of a playground quarrel between ten-year-olds, but does show that these nobles would still rise petulantly to violent action if their 'honour' was at stake. Meanwhile, an artillery detachment from Dundee arrived to attack Leith, but a spy advised the French of when the Dundonians were at dinner, and, under attack, they fled without a stroke being offered. The Dowager's forces became richer by the guns they abandoned. Knox himself felt under direct threat and tried to make sure that his brother-in-law George Bowes kept a 'good and assured horse' standing ready, since 'great watch is laid for my apprehension, and large money promised to any that shall kill me'. The jump from pamphleteer to activist had brought the shadow of the assassin nearer. His continued demands for money and matériel caused even the fair-minded Sadler to write, 'I cannot but marvel, that you, being a wise man, will require of us such present aid of men, money, and ammunition, as we cannot minister to you without an open show and manifestation of ourselves as enemies'.

Knox also set about adding fuel to the fire in a letter to Gregory Railton on 23 October, which he knew would be passed directly to Cecil and the information given to Elizabeth in person. Railton was a Protestant whom Knox had known in Frankfurt, now living in the North of England. He provided a useful unofficial conduit of gossip and intelligence. Back in May, when Knox was ship-bound for Scotland, he was shown in great secrecy a jewelled silver-gilt sceptre and a great seal also encrusted with jewels. More importantly they bore the arms of France, Scotland and England and he had touched both objects. Cecil had obviously heard rumours of the existence of such objects, 'with a style for the French King and Queen, naming them King and Queen of France, England and Scotland' and now Knox had turned rumour to fact. Obviously, all corre-spondence between Knox and England was being forwarded to Cecil, as were the answers. On 3 November, Cecil wrote to Sadler, 'I like not Knox's audacity which was well tamed in your letter. His writings do no good here, and therefore I do rather suppress them, and yet I mean not but that you should continue in sending of them.' This attitude would not have surprised Knox.

The skirmishing continued between the sides with the Regent's forces always coming off best, until in a confrontation half way between Restalrig and Holyrood Abbey the congregation suffered a humiliating defeat with their retreating cavalry riding over their infantry. In a rare moment of middle-class snobbery Knox points out that 'there were slain to the number of twenty-four or thirty men, the most part poor. There were prisoners of the laird-like sort taken.'

More significantly on 31 October the ranks of the congregation were swelled by the defection of William Maitland of Lethington. He had been secretary to the Queen Regent, Knox's exact counterpart in her forces. He,

perceiving himself not only to be suspected as one that favoured our part, but also to stand in danger of his life if he should remain amongst so ungodly a company; for whensoever matters came into question, he could not speak his conscience; which liberty of tongue, and gravity of judgement, the French did highly disdain. Which perceived by him, he conveyed himself away in a morning . . . assuring us that in the Queen there was nothing but craft and deceit.

Lethington, who had already dined and debated with Knox on his previous visit to Scotland, was the most brilliant political mind in Scotland. He would earn the nickname 'Michael Wylie', a corruption of Machiavelli, and a brief look at his life up to this point may help us to understand this pivotal figure.

William Maitland was born in Lethington Tower, the medieval seat of his family and now renamed Lennoxlove, the seat of the dukes of Hamilton. His father was Sir Richard Maitland, a country gentleman devoted to gardening and literature. Sir Richard was a minor poet and held some crown offices, rising to become Lord Privy Seal under Mary, Queen of Scots, but blindness forced his retirement until his death, twenty years later, aged ninety, in 1586. William was the eldest of seven children, born in 1528, and so was Knox's junior by fifteen years. His early education followed the pattern of Knox's, first at the local Haddington grammar school and then at the university of St Andrews, but their paths then diverged as William almost certainly travelled widely in Europe to acquire his considerable learning. He was fluent in Latin and probably Greek – a rarity for his time and background – as well as speaking French and Italian, and having an equal familiarity with the Bible. His family circumstances gave him not only a considerable library at home, but the leisure to acquire a wider culture than Knox could have dreamt of. He was called the 'flower of the wits of Scotland' by no less than Elizabeth, but by the time he met the Tudor Queen he had undoubtedly conquered the arts of flattery. If one were short of lavish presents of jewellery, flattery was always a quick route to Elizabeth's favour. Lethington married in 1553, as expected, into the nobility, his first wife being the daughter of Menteith of Kerse. The next year he was appointed assistant and successor to the bishop of Ross as secretary of state. The speed of his rise to immediate high office was brought about by the Queen Regent's wish to appoint a Frenchman, since she knew of no suitable Scot. This would have disturbed the delicate balance in her government and she was persuaded by Lord James and the earl of Cassilis to select young Lethington instead. Also both men were Protestant, as was Lethington. By 1558, he did in fact succeed to be secretary of state and a member of the privy council at the age of thirty. A year later the Spanish ambassador in London said that he ruled the Queen Regent, 'body and soul'. He had, as we have heard, already met Knox in 1555, but by October 1559 he was becoming disenchanted with the policies of the Queen Regent a disenchantment that drove him into the arms of the congregation. The slur that he merely calculated which side would be the victors is too obvious for such a subtle man. He was Protestant, aristocratic, but above all, devoted to maintaining the rule of law in Scotland, and he could see that the Queen Regent was distorting that rule. He would remain true to his country and its traditions, since as an aristocrat and landowner, he was part of that tradition. His portrait shows us a handsome man with neatly trimmed beard and moustache, fine linen and lace at his throat with a scattering of pearls in his hat – that very embodiment of the sixteenth-century man of discreet fashion – but his eyes have no smile in them and are fixed in the steady gaze of an ice-cold intellect. For once the portrait gives a true picture of the man. It gives us no hint of the terrible end that awaited him.

However, it became clear that the congregation could never overcome in the present situation, and so on 6 November they withdrew again to Stirling, under cover of darkness, having achieved very little, apart from the formal and ineffectual suspension of Mary's regency. They had set up a formal structure for payments to garrisons by levying taxes and appointing treasurers to pay on warrants signed by at least three lords 'whereof the Duke, Arran or Lord James must be one'. Astonishingly, Knox was named as a 'counsel' to supervise receipts and payments and 'to see the same duly employed, and not [put] to any private use'. He was still an influential member of the congregation's secular apparatus, although Lethington was wisely taking over as ambassador to England, where among other things he suggested to Elizabeth that there could be a union of the crowns, creating the new kingdom of Great Britain. Elizabeth was 'not seduced'.

The congregation's forces had continued to bleed away, although young Arran and Lord James declared their willingness to stay in Edinburgh if 'any reasonable company would abide with them. But men did so steal away, that the wit of man could not stay them. Yea, some of the greatest determined plainly that they would not abide.' Knox was appalled at the fickleness of the citizens of Edinburgh, some of whom even called the congregation traitors and heretics. The cry was, 'Give advertisement to the Frenchmen that they may come, and we shall help them now to cut the throats of these heretics . . . we could never have believed that our natural country men and women could have wished our destruction so unmercifully, and have so rejoiced in our adversity. God move their hearts to repentance!' The citizenry of a mercantile city tend to cling to the status quo while business is sound, and all the congregation had done for business was to have the city bombarded and cut off from its port. The citizens followed where their pockets led them and a civil war was the last thing they wanted. The Catholic Church had caused no great interruptions in trade, domestic or foreign, and the merchants probably felt, to parody the yet-to-come words of Henry of Navarre, 'Profit is worth a Mass.' In fact, by November, the bishop of St Andrews had arrived to resanctify St Giles – 'with his masquing goods, cross, cap and mitre, and after he had mumbled some words in Latin, he began to cast his holy water in all parts of the said Kirk, and then immediately set up an idolatrous Mass'. Four months later the altars were all smashed and the idolatry purged. This may have seen the last of the relic of St Giles's arm.

But before all this Knox had stayed briefly to preach in St Giles. He gave a sermon on verses four to eight of Psalm 80 – a sermon that he continued in front of the Lords of the Congregation in Stirling. It was a direct address to the lords, asking them, 'What shall we think to be the very cause that God hath thus dejected us? . . . our sins and former unthankfulness to God.' He then reminded them that when the Israelites humbled themselves before God they received an assured promise of victory. In the past, before they had either earl or lord, they took God as their only refuge, but now the congregation has too much trust in the power of the nobles. After a side-swipe at Chatelherault he reaffirms his faith that their cause will prevail in Scotland. This appears to have had a stiffening effect on morale, for a council was immediately held with a telling division of labour. Knox was called to make an invocation in the name of God, and Lethington, who had now formally replaced Knox as spokesman, was dispatched to London to meet with Elizabeth and her council. His instructions were first, to tell of the French tyranny; secondly, to tell of the Dowager's intent to conquer Scotland for France; thirdly, to preserve the families of the successors to Mary, in other words, the families of Lord James and the Hamiltons; fourthly, to stress the danger to England of direct invasion. This was a distinct possibility given Mary's claim to the English crown and the provocative quarterings in her coat of arms. Fifthly, to point out that Scotland would shortly become part of France and lastly, to repeat the fore-going as well as 'a plea to procure perpetual love betwixt the people of the two realms, a thing much desired of all Christians, saving the French only, and thus acquire perpetual fame'. The last might appeal to a Queen only a year into her reign and would certainly give scope for Lethington's powers of flattery.

Sadler and Croft dutifully told Cecil that Erskine,

> though pressed with offers and threats by the Dowager, utterly refuses to yield the castle [of Edinburgh] without consent of Parliament. His keeping of this castle is of great importance, for, if the French got it, they would be master of Edinburgh and Leith and this side [of the] Forth. The Queen Dowager still languishes in great sickness, and her physicians have no hope of her recovery.

The congregation broke up to meet again on 20 December and Knox left for St Andrews and the comfort of his wife Marjory and his sons, who had arrived in September. Knox was well aware that Marjory would be watched and could be in physical danger. Even when she managed to join him in St Andrews, her rest was 'so unrestful since her arriving here, that scarcely could she tell upon the morrow what she wrote at night'. Although we have no other evidence for it, we may deduce from this comment that Marjory acted as a secretary for Knox, if not as a brake on his overly direct tongue. Now, at least, he had a regular home in the priory of St Andrews with only occasional needs to journey, usually to Edinburgh. This was fifty miles, or a two-day ride, allowing for uncertain ferries. At any rate, he was most probably relieved that Lethington had been sent south as he was well aware of his shortcomings as a diplomat. Having, for example, asked Sir James Croft for support to prevent a total French subjugation and also to help his friends in England, he was rebuffed. Croft wrote to Knox,

> And touching the support of such as you have often written for, I could find the means that they might have some relief at their friends' hands here, if I knew how the same might be conveyed to them in such secret and close manner, as none other have notice and knowledge of the same.
>
> But, to be plain with you, you are so open in your doings as you make men half afraid to deal with you, which is more than wisdom and policy does require.

Knox obviously took this to heart:

> I am judged among ourselves too extreme, and by reason thereof I have extracted myself from all public assemblies to my private study.

And in the same vein,

> I hope that God hath delivered me from the most part of these civil affairs,
> for now are men of better judgement and greater experience occupied in these
> matters. Young Lethington, Secretary . . . I trust shall relieve me of the presup-
> posed journey.

The journey in question was daily becoming more crucial as the Dowager
first occupied Edinburgh and then moved north, splitting the congregation
forces: Argyle and Glencairn headed west for Glasgow (and their own
lands), while Arran and Lord James Stewart made for St Andrews. The
French admiral, Martigue, had his ships taken, and according to a letter, 'he
rent the hair from his beard as though he had been shaved and she [the
Queen Dowager] has wept very sore . . . but she wept not that she would
die of fat, seeing no other disease is able to take her out of this world.'

In mid December Knox preached resistance and stiffened the spirit of the
eastern congregation to march out against the now overwhelming enemy
forces. The Dowager, with her French support, tore through Fife in a
campaign of rape and pillage that, according to Knox, included hanging
two children from the church steeple in Kinghorn. She is said to have
proclaimed, 'Where is now John Knox's God? My God is now stronger
than his, yea even in Fife.' This was one of Knox's lowest points since he
was seeing for himself the effects of what was, in all but name, a civil war
– a civil war that he had supported with all his vigour and eloquence. The
time for debate over all the niceties of magisterial responsibility had passed,
as had the episodes in which only the armed men of each faction faced each
other. Now farmsteads were being burnt, animals slaughtered and crops
destroyed – the French 'wasted the country about', and Knox had taken a
large part in launching this carnage.

Near to despair, he wrote to Mrs Lock on 18 November,

> We trusted too much, dear sister, in our own strength and especially when the
> Earl of Arran and his friends were joined to our number. Amongst us also
> were such as sought the purse more than Christ's glory. We by this overthrow
> are brought to acknowledge what is a multitude without the present help of
> God, and the hollow hearts of many are now revealed . . . Our dear brethren
> and sisters of Edinburgh and the Lothians, who lie nearest these blood thirsty
> tyrants, are so troubled and vexed, that it is pity to remember their estate.

Only God comfort them. We stand universally in great fear, and yet we hope deliverance.

And again he wrote to her at the end of December:

I have read the cares and temptations of Moses, and sometimes I supposed myself to be well practised in such dangerous battles. But alas! I now perceive that all my practise before was but mere speculation; for one day of troubles, since my last arrival in Scotland, hath more pierced my heart than all the torments of the galleys did [in] the space of nineteen months; for that torment, for the most part, did touch the body, but this pierces the soul and inward affections. Then I was assuredly persuaded that I should not die till I had preached Christ Jesus, even where I now am. And yet, having now my hearty desire, I am nothing satisfied, neither yet rejoice. My God, remove my unthankfulness! From St Andrews the last of December 1559.

Here is the rank desolation of a man fearing that a life's struggle has turned out to be in vain; that personal ambitions achieved are worthless if the victory is not complete; and possibly that personal ambitions have brought about unnecessary slaughter. Knox was back in that town where the first seeds of reform were planted in his mind, and yet in principle nothing had changed. The ashes of Hamilton, Wishart, Mill and the rest were all around him and he was most likely going to join them in martyrdom. But rather than fearing death, he feared that he had been guilty of pride in achieving his 'hearty desire', and that his ambitions had led others to death and invoked a savage revenge on innocent people. Comforting such despair in the December loneliness of their wind-swept lodgings cannot have been an easy task for Marjory Knox that night.

Still attempting his dare-devil feat of riding two horses simultaneously, on 25 January Chatelherault wrote to Francis II pleading for a pardon in view of his support for the congregation. He offers to send the Queen Dowager his personal seals as a token of his good faith, and suggests that his younger children be kept by the French King as hostages. The letter went via the Queen Dowager, who passed it on to de Noailles in London, with the sarcastic suggestion that he show it to Elizabeth.

Knox had agreed to England holding Scotsmen hostage as an earnest of good faith, before they would send ground troops north and in the same letter, on 26 December, he pleaded desperately for help from the sea to prevent the French forces being strengthened.

But Knox's spirit was still unquenched, for he put heart into the Protestant leaders in a sermon he preached at Cupar with a text from St John's Gospel, telling them that this was 'the night on the sea of Galilee, their master was absent and the fourth watch was not yet come'. But, in fact, the pleas had worked. Help was at hand and delivery would appear upon the waters. Whether he personally believed this or whether he was simply putting on a brave front we have no way of knowing, but the fact remains that he was somehow able to conquer his fears and quiet those of others. Only wholly committed champions of great causes have this kind of extraordinary resilience.

The congregation were in reality so inspired by this that the Earl of Arran and Lord James Stewart were sent to Dysart (now a near-suburb of Kirkaldy) on the coast to prevent the French occupancy of all the southern harbours of Fife. There, with 500 horse and an equal number of foot soldiers, they kept 5,000 French at bay for three weeks, at all times sleeping fully clothed and booted. With little food and capable only of ambushes and night forays, the puny congregation forces froze in lashing rain through most of January, until the French decided on a final thrust to extinguish them once and for all. On 23 January they marched in full force from Dysart to destroy St Andrews and Dundee. The French army, itself running low of supplies, kept close to the shore hoping to be victualled by sea. About noon they sighted sails.

Thirteen years before and six miles away at St Andrews, Knox and the Castilians similarly had sighted sails and had hoped that they were those of English reinforcements. Instead they were a French force under Strozzi that would carry them off to the galleys. Now the reversal was complete as the Queen Dowager and her force realized that the sails were instead those of an English fleet, under one Admiral Winter. Winter had sailed from Lowestoft with twelve men of war, but, thanks to storms, only seven ships reached Bamborough in Northumberland. He embarked arquebusiers at Eyemouth and received orders to sail to the Forth estuary and 'annoy the French and hinder any landings by them'. When he arrived between the May Island and Inchkeith he saw cargo ships and a 'hoy' – a coastal cargo ship. These were the supply ships so eagerly awaited by the Queen Dowager, but they were either seized by Winter or driven ashore into the hands of the congregation.

Winter took his prizes south to Edinburgh, and wrote that, 'The country gather courage by our arrival, those neutral are now become partakers, and those who favoured the French desire the Congregation to receive them.' Whether Knox's desperate plea had any effect we shall probably never know, but his reports of events on the ground combined with Lethington's diplomacy must have moved Cecil from caution to action. There had been an old prophecy that there should be two winters in one year, which would be a great felicity in Scotland, and this was now thought to have been fulfilled. Cecil was told, 'with such follies men sometimes recreate their spirits'. Knox's sermon, however, had been truly prophetic, since now the Queen Dowager was in full retreat. This was 'no little comfort' to Knox as the Dowager had been within fatally easy reach of St Andrews. Lethington's mission had succeeded and the duke of Norfolk, having been told by Elizabeth to 'use Lethington favourably', was approaching Berwick to negotiate with the congregation on behalf of his mistress. Norfolk, who was clearly being accommodated by the shadowy Railton, regularly sent reports of all the action and negotiations to Cecil. As we hear in a post-script to one of these dispatches he found this secretarial duty somewhat onerous, 'I had written this in my own hand, but when I could scant read it, I made Mr Railton copy it.'

Knox also wrote to Railton:

> The French were within 8 miles of this [St Andrews] and thinking the ships were the army . . . they approached within 6 miles, but the certainty known, retired as much in one day as they advanced in two. If God's mighty hand had not defended these two young plants [Lord James and Arran] they had both perished in this last same danger. God is highly to be praised in the prudent boldness and painful diligence of the laird of Grange, who constantly annoyed the enemy, cutting off their victuals by land except when they moved their camp. He has been in great danger, and was shot under the left breast, yet God preserved him.

It was as if Knox were sending dispatches with recommendations for decorations, although there would be none for the infantry: 'I count our footmen as ciphers!'. He also reminded Railton that he was still in need of a good horse.

The weather improved and the Queen Dowager and her forces were harried all the way back to Leith. Knox ends the story of this campaign with a typically homespun story. A French soldier, resplendent in a red cloak and gilt helmet, invaded the cottage of a poor woman and demanded food. She offered him the bread she had just prepared, but instead he took the salt beef that was to maintain her and her children. Then he went on to ransack her 'tub' [probably a barrel of salt meat] and when he had bent over it, she tipped him into it headfirst where he ended his unhappy life. Knox says, 'Let all such soldiers receive such reward, O Lord, seeing that thou are the avenger of the oppressed.' The fact that there are similar stories accompanying all military campaigns, where they walk hand in hand with the atrocity tales of bayonetted babies, does not invalidate it, but Knox uses it as a text to exemplify God's helping the underclass.

Fife now being freed from 'the bondage of those bloody worms' a service of thanks was held in St Andrews, while the Queen Dowager carried out a petulant campaign of revenge in the Lothians. After a certain amount of prevarication the Lords of the Congregation met the duke of Norfolk at Berwick in February 1560.

Knox, rather wistfully, reprints his unsuccessful letters to Cecil at this point in the *History*, as if he felt that his efforts might be ignored when victory seemed at hand, with the English fleet now commanding the entire Firth of Forth. It might also seem as if the entire rescue had been masterminded by Lethington. The treaty was all that the congregation could have wanted, with a firm pledge by England to drive the French out of Scotland, and, most importantly, a further promise never themselves to fortify within the ground of Scotland. The duke of Norfolk signed on behalf of Elizabeth and the lords on behalf of Scotland, and the English army began to assemble at the border. By April it was ready to march on Edinburgh. The Queen Dowager wisely withdrew into the protection of Edinburgh Castle, pursuing a policy of destruction behind her, and she somewhat optimistically wrote to Elizabeth asking for reparations for the damage done by English soldiers. Elizabeth said she would look into it most thoroughly.

Leith was now approached by the extraordinary sight of a combined English and Scottish army marching over ground that they had disputed by force of arms in the very recent past, and where the Scots had been crushed under English savagery during the 'Rough Wooings'. They even camped together at the spot where, less than 200 years later, a Scottish army would rout Sir John Cope's forces at the battle of Prestonpans. But, for the moment, the Scots were united with the Auld Enemy to fight their erstwhile partners in the Auld Alliance. It was, needless to say, a fragile bond in which no one trusted anyone else.

The Dowager sent embassies to try to convert the English, as well as treating for peace with the congregation, and Knox drew up a bond of loyalty for the Scots which carried forty-nine signatures. The effect of this on the Queen Dowager was to lower her morale,

> she stormed not a little and said, 'the malediction of God I give unto them that counselled me to persecute the preachers ... it was said to me that the English army could not lie in Scotland ten days; but now they have lain near a month, and are more like to remain than the first day they came.'

Knox was now, as well as being the nominal minister of St Giles, established in St Andrews. He set about tackling some of the spiritual problems he would later codify in the *Book of Discipline*. The principal problem of displaced priests was that, since they had sinned grievously by taking part in the idolatry of the mass, they could not now be admitted to the reformed Church until they had made a complete repentance. Knox could not ask that they be automatically excluded from admittance to the Church as ministers without personal hypocrisy of the greatest sort, since he himself had once been one of that very breed of apostate. Added to this was the dilemma of how to deal with numbers of former priests who had no learning or skills of any sort. He consulted Calvin, who agreed that they should not be paid from the public purse, 'in order that they may live in useless ease', but that any who were worthy of office inside the Church should be called to 'labour therein'. The remainder, whom Calvin felt were 'for the most part unlearned and destitute of all skill', should be admonished to support themselves by honest labour, and if that failed, funds should be found from the richer benefices to support them. A surprising show of liberality from one who once had supported beheading for adulterers. Many in St Andrews did convert after confession, the most eminent being John Winram, the sub-prior who had had a hand in the trial of Wishart and had already met Knox during his time with the Castilians. He had been present at Knox's first sermon and heard his debate in the courtyard of St Leonard's.

In Knox's community every parishioner was obliged to attend church on Sunday or be exposed to the public humiliation of being sat on a stool before the congregation while his sins were read out and his confession and repentance was heard. This, for its time comparatively benign, punishment was used especially for fornicators and over 200 years later, the poet

Robert Burns would occupy the 'cutty stool' on a more or less regular basis. The elders of the Church, elected by the congregation, formed the kirk session, which became, in effect, an ecclesiastical court with powers of excommunication. In practice, even the humiliation of the stool of repentance was rare and excommunication even rarer. Jasper Ridley in his *John Knox* tells us of a case of divorce petition being tried by the session, with both Winram and the rector of the university in attendance. The husband claimed adultery on the part of his wife and produced two witnesses. These women had been standing on a stool outside the husband's house at night peering into the bedroom in the best tradition of private detectives. They testified enthusiastically that they had seen the wife with the accused lover. They then saw him remove his hose and, to their disappointment, blow out the candle. Astonishingly the session found the wife not guilty of adultery and disallowed the divorce.

However, by mid April Knox clearly had to attend to his duties in St Giles and he left for Edinburgh to be succeeded by Goodman, under whom the regime became more strict. The hoseless lover would have been lucky merely to be sat on his stool of repentance confessing his adultery.

The siege of Leith was ineffectual although the blockade was complete and the inevitable skirmishes went backwards and forwards. On 1 May an English report states, 'this present Tuesday night about supper time a very terrible fire arose among the houses on the SW part of Leith and continues burning vehemently, which we helped by shot of artillery to increase. It happened by chance.'

By the 3rd the blockhouse of Leith was surrounded and on the 5th a night assault was made, but the scaling ladders proved to be too short for the task and 'cruel slaughter' resulted. Knox gives us a vivid description of the 'French men's harlots, of whom the most part were Scots whores, [who] did no less cruelty than did the soldiers.' They were loading and carrying guns as well as throwing fire and stones from the top of the walls. He goes on the tell that the Queen Dowager watched the progress of the siege from the walls of Edinburgh Castle. She saw, with satisfaction, the French standards on the walls of Leith and went to hear Mass said by one Friar Black, whom, we are told, she had recently surprised *in flagrante* with his whore. Knox was not surprised by this, since 'whoredom and idolatry agree well together'. The French were also alleged to have stripped the corpses of their slain enemies and hung them from the walls, causing the Queen Dowager to say they were 'the fairest tapestry I ever saw. I would that the whole field that is betwixt this place and yonder, were strewn with the same stuff'. Knox pushes the tale further by telling us that everybody saw this and her words were heard by many. The distance from the castle to the walls of Leith is over two miles and the Queen Dowager was in extremely poor health, so this report has all the hallmarks of propaganda. The game remained a stalemate until June when, it might be said, God took a hand in it.

Mary of Guise, widow of James V, mother of Mary, Queen of Scots, and erstwhile Queen Regent, died on 10 June. In April she had written to D'Oysel, 'my health is better, but I am still lame and have a leg that assuageth not from swelling. If any lay his finger upon it it goeth in as into butter. You know there are but three days for the dropsy in this country'. She was to last longer than that, for on 7 June it was reported, 'The Queen worse than yesterday, her lips, hands, and legs very cold, and her tongue and wits fail her greatly.' The precise cause of her death is unknown, but the symptoms were indeed those of dropsy, a morbid accumulation of fluid that had swollen her legs enormously and itself is often a symptom of vascular disorder. It is therefore, probable that she died of a heart attack after lengthy circulatory problems. Her corpse, 'lapped in a cope of lead', sailed for France on 19 October, and was buried in the convent of Saint-Pierre-les-Dames in Rheims where her sister Renée was Abbess. Oddly enough, there were no rumours of foul play, and astonishingly she called for the ministrations of John Willock, accepting that there 'was no salvation, but in and by the death of Christ'. This appears to have been a result of her summoning several of the congregation lords for a final rapprochement, although they were deeply suspicious of some devious Guisian practice. Knox hints that she also received the last rites of the Catholic Church, and it would be surprising if she did not. He also says her life was unhappy both for her, and for Scotland, but he spares her the hysterical attacks he had launched upon Mary Tudor. Even George Buchanan in his *History* allowed that 'she possessed an uncommon genius, and a mind strongly inclined to justice,' but that she was much under the influence of the Guise clan, who 'marked out Scotland as the private property of their family'.

Her life had been unhappy and had taken an unexpected course, having been born to a father who, as one of the leading nobles of France, was the boon companion of Francis I. She then married into another noble family and would have spent her life happily running her husband's estates from her fairy-like castle at Joinville except for his early death.

Francis I then, more or less arbitrarily, gave her as wife to James V of Scotland, also recently widowed. So she left the warmth of France for the chillier climate that had killed her predecessor. She bore James a daughter, upon which he died, prophesying doom for the crown. This daughter went to France as their future Queen, leaving Mary of Guise alone in a foreign country with a parcel of self-seeking cut-throat nobles, a principal one of whom, Lord James Stewart, was her ex-husband's son by a favourite mistress. At first she allowed the vacillating governor, Arran, his Protestantism, but when it threatened France, she ousted him and became Regent. She always ruled Scotland as a province of France with the arrogance of a great magnate. It also must be said that she was an extremely capable woman, but her determination gave her no room for compromise. When she came into conflict with Knox it was a head-on confrontation, since his deep convictions gave him a similar lack of flexibility. But with her death the impetus to crush the congregation was lost by her supporters. No help could now be expected from France, since a Protestant rising under Louis, duc de Condé, and even including de Beza from Geneva, had attempted to free the King from the Guise influence. Starting in Brittany, it had spread south to Amboise, on the Loire, where it was put down with merciless butchery. From the cliff-top castle one would have seen 1,200 hanged, decapitated or drowned in the Loire. 'The streets of Amboise ran with blood, the river was covered with corpses, and all public places had gibbets.' The violence of the repression only served to strengthen Protestant feeling in France. In Scotland, seven days after Mary's death an armistice was agreed and negotiations for a peace started, with Cecil himself, accompanied by Dr Wotton, the archbishop of York, coming from England to the tripartite talks. Cecil wrote to Elizabeth that 'the treaty would finally procure that conquest of Scotland which none of your progenitors, with all their battles, ever obtained, viz., the whole hearts and goodwill of the nobility and people, which surely was better for England than the revenue of the crown.'

The bishop of Valence and the sieur of Randan came to represent French interests, meaning, 'nothing but mere falsehood', according to Knox, who was by now merely an observer. The result of the negotiations was the Treaty of Edinburgh, signed on 8 July, in which the French and English agreed to a withdrawal, (except for 120 French at Dunbar), and the destruction of all recent fortifications. It was agreed that Francis and Mary should cease to quarter their French and Scottish arms with those of England (although the royal couple had no part in the negotiations). A Convention of the Estates of the Realm would be summoned for 10 July 1560. In effect this would be a parliament. The estates would then choose five people from a list of twenty-four and the monarchs would choose seven to make up a council of twelve, who had, along with the high officers of state, to be subjects born in Scotland. This council would have the executive powers previously exercised by the Lords of the Articles. There would also be a complete amnesty on all deeds done during the rising, provided that the estates deemed the deeds worthy of amnesty. This did seem to allow the estates a certain amount of leeway for revenge. Wisely the commissioners made no allowance for religion in this treaty, since this could safely be left to the Estates after the English and French had returned home, and it would not be forgotten that it had been Protestantism that had initiated the rising, a Protestantism which had been driven on by Knox.

9   The Book of Discipline

The establishment of the council drawn up, in theory, by commonalty and royalty together was at least a step towards the democratization Knox had been advocating, although it was little more than a formalization of the system by which the Lords of the Articles, also known as the lords of secret council, had been elected previously. At least it was enough of a step forward for him to endorse it in a sermon in St Giles giving thanks for deliverance. Knox also must have been satisfied at this time to know that Christopher Goodman, his old colleague from Geneva and author of *How Superior Powers ought to be Obeyed*, had been formally installed as minister at St Andrews. When the estates met after a delay on 8 August, Knox was preaching in St Giles that 'we must now forget ourselves, and bear the barrow to build the house of God'. He was urging the need for a religious settlement, since the congregation's victory would be hollow without it. This took the form of a supplication setting out the errors of transubstantiation, indulgences, purgatory, pilgrimages and praying to saints:

We humbly crave of your honours, that such doctrine and idolatry as by God's word are condemned, so may they be abolished by Act of this Parliament, and punishment appointed for the transgressors . . . Also because the true discipline of the ancient Kirk is utterly now amongst that sect [Rome] extinguished: for who within the realm are more corrupt of life and manners than are they called the Clergy, living in whoredom, adultery, deflowering virgins, corrupting matrons, and doing all abomination, without fear of punishment; we humbly therefore desire your Honours to find remedy against one and the other . . . the true ministers of God long time have been altogether neglected, the godly learning despised, the schools not provided, and the poor not only defrauded of their portion, but also tyrannously oppressed; we likewise hereof desire remedy.

He also begged the Estates to exclude the Roman clergy from the new parliament, since they were 'unworthy of honour, authority, charge or cure within the Church of God'. Knox was back in his stride and demanding that the nettle be grasped. No wonder Thomas Randolph, nominally Elizabeth's ambassador, but in reality another of Cecil's gossip gatherers and spies, wrote to his master that 'Mr Knox spareth not to tell it them.'

It is difficult to appreciate the atmosphere of excitement that must have infected Edinburgh as this parliament assembled. Randolph told Cecil that the 'number of noblemen is greater than of long time it has been at any parliament'. Final numbers of any accuracy are difficult to come by, but the total number of members of parliament would appear to be eighty in all; twenty-five clerics, thirty-three members of the nobility with twenty-two burgesses. There would be a later addition of 100 lesser tenants-in-chief – the 'small barons'. The houses of the High Street would have been filled with their trains of servants, while their masters occupied themselves with lobbying and making accommodations where they could. Private dinners were hotbeds of plotting and the delighted vintners and victuallers saw their profits soar. Randolph told Cecil, 'the town all is in armour, the trumpets sounding'. Clearly the nobility was keeping as much pomp as they could muster. Bishops and the other great prelates either endorsed Protestantism or made their defiance seem politic. The bishop of Dunkeld, however, remained obstinate, declaring that he would never hear an old, condemned heretic, such as Knox. For some it was a first breath of the fresh air of religious liberty, while for others it was a question of calculating the most profitable way of climbing on to the new bandwagon. The idea that a new ethos for the nation was about to emerge was heady stuff, and as the summer sun lit the velvets and silks of the great magnates, it was easy to forget that the same machinery of Government was in place and that the heads of state were still a committedly Catholic king and queen. There must have been a certain feeling of the mice playing while the cat was still in France.

Lethington, with a calmer head, also reported to Cecil, calculating that only three of the clergy would give any opposition, and all others 'continue in good amity'. He ends by asking to be remembered to 'his Lady, Cecil's bedfellow, to whom with you I wish your hearty desire'. To include such a social nicety in a political dispatch would never have occurred to Knox.

The parliament met in the Tolbooth, a two-storey building in the Canongate halfway between the eastern boundary of the city and the royal palace of Holyrood on 8 August, with each member sitting according to a rigid hierarchy of seniority, and with the crown, mace and sword of the honours of Scotland laid on the vacant throne. (Knox and the *Diurnal of Occurents* specifically deny the presence of these royal symbols, but Randolph definitely reports their presence.) Lethington was appointed as speaker or 'harangue maker'. With an attendance that could have reached nearly 200 in a room measuring about 60 feet by 25 feet, he must have had his work cut out to maintain any kind of order. After the first sitting the members processed up the Canongate to the Netherbow, and then on to the duke of Chathelherault's palace half a mile away in Kirk o'Field, presumably for a celebration.

The estates quickly instructed Knox, with a committee of five others, to draw up a *Confession of Faith*, codifying the reformed faith. The committee, nicknamed the 'Six Johns', consisted of Knox, Winram, Row, Willock and Douglas, the rector of St Andrews University, and the work was presented to the Lords of the Articles in the astonishingly short time of four days. By 15 August Knox, although not a member, was presenting it to the parliament in full.

And a full parliament it certainly was, with not only the great nobles attending in unaccustomed force, but also the minor lairdry. There were objections to the presence of these 'small barons', but their attendance was assured to them in laws dating back to 1427 in the reign of James I. There was also considerable debate as to whether or not this assembly of the estates was a legal parliament, since it had not been summoned by the sovereign. These procedural points were debated for a full week, before parliament accepted its own legality by the simple fact of its existence. Francis and Mary, after all, had had time to object to parliament's assembly and nothing had been heard from them. So the rule of *tacere consentire* – to be silent is to consent – could be said to apply. After agreeing that it was a legal assembly, parliament, under Speaker Lethington, turned to religious settlement and considered the *Confession of Faith* that had been submitted to it. It is a cogent statement of the doctrines that form the basis of Presbyterianism and could easily have been written in Geneva, with some notable exceptions. The speed with which it was produced shows that there can have been very little argument within the committee. They were the group who would be responsible for the *Book of Discipline*, but it seems likely that Knox himself had the major hand in its creation.

Admirably clear, it was later divided into twenty-five chapters, moving from the creation of man and his early sins as Adam to Christ's sacrifice for the redemption of these sins. It defines the duality of God and man united in Christ, 'two perfect natures united and joined in one person'. All other heresies are 'damnable and pestilential'. The *Confession* asserts that the sole authority for any kirk is to be found in the writings of the prophets and apostles and that there are only two just sacraments, baptism and the Lord's Supper. It settles the argument of transubstantiation and consubstantiation by saying, 'we make a distinction betwix Christ Jesus, in his natural substance, and betwix the elements in the Sacramental signs; so that we neither worship the signs in place of what is signified by them'. This definition has its roots in the *Helvetic Confession* brought by Wishart and underlines Knox's objections to kneeling in adoration.

Then in chapter twenty-four the *Confession* turns to the civil magistrates, from emperors to civil officials, who hold their places by God's ordinance and, 'for the singular profit and commodity of mankind'. To them the 'purgation of religion appertains'. This is a slightly more guarded restatement of the thesis that power lies in perceived justice, and if justice is not perceived then the power may be removed. Goodman in St Andrews would have cheered mightily, although he had just spent ten days in the Isle of Man and found it sadly wanting in Reformation.

The *Confession* was adopted along with two acts abolishing the celebration of the Mass and denying papal authority. The aged lord of Lindsay, 'as grave and Godly man as ever I saw,' reported Randolph, declared that, 'I have lived many years, I am the eldest in this company of my sort, now that it has pleased God to let me see this day where so many nobles and other have allowed so worthy a work, I will say with Simeon, *nunc dimittis*.'

So the *Confession* was well received by the parliament. Randolph reported that he 'never heard matters of so great import, neither sooner despatched nor with better will agreed to'. There were only three bishops and five lords dissenting and Scotland was now, Knox had reason to think, a totally Protestant country. And it had voted to be so by democratic means. But such dissent as there was came from the apex of the parliamentary pyramid. Knox knew that other great magnates had supported reform, not so much from any spiritual reason, but because it would mean an end to the proxy rule from France, and the remainder were largely content to follow the majority provided they were not hurt by it. This was not a reliable power base for the future, but Knox would never understand the reason for this. He acted from deeply felt motives based on close spiritual examination, and his faith was totally resolute. Like all converts, he fled at once to the extreme and he felt that anyone who agreed with him did so with the same unshakeable candour. If Knox, like the nobility, had waited to see where the greatest personal advantage lay, he would never have followed Wishart. The majority of his support came not from earls and lords, but from the burgesses and lairdry, in other words, from the very people that shared his original background. The great nobles had always observed the rituals of the Church, but their power, breeding and wealth would let them laugh at excommunication, and prepare to negotiate with Satan when the need arose. Not so the lairdry or common people, who could be starved by exclusion from the Church and from whom the greatest financial exactions were made. Knox's head was untroubled by these niceties and he preached with totally unclouded commitment from the heart.

At the same time Randolph was to assure his master Cecil that the voice of Knox 'is able in one hour to put more life in us than five hundred trumpets continually blustering in our ears'. But he would have noticed that Lethington had tried unsuccessfully to have the sections on the obedience or disobedience that subjects owe withdrawn from the document. In the final draft this section stressed duty to emperors and magistrates without any qualifications as to the duty owed by magistrates. Randolph told Cecil that 'though they [Lethington and Winram] could not reprove the doctrine, yet did they mitigate the austerity of many words and sentences which sounded to proceed rather of some evil conceived opinion'. This was a first sign that, while Knox may have been given the upper hand in spiritual reformation, any meddling with the temporal aspects of power would be fiercely resisted.

However, within that week the Pope's authority was removed, the Mass forbidden in Scotland, as was all religious activity that did not conform to the new faith. It would seem that the Protestant revolution was now complete, but to hold the full authority of law all these acts had to be ratified by the sovereign, who still had failed to put the royal seals even on to the treaty of Edinburgh. To this end a commission headed by Sir James Sandilands and Lord St John set out for France on 23 September but, after lengthy Stewart prevarication, returned empty-handed. More precisely focused was another commission which was awarded £20 to propose to

Elizabeth that she might marry the earl of Arran. The commission comprised the earls of Morton and Glencairn, with Lethington and fifty-four horsemen in attendance.

A month earlier Francis II was being strongly encouraged to support this marriage and to send embassies to Elizabeth giving his support. He was also asked to do this with all speed since the prince of Sweden, an extreme Protestant, was also sending representations. Arran, for various reasons, appeared now to be high in everyone's estimation. Unfortunately, not high enough in Elizabeth's, since the delegation returned in January with the news that, while full of friendship for Scotland, Elizabeth was not 'presently disposed to marry, unless political necessity may afterwards constrain her'.

Randolph was clearly in personal touch with Knox over this period, since he led the faction that had been encouraging Knox to write a history of the Reformation movement. By September of the previous year 1559 Knox was about halfway through the task, although he would not live to see its completion. Randolph reported Knox as having said that he must have further help than could be found in Scotland for 'more assured knowledge of things past'. He thought it was a work 'not to be neglected', and Knox 'greatly wished that it should be well handled'. It certainly would win no prizes for historical objectivity, but in it we can read the account of an eye-witness, with all the vigour, and often the outrageous hyperbole, of Knox's 500 trumpets.

The spring and summer of 1560 were now busy times for Knox, for the Reformation parliament realized that although the *Confession of Faith* codified their spirituality, they had no formal structure by which they could put it into practice. There was, however, a long deserved peace in the city, with Pitscottie reporting that 'the rest of this year was good quietness and good justice kept'.

Knox and his colleagues had been commanded to write down their views touching the reformation of religion. This early request explains the speed with which the *Confession of Faith* was produced. In the preface to this latter publication we are told that it contains 'the order and uniformity to be observed concerning doctrine, administration of the sacraments, election of ministers, provision for their sustenation, ecclesiastical discipline, and policy of the Kirk'. In other words, having removed the hierarchical author-ity of Rome, this would now be the formal structure of its replacement. Clearly Knox was supremely qualified to undertake such a task, and even although the work was that of a committee it has the ring of Knox, at last being able to put forth his long-held theories and beliefs in a practical manner. The work was the *Book of Discipline* and like much of his work, it is often referred to and seldom read. It is usually thought of as a vast and dreary tome, full of dark condemnation, but nothing could be further from the truth. In a modern edition it runs to only forty-three pages and has all the briskness that one hopes for, though usually in vain, in a government Green Paper. Far from condemning what was past it concentrates on proposing the actions for the future that the committee had been asked to clarify.

But it went much further than the original brief or the preface would have led us to believe, causing Professor Croft Dickinson to claim, 'it reveals a concept of society, that more rightly than any other, may be termed "Christian Socialism".' Under the old order, power had been divided between the crown, the nobility and the Church, but now the crown was in the girlish hands of an eighteen-year-old absentee; the nobility, having been deeply divided, was uncertain of its power; and the old Church had been swept aside. Into this partial vacuum came Knox to codify the position of the reformed Church and place its greatly expanded power directly in the hands of the common people of Scotland. Its opponents called it a 'devout imagination'.

The book is divided into nine headings of widely varying lengths, the first three of which, on doctrine, the sacraments, and the abolition of idolatry, repeat and emphasize what has already been said in the *Confession of Faith*. The fourth head concerns the ministers and their lawful election. This power of election, 'appertaineth to the people, and to every several congregation to elect their minister'. The candidate would then be examined as to doctrine, either in St Andrews or in Edinburgh, before preaching 'in open audience of his flock' and being accepted by the congregation. Then follow qualifications as to the power of the council of the kirk, which will always be subservient to the wishes of the congregation. Knox then goes on to list the conditions that would disqualify any man from being a minister. (Women hardly figure at all in the *Book of Discipline*.) The list of disqualifying offences includes murder, adultery, theft, and so on, as well as simply being 'a contentious person'. Presumably this is not meant to include the way in which Knox himself had been contentious in Scotland, England and most of Europe. He also allows for the provision of readers, who can read the Common Prayers and the scriptures, 'till they grow to greater perfection . . . and by consent of the kirk and discreet ministers, may be permitted to administer the sacraments'. This acknowledges the shortage of suitable ministers for the parishes now bereft of their priest. The very word 'reader' comes from the Old Norse 'raða', meaning to advise, and by 1519 universities were using it to mean an instructor or counsellor. Whether Knox meant this usage or not is debatable.

The fifth head lays down the rewards necessary for the minister's upkeep in monetary stipend as well as housing him and supplying what turns out to be enough malt to deliver a daily pint of beer. Pensions for widows and dowries for daughters are mentioned, but there is also the useful phrase 'the modification wherof is referred to the judgement of the kirk'. Stipends for readers are suggested at a hundred marks, or more, at the discretion of the kirk, so that, 'difference be betwix them and the ministers'. Differentiation of pay scales is not new. But Knox now moves out of the strict area of his remit to deal with the poor.

> We are not patrons for stubborn and idle beggars who, running from place to place, make a craft of their begging, whom the Civil magistrate ought to punish; but for the widow and fatherless, the aged, impotent, or lamed, who neither may travail for their sustenation, we say that God commandeth his people to be careful . . . God shall show you wisdom and the means . . . but the stout and strong beggar must be compelled to work . . . to repair to the places where they were born, or of their residences, where their names and number must be taken and put in a roll; and then may the wisdom of the Kirk appoint stipends accordingly.

This is, in effect, an early form of registered unemployment benefit. Knox's concern for the deserving poor is a pre-echo of Samuel Johnson's belief that a nation's treatment of its poor was a mark of its civilization.

Knox then divides the country into ten provinces, each to have a super-intendent who would preach at least three times a week and travel every twenty or thirty days, examining the life, diligence and behaviour of their ministers. They would also examine the order of the churches, the manners of the people, how the poor are provided and the youth instructed. 'These men must not be suffered to live as your idle Bishops have done heretofore, neither must they remain where gladly they would.'

In July 1559 Cecil had recommended that the congregation look care-fully at the *Ordinatio Ecclesiastica* of Denmark, which had been presented to Henry VIII in 1537, read by Cranmer and was undoubtedly known to the reformers. In it were provisions for superintendents as well as other recommendations very similar to the *Book of Discipline*. Given that there were very few people qualified at the time ('the harvest is great but the labourers are few'), Knox suggested that for the present, their appointment should be a prerogative of parliament, but that after three years, the term of office recommended, a system of popular election would take over, involving the Church and magistrates of the province. The superintendents would also be subject to the scrutiny of the very ministers they superintended. It has been alleged that the superintendents were bishops in all but name, but there was a crucial difference, in that they were not appointed directly by the crown, but elected by the ministers from among their own number. This codified the basic organization of the parish appointing the elders to sit on the kirk session, with the minister himself approved by the parishioners and the lay administration of the parish in the hands of a deacon. This group would have the task of appointing the superintendents. Governmental, or royal, control of the Church was totally abolished.

The remainder of the fifth head concerns itself with the setting-up of a system of education available to all, in which a key word is 'docility' or the aptitude for learning. Once again Knox starts at the roots, with the need for every congregation to appoint a schoolmaster who can teach Latin and grammar as well as the catechism.

And further, we think it expedient that in every notable town . . . [there] be erected a College, in which the Arts, at least Logic and Rhetoric, together with the Tongues [Greek and Hebrew – which, it will be recalled, Knox himself did not learn until late in his life, and then only partially], be read by sufficient Masters for whom honest stipends must be appointed: as also provision for those that be poor, and be not able by themselves, nor by their friends, to be sustained at letters, especially such as come from landward [the rural areas].

Forster's Education Act for universal primary education was not passed until 310 years later.

The children of the poor must be supported . . . till trial be taken whether the spirit of docility be found in them or not. If they be found apt to letters and learning, then may they not (we mean neither the sons of the rich, nor yet the sons of the poor) be permitted to reject learning; but must be charged to continue their study, so that the Commonwealth may have some comfort by them.'

He then goes on to delineate the courses for the three universities of St Andrews, Glasgow, and Aberdeen, including physics, medicine, mathematics, economics, and politics, depending on 'docility'. This marked a huge change from the medieval system of education and really is the foundation for the basic syllabus at many modern universities. Taken with everything else, it looks forward to a future of liberal prosperity in what was, after all, one of the poorest and most backward countries in Europe. This section also enumerated the staff required, their stipends and the student fees. These varied from forty shillings for an earl's son to five shillings for a student of the lowest degree.

In the sixth head he returns to affairs of the Church directly, restating that the charges for the ministers, the poor, and education must fall on the Church. He first condemns the lairds that have simply abrogated the tithes [tiends] previously payable to the Catholic Church to themselves and in an addition he states that this condemnation was in fact finally endorsed by the lords. The *Book* as well calls for a cancellation of the burial charges, Easter offerings and various other church levies previously in force. The remaining tithes should be gathered, not by the ministers, but by deacons and treasurers, appointed annually, and supervised by the individual parish church. He accepts that the existing tithes will not be sufficient for the expanded responsibility he has proposed, and therefore the endowments of the various orders, chantries, and almshouses will transfer to the churches of the relevant towns, while the universities and superintendents will be supported by the income from the rents of the temporal land holdings of the bishops and cathedrals. And, 'merchants and rich craftsmen in free Burghs, who have nothing to do with the manuring of the ground, must make some provision in their cities, towns, or dwelling places for to support the need of the Church'.

This passage does not, as it might seem, give a preference to agriculture, but since craftsmen and merchants in free burghs would be largely exempt from local taxation, and would therefore give little back to the municipal funds, Knox felt that they should be asked to contribute directly to the Church's increased responsibility. There is also an addition whereby the lords 'condescend that the Manses and Yards be restored to the Ministers,' each to have at least six acres of land. The section ends with strict measures for financial accounting by the deacons to the superintendents. (The additions mentioned here were probably added after the *Book* had been considered by the Lords.) The existing structure whereby the right to collect revenue was leased to individuals would be dismantled. Knox must have known that most of this section represented an unachievable ideal since demolishing the existing profitable structure was wildly impractical and any attempts to do so would be strongly resisted.

The seventh heading takes us firmly into the area of doctrine and ecclesiastical discipline. There is an immediate division between offences such as blasphemy, adultery, murder, perjury and other crimes the transgressors of which

> ought to be taken away by the civil sword. But drunkenness, excess (be it in apparel, or be it in eating and drinking), fornication, oppression of the poor by exactions, deceiving of them in buying and selling by wrong mete or measure, wanton words and licentious living tending to slander, do properly appertain to the Church of God, to punish the same as God's word commandeth.

It may seem odd to us that this early attempt to administer a Trades Description Act should fall into the power of the Church, while blasphemy remains a civil offence, and that wantonness and licentious living were only to be punished if they 'tended to slander'. But we must remember that Knox viewed life as a spiritual totality and that all actions were constantly subject to God's scrutiny, so that his demarcations are often seemingly arbitrary with, for such a spiritual source, surprisingly worldly and practical aspects. Interestingly, licentious living that does not 'tend to slander' would grow into the acceptance of common-law marriage as being marriage by 'habit and repute'. Also much of what might to us seem extreme would have then been accepted as normal rhetorical hyperbole. For example, overcharging passengers on the Firth of Forth ferries was punishable by death, but there are no records of such a punishment being carried out and so many of Knox's strictures would be expected to be more honoured in the breach than in the observance. His systems of checks and balances were simply designed to reverse the excesses that the Roman Church had inflicted.

If the sinner is truly penitent, and declares his sin before the Church in public, then he may be forgiven and accepted back into the congregation. But if he refuses to repent after thorough examination he must be excommunicated. This would mean being totally excluded from society, apart from his wife and family, for all purposes both social and commercial. Also, and extremely severely, children born while the father was excommunicate would not be baptised until they became old enough to demand the sacrament for themselves, or the mother presented the child with a personal condemnation of her husband's sin.

The same strictures for penance would apply to those that had been condemned by a civil court, and Knox gives an entire (though short) section to establish that all of this applies equally to rulers and ruled, rich and poor alike.

Conduct by the ministers, elders and deacons and their method of election are dealt with summarily. 'They must be sober, humble, lovers and entertainers of concord and peace: and, finally, they ought to be an example of godliness to others.'

The ninth, and last, head deals directly with the policy of the Church. In this Knox is at pains to point out that what is contained is a *suggested* structure for what is essential – that is, the preaching of the Word, the administration of the sacraments, the common prayers, instruction of children in religion and the correction of offences. These things, he says, be so necessary that 'without them there is no face of a visible Kirk', but the frequency of these can vary with either a sermon, or prayers, or a reading of scripture daily in the great towns and on one day apart from Sunday in lesser towns, and on Sunday observed in all towns. This would be in accordance with his *Book of Common Order*, first drawn up in Geneva in 1556 and reprinted in 1562, when it became known as *Knox's Liturgy*. However it was intended to be no more than a guide with sample prayers and no whiff of ritual. He thinks it expedient that the Lord's Supper be held four times a year, avoiding Easter when 'superstitiously people run to that action at Pasche . . . and how the rest of the year they are careless and negligent'. His expediency extends to the saying of prayers at morning and night in all homes, and the master of every household instructing his children, family and servants in the principles of religion. In towns where 'schools and repair of learned men are' there should be a public debate, or prophesying, one day a week, but this would be under strict control with no contentious subjects voiced. In other words, a public debate for reinforcement but not for exploration.

Marriage is called the work of God, 'when two hearts (without filthiness before committed) are so joined that both require and are content to live together in the bond of holy matrimony'. Fornicators are excluded and deflowerers can be forced into marriage, or forced into paying a fine to the father of the victim to the value of her dowry. Men were not to marry until their fourteenth birthday and women until their twelfth. Adultery would be the only ground for divorce, but if the offender's life were spared by the civil power, genuine penitence would allow them back into the Church, even in extreme cases, to remarry.

On burial Knox, naturally, rejects the singing of dirges and saying of prayers over the dead, since they are superfluous and vain, but recommends that the dead are committed to the grave with some honest company of the Church, with gravity and sobriety. He thinks it unseemly to use churchyards, but rather 'some other secret and convenient place, lying in the most free air . . . well walled and fenced about, and kept for that use only'. More will be said later about Knox's delivery of funeral orations, as well as his own final resting place. Reasonable recommendations are made for the upkeep and maintenance of the fabric of churches.

Before reaching a conclusion there is a section on false preachers, in which Knox calls for the civil authorities to impose a sentence of death on such. He reiterates that only those who answer the definitions in the *Book* can be called to administer the sacraments. The conclusion itself is remarkably restrained and he has no doubt that many of the recommendations will seem strange, but he assures his masters that nothing is asked which is not required of God. The *Book* was formally presented on 20 May 1560.

That the work is a blueprint for a reformed Church is obvious and also that it contains a distillation of Knox's beliefs, both purely spiritual and liturgical. Although, like the *Confession of Faith*, it is the work of a committee, they were completely like-minded men, and there is no reason to think that they were browbeaten into their conclusions. Many of its recommendations had already been put into action by Knox in St Andrews when Winram had been a fellow member of the kirk session. But it goes much further than the formal delineation of a Church; it is a highly political document, giving a breadth of control to the ordinary populace beyond anything that had previously been imagined. All education would be monitored by the Church and the composition of that Church would be determined by popular elections. Thus the permitted range of debate and available knowledge would inevitably expand, and regulation of this debate would pass from a hierarchical Church under a Pope in Rome to a truly popular one. This expansion would be monitored by superintendents, themselves answerable to the electorate, but with sanctions at their disposal applicable to the ruler as well as the ruled. This was democracy in striding action, with each man's conscience answerable only to his God, without any false humility, kneeling or artificially created ceremony. Each person would be responsible for his own actions and free to express his opinions, either by voting or in open criticism of his supposed superiors. It is clear that Knox felt that there could be no superior to the common man in the full spirituality of his personal belief. If there was nothing between the face of man and the face of God, who but God could call man to account?

To the twentieth-century eye all of this may seem not only idealistic, but even dangerous. How close were Knox's parishes to Lenin's soviets, and how similar were superintendents to the political commissars of Stalinism? Certainly the *Book of Discipline* went further than Luther had ever preached and went further into democracy than Calvin would have wished. It would, if fully implemented, have brought democracy to Scotland. The system of religion that it overthrew was strictly hierarchical and supported by rigorous monarchies under the watchful eye of Rome. The savagery of the opposition to its beliefs was reaching a climax, with the first two major autos-da-fé, the mass burnings of Protestants having taken place in Valladolid and Seville. Knox's proposals struck at the structural roots of the existing church and had dangerous indications of a radical change in the basis of political government.

The *Book* also advocated the transfer of Catholic-held land and benefices to the reformed Church, including that which had already been seized by the nobility, and it was probably this recommendation more than any other that cooled the ardour of the parliament. More widereaching than anything perhaps were the recommendations for an educational system that had a complete union of Church and state at its root. The electoral power of the parishes passed upwards through various levels until they, in theory at least, would control the syllabuses of the universities, as well as being responsible for the appointment of every teacher, at every level. Children would be led by their 'docility' to follow the studies in which their natural aptitude might be of the greatest value to the state. Thus the Church would supply the civil servants and officers of State, educated according to its own precepts as laid down by the parishes. Labour would be directed to where there was a need, and the poor would be the recipients of charity provided at a local level, where its effectiveness could be best monitored.

As the reforms worked their way through the system in time, and they would take a considerable time to take effect, the power of the state would diminish and that of the Church would be all-encompassing. But it would be a Church of the parishes, of the people themselves – a parish democracy controlling all the most important aspects of life. The state would be left with foreign policy, some aspects of criminal and civil law and not much else. It would also be asked to transfer the bulk of existing Church income. So it is no surprise that the reception of the *Book* was by no means unanimously positive, and the dissenters were led by Lord Erskine, lately commander of Edinburgh Castle. Apart from Knox's dislike of Erskine's wife – 'a very Jezebel and a sweet morsel for the Devil's mouth' – he stood to lose more than most from the transfer of Church lands, and as Knox put it, 'the belly has no ears'. The formal debates and consideration of the *Book* were not to take place until the next parliament in January 1561, but by then it had been translated into Latin and sent to Calvin, Viret and de Beza in Geneva, as well as Bullinger in Zurich.

But before that happened two deaths were to influence Knox's life. The first was that of the nominal King of Scotland, the sixteen-year-old Francis II of France, and husband to Mary. Francis had already let the estates of Scotland know of his displeasure with their activities, but magnanimously told them that he was willing to forgive past faults. Sadly, he had no time for forgiveness. Knox tells us that, 'as the said King was sat at Mass, he was suddenly stricken with an aposthume in that deaf ear that never would hear the truth of God.' There was certainly an abscess, but the King had been ill for some weeks with a severe infection of the ear that spread internally to his brain, causing him severe pain and, on 5 December, death. He was succeeded by his ten-year-old brother Charles IX; Mary was now a widow and Queen Dowager of France at the age of eighteen. She was endowed with 60,000 livres annually, representing the incomes from Touraine and Poitou. Knox had 'great intelligence both with the churches and some of the court of France, and so was the first in Scotland to receive the news', which he immediately took to Chatelherault and Lord James at Kirk o'Field, Chatelherault's palace in Edinburgh. Lord James seems to have been reluctant to believe the news at first, even though Knox's informant was the same that had brought the news of Henry II's death. Lord James was clearly distressed at the news, but did find time to comfort Knox on his recent more personal brush with death.

This was much closer to home, for, at about the same time, his wife Marjory, died. 'He was in no small heaviness by reason of the late death of his dear bedfellow Marjory Bowes.' There are no details of the reasons for Marjory's death, but it was undoubtedly a great blow to him, and he later described her as 'dearest mother . . . of blessed memory'. She had been with him in his Geneva exile and come to be beside him in the time of his coming to power. But having become the spiritual leader of his country, he was suddenly alone. It is tragic that, at the pinnacle of his success, his beloved Marjory should have died, aged about twenty-five. For all that she is hardly mentioned by Knox, we can put together his tantalizingly few references with those of Goodman and Calvin to see a happy marriage, with Marjory as help-mate and supportive colleague as well as loyal wife and mother. How sad that she didn't live long enough to see him installed in his new manse, the unquestioned spiritual leader of his country. Indeed, his eminence must have seemed hollow, as he was now alone with his mother-in-law, Elizabeth, and his sons Nathaniel, aged three, and Eleazar, aged two. Marjory had been with Knox during most of his days of exile and hardship. It would only have been just if she could have lived long enough to experience some of his days of comfort.

The city of Edinburgh had been at pains to look after the minister of its high kirk, as well as providing stipends for at least three prebendaries and one priest of the old religion. The other prebendaries received nothing since they had no congregation. Knox was well rewarded by the city, with a stipend higher than the judges of the court of session, we are told. It amounted to about £200 annually, some paid from the rental of the burgh mills, and some in ready cash. Over and above this his accommodation was entirely provided, with his reader John Cairns acting as an agent. The quality of this accommodation can be judged by the fact that his first lodging was in the house of David Forrester, which would in time house the ambassador of Queen Elizabeth, so it can be presumed to be of the highest standard available. By September 1560, a tailor, John Durie, was paid to move out of his house. Knox would stay in this house, as his rent-free manse, on the north side of the High Street to the west of St Giles – the house no longer exists, the area having been destroyed in the civil disturbances of 1571. But through 1560 and 1561 Knox was given new locks, a specially constructed lectern (did he rehearse preaching at home?), and the house was repointed – not very successfully, since in 1562 his roof had to be repaired after rain leaked on to Knox's bed. A carpenter, Patrick Schange, was paid forty shillings for shelves, desks and seats, and he also constructed a great four-square desk with locks for which he got thirty-six shillings, 'to include the troubling of his spirit in the inventing on the concept'. By November 1561 Knox had 'a warm study of daillis [deal panelling] . . . within his lodging above the hall of the same with lights and windows thereto and all other necessaries'. The city treated Knox as a nobleman, more than just a preacher, to reflect his position as a leader of the Reformation. To some extent this position of eminence cut him off from the poorer citizens and especially from the members of the craft guilds, who tended to cling to the old faith through their particular patron saints. Their apprentices were a constant thorn in the side of reform, occasionally taking the law into their own hands.

An assembly of the reformed Church had been held in Edinburgh on 20 December 1560 to ordain ministers and appoint readers and also to petition parliament to accept the *Book of Discipline*. The list of those attending what was, in effect, the first General Assembly of the Kirk of Scotland is headed by the name of 'John Knox, minister', and it met in the parish hall of the church at Restalrig, north of Edinburgh.

Somewhat churlishly the assembly ruled that the adjoining parish church was a place of idolatry and should be 'razed, utterly cast down and destroyed'. The minister of Restalrig was an acknowledged papist and later would marry Mary, Queen of Scots to her ill-fated husband, Lord Darnley. The assembly decided to reconvene on 15 January, prior to meeting twice a year as a supreme assembly of the Church. (In fact the second assembly was on 27 May 1561) This assembly had not, of course, been suggested in the *Book of Discipline*, but it marked the start of a separation of the estates of Church and state. In fact, with the disappearance of the reformed clergy from the parliament, the General Assembly became the clerical estate.

The parliament which met in January was legally in a state of suspension, since it still had no authority for its existence from the sovereign. Mary had not, to the increasing fury of Elizabeth, even ratified the Treaty of Edinburgh, and by virtue of her recent widowhood, was now an eligible candidate for a political marriage. The leading prospect for this was the revolting Don Carlos, heir to the throne of Spain. He was an epileptic, grossly misshapen and given to homicidal rages – he attempted to rape a servant, but fell over in the attempt and had to undergo a primitive form of brain surgery to alleviate the results of the fall. But Mary was half a Guise and understood the importance of dynastic alliances better than most. After all, politics, not romance, had taken her to France in the first place, and so Europe held its breath. Mary's chances of physical consummation with this disgusting wretch would have been even less than with her late husband Francis, who had at least been affectionate. There was also enthusiastic speculation as to the marriage plans of Queen Elizabeth, but she was now embroiled in scandal. Her favourite courtier was Robert Dudley, her master of horse, whose wife Amy Robsart had died in extremely suspicious circumstances the previous September. This caused Mary to comment that 'the Queen of England is going to marry her groom. And he has killed his wife to make room for her!' Although Elizabeth would remain friends with Dudley, ennobling him as earl of Leicester, marriage to him was now out of the question. Astonishingly, Knox decide to play a hand in the marriage game and supported Arran, already rejected by Elizabeth, in a proposal to marry Mary. This was so secret that none of the lords knew of it, but Randolph naturally kept Cecil informed. This letter also contains the first attempt by Randolph to gain his recall to London. 'I hope Lethington may bring orders for my return. I have been six years out of my country, before the Queen came to her crown [that is, nine years ago] and the space I have been here is little to my content, saving for my duty.' He would continue in this vein for some time with no response whatsoever from Cecil. Mary and her advisers had earlier toyed with the idea of detaching Arran from the congregation by the offer of marriage, not to Mary herself but into the upper reaches of the French nobility. That had come to nothing, and this time Arran sent a letter and a ring, but both were returned and he 'bore it heavily in heart, and more heavily than many would have wished.' It is extraordinary that Knox would have supported such a marriage, with the likelihood that Arran would have had to convert to Rome.

Opinion was starting to form that Mary should return to Scotland, and at the end of January 'there were certain commissioners chosen to pass into France to desire our Queen's grace to come to Scotland, but that took not effect'. So says the *Diurnal of Occurents*. Lethington suggested that Mary might pass through England and have a meeting with Elizabeth, 'such as shall breed quietness for our times'. Cecil made no comment. Randolph also told him, 'the King's death has bred in us here such security that were it not that sometimes Mr Knox . . . or the Laird of Lethington . . . [who] puts us in remembrance where and in what case we were not long since, we should grow stark dull or forget ourselves.' Clearly Knox, always a facer of unpleasant facts, was thundering threats of disaster to come, while Lethington was solidifying support in parliament. At least for the time being, they were pulling in the same direction. Obviously, there still were doubts as to whether the parliament, without the official endorsement of the sovereign, had any legal validity. Later in the month Mary was reported to be wanting to return but only 'by the request and suits of the people of Scotland'. On 20 February she said that she will summon a parliament on her return while granting a general amnesty to all wrongdoing in her absence. It is doubtful if anyone believed this.

Legal or not, however, the parliament debated the *Book of Discipline*, and inevitably there was some some dissent. 'Some approved it, and willed the same to set forth by a law. Others, perceiving their carnality and worldly commodity somewhat to be impaired, grudged, insomuch that the name of the *Book of Discipline* became odious unto them.' With this amount of disquiet, implementing its recommendations would be a greater problem. This would have meant much power passing from the nobles to the parishes, with the concomitant loss of revenues, and however vehemently the nobles professed Protestantism this was unthinkable. Discussion was postponed. This parliament made no new laws, but dispatched Lord James Stewart to France to apprise Queen Mary of opinion in Scotland – also, said Lethington, 'to grope the mind of the young Queen'. He was well warned of the malice of her advisers and was also instructed to forbid her to hear Mass in public on her return. He agreed to give her this message, but pointed out that if she chose to hear Mass secretly in her own privy chamber, who could stop her? He was rumoured to have been offered a cardinal's hat if he would convert to Rome. Lethington was also afraid that French gold would soon pour into Scotland and he had no resources with which to answer such bribes. Quoting Chaucer, he complained that 'with empty hand men no hawks lure'. He summarized the situation to Cecil on 26 February, dividing Scottish influence into three. The first part were 'neutrals' who would follow the majority without any fixed adherence to principle; the second were the part of the nobility led by Chatelherault and under the influence of Knox; while the third faction favoured the return of Mary, on the unlikely condition that she govern by the consent of her subjects, favour the Protestants, confirm the Treaty of Edinburgh, and reform clerical abuses. This was hopelessly optimistic. Lethington went on, 'I pray you consider what danger it is for me to write. Many men's eyes look upon me. My familiarity with that realm [France] is known, and so misliked that I learn it shall be my undoing, unless the Queen be made favourable to England, which I fear shall be hard to do'.

Ambassadors arrived in Scotland, firstly from Charles IX, the eleven-year-old King of France, to announce, in a 'harangue', the dissolution of all treaties, at the same time expressing the king's continued amity with Scotland, and assuring the parliament of Catherine de Medici, the Queen Mother's, concurrence with all the foregoing. Rather frostily the parliament assured him that no subjects were more ready to serve their sovereign and they thanked the Queen Mother for her good will. In the same month Lord James's path had crossed that of Gilles de Noailles, who arrived on 11 March as another ambassador from Mary. He demanded that the friendship with England should cease, that the league with France be reinstated and that the Catholic bishops be reappointed. Buchanan gives us a cogent summary of the answers he received from the Scottish parliament.

> With regard to the ancient league with France, they were not conscious of having violated it; on the contrary, it had many times been neglected by the French, especially very lately, by their fighting against the liberty, and endeavouring to reduce to humiliating slavery, their unoffending ancient ally. The treaty with England they could not dissolve, without being considered the most ungrateful wretches, who repaid the greatest favour by the most grievous injustice, and who conspired against the welfare of the preservers of their own liberty. And with regard to the restoration of the priesthood, they neither acknowledged the order, nor the use of those he called priests.

However, de Noailles' arrival gave a focus to the still considerable Catholic adherents in the land and, ever fickle, Edinburgh trembled on the brink of revolt. In April it had been even suggested to Mary that she should land in the north where an army of 20,000, led by the Huntlys, would welcome her. She wisely rejected the offer.

Also in April letters arrived from Geneva for Knox and Goodman. Calvin praised the efforts of the Reformation, but expressed grief that 'your noblemen are divided by intestine disputes; and you are more justly vexed and tormented, because Satan is plotting in the midst of you, than you were formerly troubled by the movements of the French'. On a more personal note he continues, 'Your widowerhood is to me grief and bitterness, as it ought to be. You found a wife whose like is not found everywhere, but as you have rightly learned whence consolation in sorrow is to be found, I doubt not that you will bear this calamity with patience.' He continues this theme in the letter to Goodman: 'Although I am not a little grieved that our brother Knox has been deprived of the most delightful of wives, yet I rejoice that he has not been so afflicted by her death, as to cease his active labours in the cause of Christ and the Church.' Goodman had clearly been thinking of leaving Scotland, but Calvin pleads that, given the 'scarcity of labourers', he should remain. These letters show not only that Calvin had a gentler side than he is usually accredited with, but also that he was well informed about affairs in Scotland.

An attempt was made to move on these affairs when the second General Assembly met in the Tolbooth on 27 May 1561 and put forward a Supplication to the lords of secret council asking for the execution of some of the clauses from the *Book of Discipline*. The *Diurnal of Occurents* gives its purpose as 'suppressing idolatry, and punishing the users, maintainers, haunters and frequenters thereto, punishing such as purchase, bring home, and execute the Pope's Bulls'. The supplication also sought to condemn the persecution of Protestants and their relatives. This supplication was again accepted in theory, and then lost in the application, except for the burning of Paisley Abbey and various depredations in the west and Fife.

By July a riot broke out in Edinburgh, when a certain John Gillon was sentenced to be executed for having taken part in a game of Robin Hood, (part of a Feast of Misrule outlawed in 1555). Knox had in the past often interceded in similar cases, but in this case he was obdurate, in spite of warnings from a deputation. He plainly stated that 'he would not hurt his conscience for fear of any man'. But the Edinburgh mob seized the Tolbooth Prison and set free Gillon, along with the other inmates.

About this time Knox was shown an account of the meeting between the English ambassador and Mary, which Elizabeth had sent to Randolph. Mary was asked why she had not ratified the Treaty of Edinburgh, but she said that she was powerless without the advice of the nobles of Scotland. She looked forward to receiving this when she returned and hoped that Elizabeth would not encourage any of Mary's subjects in disobedience, for there was 'much ado in my kingdom about matters of religion'. She went on, 'God does command subjects to be obedient to their princes.' The ambassador cautioned her, 'Yea, madam, in those things that be not against his commandments'. She replied, 'The religion that I profess, I take to be most acceptable to God; and, indeed, neither do I know nor desire to know any other. Constancy does become all folks well, but none better than princes, and such as have rule over realms, and specially in matters of religion.' She then begs for the amity of her sister-queen. Knox tells us that, 'these advertisements somewhat exasperated the Queen of England, and not altogether without cause', resulting in a lengthy letter from Elizabeth to the estates, beseeching them to exhort Mary to ratify the treaty, with an overt threat of what might happen if she did not. 'The Queen your Sovereign shall enjoy her state with surety; and you yourselves possess that which you have with tranquillity, to the increase of your families and posterities which by the frequent wars heretofore your ancestors never had long in one estate.' The reply assured Elizabeth that the estates would do all they could, but if they failed, she was not to blame them. Interestingly, Knox describes this as 'our reply', making it clear that he was acting not only as chronicler and minister of St Giles, but as a member of the councils of state.

Lord James had not been the only one to 'grope the young queen's mind', since she wrote to Lethington:

If you employ yourself in my service and show the good will whereof you assure me, you need not fear calumniators nor talebearers, for such have no part with me. I look to results before believing all that is told me . . . and nothing passes among my nobility without your knowledge and advice. I will not conceal from you that if anything goes wrong after I trust you, you are he whom I shall blame first. I wish to live henceforth in amity with the Queen of England and am on the point of leaving for my realm. On arriving I shall need some money for my household and other expenses. There must be a good year's profit from my mint and other casualties . . . For my other intentions, being on my departure, I remit them to my arrival, when I see and hear from you how things have passed . . .

This letter makes absolutely clear that Mary was intending to return two months before she actually did, and that Lethington, no matter what public statements of doubt he put out, was petitioning strongly for a place in her government. There is also undisguised steel in the letter that sits uneasily with the image of the teenage weeping widow. Information as to Mary's frame of mind was also regularly reaching Elizabeth and Cecil, thanks to her able ambassador to France, Nicholas Throckmorton.

I understand that the Queen of Scotland is thoroughly persuaded that the most dangerous man in all her realm of Scotland, both to her intent here and the dissolving of the league between your majesty and that realm, is Knokes [sic] and therefore is fully determined to use all the means she can devise to banish him thence, or else to assure them that she will never dwell in that country so long as he is there and to make him the more odious to your majesty ... she mindeth to lay before you the book that he has written against the government of women ... thinking thereby to animate your majesty against him. I take him to be much of your Majesty's purpose ... and therefore not to be driven out of the realm.

Throckmorton had also seen the harder side of the young Queen, when questioning her about the continued quartering of England on her arms, and therefore her claim to Elizabeth's throne. Elizabeth had tentatively agreed to Mary's passage through England and a meeting if these obstacles were removed and the Treaty of Edinburgh ratified.

Throckmorton had said to Mary, 'You will give the Queen my mistress occasion greatly to suspect your well meaning unto her.'

She replied, 'Mine uncles have sufficiently answered you in this matter; and for your part, I pray you, do the office of a good minister between us, and so shall you do well.'

Then he went on, 'And so the Queen dismissed me and M de Lansac brought me to my horse.'

There would be no need for Knox to draw up battle-lines. Mary herself would be arriving with hostile preconceptions enough .

Mary's arrival seemed now to be inevitable, although on 9 August Randolph wrote to Cecil that Lord James Stewart, the earl of Morton, and Lethington had all told him that they wished 'she might be stayed' and cared not if they never saw her face again. Lethington had also told him that the royal treasury held only 20,000 crowns, which was insufficient for trouble-free rule, but that she should find obedience if she embrace Christ and deserve peace with her neighbours. Of course, Lethington may have been trying to forestall the blame that might fall on him when Mary arrived to find a less than lavish treasury. Randolph goes on to report that 'Mr Knox is determined to abide to the uttermost and others will not leave him until God have taken his life and theirs together.' He continues, 'It might please you to comfort him with letters, that the Queen's Majesty doth not utterly condemn him ... it will be a great comfort to him and others. His daily prayer is for amity with England, and that God will not suffer men to be so ingrate, and will not run headlong to destroy them that saved their lives and gave their country liberty.' He repeats his rather sad request to be allowed to 'quit this place for one of more quiet'. Privately Cecil is given the gossip that the Earl of Huntly's wife had consulted her 'familiars' who promised her that the Queen will never set foot on Scottish ground. Randolph added that if the prophecy were false, 'I would she were burned as a witch'.

Knox had, it seemed to him irrevocably, offended Elizabeth by *The First Blast*, thereby alienating his most powerful Protestant neighbour, and now could only look forward to the arrival of an implacably Catholic enemy. The totality of his reforms depended on the whims of a parliament who would easily bow their necks under the yoke of preferment and riches promised by a new sovereign. For the moment the Reformation seemed secure, but Randolph had obviously sensed the effects of devastating insecurity on Knox and realized that a simple reassurance from Cecil would go a long way to restoring his morale. However, for the moment, all did seem secure and Scotland held its breath. The seemingly ever-increasing hostility between Mary and the Protestant lords, led by Knox, could not, however, prevent the inevitable and on Tuesday, 19 August 1561 Mary Stewart landed in Leith to claim her kingdom.

10 A New Queen

Mary, Queen of Scots, was just three months short of her nineteenth birthday, already a widow and most probably also still a virgin. It is difficult to conceive of a more artificial upbringing than that received by Mary Stewart. When only five-and-a-half she was despatched to a foreign country to marry the heir to its throne. Her prospective husband was deformed and sickly, and kept under the watchful eyes of his dominating mother Catherine de Medici. Mary's sole purpose in life now was to be educated as a brood mare, to produce a son that would, in turn, rule France and Scotland. But all was not gloom for the little princess, since she was adored for her beauty by the entire French court, where her interests were well protected by her Guise uncles. She was also admired for her intelligence, mastering French to the point that she claimed to think in the language for the rest of her life – although by having her own Scots servants, the four Maries, and bodyguards, she also maintained her ability to speak Scots. Later, in captivity in England she would speak English equally well, but with what accent we can only guess. When only thirteen years old she astonished the court by delivering a public oration in Latin.

Mary undoubtedly fell under the conflicting influences of both Catherine de Medici and the royal mistress Diane de Poitiers. This conflict can be graphically seen at the château of Chenonceaux, where there are two gardens, one in the Italian style for Catherine and one in the French style for Diane. The royal monograms in the palace have an 'H' for Henry II entwined with a 'C' for his Queen Catherine, but the 'C' has the pointed ends of Diana's moon. It was in this atmosphere of intrigue and power struggles that Mary grew up, taught by Diane to get what she wanted by charm and by Catherine to use guile and politics. Totally drenched in the Catholic faith and surrounded by the adulation of her Guise uncles, it was a surreal, sunlit existence, in fairy castles, with flattering courtiers on every hand. Brantôme says, 'Oh Scotland! Your days must be shorter and your nights longer since you have lost the princess who was your light.' She read the poetry of Ronsard and du Bellay 'with tears and sighs . . . possessing gracious worldliness . . . a true goddess'. She became an accomplished musician on the lute and the virginals. In her white mourning clothes, after the death of her poor husband, her beauty was praised by all as breathtaking. None of this was in any way a useful preparation for ruling Scotland.

In the spring of 1561 Lord James, her half-brother, had visited Mary to apprise her of affairs in Scotland. While with her in Joinville, a Guise country house in the beautiful countryside of Champagne, he set about persuading her to return to Scotland, where he and Lethington would guide her. Contrary to his instructions he agreed to her hearing Mass strictly in private, with only herself and her household attending. However much she might fear Knox raising the country against her, there was Guise blood in her veins, with the accompanying sense of duty, and she therefore realized that she could no longer remain a dowager in France. Marriage was not imminent and so, tearfully, for she feared the sea voyage, and wished a hundred times to stay as a dowager in the warm beauty of Touraine and Poitou rather than her 'uncivilised homeland', she steeled herself for the journey to her northern kingdom. So on 14 August, accompanied by three uncles and her 'Four Maries', as well as the poet Châtelard and Pierre de Bourdielle, abbot of Brantôme, she set sail from France. Brantôme was a fanatical admirer of Mary, having described her at her wedding, as 'a hundred times more beautiful than a Goddess of Heaven'.

Unfortunately Mary witnessed the loss of a ship outside Calais harbour and took this as a bad omen for the voyage. She clung to the rail of her galley, repeating over and over, 'Adieu France! Ma chère France!' and weeping uncontrollably. She does appear to have been one of the great weepers of history.

The voyage was uneventful, that is to say, there was no intervention from Elizabeth, and with helpful following winds. Even though Mary forbade the use of the lash on the rowers her little fleet arrived in Scottish waters earlier than expected. On the night of 18 August 1561 her two galleys were in the Firth of Forth in thick fog and torrential rain. This was not the sunlit glitter of the Loire. Seeing the crew lighting lanterns, Châtelard told them to desist, since 'the Queen's eyes will light the whole sea'. By next morning things were no better, and Brantôme could not see from poop to main mast, 'a sign that we had landed in an obscure country'. Knox tells us with less lyricism, that 'scarce might any man espy another the length of two pair of boots'. He also saw an omen in the weather – 'what comfort was brought into the country with her, to wit, sorrow, dolour, darkness and all impiety'. Cannon sounded, and still in mourning dress, accompanied by her ladies-in-waiting, Mary Stewart stepped on to the soaking soil of her kingdom.

Because of her early arrival there was no one on the quayside in Leith to meet the royal party and she went first for shelter to the house of an astonished merchant, Andrew Lamb, where she dined. Finally, after an uneasy two-hour wait, an embarrassed Lord James Stewart arrived with Argyll and Erskine, and the royal party set off by horse for a hastily prepared Holyrood. Mary wept at the lack of pomp and magnificence she had enjoyed for so long in France. Brantôme tells us that she felt she had exchanged paradise for hell.

In the drenching rain on the way to Holyrood, a distance of about three miles, she was met by the rebels who had broken open the Tolbooth and saved John Gillon from hanging. She was told that all they had done had been 'in despite of the religion' and she granted them a royal pardon. This all sounds so convenient to demonstrate her grace towards her people, and especially the fickle people of Edinburgh, that one can be forgiven for suspecting a politician's hand in the event, even though there is no evidence for such an action. Today it would have been a photo-opportunity. The news was not long in reaching Knox.

The first view of her palace would have been from the top of what is now called the Abbeyhill, where the building nestled in a gentle valley beside the abbey in the royal park. Though pleasant enough, it would have been a great contrast to the palaces she had left in France. The abbey of Holyrood had suffered under the English depradations of the Rough Wooings and the lead had been stripped from the roof. The palace itself was small by French standards and Mary would have been surprised to see the windows barred and fortified. The park was largely treeless, dramatically dominated by the 800-foot-high volcanic plug of Arthur's Seat. It was also, as a royal demesne, a debtor's sanctuary, and several debtors lived semi-permanently in the park, sleeping in shelters, living off fish and what birds they could catch, supplemented by provisions brought in by relatives or friends. Shrouded by fog and rain it must have presented a grim and cheerless picture.

The geography of her private apartments has changed very little over the years. Situated on the second floor of the north-west tower, they comprised a bed-chamber and tiny private supping-room, with a 'privy' staircase from the bed-chamber giving access to the floor below. During the day Mary's bed would have been dismantled. Beyond this bed-chamber was an audience chamber as well as a private chapel. The chapel has now been lost in seventeenth-century rebuilding.

These were functional rooms, the largest being only about 50 feet by 20, and somewhat dark, facing north-west, but they were her private realm. They were a very far cry from the pomp of the Louvre. In time Mary would import canopies and hangings, tapestries and linen as well as two male embroiderers and three upholsterers from France. However, she settled in with her attendants lodged wherever they could find space elsewhere in the palace, to spend her first night in her new realm.

Bonfires of celebration blazed throughout the capital, and rest was denied her when 'a company of the most honest, with instruments of music and with musicians, gave their salutations at her chamber window. The melody, as she alleged, liked her well; and she willed the same to be continued some nights after'. Or so Knox says. Brantôme tells a different story, of wretched amateurs singing psalms out of tune and hideously disturbing any thought of sleep.

It seems unlikely that Knox slept much that night either, for Scotland was no longer ruled by a nominally Protestant council, technically under the authority of an absent Catholic queen. That queen was in her capital and in full state. Knox says that 'with great diligence the lords repaired unto her from all quarters'. Now he had seen that the parliament was willing to accept an end to Catholicism, but drew the line as yet at transferring individual riches to the reformed Church. If, as true nobility, they now gave their total loyalty to the Queen, might she prove to be a useful protector of their fortunes? And if that meant returning to the Roman Church, was that too high a price to pay? After all, Knox had said, 'the belly hath no ears', and the nobility of Scotland had a very great regard for their bellies. What if the practice of hearing Mass spread from the palace where Lord James Stewart had already agreed to Mary celebrating the ritual in the privacy of her chapel? Would the pattern of Mary Tudor be repeated? The hold of reform was fragile, with priests still in place and the bulk of the population continuing to adhere to the old Church. Knox relied heavily on the support of the nobility and had been at their head since his return, through all their campaigns of reform. But was their protest as much against the rule of the

Queen Regent as against the rule of Rome? Undoubtedly, the increasing influence of France had been deeply resented, while receiving the revenues of sequestered Church property did much to hold their loyalty. It was abundantly clear from the reception given to the *Book of Discipline* that while setting up a new religion was welcome, losing wealth to pay for it was not. And the plans for universal education had hardly seemed worthy of debate. The nobility of England had, by and large, moved from Protestant reform under Henry VIII to a restoration of Rome under his elder daughter, and back to Protestantism under Elizabeth. There were dangerous precedents for the religion of the sovereign being the religion of the people. Knox was justified in having real fears that his whole mission could be in jeopardy as the hard-won Reformation went into reverse. Being immune to her charm, he had a better grasp of the realities that Mary might impose on the greedy and fickle politicians. Elsewhere, it is no exaggeration to say that Europe watched the unfolding events in Scotland with bated breath. France and Spain both hoped for a volte-face and for Scotland to return to Rome.

Elizabeth had most to fear from this, since Mary could easily provide a focus for Catholic dissent in England, and Elizabeth dared not act overtly aginst her. But her northern border was dangerously vulnerable, and she was still well aware that Mary had never relinquished her claim to the English crown, nor had she ratified the Treaty of Edinburgh.

The only concession so far – that Mary could hear Mass in the privacy of her own chapel – had been negotiated by Lord James Stewart. He had previously pointed out that it would in any case be impossible to prevent her. So on Sunday 24 August Mary heard Mass in Holyrood, with Lord James guarding the door of the chapel, ostensibly to prevent any Scotsmen from entering. In fact he was there to protect the officiating priest from the 'godly', who, led by the master of Lindsay (son of the Lord Lindsay who had been so well pleased by Parliament's acceptance of the *Confession of Faith*), were starting to shout that 'the idolater priest should die the death'. The priest was, however, safely conveyed to his chamber while the godly gathered in the abbey to voice their complaints against the court. The court, meanwhile, along with the Guise uncles, vowed that they would immediately return to France, since living without the Mass was impossible. Knox fervently agreed with their wish to return, 'for so had Scotland been rid of an unprofitable burden of devouring strangers, and of the malediction of God that has stricken and yet will strike for idolatry'.

The English agent Randolph had attended Knox's 'thundering' sermon on the same day and clearly shared his misgivings, for all that Knox 'ruleth the roost and of him all men stand in fear'. St Giles had been packed, by citizens and nobility alike, to hear Knox's reaction to Queen Mary's arrival. His was an unequivocal diatribe condemning her as an idolator. Randolph feared 'that one day he will mar all', since Knox's unbending fervour could have a negative effect on the developing situation. Mary had no intention of renouncing her Catholic faith and regarded her arrival in Scotland as one step closer to her accession to the English throne, aided by France. Lethington and Lord James had negotiated the treaty of mutual interest with England, but were prepared to be flexible, notwithstanding they now had a sovereign who was as unbending as Knox. As we have seen, compromise was as foreign to him as it was to the Guise clan. The Scottish nobility would, as usual, try to calculate which side offered them most advantage. The people had been cheered by the sight of their new Queen, young, beautiful and given to pleasure. So the next developments would be the first moves in a complex game in which the opposing sides were playing by different rules.

And the first development was exactly what Knox feared, for on the 25th, the day after Mary had used the thin edge of the wedge and had heard her first private Mass, an Act was proclaimed forbidding any change in the religious state of Scotland at the time of her arrival, but also forbidding any molestation of her servants, 'or persons whatsomever come forth of France in her Grace's company at this time'. In other words, while there was a concession to the reformers of the maintenance of the status quo, the brotherly concession that she might hear Mass in private was now extended to her court and enshrined in law as a right. The wedge was being firmly hammered in.

But not before Arran replied to Mary's Act in a protest to the heralds that while Mary's servants would be protected from molestation, the celebration of the Mass by them was still a capital offence. This protest was probably the work of Knox himself and, certainly from the pulpit on 31 August he preached 'that one Mass was more fearful to him than if ten thousand enemies were landed in any part of the realm, of purpose to suppress the whole religion'. The 'guiders of the Court' mocked this as a very 'untimely admonition'. But Knox had diplomatic practice on his side. Charles V had forbidden the English ambassador to hold a Protestant service even in the confines of the English embassy, and Elizabeth had been adamant in forbidding the freedom to hear Mass to her various Catholic suitors.

The doors of Holyrood were now coming to resemble those of number 10 Downing Street when a Cabinet reshuffle is looming. The earl of Cassilis, previously a devout reformer and member of the congregation, attended St Giles on the Sunday but heard Mass on the Monday. Randolph writes that the rumour was that he had repented by Tuesday. The earl of Huntly had arrived with sixteen horses, and the bishops of St Andrews and Dunkeld had appeared, gowned and hatted, but now were afraid to venture from their lodging. Significantly, Bothwell was forbidden to appear on account of the smouldering rancour between him and Arran, while Lord James and Lethington were thought to be most in credit with Mary. Knox does make clear that the Lords arrived full of righteous indignation, which quickly wore off in the presence of the Queen. He quotes Robert Campbell saying to Lord Ochiltree,

> My Lord, now ye are come, and almost the last of all the rest; and I perceive by your anger that the fire-edge is not off you yet; but, I fear that after the holy water of the Court has been sprinkled on you, that you shall become as temperate as the rest. For I have been here five days, and at the first I heard every man say, 'Let us hang the priest'; but after they had been twice or thrice in the Abbey, all that fervency was past. I think there be some enchantment whereby men are bewitched.

Much has been made of Mary's personal magnetism. Carlyle calls her 'this ill-starred, young, beautiful, graceful and highly gifted human creature, planted down into so unmanageable an environment,' and so places himself immediately with Brantôme and the Mariolators. Even allowing for the fact that most royal portraits tend to flatter, she does appear to have been a beautiful woman. She was tall and athletic, with a ready wit and intelligence. She could never have existed at the French court without being an expert in the art of flattery, and would have learnt that her sexuality could make her useful friends without her having to give more than promising smiles, but like many people who have relied on beauty and wit, when she found it ineffective, she lapsed into the petulant ill-humour of the spoilt child. She had the Stewart [and Guise] belief in absolutism but lacked the political skill to use moderation when needed. Here she showed a contrast to her mother's calm consideration of what was politically expedient. Mary's later correspondence is a constant stream of whingeing complaint at petty trifles, although by then she was painfully arthritic and daily expecting the inevitable end. But here in Holyrood she was Queen in her own right and determined to win over her headstrong noblemen by exercising her seemingly hypnotic charm.

She had not, however, had the chance to expose Knox to this charm. The citizenry of Edinburgh still supported him and there had been demonstrations against Mary. As spiritual leader of Scotland and an influential voice in the council, protocol would have demanded that he pay his respects to his sovereign. But as yet he had not done so and therefore Mary took the initiative and Knox was summoned to Holyrood on 4 September 1561.

This interview took place in the morning at Holyrood Palace, either in the Queen's audience chamber or her bed-chamber on the second floor. Her bed would have been dismantled during the day. Mary was attended by two ladies-in-waiting and Lord James Stewart was also present as, it seems, a sort of referee, having a foot in both camps. Our knowledge of what took place depends entirely on the written version in Knox's *History*, and, unsurprisingly, he has the best of the argument.

Mary would have been seated throughout, with Knox, who was of medium height, a respectful distance away, so he would not, as Marian apologists have so often misstated, have 'towered accusingly over the Queen'.

Mary took the offensive immediately. She started by accusing him of raising a part of her subjects against her mother and herself, of writing a book against her, *The First Blast of the Trumpet aginst the Monstrous Regiment of Women*, and of causing sedition and slaughter in England. Moreover she had heard that he did it all by necromancy. Mary had clearly done her homework, and Knox's reputation would have been familiar to her in France. It was, we know, one of the reasons for her reluctance to make the journey, but now that she was here, in her own kingdom, Knox was a snake that had to be scotched. She certainly lacked no courage in taking the battle directly to him. He begged her patience to hear his simple answers and said,

If to teach the truth of God in sincerity, if to rebuke idolatry, and to will a people to worship God according to His word, be to raise subjects against their princes then I cannot be excused; for it hath pleased God of his mercy to make me one (amongst many) to disclose unto this realm the vanity of the Papistical religion, and the deceit, pride and tyranny of that Roman Antichrist . . . And touching that book which seemeth so highly to offend your Majesty . . . [I] am content that all the learned of the world judge of it.

He gives a faint hint that he does not consider her as one of 'the learned'. Mary then asked if he thought that she had no just authority as a sovereign, and Knox neatly side-stepped this with a two-edged justification.

> If the realm finds no inconvenience from the regiment of a woman ... [I] shall be well content to live under your Grace as Paul was to live under Nero: for in very deed, Madam, that book was written most especially against that wicked Jezebel of England ... Now, Madam, if I had intended to trouble your estate because you are a woman, I might have chosen a time more convenient for that purpose than I can do now, when your own presence is within the realm.

This has neither the diplomacy of Cecil nor the subtley of Lethington, not least becasue he equates her with Nero. He seems to feel that, having been instrumental in having the Catholic religion outlawed, he had in no way 'troubled her estate'. He flatly denies having caused any unrest in England, but affirms that

> during the time that I was there [if] any man shall be able to prove, that there was either battle, sedition or mutiny, I shall confess that I myself was the malefactor and the shedder of blood ... God so blessed my weak labours that in Berwick (where commonly before there used to be slaughter by reason of quarrels that used to arise among the soldiers) there was as great quietness all the time I remained there as there is this day in Edinburgh. And where they slander me of magic ... I have witnesses ... that I spake both against these arts and against those that use such impiety.

Mary then moved to a subject close to Knox's heart, by asking if he had not taught people 'to receive another religion than their princes can allow'. 'And how can that doctrine be of God, seeing that God commands subjects to obey their princes?'

Knox had no difficulty in answering that one, since, he argued, religious authority comes only from God and not from princes, so subjects are not bound to take religious belief from their rulers. True belief may occasion disobedience, but if the belief is a true one, then there can be no sin, otherwise Abraham would have sinned for not worshipping Isis and Osiris, and the Apostles should have followed the Roman emperors.

He concluded, 'And so, Madam, ye may perceive that subjects are not bound to the religion of their princes, albeit they are commanded to give them obedience.'

She attempted to qualify this answer and stepped on to very thin ice indeed: 'But none of these raised the sword against their princes.'

Knox brushed this aside. 'They resisted; for those that obey not the commandments that are given, in some sort resist.'

'But yet, they resisted not by the sword?'

'God, Madam, had not given unto them the power and the means.'

This was very near to a direct threat and Mary jumped on it at once. 'Think ye, that subjects having power may resist their princes?'

'If their princes exceed their bounds, Madam, and do against that wherefore they should be obeyed, it is no doubt but they may be resisted, even by power.'

Then the ice broke under Mary as Knox drew a parallel with a father, who, stricken with a frenzy, threatens to kill his own children. He is due obedience as allowed by God, but, in this case, should be restrained by any method until the frenzy passes. So there is no disobedience in resisting 'princes that would murder the children of God that are subject to them. Their blind zeal is nothing but a very mad frenzy, and therefore to take the sword from them, to bind their hands, and to cast themselves into prison, till they be brought to a more sober mind is no disobedience against princes but just obedience, because it agreeth with the will of God.'

At this point Knox tells us that Mary 'stood as it were amazed, more than the quarter of an hour. Her countenance altered, so that Lord James began to entreat her, and to demand, "What has offended you, Madam?" ' Clearly no one had ever spoken to her in this way before or engaged her in a debate with any intention of contradicting her. Up to this point in her life she would have had very little contact with affairs of state and all philosophical questions would have been answered by the Church. Direct questioning of the Queen would have been forbidden except by her closest courtiers, and they would have made very sure that everything asked of her would have been for her own pleasure or reassurance. But as she had quickly discovered, Scotland was not France. Her mother had learned the same hard lesson with much greater speed and used her learning to greater advantage than Mary ever would. Her prolonged silence tells us, not only of her shock and outrage, but her realization that she could only cope with people of Knox's intellectual calibre and fervency of belief by equalling their arguments. But her reply, when it came, was lame.

'Well then, I perceive that my subjects shall obey you and not me; and shall do what they list, and not what I command; and so must I be subject to them, and not they to me.'

This had a mixture of girlish petulance and outraged Guise majesty. Since he had rattled Mary almost to the point of temper loss, Knox could now afford to be at his calmest. He assured her that he never sought to have anyone obey him, for everyone was liable to obey God, who 'craves of Kings that they be as it were foster-fathers to His Church and commands Queens to be nurses unto His people'.

Mary had no choice but to retreat behind the bastion of her upbringing. 'Yea, but ye are not the Kirk that I will nourish. I will defend the Kirk of Rome for I think it is the true Kirk of God.'

Knox replied, 'Your will, Madam, is no reason; neither doth your thought make that Roman harlot to be the true and immaculate spouse of Jesus Christ. And wonder not, Madam, that I call Rome a harlot; for that Church is altogether polluted with all kind of spiritual fornication, as well in doctrine as in manners.'

'My conscience is not so.'

'Conscience, Madam, requires knowledge; and I fear that right knowledge ye have none.'

'But I have both read and heard.'

'So, Madam, did the Jews that crucified Jesus Christ . . . Have ye heard any teach but such as the Pope and his Cardinals have allowed? And ye may be assured that such will speak nothing to offend their own estate.'

'Ye interpret the Scriptures in one manner, and they interpret in another. Whom shall I believe? And who shall be judge?'

Knox answered her by telling her that the 'word of God is plain in the self', and restates the principles of the *Confession of Faith* that the Mass is man-made and therefore idolatrous. 'Now, doth not the word of God plainly assure us that Christ Jesus neither said, nor yet commanded Mass to be said at his Last Supper, seeing that no such thing as their Mass is made mention of in the whole Scriptures?'

At this Mary admitted that Knox had had the better of the argument, but that if her authorities were present they could answer him. But Knox assured her that he would be glad to argue the matter to a conclusion with the best papistical authorities. Mary replied that he may get the chance sooner than he thinks, and Knox turned the point by saying that if it ever happened in his lifetime it would, indeed, be sooner than he thought since ignorant papists could not patiently reason, and were not able to sustain an argument except by fire and sword. Much to her relief, Mary was at this point called in to dinner and Knox prayed to God that she would be as blessed in the commonwealth of Scotland as ever was Deborah in the commonwealth of Israel. Such a blessing after such an interview cannot have improved her appetite.

Knox admits that he has left us with an edited version of this 'long Conference' in his *History*, but since Mary would have dined at noon and the meeting would probably have started after half-past nine it cannot, in reality, have been over-long. But Knox, who would have been standing throughout, clearly found it so. More than physical discomfort would have been the conflict of intellects between them. Here was a young girl, raised as a devout Catholic, and totally unused to debate, being challenged by a middle-aged cleric. His use of logic, backed by copious scriptural instances, would have been completely alien to her. And her simple unshakeable belief, based entirely on faith without any recourse to theological reason, would have seemed equally bizarre to Knox. Her long silences were in all probability a product of bafflement both at the often syllogistic arguments and the fact that her very sovereignty was a matter for debate. Knox, being used to nimbler minds and subtler argument, presumed an ulterior motive. 'If there be not in her a proud mind, a crafty wit, and an indurate heart against God and His truth, my judgement faileth me.'

Randolph's account of the meeting was that

> Mr Knox spoke unto the Queen and knocked so hastily upon her heart that he made her weep. As you well know there be [some] of that sex that will do that as well for anger as for grief. She willed him to use more meekness in his sermons. The bruit that he has talked with her makes the Papists doubt what will become of the world and they like not that I resort so often to the Court. She wishes to enrich her crown with Abbey lands, which, if she do, what shall there lack in her, saving a good husband, to lead a happy life.

Not possessing her mother's political intelligence and the skill to *reculer pour mieux sauter* Mary attempted to achieve her ends simply by a determined charm fuelled by instinct. It was a strategy that would lead her, twenty-seven years later, to the axe in Fotheringhay Castle, but at the moment she was a young Queen with a kingdom to explore. She had appointed a privy council, including the troublesome earl of Bothwell, and

Professor Rait in his *Parliaments of Scotland* tells us that 'with the return of Queen Mary Parliament relapsed into its old position as a mere court of registration'. Most of the Queen's French attendants left for home with gold chains as rewards. An Edinburgh goldsmith, James Mossman, was paid £29.10s for making them, while his servants got 20 shillings in 'drink-money'. We will meet Mossman again. Mary paid off her ships, and having to a certain extent severed her links with her past, she set out to show herself to her new kingdom.

She visited Linlithgow, Stirling, Perth, Dundee and Saint Andrews, all of which she 'polluted with her idolatry'. Knox also tells us that, 'fire very commonly followed her in that journey', a comment that is doubtless meant to lead us to believe that heretics went screaming to the stake in Mary's train. There is no evidence whatsoever for this accusation. Randolph gives us a truer picture: while Mary was asleep at Stirling, her candle set the hangings of her bed on fire – swiftly extinguished with much nocturnal fluster. The ordinary populace would have greatly enjoyed the spectacle of the young, glamorous and controversial Queen riding with her glittering entourage through the streets, and the burgesses also used the opportunity to pledge loyalty to their new monarch with lavish offerings, such as a golden heart at Dundee. Extravagant masques and pageants littered the route, too, often, surprisingly, openly supporting the Reformation. During one progress she fell sick and was carried from her horse to her lodging. She was, 'troubled with such sudden passion after any great unkindness or grief of mind'. There was adoration of her beauty but by no means wholehearted support for her religion, as she used the indulgence gained from Lord James to hear Mass as she travelled throughout Scotland. Knox accuses the French of enriching themselves on this progress, and although many of her train had already left for France, the remark shows that Mary was still regarded as her mother's daughter – the likelihood of a French seizure of Scottish sovereignty was never far from people's minds. Randolph also reports that when she spent the night as a guest of the earl of Rothes, 'it is said that he lost both plate and something else easy to be conveyed, and it is true that where they have been they paid little for their meat'.

She returned to Edinburgh on 29 July, and on 2 August she rode out of Holyrood to take formal possession of her capital and its castle. She was met at the entrance to the city by 'five black slaves, magnificently appar-elled' and twelve of the chief citizens carried a canopy over her head.

Accompanied by most of the nobility of Scotland except for the duke and his son Arran, 'she rode up the castle bank to the castle and dined therein; and when she had dined at 12 o'clock, her highness came forth of the said castle toward the said borough at which [moment] the artillery shot vehemently.' After this *feu de joie* came the inevitable pageants at the butter and milk trons (market places). During the first of these, with fountains running with wine, a boy emerged from a Globe and presented her with the keys (presumably of the city) and a Bible and psalter. 'She began to frown: [but] for shame she could not refuse it'. Indeed at one of the pageants it had been planned that there should be a comic parody of the Mass, with the burning of the priest, but thanks to the intercession of the Catholic earl of Huntly this was cancelled. One of these pageants took place at the Butter Cross, some hundred yards from Knox's own window in his new manse. He would have found it impossible to keep his infant sons from watching the glittering spectacle below, as the most glamorous Catholic in Scotland was cheered to the echo by the citizens of Edinburgh. Even the officially contrived reminder that this was nominally a Protestant country may well have passed unnoticed. It is difficult to imagine how Knox would have explained the perfidy of the heroine of the day to his sons.

As a background to the glamour and glitter of the progress the magistrates of Edinburgh enacted their time-honoured custom of having the statutes of the city read in public. They commanded that all 'fornicators, noted drunkards, mass-mongers, obstinate papists that corrupted the people, such as priests, friars, monks and others of that sort' should leave the town within forty-eight hours. Those who disobeyed this would be branded on the cheek and paraded in a cart. Mary was apparently furious at this desecration of her religion in her own capital city and immediately commanded that the provost and bailies of the city should give themselves up to imprisonment in the Tolbooth and new elections held. Knox implies that Lord James Stewart and Lethington were behind Mary's actions. There are no accounts of any punishment being meted out to the provost and bailies, but they were replaced on 8 October.

At the end of the week, Knox wrote to Cecil with a summary of the general situation.

Men delighting to swim betwixt two waters, have often complained upon my severity . . . But I do fear, that that which men term leniency and dulceness [sweetness of nature], do often bring upon themselves and others most fearful destruction, than yet hath ensued the vehemency of any preacher within this realm . . . This I write from the dolour of heart. Some of no small estimation have said, with open mouth, the Queen neither is, [nor] neither shall be of our opinion, and . . . the Cardinal's lessons are so deeply printed in her heart, that the substance and quality are like to perish together. I would be glad to be deceived, but I fear I shall not. In communication with her, I espied such craft as I have not found in such an age. Since then the Court has been dead to me and me to it.

There is no doubt that Knox now felt that all his work since he first preached during the siege of St Andrews was being undone and that the Reformation was in danger of decline. He was recently widowed, his testament of democracy in the *Book of Discipline* was being watered down by pragmatism, and the honour shown to him by the city of Edinburgh must have seemed hollow. In despair he had written to Mrs Lock a few days before his letter to Cecil:

The permission of that odious idol, the Mass, by such as have professed themselves enemies to the same doth hourly threaten a sudden plague. I thirst to change this earthly tabernacle, before that my wretched heart should be assaulted with any new dolours.

I fear this my long rest shall not continue . . . We have discharged our consciences, but remedy there appeareth none, unless we would arm the hands of the people in whom abideth yet a spark of God's fear. Our nobility . . . can well enough abide the Queen to have her Mass, in her own chapel if she like. I have finished open preaching the Gospel of Saint John, saving only one chapter. Oft have I craved the miseries of my days to end with the same; for now, sister, I seek for rest . . . My only comfort is, mercifully, with an assured expectation for the end of such miserable corruption. My mother saluteth you . . . Our Queen weareth the doole [French 'deuil', or mourning] but she can dance daily, doole and all.

This is Knox at his very lowest, and he writes in similar tone to Calvin. 'I never before felt how weighty and difficult a matter it is to contend against hypocrisy under the disguise of piety . . . my strength daily diminishes.'

On Sunday 14th, 'her Grace's devout chaplains' had set about singing High Mass in Mary's chapel, but Argyll and Lord James, 'so disturbed the choir that some, both priests and clerks left their places with broken heads and bloody ears'. Randolph thought it good sport for those that beheld it. Meanwhile Knox preached that it was the duty of all magistrates to uphold a good reformed commonwealth. Mary's rumour machine spread it about that Lord James seeks 'too much his own advancement which hitherto little appears for anything he ever received worth one groat', while Lethington is too 'politique'. Randolph comments, 'take these two out of Scotland and those that love their country shall soon feel the want of them!' Yet he was, as a good spy should be, so trusted that he sat with her in the council chamber while she was sewing some work or other and talked together in the garden of the palace. However, his good reports of her cut no ice with Knox, who still felt that 'many men are deceived in this woman'. Knox also felt that *posteriora erunt pejora primis* (Later things will be worse than first things). But Randolph's admiration for Knox was similarly unshaken. 'His severity keeps us in marvellous order; I commend better the success of his doings and preachings than the manner thereof, though I acknowledge his doctrine to be sound.' Three days later Randolph tells Cecil that his father has died, his legacies in England have to be claimed, and reminds Cecil of the fact that he has not seen his now widowed mother for eight years, so could he have a leave of absence? The plea was ignored.

Lethington had written to Cecil stressing Mary's continued friendship for Elizabeth, even though she was still reluctant to ratify the Treaty of Edinburgh. He also starts subtly to attack Knox's position by suggesting that although he is incapable of diplomacy, Knox was still a man of great influence in secular affairs and should be watched closely.

> You know the vehemence of Mr Knox's spirit, which cannot be bridled; and doth sometimes utter such sentences as can not easily be digested by a weak stomach. I would wish he would deal with her more gently, being a young Princess unpersuaded, for this I am accounted to be politic, but surely in her comporting with him she doth declare a wisdom far exceeding her age. God grant her the assistance of His Spirit. Surely I see in her a good towardness, and think the Queen your sovereign shall be able to do much with her in religion, if they ever enter in a good familiarity.

The Queen heard Mass for All Saints Day and in a marginal note in his *History* Knox comments, 'The Devil getting entry with his finger will shoot forth his whole arm.' But doubts were beginning to be heard as to 'whether that subjects might put to their hand to suppress the idolatry of their Prince'.

In the house of the register clerk, Sir James McGill, a meeting took place with Lord James, Secretary Lethington, the earl of Morton and others, arguing that subjects could not lawfully prevent the Queen from hearing Mass. Knox, along with John Row and other ministers, naturally opposed this argument. Knox offered to write to Calvin for a ruling, even although he had asked the same question in a letter to Calvin a week earlier. Lethington insisted that he himself should write the letter, since the wording of the question could influence the answer. As the debate continued, 'neither could reason nor threatening move the affections of such as were creeping in credit. And so did the votes of the lords prevail against the ministers.' Knox comments, 'that her liberty should be their thraldom ere it was long'.

The credit that some lords were creeping into was demonstrated vividly when Lord James was made lord lieutenant of the borders and set about a swift campaign to subdue that lawless region. In spite of the usual bribes he hanged over twenty and imprisoned twice that number before reaching an agreement with his English counterpart, Lord Grey of Wilton, for, 'good rule to be kept upon both the Borders'.

The capital now had all the ingredients for a major explosion. The archbishop of St Andrews had arrived with a retinue of eighty horsemen, making a detour half a mile out of his way to parade his strength along the length of the high street, and the bishop of Ross was made a privy councillor.

Mary demonstrated her ability to manipulate events to her own advantage on 16 November by 'taking a fray [fright] in her bed as if horsemen had been in the close and the palace had been enclosed about'. No evidence was ever found for such an intrusion, as Randolph, who thought that the entire affair had been engineered by Mary herself, asked, 'What doth your honour think of the poor damsels that were left alone whilst others sought corners to put their heads in? They come to themselves – take counsel what to do – every man takes his armour – watch appointed, scouts put forth, nothing seen or heard!' Suspicion was diverted to the earl of Arran as coming with 'a stark company' to seize the Queen. The 'hurlyburly' had the makings of a dangerous situation for 'the town is packed and pestered with papists, though I am sure there is not one of them who will die for Christ, yet to save their Queen from stealing they would not stick to strike a stroke or two'. The long term result was, however, that from now on Mary was provided with a personal bodyguard of twelve halberdiers that she shortly intended to double.

Possibly she had reason on her side, for Edinburgh was still a dangerous city. William Balfour, described as an 'in-dweller' in Leith, had appeared under threat of £1,000 forfeit to answer three charges. The previous November he had 'raised a tumult' in Lord Invernethie's place, then interrupted the examination of a minister, John Cairns, in St Giles. He had 'laid his hand on his weapons' on that occasion, but had not been arrested. Finally on 10 December, 'in the presence of a great multitude, he had interrupted a celebration of the Lord's Supper in the Tolbooth with an outburst, "Is that your communion? The devil burst me if ever it comes into my belly! And the devil burst them in whose belly it comes for it is a very devil!"' This time he was arrested as 'a common blasphemer of God and his Holy Evangel and for a seditious person'.

Religious hooliganism apart, there were still plenty of the secular sort, even among the nobility. Bothwell, along with Lord John Stewart, Lord James's brother, and Mary's uncle René d'Elbeuf, had manage to gain entry to the house of Alison Craik, a merchant's daughter, 'a good handsome wench' and reputedly Arran's 'hoor'. What took place we do not know – perhaps Alison had two friends as a welcoming party for the three noblemen – but when they returned on the following night the noble trio were refused admission. Arran called out his Hamilton supporters, d'Elbeuf seized a halberd and claimed that ten men could not restrain him although he was nearly a mile away by now, safely inside the royal palace. The result was a riot, with the town guard called out and ambassador Randolph nervously noting, 'I thought it as much wisdom for me to behold them out of a window as to be in their company.' Arran and Bothwell had clearly not made up their differences, and although Mary declared herself willing to try to mend the controversy, nothing was done for the moment. However Bothwell was, with his friends, temporarily exiled from Edinburgh.

Mary continued to annoy Knox with her hypocrisy, dressing herself in solemnity as a mourning widow, while secretly dancing and decrying Scotland for its gravity after the gaiety of French court life. Her Scottish noble dancing partners did not follow her lead and wear mourning for their Queen's husband. Mary's decrying of Scotland is totally unauthenticated but declared by Knox to be the actual truth, while her avowals of love for her native land were false. Declaring the apparent truth to be a lie, while the real truth is a secret that would reveal an altogether different aspect – a secret known to the propagandist alone and therefore unprovable – is a well-tried tactic and Knox has no shame in using it. Since Mary is so often accused of holding excessive balls and other celebrations, in contrast to her ailing and embattled mother, it should be remembered that she was a high-spirited nineteen-year-old at last freed from governesses and uncles. Her apartments at Holyrood were small by her previous standards, as was her circle of close friends, but at least she could create a splash of colour to contrast with the gloom outside.

The gravity of Scotland displayed its full weight in December, when the General Assembly met. This would have been the third assembly, but for some reason, the *Booke of the Universal Kirk* does not record its meeting. This was, however, the first General Assembly of Mary's reign and would require several of the main characters either to nail their colours to the mast of reform or be seen as aligned with the Queen's party. Knox tells us that the rulers of the court began to draw themselves apart from their brethren and 'to stir and begrudge that anything should be consulted upon without their advice . . . The courtiers drew unto them some of the lords, who would not convene with their brethren . . . but kept them in the Abbey. The principal commissioners of the churches, the superintendents, and some ministers passed into them where they convened in the abbot's lodging.' The lords complained that the ministers acted in secret; they denied this and, in their turn, accused the lords, whom Knox calls the 'flatterers of the Queen', of not honouring the pledges they gave in subscribing to the *Book of Discipline*.

Some of the lords then denied they had ever heard of the *Book of Discipline*, and questioned whether such assemblies were lawful, since the Queen would gladly have them all disbanded. If Knox at St Andrews had 'struck at the very root of Papism', this struck at the root of the Reformation, and in very short order the debate distilled itself into a dispute between Knox and Lethington. 'The reasoning was sharp and quick on either part.' The Queen's faction asserted that it was suspicious to princes that subjects should assemble themselves and keep conventions without the knowledge of the sovereign. Knox countered that since the Queen knew very well that there was a reformed Church in Scotland and what its times of convocation for an assembly were, they could hardly be accused of meeting secretly. Lethington rapidly shifted ground, admitting that the Queen knew all this full well, but the question was whether or not she allowed it. The reply was that if the liberty of the Church depended on the Queen's allowance, all assemblies and the public preaching of the Evangel would be forbidden. Without assemblies the judgement of the many could not concur to correct the errors of a few. This point seemed well taken, even by the nobility, and it was suggested to the Queen's party that she might send observers to hear the deliberations of the assembly. The first round seemed to have gone to Knox.

Next the assembly asked if the Queen would ratify the *Book of Discipline*. This was treated with derision, and Lethington asked how many who had subscribed to the *Book* would be bound by it.

'All the godly' he was told.

'Will the Duke [of Chatelherault]?' asked Lethington.

'If he will not', answered Andrew Stewart of Ochiltree, 'I would that he were scraped out, not only of that book, but of our number and company. For to what purpose shall labours be taken to put the Kirk in order, and to what end shall men subscribe, and then never mean to keep word of that which they promise?'

'Many subscribed there *in fide parentum*, as the bairns are baptised,' answered Lethington.

'That book was read in public audience,' said Knox, 'and by the space of divers days the heads thereof were reasoned, as all that here sit know well enough, and ye yourself cannot deny; so that no man was required to subscribe that which he understood not'.

Lethington crushed this: 'Stand content that Book will not be obtained'.

Lethington had taken the gloves off and was now using naked power. Knox was capable only of a prayer: 'Let God require the lack this poor commonwealth shall have of the things therein contained, from the hands of such as stop the same.' He knew he had lost this round, and he must have realized that there was no possibility of Mary accepting the strictures of the *Book*, even with the support of the nobility, which itself was now unlikely. The total support he had hoped for was now denied him, a move that forced him to attack piecemeal, requiring the suppression of idolatry and, most importantly, the provision of stipends for ministers, 'for unto that time the most part of the ministers had lived upon the benevolence of men'. The greater part of the wealth of the Church was still in the hands of the Catholic clergy, and lay nobles held rich endowments. The immediate threat from the assembly was that they would withhold all revenue distribution until a settlement could be found, and as usual the appeal to the pocket was more potent than the appeal to the head. Also, if the threat to withhold money was carried out in the Queen's name, it could be said that she was affecting the state of religion as she had found it. 'This somewhat

The ruins of St Andrews Cathedral.
Knox preached below the triple window

The site of Knox's burial. It is an anonymous square of yellow paint
in a car park

William Maitland of Lethington by the 11th Earl of Buchan after an unknown artist. Nicknamed 'Michael Wylie, Scotland's Machiavelli', the most brilliant diplomat in Scotland, whose expediency brought him into conflict with Knox's faith. Their debates were evenly matched, but Lethington could, and did, manipulate raw political power

James Stuart, Earl of Moray by Hugh Munro after an unknown artist. (Often spelt Stewart.) An illegitimate son of James V, he was therefore half-brother to Mary, Queen of Scots. As Lord James Stewart he was a strong supporter of Knox and the Protestant reformers. He acted as Mary's chief minister and she created him first, Earl of Mar, then, Earl of Moray. He opposed her marriage to Darnley and defeated the Queen's forces at Langside. He was shot by the Hamilton faction in 1570

George Wishart, by an unknown artist. This reformer and martyr brought systems of continental thinking to Scotland. Knox first met him after an assassination attempt and became his bodyguard and sword carrier. He had a profound influence on Knox's thinking and actions, but was burnt at the stake in St Andrews in 1546

St Andrews Castle. Cardinal Beaton would have watched Wishart's execution from the lower of the two windows

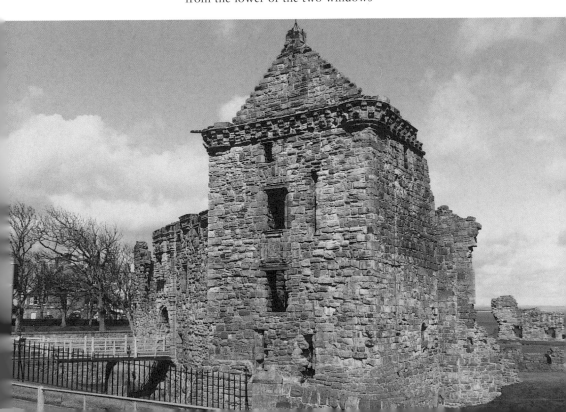

✳✳✳✳

X

O

THE FIRST AND

SECOND BOOKE OF DISCIPLINE.

Together with some

ACTS OF THE GENERALL ASSEMBLIES,

Clearing and confirming the same : And

AN ACT OF PARLIAMENT.

EXOD. 25. 9.
According to all that I shew thee, after the paterne of the Tabernacle, and the paterne of all the instruments therof, even so shall yee make it.

This book of Disciplin was penned anno · 1560·

Printed Anno 1 6 2 1.

Title page of the first and second *Book of Discipline*. Although nominally written by a committee, the first book encapsulated Knox's spiritual and political thinking. Not publicly published until 1621 this edition included Andrew Melville's additional book. Had the original been put fully into action there would have been progress in education and social security well in advance of Scotland's current legislation moved the Queen's flatterers . . . and so began they to practise how they should please the Queen and yet seem somewhat to satisfy the faithful.'

This was a crucial point of acceptance for the reformers, since the Catholic clerical establishment was still in place, although forbidden to say Mass or to preach. The nobility held much of the wealth – Lord James possessed the holdings of St Andrews – and the poorest constituents of the equation were the ministers of the newly established Church. Henry VIII and his chancellor Cromwell had seized the wealth of the English Church before they reformed the religion, but Scotland had taken a more difficult, if more spiritually correct, route. There was no possible way that would be painless for the nobility, but there was a solution which allowed them to save face, and which, if still painful, was at least acceptable. No subvention had yet been made by the reformers to the Queen, since she was implacably opposed to all that they stood for, but gaining favour of one's sovereign was of supreme importance for the aristocracy. It was thus decided that one third of all ecclesiastical benefices should be awarded to Mary who would then remit half of these sums to paying the ministry of the reformed Kirk. The remaining two-thirds would continue to be employed by the current holders. Knox may have felt that Mary had no right to claim any part of these revenues, but it is more extraordinary that a Catholic monarch should agree to be the redistributor of revenues from her, for the moment, persecuted Church to the Church of her persecutors. But two advantages would have been apparent to her. She was attempting to recreate at Holyrood the glitter that had been normal for her court at Fontainebleau, and the payments of her widow's dowry from France were intermittent at best. Secondly, it brought her some peace and gave a sign of compromise towards reform.

And so the Acts were passed that enshrined the taxation of the 'thirds' in law. Knox had in the *Book of Discipline* asked for all the revenues to found the new equality, but now was to receive just one sixth. From the pulpit of St Giles he made his feelings clear:

> If the end of this order, pretended to be taken for the sustenance of ministers, be happy, my judgement fails me; for I am assured that the Spirit of God is not the author of it; for, first, I see two parts freely given to the Devil, and the third must be divided between God and the Devil: well, bear witness to me, that this day I say it, or it be long that the Devil shall have three parts of the third; and judge you then what God's portion shall be.

As with all political compromises, neither party was happy. Lethington reported the opposing view that, 'The ministers being satisfied, the Queen will not get at the year's end to buy a new pair of shoes.' Antonia Fraser tells us that in 1560 Mary's royal revenues were in the region of £10,000 sterling, as opposed to Elizabeth's £200,000! On 10 August 1562 Mary would write to the superintendent of finances in France complaining that her pensions had not been paid.

In his *History* Knox calls this 'an unpleasing matter' for the assembly, with everyone complaining of poverty. On the part of the ministers, Knox pointed out that they required books, peace to study and travel while edifying the Kirk of Christ – an echo of his own previously unachieved ambitions – and yet had no other income but their stipends. The lords and others, by contrast, had worldly business and could augment their incomes by 'some other industry'. Appeals were met with, 'The Queen can spare no greater sums.' Knox complained bitterly:

> O happy servants of the Devil, and miserable servants of Jesus Christ, if that after this life there were not hell and heaven. For to the servants of the devil, to your dumb dogs and horned bishops, to one of these idle bellies (I say) ten thousand was not enough; But to the servants of Christ that painfully preach his evangel, a thousand pound; how can that be sustained?

Lethington wondered if ever there was a minister that gave thanks to God for the Queen's liberality or gave her 'grand-mercies'. He was rebutted anonymously by one who said that anything given freely by the Queen should be acknowledged. But the ministers had received nothing freely, and no previous monarch had been awarded anything. The present Queen was no more entitled to these revenues than those who had divided Christ's raiment at his crucifixion. And at least they waited until He was dead, while Mary was taking His revenue while His message was still being preached. The papists had done well by their flatteries, but the poor preachers would not flatter 'for feeding of their bellies'. Knox tells us that these words were judged proud and intolerable, and engendered no small displeasure to the speaker. But while maintaining the speaker's anonymity through a third person, there can be little doubt that it was the voice of Knox that spoke. It was an attempt to put forward a strong personal view while still maintaining that he was writing an objective history.

Knox could still count on his popularity in Edinburgh, for, when he was granted permission to leave a substitute in St Giles while absent on business, the town council begged him 'to hasten home that the Kirk be not desolate'.

On a similarly happy note, Knox had officiated at the marriage of Lord James to Agnes Keith, daughter of William, earl of Marischal. It was a glittering occasion, Lord James having been created the earl of Mar on the previous night, before the entire nobility of Scotland. Now the same nobility, except, of course, for the Queen, crowded St Giles to hear Knox preach. Knox exhorted the couple to behave moderately in all things, and acknowledged the good that Lord James had done for the comfort of the Kirk of God. The wedding party then moved to Holyrood Palace for a banquet given by the Queen for everyone, though this time, of course, excepting Knox. At Holyrood Mary awarded ten knighthoods and there were fireworks and displays of equestrianism. Randolph notes that Mary drank Elizabeth's health from a gold cup that she later gave to Randolph as a gift. This from a Queen who might not afford a pair of shoes in future. Knox was appalled, with many of the godly, at the vanity of the masqueing and banqueting. But the event serves to illustrate the polarity that had already taken place, with Knox all-powerful spiritually in St Giles, while Mary sat discontentedly in the palace, ruling secularly in royal style. The question was who could wrest most power away from the other.

Randolph was still keeping Cecil well informed of how, as far as the assembly was concerned, 'Our Papists greatly mistrust the meeting'. Knox, he also conveyed, was still more vehement than discreet or learned, 'which I heartily lament'. There was also a slight rumour that Mary was being advised by her uncle, the cardinal of Lorraine, to convert to the Anglican faith as a precursor to greater friendship with Elizabeth. This rumour had been received with horror by the reformers since it would have meant that the nascent Kirk would have been strangled at birth. Knox had preached against the Anglican rite, 'on Sunday last, [he] gave the cross and the candle such a wipe [he so declaimed against the ritual objects], that as wise and as learned as himself wished him to have held his peace,' but then made ample amends with a vehement prayer for greater amity with England.

Mary's reliance on support from France suffered a severe setback on 1 March, when a barn at Vassy in the Champagne region, filled with worshipping Huguenots, was burnt down and any escaping worshippers were massacred by troops of the duke of Guise. This was sufficient spark for Louis de Condé to start what would be the first of France's seven wars of religion. Scottish volunteers besieged Randolph to arrange for passage to France, and about a thousand volunteers did fight for Condé in a campaign that seemed to carry all before it in the spring of 1562. This also meant that all expressions of friendship between Mary and Elizabeth ceased, at least until the summer when Cecil and Lethington set about arranging a meeting between the two queens. It was a meeting for which Mary was keener than her cousin. Back in January Lethington had joked with Cecil, 'Let us not weary to push forward till they have met, when I doubt not that one of them shall govern the other, that they shall thereafter need no mediators, then will I say, "*Nunc dimittis servum tuum Domine!*" ' (In the gospel of Luke, Chapter 2, the aged Simeon sees the baby Jesus, and exclaims, 'Lord, now lettest thou thy servant depart in peace'.) Lethington does not hazard a guess as to who would govern the other.

A glimmer of prudence among Mary's squabbling nobles came when Knox was approached by an old friend, James Barron. Barron was a magistrate and commissioner to the General Assembly; and was also the widower of Elizabeth Adamson, whom Knox had comforted in 1555 and had written to from Lyon. On this occasion, Barron came as an ambassador for the earl of Bothwell, who wished to end the feud between himself and Arran. The two hot-heads had exchanged challenges to a duel in 1560, and Bothwell had caused a riot when trying to usurp Arran in the favours of Alison Craik, much to the latter's delight. It is a mark of the esteem in which Knox was held, even by such aristocratic egos, that his impartiality would be called upon. Knox and Bothwell met at Barron's house and Bothwell immediately repented of his previous affiliation with the Queen Regent, and of his various other feuds. With refreshing candour he gave a supplementary assurance that if the feud could be patched up he could live without his bodyguard of 'wicked and unprofitable men'. Knox declared his family's loyalty to the house of Hepburn and, with amazing tact for Knox, avoided all mention of Bothwell's father's perfidy in devising the arrest of George Wishart. Knox was delighted that Bothwell was embracing peace and the reformed Church, and at a second meeting it was agreed that Knox would arrange an encounter with Arran. Before that could happen, however, Bothwell attacked Cockburn of Ormiston and his family, friends of Knox, when they were out hunting and unsuccessfully attempted their capture for ransom. Bothwell apologized for this lapse and the warring pair shook hands publicly at Arran's father's town house, and they were seen in public together at St Giles. The two families had, in the best traditions of the Mafia, ended the feud.

But the story did not end there. On the Friday after the conciliatory visit to St Giles Arran came with two friends, Richard Strang, an advocate, and Alexander Guthrie, the town clerk, to interrupt Knox at his house, where he was making notes from his past sermon. 'I am treasonably betrayed,' declared Arran. He told the amazed Knox that Bothwell had come to him and said, 'I know that you are the man most hated of any man in Scotland with the Queen . . . I know this to be true upon such conferences as I have had with the Queen's self and other, therefore it stands you upon to see to your self. If you will follow my counsel and give me credit, I have an easy way to remedy the whole, that is, to put the Queen into your hands and take away your chief enemies the earl of Mar and Secretary Lethington.'

It was concluded between them that they should ride together to Falkland Palace in Fife, where the Queen was in residence with Lethington and Mar. The noblemen would be killed, the Queen should be taken by force and brought to Chatelherault's castle at Dumbarton. There a forced marriage with Arran would take place. Arran confessed his love for the Queen, but feared that Bothwell was trying to implicate him in a false plot, which he, Bothwell, would then reveal, condemning Arran as the instigator.

Knox was highly skilled in dealing with female parishioners who had doubts about their faith, but here was a clearly stark mad aristocrat spinning tales of treason in front of witnesses. His astonishment must have been complete. He asked first if Arran had consented to any part of the treason and was told that Arran had said 'nay' to it all. Knox then declared that Bothwell could not accuse you of 'that which he had devised, and whereto you would not consent'. Knox clearly had no understanding of Bothwell, and Arran went on, 'You understand not what treason is used against me: it is treason to conceal treason'. Knox counselled Arran to wait, depending on his own innocence, and see what happened next, probably because Knox could supply no immediate answer to his dilemma. Arran went to Kinneil House, his father's country mansion near Edinburgh, and told the tale again to his father. Randolph reported that 'this put the Duke in such a rage that he would have slain his son,' but instead he, sensibly, locked him up. From his room, now clearly totally demented, he then wrote a letter in cipher for Mar and smuggled it via a servant to Randolph, who was close to Mar. Randolph received and read it while hunting with Mary, and immediately told her of the news. The abbot of Kilwinning promptly appeared with the news that Arran had escaped, 'out of his chamber with cords made of the sheets of his bed, and no man wist where he had become'. But Knox had informed Mar of Arran's dangerous madness, 'stricken with frenzy', and with a speed untypical of the Stewarts, he managed to arrest Bothwell, Arran and the abbot, who, as a Hamilton, was related to Arran, and have them locked up in Edinburgh Castle. Arran's love for Mary had now grown into sexual fantasies – he believed she was lying beside him in his bed. Bothwell, in his typical swashbuckling manner, escaped to his grim fastness of Hermitage Castle at Liddesdale on the English border. Arran, meanwhile, was kept in all the rigour of the harsh treatment thought suitable for lunatics. After a few years he was released, a gibbering maniac, into the care of his family. The care must have been considerable since the lunatic earl lived until 1606.

Arran's madness and removal from the scene also removed Knox's main champion at court. Lethington and Mar were now devotedly carrying out royal wishes, so, with parliament reduced to a cipher, the pulpit of St Giles and the meetings of the General Assembly had become his chief areas of influence. Mary, having circumvented the non-existent plot of Arran's, was still keen to arrange a meeting with Elizabeth, but the growing success of the Catholic powers in France meant that the meeting was postponed indefinitely by Elizabeth 'for divers weighty and great considerations'. There was no need to give any detail.

A sign of the fragility of the peace in Scotland was seen when Mar made an incursion into the border country and arrested fifty thieves. Seventeen were drowned, owing to the lack of suitable trees to hang them from, others were executed in Jedburgh and the principal offenders were hanged on the Borough Muir in Edinburgh.

It may have been Knox's presence in Dieppe in 1559 that had caused an increase in piety, but in Edinburgh in 1562 his presence seems to have had no such effect. Indeed, in May the council had to order the digging of a deeper hole in the Nor' Loch for the 'dipping of fornicators', and the increase in this activity led, by November, to threatening them with bread and water in the 'iron-house', banishment from the city, or scourging at 'the cart's arse'.

The General Assembly met on 29 June. There was concern over the 'good order to be kept in the Church, for the Papists and the idolatry of the Queen began to trouble the former good order'. Also acts were made against some ministers who had left the Church for 'other vocations more profitable to the belly'. John Sharp is singled out for mention by Knox. In fact, he took up the law as an advocate, eventually being knighted by King James in 1604. But far and above all this, the assembly made a supplication to the Queen, setting out the principal headings of the *Book of Discipline* and demanding her endorsement of them. Although the assembly had a love for tranquillity 'nothing be more odious to them than tumults and domestic discord, yet will men attempt the uttermost, before that in their own eyes they behold that house of God demolished, which with travail and danger God hath within this realm erected by them'. The 'monsieurs of the court and Secretary Lethington above others' could not abide such hard speaking. The assembly asked what they should do, and Lethington simply answered, 'complain'.

'To whom?'

'To the Queen's Majesty.'

'How long shall we do so?'

'Till you get remedy,' said the Justice Clerk.

'If the sheep shall complain to the wolf, that the wolves and whelps have devoured their lambs, the complainer may stand in danger; but the offender, we fear, shall have liberty to hunt after his prey.'

'Such comparisons,' said Lethington, 'are very unsavoury; for I am assured that the Queen will neither erect, nor maintain Papistry.'

'Let your assurance serve yourself, for it cannot assure us, for her manifest proceedings speak the contrary.'

The supplication was never going to get past Lethington in its present form, and the assembly decided to allow him to rewrite it in a gentler manner while still maintaining the substance. His editing was so severe that when it was presented to the Queen, she said, 'Here are many fair words, I cannot tell what the hearts are.' Sadly Knox bemoans that 'for our painted oratory, we were termed the next name to flatterers and dissemblers'.

In the next month Mary greeted an unexpected visitor whose activities in Scotland find a parallel with Knox's life as an exile in Europe. The Council of Trent was holding its third session to right some of the perceived wrongs of the Church as part of the Counter-Reformation, and unsurprisingly there were no Scottish bishops in attendance. Pope Pius IV set about to try and alter this by sending a nuncio to appeal directly to Mary. So Father Nicholas de Gouda, a Jesuit, was called to Louvain where he received apostolic letters for Mary, formally summoning the Scottish bishops to the Council of Trent. At Louvain he met Edmund Hay and William Crichton, both Scottish priests. Crichton went ahead to Scotland while de Gouda and Hay went to Antwerp where they took boat for Scotland accompanied by 'suspicious and heretical' fellow passengers. On arrival Hay took de Gouda to the private house of a kinswoman in Leith and sent to the Queen asking for an appointment, as well as asking for advice on effective disguises.

This secrecy gives us an excellent picture of the sort of conditions under which Knox would have travelled in Europe. Mary replied that the meeting would have to be in private, since her council consisted entirely of 'heretics and enemies of the Apostolic See'. Thanks to spies and careless gossip the arrival of a nuncio was soon common knowledge – Randolph reported it, along with Knox's reaction, to Cecil on 26 June.

The report de Gouda delivered to the Pope on the completion of his mission in Edinburgh stated,

> the leader of the heretics and most famous preacher in the royal city raged wonderfully in almost every sermon against the Pope as Antichrist and against me as an emissary of Satan, and a nuncio of Baal and Beelzebub. The whole populace and all the chief men of the realm solemnly attend his sermons in great numbers, where he excites them, not against me only, but against the Queen as well, for admitting such a man as me into her realm, and giving audience to those who were bent on corrupting the pure Gospel, the light of which had now at length dawned upon them.

His mission was one of great danger, since the cry in the streets was to make 'a noble sacrifice to God and to wash their hands in his blood. If the Pope had sent a devil with horns he would have found a Scotsman to guide him as de Gouda had found Edmund Hay.' Hay having been unmasked, his fellow priest Crichton took over guarding de Gouda and he was transferred to a safer house at Megginch in Perthshire for two months. They eventually came to Edinburgh with an escort of three horsemen, then once in the city dismissed the guard, and entered on foot by fields and around the town walls to the house of the Queen's almoner. This was probably in the present-day Abbey Strand, a few yards outside the palace precincts. Next day, Mary met de Gouda and Hay in a private chamber an hour before Knox started preaching, the time chosen to guarantee the absence of the 'heretical courtiers'. Knox and Mary's council were now safely ensconced just under a mile to the west, while Mary could set about her secret business with, legend has it, her four Maries guarding the door. The interview was carried out in Latin, which the Queen understood, though not well enough to reply, so Edmund Hay translated. This seems to put into doubt Mary's reputed fluency in the tongue, even allowing for her teenage address in the Louvre. She told them that it was very unlikely she could send a delegation to the Council of Trent, but vowed that she would rather die than abandon her faith. De Gouda noticed her anxiety over the time. Knox's sermons cannot have been the two-hour marathon we have come to expect.

She refused to accept the letters to her bishops personally, for 'she feared delivering them would be a sign for a revolution'. She arranged that all the letters could be sent to the bishop of Ross. She said she would try to arrange an interview with Lord James, but afterwards learnt that so great was the seeming bitterness against the Pope that this was impossible. She refused de Gouda a safe conduct or even royal protection since if he was found with such documents on his person it would do him more harm than good. She said, 'Do not go abroad, but keep in some secret chamber.' She was now very anxious about the ending of the sermon, and saying that in time she would try to establish a Catholic college in Scotland, she dismissed them.

She later sent for the letters to the bishops and gave the nervous nuncio a formal receipt for them. The bishop of Ross refused to receive the letters from the Queen, even after an appeal by a Carthusian prior on behalf of de Gouda. The prior lived in permanent secular disguise while petitioning for the return of the order's lands; however the bishop of Ross refused categorically to have any contact whatsoever. De Gouda says finally, '*Hoc de illo!*' – 'so much for him!'

Next he visited the bishop of Dunblane, disguised as one of the bishop's servants, since he had heard that the bishop was keen to join the Society of Jesus. He was again rebuffed without an interview. He did, however, manage to meet the bishop of Dunkeld, this time disguised as a banker's clerk, and although entertained to dinner, had to carry on with the imposture by discussing only finance, presumably in Latin, throughout the meal. *Et haec quidem de Episcopis* – so much for the bishops.

As Knox had seen the ecclesiastical reverse in England under Mary Tudor, de Gouda observed the complete rejection of Rome and all things Catholic, as well as the apostasy of priests. He was horrified to find superintendents marrying. An unfortunate French merchant, mistaken for de Gouda, was seized by a mob, and very nearly beaten to death. De Gouda noted that some of the nobles heard Mass in secret and that a large number of the common people were still Catholics and were sustained by a strong hope that one day they would be set free. He decried the multiple holdings of benefices and inveighed as much against them as did the reformers. His description of a flock betrayed by its shepherd and so taken by wolves could have come straight from the pages of Knox. He concludes that Mary should marry some strong Catholic prince, appoint a Catholic council, found a Catholic college, and use Philip of Spain to control the English. Finally with Hay, disguised as sailors, he returned to Louvain in a ship hired by the redoubtable Crichton.

Although the waters of history closed over the event without a ripple, it does demonstrate that Knox still dominated to a great extent and that Lethington, the earl of Mar, and the rest of the council would abandon the Queen spiritually to hear Knox preach. The Queen was thus isolated, although there were still adherents to the old faith and the nobility still relied on her patronage. The common people, certainly in the vicinity of the capital had no love for papacy, certainly not when it came into their midst as a poorly kept secret.

Domestically Knox, now a 'sole man', set out to relieve the burden of his household in which he had two young sons to bring up. On 4 August Randolph, at Knox's request, asked Cecil for a licence for Mrs Bowes to go back to Scotland with her man, a maid and two horses, which she would return, as well as £100 of her own money. Not so long ago Knox would have petitioned Cecil himself, but he had been thoroughly supplanted by Lethington. The licence was granted, although Knox, as we have seen, was now only the spiritual leader of the Protestant reformers, without his previous political authority. Although he still had a considerable following, Scotland was ruled in fact by Mary, with Lethington making sure that no one rocked the boat. Knox's ideas were laudable in theory, and had support in the middle classes and with some of the nobility. But where they represented a threat to the status quo, the real powers in the land would do everything they could to make sure that, while they may have been endorsed in principle, they would never be put into practice.

11 Royal Conflict

In the autumn of 1562 Mary and Knox were both on the move, with Knox reassuring himself of Protestant support in the country at large and the Queen paying him no heed whatsoever as she sought to bring at least one of her unruly nobles to heel.

The north of Scotland was dominated by the figure of George Gordon, the earl of Huntly, a dynastic chieftain in the best medieval mould, and above all a devout Catholic. It had been he who had suggested an early return by Mary, backed by Gordon arms, and he was less than happy about her seeming compliance with the Protestant council. The present cause of Mary's discontent was no more than another Edinburgh street brawl between Sir John Gordon, Huntly's son and one Lord Ogilvie. Sir John was arrested, but fled from prison to his family's stronghold in the north; there he seized the lands of Mary's own master of the household. Mary could not ignore this slight to her authority and set off, aiming for Inverness, a Huntly stronghold, and insisting on Randolph's presence on the journey. He was an unwilling traveller – 'a terrible journey both for horse and man, the countries are so poor and the victuals so scarce'. With the Queen in this martial mood and the uncertainty of the conflict in France, the nobility felt that they stood in a dangerous state. Knox, who was briefly in Stirling, had written to them to hold firmly to their cause. He had also written to Mary, on behalf of the whole Church, to keep her promises of toleration.

However, Mary's pursuit of Sir John provoked a full-scale rising by Huntly. Mary took Inverness Castle, hanging the corpse of Captain George Gordon over the bridge – Randolph declared that his head was set up on the castle. Mary now had Lord James, whose title as earl of Mar was in dispute, created earl of Moray. The Moray revenues had been in the hands of Huntly for thirteen years, and egged on by his terrifying wife – she was permanently surrounded by her personal witches – Lord James embarked on a campaign of attrition that ended on the field of Corrichie, twenty miles west of Aberdeen, with the old Earl's death. The likely cause was a stroke: 'He suddenly fell from his horse stark dead – he burst and swelled.' Seven months later, in May 1563, his mummified corpse was tried for treason in front of Mary sitting in parliament. After this bizarre episode Mary was back in Edinburgh by September 1562. Later she would have to witness the execution of Sir John Gordon, the originator of the trouble. Unfortunately, the executioner was inept and the protracted butchery caused Mary to faint and remain in bed for two days.

Knox, meanwhile, continued to supply England, through Randolph, with information about Catholic agitators. For example, here is Randolph to Cecil on 31 August:

I send a letter from Mr Knox, what men he writes of I know not, but am assured they came in at the West Border. They may work much mischief; and divers are greatly offended with them. If my sovereign please I doubt not to have them fast enough. Knox has often warned me of 'practisers', but these are the first he or any other could assure me of.

Knox obviously had his own intelligence network, possibly through the parishes, but what is astonishing is the confidence with which Randolph feels he can effect the arrest of these 'practisers', who may well have been clandestine priests. Cecil would certainly have had an interest in any such who thought of entering England from the north.

Francis Walsingham, who ran Elizabeth's secret service with cold efficiency, would be doubly keen and could, through Randolph, act more ruthlessly than Knox via Secretary Lethington. Randolph wrote the letter from Aberdeen, where he was reluctantly following the royal campaign.

With the royal power moving north, Knox took the opportunity to go to Galloway in the west, a time-honoured stronghold of dissent. His purpose was to stiffen resolve among the nobility, and he exhorted them to 'put themselves in such order as that they might be able to serve the authority, and yet not to suffer the enemies of God's truth to have the upper hand'. His exhortation was certainly successful, for on 4 September at Ayr, the earl of Glencairn led over a hundred lairds and burgesses in signing a 'band'. They confirmed their support for the reformed Kirk and vowed to maintain its ministers – albeit only spiritually. Apart from the earl, the signatories were from the traditional middle class. But why did Knox choose this particular moment to go to the country, even if it was to a constituency where he was sure of solid support? He obviously felt that with the Queen absent, Edinburgh could be regarded as a constituency that could be safely left alone.

In Edinburgh the council divided its time between St Giles and Holyrood palace. It was giving support to Knox as spiritual leader, but at the same time giving obedience to the secular governance of the Queen. In Edinburgh in 1556, six years previously, Knox had been asked if it was possible to hear Mass and then attend the Protestant church, and the man who had asked the question was Secretary Lethington. The Queen could offer tangible rewards for loyalty, whereas Knox asked for financial sacrifice. Loyalty to the sovereign was inherent in the great nobles, and where it was found to be lacking, the recent example of the earl of Huntly was a vivid reminder of the consequences. Also the religious wars in France were going the way of the Catholic forces, and this could give Mary greater confidence to attempt active proselytization in her own realm. Removing his voice from St Giles could be risky for Knox, but the Queen's absence did give him an opportunity to preach outside the capital.

His preaching in Ayrshire, however, came to the attention of one Quentin Kennedy, the abbot of Crossraguel, and son of the earl of Cassilis. The abbot had in 1558 published a tract putting forward a case for the Catholic Mass, followed by an answer to the arguments put forward by Knox in 1550, when he was called before the bishop of Durham. Abbot Kennedy had also challenged John Willock to a public debate that never took place, but now he had the very fount of Reform only a few miles distant and he promptly issued a fresh challenge.

In a time before mass communications these gladiatorial displays of argument were popular – Knox had publicly debated with John Winram, sub-prior of St Andrews in 1546 – and he had been challenged by others in the past, notably one Ninian Winzet. Winzet had written to Knox on several occasions and Knox had replied to him loftily, from the pulpit of St Giles. Knox refused this challenge to a public debate and Winzet replied with *A Last Blast of the Trumpet of God's Word against the Usurped Authority of John Knox*. Winzet's printer in Edinburgh was one John Scot, who must have regretted having taken on the work, since his print shop was raided, he was imprisoned and all copies of the work were burnt. Winzet wisely left Scotland for Ratisbon, but pestered Knox with further pamphlets containing increasingly personal attacks on Knox's apostasy from his ordination into the Catholic Church. Finally he resorted to the childish insult that Knox had betrayed his nation by now having an English accent. Meeting Winzet for a public debate would only have accorded the 'oxygen of publicity' to the opposition.

Abbot Kennedy was a different matter, however. Knox was 'informed that you are come in this country to seek disputation, and in special to make impugnation to certain articles which were pronounced and rehearsed by me to my flock in Kirkoswald'. Knox denied that his first purpose was disputation, but agreed to meet the abbot after a lengthy and increasingly bad-tempered correspondence. Knox was rightly afraid of capture, if he visited the abbey of Crossraguel, and the abbot had similar misgivings about entering Ayr. The provost of Ayr had been the first signatory of the recent Band. Since the provost foresaw violence wherever the debate took place, the earl of Cassilis hoped they would both desist, but the demagogic blood was up, and with limits on how many supporters each side could bring, the debate took place in the provost's house in Maybole, two miles from Crossraguel. It lasted for three days.

Abbot Kennedy's position was that there was scriptural warranty for the Mass, thus striking at Knox's central tenet that since the Mass was man-made, it was idolatrous.

> I define the Mass, as concerning the substance, and effect, to be the sacrifice and oblation, of the Lord's body and blood, given and offered by Him in the last Supper; and take the Scripture to be my warrant . . . and, for the first confirmation of the same, grounds me on the sacrifice of Melchizedek.

Melchizedek had offered bread and wine to Abraham in Genesis. This was too easy for a skilled debater such as Knox. The bread and wine could be seen as refreshment only, and certainly had no divine origin.

> The opinion conceived by my Lord Abbot, concerning bread and wine, brought forth by Melchizedek to be offered unto God, is not expressly contained in God's Scriptures, therefore it is utterly to be rejected. Beware, my Lord, that ye be not beaten with your own baton, for then must the Mass, yea, the best part of the same, stand upon an unsure ground, that is to say, upon the opinion of man, and having no assurance of God's expressed word.

Even when Knox published the dispute in 1563 it is difficult to see how it could have occupied three days, and there is way of knowing how many of the audience, near to a hundred at the start, remained at the end. But Knox was triumphant: 'The Mass stands groundless, and the greatest patron thereof, for all his sicker [expert] riding, hath lost one of his stirrups, yea, is altogether sat beside his saddle.'

Knox returned to Edinburgh in mid November and gave a dinner for the aged duke of Chatelherault and Sir William Randolph, whose presence had been requested by the duke. Knox, as he had done in Galloway, was reassuring himself of his support, and Chatelherault could possibly have some influence with Moray and Lethington. Knox was no longer certain of their support. He extracted three promises from the duke: first, to profess Christ's word; second, in all ways to show himself an obedient subject to his sovereign; and third, never to alter from that promise he had made for the maintenance of peace and amity between both realms. Knox still held fast to the belief that reform could only be assured with concord between Scotland and England. In this, in fact, his fears of opposition were groundless, since Moray and Lethington were working towards that end as well.

Randolph, wisely, said of Chatelherault's promises that he would believe them when they took effect, but hoped that the conclusions would not depend on his word alone. To Cecil he reported Knox's thinking in some detail:

> I know his good zeal and affection to our nation, and his great travail and care to unite the hearts of the princes and people in perpetual love and kindness. I know that he mistrusts more of his sovereign's part than he does of ours. He hath no hope (to use his own terms) that she will ever come to God or do good in the commonwealth; he is so full of mistrust in all her doings, words and sayings, as though he were either of God's privy counsel, that knew how he had determined of her from the beginning, or that he knew the secrets of her heart so well, that neither she did nor could have for ever one good thought of God or of his true religion! . . . he fears that new strangers be brought in to this realm . . .'

The Queen had also returned from her military adventures, 'and then dancing began to grow hot, for her friends began to triumph in France'. She was reputed to have received news of new Catholic victories in France, and excited by this, 'danced excessively, till after midnight'. In July a decree had been passed in Paris encouraging the summary dispatch of 'heretics without interference by officers of the law'. Then Catholic forces under Guise leadership ended the siege of Rouen on 26 October with an unparalleled outbreak of murder, rape and looting. In a Protestant country Mary's behaviour was undoubtedly provocative, but reports of her unfeelingness would have been swollen by rumour. However, Knox inveighed strongly against these antics in St Giles, when some of Mary's private guard were present, and he was promptly sent for to have his second interview with Mary.

This interview differed from the first in that, although it was held in her bedchamber, the company was much different, the Queen being attended by her ladies, the four Maries, some 'common servants', as well as the earls of Moray and Morton along with Secretary Lethington. The guard members who had reported Knox's sermon were also standing by, should their testimony be needed, and indeed the whole arrangement smacked much more of a formal trial than had the first meeting. Knox was called and accused of speaking irreverently of the Queen and of working to bring her into the hatred and contempt of the people. All of these charges were delivered by the Queen personally, in a long harangue, to which we imagine Knox listened respectfully, before answering,

> Madam, this is oftentime the just recompense which God giveth to the stubborn of the world, that because they will not hear God speaking to the comfort of the penitent, and for amendment of the wicked, they are often compelled to hear the false report of others to their greater displeasure . . . if the reporters of my words had been honest men, they would have reported my words and the circumstances of the same. But because they would have credit in court, and lacking virtue worthy thereof, they must have somewhat to please your Majesty, if it were but flattery and lies. But such pleasure (if any your Grace take in such persons) will turn to your everlasting displeasure.

It would have been good to know at whom Knox was looking when he delivered this statement. As he went on, somewhat forbiddingly, Mary must have been glad she was sitting down:

> And because that you have heard their report, please your Grace to hear myself rehearse the same, so near as memory will serve. My text, madam, was this, 'And now, O kings, understand; be learned, ye judges of the earth.' . . .

the complaint of Solomon is this day most true, to wit, 'That violence and oppression do occupy the throne of God here on earth', for while that murderers, blood-thirsty men, oppressors and malefactors dare be bold to present themselves before kings and princes, and the poor saints of God are banished and exiled, what shall we say but that the devil hath taken possession of the throne of God, which ought to be fearful to all wicked doers, and a refuge to the innocent oppressed . . . His statutes and holy ordinances they will not understand; for in fiddling and flinging they are more exercised than in reading or hearing of God's most blessed word; and fiddlers and flatterers (which commonly corrupt the youth) are more precious in their eyes than men of wisdom and gravity . . . and of dancing, Madam, I said, that albeit in Scriptures I found no praise of it, and in profane [i.e. secular] writers, that it is termed the gesture rather of those that are mad and in frenzy than of sober men; yet I do not utterly damn it, provided that two vices be avoided . . . that the principal vocation of those that use the exercise be not neglected for the pleasure of dancing, secondly, that they dance not for the pleasure that they take in the displeasure of God's people . . . If any man, Madam, will say that I spake more, let him presently accuse me.

He tells us that the Queen then looked at some of the informers, and said,

Your words are sharp enough as you have spoken them, but yet they were told to me in another manner. I know that my Uncles and you are not of one religion, therefore I cannot blame you albeit you have no good opinion of them. But if you hear anything of myself that mislikes you, come to myself and tell me, and I shall hear you.

This represents a huge concession by Mary, given in the presence of Moray, Morton and Lethington, that the royal ear would always be available to Knox. It was probably not politic to have mentioned her uncles, one of whom, the duc de Guise, had been responsible for recent massacres of Protestants. Knox seized on the point.

I am assured that your Uncles are the enemies to God, and to his Son Jesus Christ; and that for maintenance of their own pomp and worldly glory . . . But as to your own personage, Madam, I would be glad to do all that I could to your Grace's contentment, provided that I exceed not the bounds of my vocation. I am not appointed to come to every man in particular to show his offence; for that labour were infinite. If your Grace please to frequent the public sermons, then I doubt not but that you shall fully understand both what I like and mislike . . . Or if your Grace will assign unto me a certain day and hour when it will please you to hear the form and substance of doctrine which is proponed in public in the churches of this Realm, I will most gladly wait upon your Grace's pleasure, time and place. But to wait upon your chamber-door, or elsewhere, and then to have no further liberty but to whisper my mind in your Grace's ear, and to tell you what others think and speak of you, neither will my conscience nor the vocation whereto God hath called me, suffer it. For albeit at your Grace's commandment I am here now, yet cannot I tell what other men shall judge of me, that at this time of day am absent from my book and waiting upon the court.

'You will not always be at your book,' and saying which, Mary turned her back. If a chink of light had for a moment opened up, Knox had firmly slammed it shut. Mary was thoroughly educated in her Guisian pride of power and Knox had the unbending hauteur of the missionary dogmatist. Moray and Lethington would have had their opinions confirmed, while the remaining attendants could only stand in amazement at hearing their sovereign addressed so slightingly. Some among them muttered that he was not afraid to behave thus and he replied, 'Why should the pleasing face of a gentlewoman frighten me? I have looked in the faces of many angry men, and yet have not been frightened above measure.'

Randolph dutifully reported that there was little liking between them, but they parted in such a manner that no slander might arise from the meeting. In other words, the stalemate continued. Through Randolph Knox apologized for not writing directly to Cecil, but was reported as having a strong preference for Elizabeth over Mary, also supplying information on 'certain Friars sent out of this country for fear of punishment and are received as ministers in England'.

A week later the Kirk held a General Assembly on 25 December and justifiably complained that it had received no answer to its supplication of the last assembly. They accepted that, given the troubles occurring since the last assembly, the 'practice of the Queen and her Council [was] with fair words to drive time'. They then had to deal with the case of Paul Methven.

Methven was a minister in Jedburgh in the Border country and had professed Protestantism there at a time when to do so was very dangerous. He was therefore an esteemed member of the Church. But now there were rumours and accusations that he had fathered a child with his maidservant. It was essential that the new Church be seen to be whiter than white, after the accusations it had made of Catholic immorality, and that any lapses by its ministers be investigated with all thoroughness, before being punished with severity. It was therefore with a heavy heart that Knox, in January 1563, left with elders of the Kirk of Edinburgh to join the superintendant of Lothian in an investigation of the slander. The slander was, they found, widespread with so many witnesses that the investigators suspected a prearranged campaign, visiting the places where witnesses claimed to have heard adulterous noises. So far everything was circumstantial, much less concrete than the evidence against the candle-lit and hoseless visitor in a similar case in St Andrews, and the investigators longed to find Methven innocent. True, on the alleged occasions his wife, 'an ancient matron', had been absent in Dundee, but the investigators, 'having a good opinion of the honesty and Godliness of the man, travailed what they could (conscience not hurt) to purge him of the slander'. But then, as in the best courtroom dramas, the brother of the wronged girl appeared, unaware that there was an investigation. He had taken the girl away, had the child baptized in his own name, and carried messages, money and clothes from Methven to his sister. Without waiting for the now inevitable verdict of excommunication Methven fled from Scotland. Three years later he attempted to purge himself of the crime by confession and exposing himself to retribution outside churches in Edinburgh and Jedburgh. Though he gained great sympathy for his honesty, he failed to carry the expurgation to his original parish in Dundee and he returned to England, where he became a vicar in the south-west until his death in 1606.

Knox includes the story of the fallen minister and his punishment for two reasons,

> firstly, to forewarn such as travail in that vocation, that, according to the admonition of the Apostle, 'such as stand, take heed lest they fall' . . . neither yet ought his fall anything to prejudge the authority of the doctrine which he taught . . . The other cause is, that the world may see what difference there is between light and darkness, between the uprightness of the Church of God, and the corruption wich rings in the synagogues of Satan, the Papistical rabble.

The Protestant faith had been the official doctrine of the country for less than three years. Part of its manifesto had been the correction of the

immorality going unpunished in parts of the Catholic Church. It was therefore absolutely essential that the new regime should be seen to be as
incorruptible as the leaders of any revolutionary movement. However much
Knox regretted it, Methven had to be seen to be punished.

By the turn of the year Mary was to say, 'Mr Knox is so hard at us that
we have laid aside much of our dancing. I do it more for heaviness of heart
that things proceed not well in France than in fear of him.' It is not surprising that Mary was feeling embattled since in the palace itself there was a
Protestant sermon three times a week in Moray's apartments, 'so near to
the mass, that two so mortal enemies can not be nearer joined, without
some deadly blow given to one side or the other. One of the Queen's priests
got a cuff in a dark night, that made somewhat a do!' Mary was, however,
still a loyal Catholic, and as much as she claimed that the Protestant faith
was inviolable in Scotland, her secret correspondence tells a different story.
In January 1563 she had written in Italian to her uncle the cardinal of
Lorraine, with an enclosure for Pope Pius IV. In it she vows total obedience
to Rome and pledges to restore Catholicism to Scotland, even at the risk of
her own life. She expresses her complete support for the Council of Trent
and its Counter-Reformation activities. In March she would write to the
council itself regretting that she had been unable to send any priests from
Scotland.

But there were events closer to home that must have given her sleepless
nights. As if to combine the transgression of Methven with the amorous
follies of the lunatic earl of Arran, one Pierre de Châtelard now appears
briefly in the limelight. A charming courtier who had accompanied Mary
from France, he returned there only to come back to Scotland in 1562,
where he remained in her court. He had a reputation as a poet and would
have been able to shower Mary with the stylized and high-flown verses
reminiscent of the medieval courts of love. According to Knox he was the
best-dressed of the court, and given to dancing 'to the purpose'. This was
simply dancing in couples close enough for the transmission of whispered
secrets, but Knox thought such fashions 'more like to the brothel than to
the comeliness of honest women'. Mary would have thought not of broth-
els, but more likely of sunlit evenings on the Loire, with elaborate and
fundamentally frivolous courtships in the gardens of Renaissance châteaux.
It was all a far cry from Holyrood and nobles whose idea of courtship was
physical capture and rapid marriage to avoid scandal – and thus a breath of
fresh air for the young Queen. And Knox allowed that the occasional steal-

ing of a kiss was honest enough, even though the Scottish courtiers were beginning to feel excluded from royal favour.

Châtelard's first move into madness came late in 1562 when he hid beneath the Queen's bed, 'with his sword beside him and his dagger about him', only to be discovered during a routine search before Mary retired for the night. She was told of the event the next morning and ordered Châtelard to leave the court. Instead of doing this he followed the court to Fife and managed to burst in on Mary in her bedchamber when she was attended only by her ladies-in-waiting. Mary became hysterical at the intrusion of this seeming madman, and when Moray arrived, his royal half-sister beseeched him, 'As he loved her, slay Châtelard, and let him never speak word.' Moray hesitated, saying,

> Madam I beseech your Grace, cause me not [to] take the blood of this man upon me. Your Grace has entreated him so familiarly before, that you have offended all your nobility, and now if he be secretly slain at your own commandment, what shall the world judge of it? I shall bring him to the presence of Justice, and let him suffer by law according to his deserving.

In other words he would be tried for treason, and undoubtedly executed.

But Mary went on, 'Oh you will never let him speak?'

'I shall do, Madam, what in me lieth to save your honour'.

Moray's pledge seems to have a little of, 'Trust me, I know what is going on. Your secret is safe with me'. Was there anything going on? Why was Mary so keen for Châtelard's silence? Had he been in the Holyrood bedchamber by invitation and the entire dalliance had become too much for the widowed, but still virgin Queen? We shall never know.

He was tried and found guilty, coming to the scaffold on 22 February 1563 with a copy of Ronsard's hymns – one of Mary's favourite authors. His final words were, according to Brantôme, 'Adieu, the most beautiful and cruel princess in the world.' Randolph says that Chatelard privately confessed that he hid under the bed 'to have tried her constancy, and by force to have attempted that which by no persuasions he could attain to.' According to Knox his final words were 'O Cruel dame, or Cruel Mistress'. Knox was not present, and anyway would have taken the amorous persiflage of courtly love as a tool of Satan – much in the same category as dancing to the purpose. He goes on, 'And so received Châtelard the reward of his dancing, for he lacked his head, that his tongue should not utter the secrets of our Queen.' This last hint that there were secrets yet to be discovered is completely without foundation, but we can see that Mary's undoubted beauty, combined with her vivid past as a widowed virgin, and now a beleaguered Queen, had a powerful sexual effect driving Arran to permanent insanity and Châtelard to the block. It had, however, no effect on Knox.

During this time there was continual testing of the waters by both sides. On 17 March one Sir James Arthur was charged with baptizing and marrying in 'the fashion of papistry'. At Easter, Mass was said to have been conducted by the bishop of St Andrews and the prior of Whithorn, in spite of being warned that such actions consituted a capital offence. Some priests in the west of Scotland were arrested, and Quentin Kennedy of Crossraguel, Knox's recent opponent in debate, was firmly told that if the law continued to be flouted, more arrests would be made and summary punishment meted out without reference to the council. Mary was furious at this, but in fact was impotent, since it was merely reinforcing the law of the land. She was at Lochleven Castle, which she would occupy later under much less happy circumstances, and summoned Knox once again to explain the situation.

The castle is a forbidding medieval structure set on an island in an idyllic loch, complete with its own delicious species of trout. Knox would have had a ride of some thirty miles before being rowed across the loch to meet the Queen, who was clearly in combative mood.

> She travailed with him earnestly two hours before supper, that he would be the instrument to persuade the people, and principally the gentlemen of the West, not to put hands to punish any man for using of themselves in their religion as pleased them. The other, perceiving her craft, willed her Grace to punish malefactors according to the law, he durst promise quietness upon the part of all them that professed the Lord Jesus within Scotland.

Knox went on to threaten that without application of the existing law, the people might well take the law into their own hands. Mary was appalled at Knox's seeming endorsement of this usurpation of her power.

'Will you allow that they shall take my sword in their hands?'

Knox immediately launched on familiar proofs that justice was God-given and hence did not, by definition, reside in the temporal authority. If that authority chose not to dispense justice it would fall to others to do it for them. He also pointed out that there was no sin concerning those who restrained rulers from venting their rage on the innocent. Given the activities of Mary's uncles in France at the time, this was very close to home. Biblical precedent followed as summer does the spring, starting with the story of Saul sparing the life of Agag, the 'fat and delicate' king of the Amalekites, and then God commanding Samuel to hack Agag to pieces. Knox's scriptural precedents tended to be blood-spattered. Therefore he earnestly prayed that she should let the papists understand that their offences would not go unpunished. The law gave power to judges to search out 'massmongers, or hearers of the same', and punish them. He asked that she consider the mutual contract between her subjects and herself. The people were bound to obey her, but she was bound to keep laws regarding them. She demanded service, but the people were entitled to demand protection and defence against 'wicked doers'.

'Now, Madam, if you shall deny your duty unto them (which especially craves that you punish malefactors) think you to receive full obedience of them? I fear, Madam, you shall not.'

Whereupon the Queen 'somewhat offended' passed to her supper. It is not in the least surprising that she was 'somewhat offended', since no one would ever have broached such a subject with her. Under her late father-in-law or in reach of any Guise uncle, such a statement would have meant instant death. Knox was saying that not only did rulers not have total and unquestioned power over their subjects, but also that what power they did possess was conditional on a mutual contract. The validity for the existence of sovereigns was entirely utilitarian, and when their usefulness ceased so did their *raison d'être*. This was the first time Knox had propounded his egalitarian views in person to a ruling monarch and he had stunned her into silence. Knox's flame of democracy still burned as brightly as ever.

Knox had to spend the night at Lochleven Castle, because of its island situation, and, before retiring, he relayed his arguments to the earl of Moray. Whether Moray then spoke with his half-sister we do not know, but next day Knox met a very different Mary, Queen of Scots. He was wakened shortly after half-past five, before sunrise, and asked not to leave without having a further meeting with the Queen, who was already, not only awake, but risen, dressed, and ashore, hawking near Kinross. This interview, presumably with both parties still mounted, struck an entirely different note. 'Whether it was the night's sleep, or a deep dissimulation locked in her breast, that made her forget her former anger, wise men may doubt.' Knox's distrust was deep. 'Whereof she never moved [a] word, but began diverse other purposes'. She started by telling Knox that Lord Ruthven had sent her a ring as a token of love – a love she could not reciprocate since she knew that he had used enchantment. This was doubly annoying since Ruthven had been made a member of the privy council at Lethington's request. Knox showed a glimmer of diplomacy in his response, 'That man is absent for the present, Madam; and therefore I will speak nothing in that behalf.' Almost as if she found his diplomacy had passed a test, she swiftly changed the subject, asking if Knox was about to leave for Dumfries to oversee the election of a superintendent, and that a candidate for the post was Alexander Gordon, the titular archbishop of Athens, and bishop of Galloway. When he confirmed that this was the case, she warned him never to promote that man to any office in the Kirk. Her recent experiences with the earl of Huntly, among others, meant that the very name Gordon was anathema to her. Knox assured her, however, that where free elections took place, the spirit of God was called on to decide. Mary still thought Alexander Gordon to be a dangerous man. However, Knox does admit that the bishop was found to have gained his nomination corruptly and was to continue to use corruption to attempt to gain the election. This must have been a considerable shock for Knox, who knew Gordon personally and had entertained him as a guest in his manse.

The conference continued, although Knox was eager to leave, probably confused by the change in Mary's attitude: he was now seemingly being regarded as a confidant rather than an implacable enemy.

Mary started to talk of Lady Argyll. She had been born Lady Jane Stewart, and was another illegitimate offspring of Mary's father James V, but had married the Earl of Argyll in 1554. The marriage was not happy – it would end two years later in separation, and in 1573 in divorce – but Lady Argyll was now behaving in a scandalous manner. Knox told the Queen that he had, before Mary's arrival, patched up quarrels between the earl and his wife, and having heard nothing recently, presumed that all was well. Mary corrected him and asked Knox to use his good offices to 'put them at unity', but not to let the earl know. Knox agreed, by now desperate to leave before any further embarrassing personal confidences were offered. As a parting shot, she said, 'Touching our reasoning yesternight, I promise to do as you required; I shall . . . summon all offenders, and you know that I shall minister justice.'

Knox could not resist a tart riposte: 'I am assured then that you shall please God, and enjoy rest and tranquillity within your realm; which to your Majesty is more profitable than all the Pope's power can be.'

So he sank in his spurs and was off. It does sound as if she was acting under heavy advice from Moray and Lord James to mend her quarrel with Knox, who was, after all, in the right. Her behaviour does show a willingness to appear to compromise. Knox found it a proof of her willingness to dissemble, while having a heart filled with nothing but venom and destruction.

Knox kept his word and did write to Argyll, telling him that his behaviour toward his wife was very offensive to many godly people, and that her complaint that he had withdrawn 'the use of his body' from her was grievous. He does not excuse the behaviour of Lady Argyll but warns that if the earl cannot prove adultery against her, then his behaviour is itself inexcusable. 'Sin is sweat in drinking, but in digesting more bitter than gall.' He ends by hoping that the earl will be in Edinburgh on 19 May, so that justice will not be mocked. This refers to the coming trial of the forty-eight priests who had been arrested for celebrating Mass at Easter. It seemed that Mary had likewise kept her word to Knox, but she had a trick up the royal sleeve. The defendants were found guilty but sentenced to be imprisoned during her Majesty's pleasure, which turned out to be short – most were free by early summer. There was no likelihood of protest against this, since Mary had called a Parliament, the first of her reign, for 26 May, and there were many axes to be ground there. Knox accuses Mary of 'deep craft' and quotes many as having the opinion, 'We see what the Queen has done; the like of this was never heard of within this realm; we will bear with the Queen; we doubt not that all shall be well.'

It was on the 28th that Mary took part in the disgusting farce of trying the still unburied corpse of the earl of Huntly. He was found guilty and became one of eleven other Gordon barons and lairds that forfeited his lands to the crown.

Parliament met with such great pomp and ceremony that the horrified Knox wrote,

Such stinking pride of women as was seen at that Parliament was never seen before in Scotland. Three sundry days the Queen rode to the Tolbooth. The first day she made a painted oration, and there might have been heard among her flatterers, '*Vox Dianae*! The voice of a goddess, (for it could not be *Dei*,) and not of a woman! God save that sweet face! Was there ever orator [who] spoke so properly and sweetly!'

Of course, Knox was writing in retrospect and the parliament of 1563 was not one he would look back on with any satisfaction. It had been stage-managed by Mary, probably with the help of Moray and Lethington. Unknown to Knox, and probably to Lethington, earlier that month Mary had written to the Council of Trent vowing to bring back Scotland and England under the authority of the Apostolic See, as soon as she was Queen of both countries. But back in the real world of Edinburgh, the fact that Lethington was not even present shows his confidence in the arrangements. Mary's arrival, which so enraged Knox, would have endeared her to the Edinburgh populace as Chatelherault preceded Mary with the crown. His descendant, the 16th duke of Hamilton, performed the same task to open the new Scottish parliament in June 1999. Argyll carried the sceptre and Moray the sword, and trumpets sounded as the people watched their young Queen open their parliament. But it was a parliament in which the agenda had been strictly controlled. All attempts to introduce debate on reform, or final acceptance of the *Book of Discipline* were thrown out, with the warning that any attempt to force the pace would make this the last parliament of her reign. An Act of Oblivion for past misdeeds was passed, but acts against adultery, along with legislation on the repair of manses and minister's land holdings, were so diluted as to be little more than sops to the Protestants. The grant of the earldom of Moray to Lord James was confirmed, as were various grants and rewards to loyal friends and servants. The reformers were quietened with the promise that when the Queen consulted parliament on the subject of her marriage, then religion would be the first item on the agenda. Knox was bitterly disappointed, and having lost Arran as a friend at court, could see that Moray had now changed allegiance, if not religion. In fact, 'The matter fell so hot betwix the earl of Moray and some others of the Court, and John Knox, that familiarly after that time they spoke not together more than a year and a half'. In fact Knox wrote a bitter letter to Moray, which he describes in his *History*.

He made unto him a discourse of their first acquaintance; in what estate he was when first they spoke together in London [in July 1552]; how God had promoted him, and that above men's judgement, and in the end made this conclusion, 'But seeing that I perceive myself frustrated of my expectation, which was, that you should ever have preferred God to your own affection, and the advancement of truth to your own singular commodity, I commit you to your own wit, and to the conducting of those who better can please you.

I praise my God, I this day leave you victor of your enemies, promoted to great honours, and in credit and authority with your sovereign. If you so long continue, none within the realm shall be more glad than I shall be: but if that after this you shall decay (as I fear that you shall) then call to mind by what means God exalted you; which was neither by bearing with impiety, neither yet by the maintaining of pestilential Papists.

This has all the sad spitefulness of a letter between separating lovers, but Knox expresses a totality of rupture and disappointment that would make it almost impossible to heal the rift. Once again Knox has written 'more in anger than in sorrow' and his anger is understandable as he sees the very allies he stood beside in the campaigns against Mary of Guise now allying themselves, in search of favour, with her equally unshakeable Catholic daughter. Lethington was always going to support the legal authority with the full vigour of his intellect. Randolph had said that he would do and say whatever lay within his power to serve his mistress and his advice was followed more than any other. But an alliance between Moray and Knox would have been not only formidable, but directly threatening to Mary. In the past their familiarity had caused envy, but now that the breach had been made, the 'flatterers of the said earl . . . triumphed of it', and 'they ceased not to cast oil into the burning flame, which ceased not to burn'. Knox no longer had any allies at court, but before parliament dissolved he addressed the 'most part of the nobility'.

He started by pouring forth the sorrow of his heart, reminding them that he had been with them in their lowest moments of desperate temptation. He reminded them that they should depend upon God's protection and 'prefer his glory to your own lives and worldly commodity'. He had been beside them at St Johnston, Cupar Moor and the Crags of Edinburgh, and still remembered, 'that dark and dolorous night when all you, my Lords, with shame and fear left this town [Knox is referring to November 1559 when the Lords of the Congregation left Edinburgh to the powers of the Queen Regent]'. Having stirred up feelings of guilt and set his noble auditors squirming in their seats, he turned to the absent Mary. 'The Queen, say you, will not agree with us: ask of her that which by God's word you may justly require, and if she will not agree with you in God, you are not bound to agree with her in the Devil.' The dean of Restalrig, John Sinclair, interjected that nothing of the reformed religion had been established by law or parliament. Knox described this as treasonable and deserving of the gallows, since the reformed religion was accepted by a parliament that was as lawful as any. Having put the Queen's authority into question, he turned to the question of her marriage and told the nobility that if they consented to Mary marrying an infidel – and all papists were infidels – they would bring God's vengeance on the country, a plague upon themselves and 'perchance do no small comfort to your sovereign'.

With a certain satisfaction Knox says that both papists and Protestants were offended, and his most familiar friends disdained him for speaking against the Queen's freedom to marry as she wished. Mary herself was incandescent with rage when she heard, and Knox was summoned for what would be their last meeting. He went with 'divers of the faithful' but only Erskine of Dun was allowed into the royal presence with him. Since this meeting took place immediately after his sermon, the pain from it was very fresh. It is extremely unlikely that Mary had been present in person for the diatribe, but clearly the salient points had been reported to her, giving her the ammunition to work herself up into a towering rage; Knox calls it 'a vehement fume' and goes on to recount the ensuing scene:

> The Queen ... began to cry out that never Prince was handled as she was. 'I have,' said she, 'borne with you in all your rigorous manner of speaking, both against myself and my uncles; yea, I have sought your favours by all possible means. I offered you presence and audience whensoever it pleased you to admonish me; and yet I cannot be quit of you.'

The high tide of Guise passion and arrogance was dashing itself on the cliffs of Knox's intransigence.

> 'I vow to God, I shall be soon revenged'. And with these words, scarcely could Marnock [probably a body-servant called Marna], her secret chamber-boy, get napkins to hold her eyes dry for the tears: and the howling, besides womanly weeping, stayed her speech.

Knox was obviously unimpressed by this display of fury.

> The said John did patiently abide all the first fume, and at [an] opportunity answered, 'True it is, Madam, your Grace and I have been at divers controversies, into the which I never perceived your Grace to be offended at me. But when it shall please God to deliver you from that bondage of darkness and

error in the which you have been nourished, for lack of true doctrine, your Majesty will find the liberty of my tongue nothing offensive. Without the preaching place, Madam, I think few have occasion to be offended at me; and there, Madam, I am not master of myself, but must obey Him who commands me to speak plain, and to flatter no flesh upon the face of the earth.'

Mary was willing to grant this extension of present-day parliamentary privilege as far as doctrinal matters were concerned.

'But what have you to do', said she, 'with my marriage?'

'If it please your Majesty [said he], patiently to hear me, I shall show the truth in plain words. I grant that your Grace offered unto me more than ever I required; but my answer was then, as it is now, that God has not sent me to wait upon the court of Princesses, nor upon the chambers of Ladies; but I am sent to preach the Evangel of Jesus Christ, to such as please to hear it . . . but so it is that the most part of your nobility are so addicted to your affections, that neither God's word, nor yet their Commonwealth, are rightly regarded. And therefore it becomes me to speak, that they may know their duty.

'What have you to do,' she asked again, 'with my marriage?'

Realizing, perhaps, that she was becoming repetitive, Mary then made the mistake, feared by all cross-examiners, of asking one question too many. 'Or what are you within this Commonwealth?' The Queen had set her own trap and Knox slammed it shut.

A subject born within the same, Madam. And albeit I neither be Earl, Lord nor Baron within it, yet has God made me (how abject that ever I be in your eyes) a profitable member within the same. Yea, Madam, to me it appertains no less to forewarn of such things that may hurt it, if I foresee them, than it does to any of the nobility; for both my vocation and my conscience craves plainness. And, therefore, Madam, to yourself I say that which I speak in a public place: whensoever the nobility of this realm consent that you be subject to an unfaithful husband, they do as much as in them lies to renounce Christ, to banish his truth from them, to betray the freedom of this realm, and perchance shall in the end do small comfort to yourself.

A later marginal note of 1567 says, 'Let Papists judge this day.' Knox had, with great cogency, established his belief in principles that were complete anathema to Mary. First, he argued that any subject could have equal rights to express his own critical opinions with impunity. Jasper Ridley in his *John Knox* reports an annoyingly unnamed historian as saying, 'Modern democracy was born in that answer'. Certainly the right to free speech, enshrined in the first amendment to the American Constitution, and suppressed by all dictatorships, is vigorously asserted here. Secondly, should Mary choose to marry an 'unfaithful' (that is, Catholic) husband, the nobility should, by right, prevent her from carrying out her wishes. In other words, an obscure milkmaid's marriage to whomever she chooses will attract no attention, but a Queen's choice may be criticized by the milkmaid and her wishes may be thwarted by her advisors. Knox tells us,

At these words, howling was heard and tears might have been seen in greater abundance than the matter required. John Erskine of Dun, a man of meek and gentle spirit, stood beside and entreated what he could to mitigate her anger, and gave unto her many pleasing words of her beauty, of her excellence, and how that all the Princes of Europe would be glad to seek her favours. But all that was but to cast oil in the flaming fire. The said John stood still, without any alteration of countenance for a long season, while that the Queen gave place to her inordinate passion, and in the end he said, 'Madam, in God's presence I speak; I never delighted in the weeping of any of God's creatures, yea, I can scarcely well abide the tears of my own boys whom my own hand corrects, much less can I rejoice in your Majesty's weeping. But seeing that I have offered to you no just occasion to be offended, but have spoken the truth, as my vocation craves of me, I must sustain (albeit unwillingly) your Majesty's tears, rather than I dare hurt my conscience, or betray my Commonwealth through my silence.

This was too much for Mary and Knox was ordered to wait in an antechamber, while Erskine of Dun with the recently arrived Lord John of Coldingham attempted to calm the tear-drenched Queen. Knox was kept waiting for a recall with Lord Ochiltree and Mary's ladies-in-waiting for an hour. He gives an example of the light banter with which he entertained the 'gorgeously apparelled' ladies:

O fair ladies, how pleasant were this life of yours, if it should ever last, and then in the end we might pass to heaven with all this gay gear. But fie upon that knave Death, that will come whether we will or not! And when he has laid on his arrest, the foul worms will be busy with this flesh, be it never so fair and tender; and the silly soul, I fear, shall be so feeble, that it can neither carry with it gold, garnishing, targetting [jewelled embroidery], pearl, or precious stones.' And by such means procured he the company of women; and so passed the time until the Laird of Dun willed him to depart to his house ... The Queen would have had the censure of the Lords of the Articles, if that such manner of speaking deserved not punishment; but she was counselled to desist: and so that storm quieted in appearance, but never in the heart.

Even given the fact that sixteenth-century stomachs were stronger than ours, Knox's idea of light banter to procure the company of women seems distinctly dark. Certainly as Knox walked uphill the three-quarters of a mile or so to his house he must have reflected on Mary's behaviour. He had given no ground on any of their four meetings and would continue to regard her as an pagan infidel until she rejected Rome. More importantly, her will could never be endorsed unless it coincided with the united wishes of parliament and the General Assembly. But parliament had just shown itself to be a rubber-stamp for the Lords of the Articles, controlled by Moray and Lethington, neither of whom were any longer allies of Knox. His stiffening of the nobles' morale had been essential in defeating Mary of Guise, but it was now an impediment to their prosperity. Mary, now dry-eyed, realized that while she would never curb Knox, her best plan, for the present, would be to ignore him. The tide of reform was ebbing away.

12   New Alliances

On the 8 August 1563 Christian Pinkerton, with twenty-one other 'persons moving in the lower ranks of society', had been charged with attempting to restore the Catholic religion. This was symptomatic of a dangerous shift in opinion. Knox felt that the Catholic faith was beginning to grow in popularity, and its influence was coming close even to his own family, as witness the specially composed prayer to be said after grace at his table.

> Deliver us, O Lord from the bondage of idolatry. Preserve and keep us from the tyranny of strangers. Continue us in quietness and concord amongst ourselves, if thy good pleasure be, O Lord, for a season.

When asked why he only prayed that peace should be preserved for a season and not for ever, he answered that he did not see how peace could continue while idolatry, which had been suppressed, was now on the rise again. By making public his private prayer, complete with its qualifications, he managed to voice his doubts indirectly. It also served as a warning that Moray's agreement with Mary, allowing her alone to hear Mass privately, was in danger of breaking down. When it did there was a strong possibility of violence erupting.

And break down it did, as while the Queen was in Stirling 'the Papists in great number resorted to the Abbey, [in Holyrood] to their abomination'. This was no longer a case of the Mass being said in the royal presence and in the Queen's private chapel, but a more or less public service, albeit attended by 'dontybours', or so-called courtesans, and other members of Mary's French household. Also the Mass was being said, not in Mary's private chapel, but in the abbey church of Holyrood. Moray's previous agreement with Mary was now no longer valid and the boundary had been doubly crossed. At first Knox took no part in what followed, but it is a very neat coincidence that his private prayer became public just in time for his prophecy of violence to become true. In many ways the knowledge of his prayer gave a spurious validity to events. Previously he had taken no greater action against iconoclasm than to condemn it from the pulpit, an action that in effect gave it further publicity. Now he was saying that if idolatry brought among us by strangers should spread, he prayed that there should be no resulting violence. Though Knox was never a diplomat, he did have occasional moments of guile, and this may have been one of them. By declaring his dread of what might take place, he might be seen as having instigated the idea in the first place.

At any rate the violence did occur on 15 August 1563 when some of the 'brethren' burst in on a Mass at the abbey, terrifying the priest and the largely female congregation. They had been sent merely to note the names of the transgressors, but were armed with 'pistolets'. One Madame Raulet, overseer of the Queen's maids and wife to Mary's private secretary, raced to St Giles, where the comptroller, Pittarrow, was hearing Knox preach. He panicked and with the provost and bailies, accompanied by the bulk of the congregation, left St Giles and ran down the street to stop the presumed slaughter. When they arrived at the palace, however, they found all was now quiet, if tense. A 'zealous brother, named Patrick Cranston' had approached the officiating priest saying, 'The Queen's Majesty is not here, how dare thou then be so malapert, as openly to do against the law?', and with much muttering on both sides the confrontation fizzled out. When news of this reached Mary she unwisely charged Cranston along with Andrew Armstrong and George Rynd with everything the law could find – forethought, pretended murder, felony, hamesuckin (offering violence to a householder in his own home), violent invasion of the palace, and spoliation of the same. In a counter-move twenty-two people were charged with attending Mass on the previous Sunday.

Knox had written to Cecil, voicing his fears about the wavering Council and 'the multitude of calamities that I see appearing to fall upon this isle – all because the inordinate affections of her that is born to be a plague to this isle'. Then, he wrote an open letter to the congregation summarizing the situation. He naturally plays down the part played by Cranston and his fellows – there is no mention of pistols – and asserts that the action to be taken against them is merely 'preparation upon a few, that a door may be opened to execute cruelty upon a greater multitude'. He then exhorted the faithful to be in Edinburgh on the day of Cranston's trial for 'comfort and assistance'. Obviously the contents of this letter were a less than well kept secret and, to Mary's delight, were thought by the council to be treasonous, at least in that Knox might be seen to have called a convocation of the Queen's subjects without royal consent. Knox was charged to appear and answer the allegation.

In fact the trial of Cranston and his allies was a damp squib, with little support in the streets and less enthusiasm in the courtroom. It was adjourned and eventually forgotten. There is likewise no record of the twenty-two Catholics ever being brought to trial, as all eyes focused on the forthcoming trial of Knox himself. The master of Maxwell approached Knox and threatened to end their friendship unless he apologized to the Queen. Knox refused to admit any crime: 'I never made myself an adversary party to the Queen's Majesty, except in to the head of religion.'

Maxwell took a sadly prophetic view of this statement by his old friend. 'Well, you are wise enough, but you will find that men will not bear with you in times to come, as they have done in times past.'

Knox's reply can be seen either as arrogant or as resigned. 'If God stand my friend, as I am assured of his mercy he will, so long as I depend upon his promise, and prefer his glory to my worldly life and profit, I little regard how men behave themselves towards me.'

This exchange marked the end of the friendship between Maxwell and Knox. Knox was also visited by John Spens of Condie, the Queen's advocate, who reassured Knox that as he could not be shown to have committed treason, he would merely be accused of the crime and then dismissed – also that God would help him. There was now unease in the royal camp about such a high-profile action being initiated. Maxwell had failed to persuade Knox to agree to an 'an out-of-court settlement' by apologising; moreover Spens had seen the actual detail of the charges and felt that Knox would win. Thus, as a last-ditch attempt to avoid humiliation, Moray and Lethington sent for Knox. They warned Knox that, try as they might, they could not calm Mary's fury at him, but if he confessed and apologized perhaps, even at this late stage, affairs might be concluded peacefully.

They should have known better. Knox denied the crime and stressed, 'To confess an offence where my conscience witnesses there is none, far be it from me'.

Lethington asked, 'Have you not made convocation of the Queen's lieges?'

Knox claimed he had a just defence for his accusation and when Lethington asked to hear it, Knox shook his head and allowed that he might be thought a fool if he made his defence known at this stage. Lethington, having, for once, been bested by Knox in forensic debate, left, although Moray stayed to hear Knox's opinion of his position at court.

Astonishingly Knox told him that if he felt that he, Moray, was not in good standing there was nothing Knox could do about it. 'You have the Counsellors that you have chosen, my weak judgement both you and they despise. I can do nothing but behold the end, which, I pray God, be other than my troubled heart fears.' Despite these intercessions Mary remained implacable, although in physical pain from, Randolph was sure, melancholy at the impossibility of arranging a marriage.

On 21 December Knox was summoned to Holyrood between six and seven in the evening. He arrived with so many supporters that they occupied the staircase to the royal audience chamber, spilling down two storeys and filling the inner court of the palace. Ranged against him were Chatelherault, Argyll, Moray, Glencairn, Marischal, Ruthven, Pittarrow, Bellenden, Sinclair, Maxwell, McGill, Spens and the Lethingtons, both father and his son, the secretary. Most of these had been his allies against Mary of Guise, but now sat uneasily in judgement on the man whose preaching had been their inspiration. At Knox's entry they ceased what had been an intense discussion and took their places, preparatory to the entry of the Queen. This she did with 'no little worldly pomp', and sat flanked by Maxwell and Lethington who seem to have given close advice into alternate royal ears. Knox found her pomp lacking womanly gravity, for when during the sycophantic applause that greeted her entrance she saw Knox standing bare-headed and facing her from the foot of the table, she broke into guffaws of laughter. She then said, 'This is a good beginning. But do you wonder why I laugh? That man made me weep, and wept never [a] tear himself. I will see if I can make him weep.'

Randolph on the 13th had commented on Mary's often weeping 'when there is little apparent occasion'. Lethington now produced a copy of Knox's letter to the congregation and Mary asked Knox to confirm his handwriting. The letter was passed from hand to hand, then to Knox, who willingly confirmed his authorship. Lethington said that was more than he would have done, while Knox told him that charity was not suspicious, meaning that the truth had nothing to fear. Mary put an end to this exchange by instructing Knox to read the letter aloud, which he did. She then asked Spens, as royal advocate, to read the accusation – which he did 'very gently'. Less than gently, Mary addressed the whole table, asking if they had ever heard a more disrespectful and treasonable letter. Ignoring this request for a rush to judgement, the lords sat in a silence broken by Lethington asking if Knox repented. Knox said he would if he knew the offence.

Mary was unhappy with the courteous way Knox was being treated. 'What is this? Methink you trifle with him. Who gave him authority to make convocation of my lieges? Is not that treason?'

'No, Madam,' said Ruthven. 'He makes convocation of the people to hear prayer and sermon almost daily, and whatever your Grace or others may think of it, we think it no treason.'

Mary was getting near to a royal foot-stamping. 'Hold your peace, and let him make answer for himself'.

Knox replied, 'I began, Madam, to reason with the Secretary, whom I take to be a far better dialectician than your Grace is, that all convocations are not unlawful, and now my Lord Ruthven has given the instance . . .'

Mary countered, 'You shall not escape so. Is it not treason, my Lords, to accuse a Prince of cruelty? I think there be Acts of Parliament against such whispers.'

Many agreed with this, but Knox asked again how he could be accused of this. 'I will first desire this of your Grace, Madam, and this honourable audience, whether if your Grace knows not that the obstinate Papists are deadly enemies to all that profess the Evangel of Jesus Christ, and that they most earnestly desire the extermination of them and of the true doctrine that is taught within this Realm?'

The Queen held her peace, while Knox explained at some length that he had never accused the Queen of cruelty, but rather the 'pestilent Papists' who had inflamed her against pure men. He was warned that he was not now in the pulpit, but went on that he was in the place where he was obliged of conscience to speak the truth. Scriptural examples followed and he ended with a warning of the danger of papist counsellors, 'and that your mother found'. At this Lethington smiled, possibly in admiration of one trained by medieval Schoolmen. At any rate, he realized that Mary had lost the argument, and whispered something in her ear. She composed herself and told Knox, 'Well, you speak fair enough before my Lords, but the last time I spoke with you secretly, you caused me to weep many salt tears, and said to me stubbornly that, "You set not by my weeping." '

Knox then repeated more gently his arguments of the previous meeting, tactfully omitting his assertion that as a subject in Mary's commonwealth he had every right to criticize her in whatever way he wished.

Lethington then applied himself to the royal ear again and turned to Knox. 'Mr Knox, you may return to your house for this night'.

After Knox had left, a much relieved man, a vote was taken as to whether he had offended the Queen. The Lords found unanimously for Knox and Mary swept out, while Lethington 'raged' at the verdict. Since he had been instrumental in achieving it his rage may have been a formality. The Queen returned and a second vote was demanded, which, if anything, hardened the attitudes of the counsel.

'Shall the Laird of Lethingtom have the power to control us? Or shall the presence of one woman cause us to offend God, and to damn an innocent [man] against our conscience for the pleasure of any creature?'

That night there was no dancing or fiddling in Holyrood, 'for Madame was disappointed of her purpose which was to have had John Knox in her will by vote of the nobility.'

It may be that Knox here had played a chess game of some intricacy: first, by allowing his private fears of violence against the likely spread of Catholicism to become public; secondly, by whipping up public support for the disrupters of the Holyrood Mass when they were sent for trial; thirdly, trapping Mary into arraigning him before the council, most of whom were old Protestant friends; and finally, through his acquittal, having his power endorsed and the existence of Protestantism as the established religion of the realm confirmed.

Knox was in any case risking little, for if found guilty of the treason with which Mary had charged him, what would she do with him? Executing him would have brought the country to the edge of civil war, with the possible military entry of England; on the other hand, Knox would refuse exile and become the proto-martyr leader of an underground movement that might see the earl of Moray on Mary's throne. A mere admonishment would be useless and seen by the populace as a sign of weakness. Indeed all the scenarios had attractive features for a devious schemer. But given Knox's straightforward character and lack of diplomatic skills it seems unlikely. So why did Mary attempt a confrontation? Her various meetings with Knox had resulted in stalemates, with any honours going to Knox. Mary's action in bringing Knox to trial was ill-judged, but she may have been allowed to carry it out by Lethington in order to trim her popularity and maintain a balance between the throne and Knox. He must have foreseen her defeat, and all he had to do was to fan the flames of her temper until she was beyond reason. It certainly was the style of Scotland's Machiavelli to divide and rule.

It seems that a final feeble attempt at face-saving was made by French members of Mary's court, who approached Knox at home and suggested that if he entered Edinburgh Castle and confessed he would be immediately free to return home. This was rapidly brushed aside as an insult to the 'noble men, that of their conscience, and with displeasure of the Queen have absolved me . . . [and] how can I exhort others to peace and Christian quietness, if I confess myself an author and mover of sedition?'

Mary's court was, at the same time shaken by a minor scandal when the royal apothecary, a Frenchmen, was discovered to have got one of the maidservants pregnant. Using his skill with medicine the child was 'slain in the mother's belly'. Both were hanged for murder. At the same time Knox mentions an over-hasty marriage between John Sempill, son of Lord Sempill, whom Knox called 'the Dancer', and Mary Livingstone, 'surnamed the Lusty'. The four 'Maries' had all vowed not to marry before their mistress and this precedent allowed Knox to inveigh against the current immorality. In fact this marriage was far from over hasty. It took place in March 1565 after careful grants of lands to Sempill, so here Knox is being openly slanderous. He also refers to scurrilous tracts or ballads circulating at the time that spelled out the enormities of the court. These have, perhaps fortunately, been lost.

The General Assembly held its usual December meeting and complained that, inevitably, some of the 'thirds' due had not been paid. Lethington gave them assurances that all would be done in proper order but that the expenses of her guard and kitchen were so great that there would have to be a delay. However, the stipends would be paid in the fullness of time. No one believed him and one John Craig fanned the flames by declaring:

Some time [ago] were hypocrites known by their disguised habits, and we had men to be monks, and women to be nuns, but now . . . we have a new order of monks and nuns . . . we cannot discern the earl from the abbot . . . But seeing that you shame not of that unjust profit, would [to] God that you had the cowl of the nun, the veil, yes, and the tail joined withal, so that you might appear in your own colours.

This was too near the knuckle for Lethington, whose diplomatic skills vanished as he vowed never again to care about the plight of ministers: 'Let them blow and bark as loud as they list.' Knox here felt again that the impetus of reform was being lost.

> And thus had the servants of God a double battle, fighting on the one side against the idolatry and the rest of the abominations maintained by the Queen, and upon the other part, against the unthankfulness of such as sometime would have been esteemed as the chief pillars of the Kirk within the Realm.

Knox, however, also asked for the assembly's endorsement of his defence before the queen. Sir John Ballantyne, the Justice Clerk, objected and was removed, so unsurprisingly Knox was given the support of his fellow ministers. They did, however, agree to look critically at the provisions of the *Book of Discipline* and report to the next assembly. This could mean endorsement or, more likely, dilution. No matter that the status of reform seemed to be diminishing, Knox's position as head of the Kirk still seemed assured and his credibility had survived the confrontation with Mary greatly strengthened.

Three months later, on 26 March 1564, Knox remarried. He had been a 'sole man' since the death of Marjory in December 1560 with two sons, Nathaniel, now aged not quite seven years, and Eleazar, aged five. His household had been augmented by his mother-in-law, Elizabeth, since her return to Scotland in the autumn of 1562, but he felt that it needed the presence of a wife too. His choice was Margaret Stewart, daughter of Andrew, Lord Stewart of Ochiltree, so Knox had finally moved from his roots in Haddington into the nobility – albeit the minor nobility. Knox had previously described his father-in-law as 'a man rather born to make peace, than to brag in the streets', but he was distantly related to the Queen. Margaret's uncle had married the widow of James IV, and the family could trace a direct line back to James II. The effect of the news on Mary that she was now distantly related to Knox was that 'she stormeth wonderfully that she is of the blood and name'. Needless to say we know nothing of the courtship, if there was any, or even how they met, but it seems likely that the match would have been arranged between Knox and Lord Andrew, a firm supporter of Protestantism.

Another reason for supposing that the marriage was one of convenience was that Knox was now about fifty and his bride seventeen. Marriages with such disparity of ages were not uncommon – 150 years previously Chaucer had satirized the marriage of May to December in the *Merchant's Tale* – and Calvin had been asked to give a judgement on one union with an even greater gap. But the gap was over fifty years and Calvin disapproved. We have no clues as to what took place in Knox's manse, but Margaret bore him three daughters and nursed him in his final days, so she carried out her wifely duties without attracting any controversy, apart from the inevitable calumnies that Knox had captured her by a pact with the devil. Diabolically procured or not, Knox's second marriage seems to have been as happy and peaceful as his first.

This accusation by one Nicol Burne, made nine years after Knox's death, was only one prong of the attack made on the reformer in *The Disputation concerning the Controversit Headdis of Religion*. Burne also attacked Knox, whom he spells 'Kmnox', as an apostate, which he was, and 'ane heretic', which, depending on your point of view, he also was. But Burne also refers back to Knox's challenge in March 1562 by Ninian Winzet to show the origin of his calling as a minister. Burne asks to be shown one lawful magistrate who appointed Knox as a minister – Edward VI would have sufficed – to say nothing of being called to preach by the congregation in St Andrews – and declares that Knox had publicly boasted to Winzet that his calling had been extraordinary, as had that of John the Baptist. This was not quite true, since all that Knox had asserted was that John the Baptist's calling had been endorsed by miracles occurring to presage his birth and was therefore extraordinary. He had never compared himself with the Baptist. Burne goes on to claim that Knox had privately confessed – to whom is not stated (in such cases it never is) – that his calling came not from the laying-on of hands, but from 'guns and pistols'.

Some years later in 1578, Claude Nau, secretary to Mary, Queen of Scots, wrote in his Memorials that Knox's time in the galleys came from the fact that he had been outlawed on a charge of incest and 'other grievous accusations'. Nau did, however, admit that Knox had 'a cunning and crafty wit, and was admirably fitted for exciting the mob to sedition'. Since Nau never met Knox and the bulk of the Memorials were dictated to him by Mary in her imprisonment, she must have shared in this view of a populist demagogue. All of which demonstrates that Knox's hyperboles about whoredom and Jezebels were equally to be found among the supporters of Rome.

Knox continued to preach against the Mass, addressing himself now to those 'men, not Papists, we say, but chief Protestants, [who] will defend the Mass to be no idolatry'. It is interesting that the doubters and taunters attended his services, even though they mocked his vehemence. Mary's courtiers complained, 'we must recant, and burn our bill, for the preachers are angry.' The next opportunity for this anger to become public was in the General Assembly.

On the first day of this assembly the nobility, or, as Knox calls them, the 'Courtiers', failed to attend and an emissary was sent to call for their presence. They were slightly miffed to have been thought wanting in their duty and on the next day twelve of them appeared, headed by Chatelherault and the earls of Moray, Argyll, Glencairn and Morton, with Lethington heading the civil servants. They did not join the open assembly but met in an inner room and sent for the attendance of the superintendents and 'some learned ministers' to confer with them. The assembly took the view that without their principal officers the remainder of the assembly would have to sit idle, and any decision taken between the nobility and this rump would be seen as secret machinating. The lords agreed to a compromise, promising that any decision taken would be declared again in public, and with this proviso ten of the assembly left to join the private meeting. But 'because the principal complaint touched John Knox, he was also called for'.

Lethington started the 'harangue' by arguing, first, how much they were indebted to God for freedom of religion under the Queen; secondly, how necessary a thing it was that, through the good offices of the Kirk, her subjects should have a good opinion of her; lastly, how dangerous it was that ministers should disagree on the form of prayer for her majesty, or 'in doctrine concerning obedience to her Majesty's authority'. Moving now to the meat of the matter, he especially craved Knox to moderate himself, not only in the form of prayer he used, but also in the doctrine 'touching her estate and obedience'. With heavy irony he asked Knox not to take this as a reproach, but to remember that others may propound the same views 'not with the same modesty', and that he feared what this might engender in the people's heads. It was not too difficult for Knox to see the agenda behind this argument and he replied,

If such as fear God have occasion to praise him, that because idolatry is maintained, the servants of God despised, wicked men placed in honour and authority . . . [and] if those and the like use to provoke God's vengeance against realms and nations, then, in my judgement, the godly within Scotland ought to lament and mourn; and so to prevent God's judgement, lest that he, finding all in a like security [situation] strike in his hot indignation, beginning perchance at such as think they offend not.

This difficult statement drew up battle lines, and by now it was clear to the twenty or so in that small room that a debate was launched between Knox and Lethington over ground with which everyone was familiar. Indeed Lethington started by saying that this was a subject on which he and Knox were unlikely to agree. Perhaps unwisely, he asked Knox how he could prove that God had ever punished a God-fearing people for the iniquities of their prince.

Knox did not appreciate the interruption. 'I looked, my Lord, to have audience, till that I had absolved the other two parts, but seeing that it pleases your Lordship to cut me off before the middle, I will answer your question.'

Knox gave an immediate scriptural example of such an event, and Lethington moved swiftly to his second point, of the opinion Knox delivered publicly about Mary and of his form of prayer for her.

Knox said he was driven by his conscience. 'I have called to God for her conversion and have willed the people to do the same, showing them the dangerous estate not only she herself stands but also the whole realm, by reason of her enduring blindness.'

'That is it,' said Lethington, 'wherein we find the greatest fault. Your extremity against her Mass, in particular, passes measure. You call her a slave to Satan, you affirm that God's vengeance hangs over the realm, by reason of her impiety; and what else is this but to rouse up the heart of the people against her Majesty, and against them that serve her?'

In support of this the Master of Maxwell interjected, 'If I were in the Queen's Majesty's place, I would not suffer such things as I hear.'

Lethington went on, 'You pray for the Queen's Majesty with one condition, saying, "Illuminate her heart, if your good pleasure be"; whereby it may appear that you doubt of her conversion.'

'Not I, my Lord, but her own obstinate rebellion causes more than me to doubt of her conversion.'

'She thinks that not rebellion but good religion'.

Knox was immovable. 'So thought they that sometimes offered their children to Moloch . . .'

Lethington wriggled. 'But yet you can produce the example of none that so has prayed before you.'

'I will demand a question, whither you think that the apostles prayed themselves as they commanded others to pray?'

'Who doubts of that,' came from everyone present. They were enjoying this battle of wits between the young man, arguing for a maintenance of traditional values, and the old man, proposing radical change. Knox went on to quote Peter exhorting Simon Magus to pray that his previous heresies might be forgiven and declared that he had the same wish in his heart for the Queen.

Lethington moved on to his second point, asking where the Prophets spoke so irreverently of kings or princes. The inevitable Old Testament examples were quoted and Lethington, now fighting a rearguard action, disavowed them on the basis that these long past examples did not appertain to the present. But St Paul had validated the entire scripture as written for our instruction, so precedents poured forth until: 'Secretary Lethington leant upon the Master of Maxwell's breast, who said, "I am almost weary, I would that some other would reason in the chief head, which has not been touched [upon]." ' Morton as chancellor bade George Hay, the chaplain to the council, to reason with Knox as to the obedience due to princes.

He declined to do so on the perfectly valid grounds that he agreed with Knox, and the baton passed back to the weary Lethington. Knox raised the old argument that when men oppose unjust princes they oppose not God but the devil.

Lethington tried to split a hair. 'If the Queen command me to slay John Knox, because she is offended with him, I would not obey her. But, and should she command others to do it, or if it be a colour of justice [to] take his life from him, I cannot tell if I [would] be found to defend him against the Queen and against her officers.'

Knox answered, 'I say, my Lord, that if you be persuaded of my innocence, and if God has given to you such a power and credit as might deliver me, and yet suffered me to perish, that in so doing you should be criminal and guilty of my blood.'

'Prove that and win the play,' said Lethington.

Knox, needless to say, quotes from the old Testament, citing the case of Jeremiah being sentenced to death by the people, priests and prophets, for foretelling the fall of Jerusalem. They would have been guilty of spilling innocent blood. Lethington thought that the two cases were totally dissimilar, since the King had not condemned him to death.

But Knox maintained that this did not matter since the final authority was the King's and he, with the whole city, would bear responsibility for shedding Jeremiah's blood. 'God craves not only that a man do no iniquity in his own person, but also that he oppose himself to all iniquity, so far as in him lies.'

Lethington, having been over this ground before, could see that the dam was breaking. 'Then will you make subjects to control their princes and rulers?'

'And what harm should the Commonwealth receive, if that the corrupt effects of ignorant rulers were moderated, and so bridled by the wisdom and discretion of godly subjects, that they should do wrong nor violence to no man?'

Lethington, wisely, shifted his ground. 'All this reasoning is nought of the purpose; for we reason as if the Queen should become such an enemy to our religion . . . which I am assured she never will do . . . Our question is whether we ought to suppress the Queen's Mass? Or whether her idolatry should be [laid] to our charge?'

'Idolatry ought not [only] to be suppressed, but the idolator ought to die the death, unless we accuse God'.

'I know the idolator is commanded to die the death; But by whom?'

'By the people of God, for the commandment was given to Israel.'

'But there is no commandment given to the people to punish their King if he be an idolator.'

'I find no more privilege granted to Kings by God, more than the people, to offend God's majesty.'

'I grant,' said Lethington, 'but yet the people may not be judge to their King to punish him, albeit he be an idolator.'

'God is the universal judge as well to the King as to the people; so that what his word commands to be punished in one, is not to be absolved in the other.'

'We agree in that.'

The audience were on the edges of their seats for this battle of principles.

Lethington went on, 'But the people may not execute God's judgement, but man [should] leave it to Himself, who will either punish it by death, by war, by imprisonment, or by some other plagues.'

Not so, argued Knox. 'I am assured that you have no other warrant except your own imagination, and the opinion of those who more fear to offend princes than God.'

Lethington had clearly prepared himself for this confrontation; indeed, he said that putting together his arguments had cost him more labour than seven years' reading commentaries. He now quoted Luther, Melancthon, Bucer, Musculus and Calvin, even delving into the apocryphal Book of Baruch. Knox replied with what was almost a full sermon based on God's instructions to Abraham not to defile himself with idolatry and to resist tyrants who imposed it. He warned Lethington that he and Mary 'shall drink the cup of God's indignation', for Lethington having permitted and maintained Mary in her idolatry. The debate lasted well over an hour with more or less the same arguments being deployed, fruitlessly, by both sides. Lethington tried belittling Knox by saying that he doubted if there were many learned men of his opinion. Knox produced a copy of the *Apology of Magdeburg*, asking Lethington to read the list of ministers who had subscribed to this tract exhorting the citizens to resist the rule of the Emperor Charles V. Lethington read it and said, 'Homines obscuri' ('Unimportant men') while Knox replied, 'Dei tamen servi', ('But servants of God'). Finally Lethington asked that the company vote on the rights of the Kirk to condemn the Queen. Knox objected on the grounds that this was a more or less secret meeting and the matter should be debated by the whole assembly, for 'whatever should bind, the multitude should hear'. Then, argued Lethington, 'Why may the Lords not vote, and then show to the Kirk whatever is done?' Knox thought this was doing things in the wrong order, but Lethington, who obviously thought the debate had lasted long enough, asked the lord chancellor to call a vote. Some supported the status quo of condemning the Mass while allowing Mary her right to celebrate in private, while others wanted to take by force 'a poisoned cup when she was going to drink it'.

In an attempt to break the impasse, the clerk of the register reminded them that in the past they had requested Knox to write to Calvin for his judgement and suggested that they did so now. Knox told them that Lethington had undertaken to write to Calvin with less bias than he would have felt. Lethington told them that he had had second thoughts about being a subject and asking for advice without the consent of his sovereign. The courtiers applauded this 'as if Apollo had given his response'. Knox declared that the truth of Christ had been betrayed and God would one day have his revenge. All idea of voting stopped and Knox was commanded to write to Calvin. He refused, saying he knew the minds of the most learned in Europe and was fully prepared to teach their doctrines, but no one took up his offer and the meeting broke up in sweaty rancour.

This debate, if it can be called such, marks the moment when the Reformers realized that they would make no further progress and that the report of the ministers on the *Book of Discipline* was largely irrelevant. If this report was given, it was not reported in the *History*, in favour of Knox's lengthy verbatim report of the debate with Lethington. To a twentieth-century mind Knox's arguments, especially if shorn of Old Testament authority, carry the greater validity, and Lethington's devotion to the royal prerogative looks backwards, while Knox was looking to a future already half agreed. The provisions of the *Book of Discipline* might have been accepted by parliament, they might even be law, but their implementation would never be achieved.

In terms of *realpolitik* the power of the country lay in the hands of Moray and Lethington, and they followed wherever the monarch led. Their method of government dated back to the Middle Ages and their prestige and wealth depended on its continuance. Knox and the assembly were asking for a peaceful revolution with power being devolved to the people, guided, as ever, by a Protestant God. But democracy would have to wait a little longer.

Outside the confines of Knox's manse and the debating chamber of the Tolbooth, the other great topic of controversy was undoubtedly Mary's unmarried state. Lethington was still negotiating with Spain as to the possibility of a marriage to Don Carlos, a prospect that horrified Elizabeth and Cecil. Neither of them had any faith in Knox's pious hope that Mary might renounce Rome, and so a union with Spain would mean a complete encirclement of England by Catholic powers. There were no realistic Protestant suitors available and Elizabeth, at Cecil's prompting, even suggested a marriage with her favourite, Lord Robert Dudley, soon to be the earl of Leicester. Lord Robert had the advantage of being Protestant and had been in correspondence with Knox, who, in a letter of October 1563, had summed up the condition of the Scottish nobility for him.

True it is, my Lord, that zeal, joined with knowledge, once appeared in a great part of our nobility; but alas, to the grief of many hearts, it is now judged to be waxen cold, whether it be by reason of this late calm and tranquillity, in the which every man seeks to build his own house, and to make himself great, having small care to edify the house of God: whether this, I say, be the cause, or whether because, from the beginning they sought not the truth, but their own advantage, I know not, God knoweth: but this is most certain, that there appears no such fervency in the most part of our nobility (our courtiers are the coldest) as I have sometimes seen. Yes, I am ashamed and confounded within myself, when I consider so great a mutation within so short a space.

There was no need for Knox to say that he wrote this with a heavy heart. Randolph felt that Mary might well follow Elizabeth's advice, although

To follow altogether her own fantasy, is not best to be allowed. To be ordered by her own subjects, however faithful they may be, is to yield too much, and more than can stand with a princely heart. She is most willing to follow the advice of one in grandeur like herself . . .

In the same letter Randlolph passes on a piece of gossip. 'An Italian "Piementois" a singer . . . is her secretary for French affairs. He has crept in.' His name was David Rizzio. Mary herself, in a private letter to her aunt, assured her that negotiations with Don Carlos had ceased and that she would soon find a husband elsewhere.

Moray felt grudgingly that Dudley would be a better match than anyone else. A match with 'the other' 'would breed us more trouble than commodity, and no less sorrow to our mistress than to any . . .' But Dudley had no wish to take part in the marriage game and Elizabeth certainly had misgivings over losing her favourite courtier. Mary also refused to enter into negotiations over a marriage to Dudley unless Elizabeth accepted her as next heir to the English throne. The plan of Cecil and Lethington came to nothing. But a new suitor did appear in the person of 'the other', Henry Stewart, Lord Darnley. He traced his ancestral line back to Mary, daughter of James II, and had a claim to the throne if Mary died childless, provided it could be shown that Chatelherault's father had had an invalid divorce, thus rendering his now mad son illegitimate. Darnley's father, the earl of Lennox, had married Lady Margaret Douglas, a niece of Henry VIII, so his veins flowed with copious royal blood.

At the ceremony when Dudley was made earl of Leicester, James Melville was told by Elizabeth that 'you like better of yonder long lad', pointing to Darnley. Melville returned to Scotland with presents from Lady Lennox, Darnley's mother. They were a diamond ring for Mary, a diamond for Moray and a watch set with diamonds and rubies for Lethington. Melville says she was a very wise matron, and Darnley was equally 'wise', for when

Mary Beaton and the ambassador beat the Queen and Darnley at a game of cards, he paid Mary Beaton 'a ring and a brooch with two agates worth fifty crowns'. Not only was he 'wise' he was undoubtedly a handsome young courtier. Eighteen years old, possibly over six feet tall, his graceful manners and aesthetic interests would bring back memories of Brantôme and Mary's French courtiers, but he was also a Catholic. This may have pleased Mary but it horrified Cecil, who dispatched Nicholas Throckmorton to further Dudley's cause. He was to discover how firmly Mary insisted on being recognized as Elizabeth's heir, and to tell her that it was felt that the marriage with Darnley was 'not meet for her. And if she presses to know the causes moving us, you shall say we did not open them to you'. On 26 February Darnley had dined with Moray and Randolph before hearing Knox preach. He was then persuaded by Moray to dance a galliard with the Queen. But Moray still thought, 'if she take fancy to this new come geste [Darnley] then shall thee be sure of mischief, sedition and debate at home'. But Mary had at last found a dancing partner who was taller than she was.

She continued to shock Knox and the Protestants by her behaviour, as at the feast of the resurrection she and 'divers' of her women disguised themselves as 'bourgeois' wives and went about the town selling favours to finance a banquet at which the disguises, which had fooled no one, were discarded. More seriously, when a priest was stood at the market cross for four hours, Randolph tells us that 10,000 eggs were spent on him and he was beaten by 300 or 400 men with batons, before the provost rescued him and returned him to join two others in irons in the Tolbooth. Mary commanded that they be released and their confiscated property restored, 'which is obeyed to the great offence of the whole people'.

On 1 May Elizabeth, who thought the Darnley marriage 'very strange', officially told the Scottish council that it would be 'unmeet, unprofitable and perilous to the sincere amity between the two Queens'. Moray was bluntly told by Mary to give his written endorsement of the marriage and when he refused, 'she gave him many sore words'. Darnley's rise was now unstoppable; the *Diurnal of Occurrents* tells of his elevation in the ranks of the aristocracy in 1565.

25th May, Henry Stewart was made Knight of Torbolton, Lord Ardmannoch and earl of Ross in Stirling; [Randolph dates this as happening on the 14th and adds the dukedom of Rothesay to the list.]

22nd July, Henry, earl of Ross, Lord Armannoch and Torbolton knight, was proclaimed in the parish kirk of St Giles, in Holyroodhouse, and in the Chapel Royal, to be married with Mary, by the grace of God, Queen of Scots; and the same day, between three and four in the afternoon, the said earl of Ross was made duke of Albany, with great magnificence, by our sovereign in the Abbey of Holyroodhouse. [Knox's *History* – now being written by an unknown hand, based on Knox's notes and papers – gives Darnley's elevation to the dukedom of Rothesay as happening on 23 July.]

Mary had now antagonized her previous advisers, as Randolph wrote to Leicester on 3 June: 'Her councillors now are those she liked the worst, the nearest of her kin are farthest from her heart: my Lord of Moray liveth where he list . . . David [Rizzio] is he that now works all.'

He goes on to report the universal dislike in which Darnley is held. 'When they have said and thought all they can, they find nothing but that, "God must send him a short end." ' The Queen is obviously besotted – 'her wits are not what they were' – and 'she is a woman more to be pitied than any that ever I saw'. He also repeats the standard rumours of witchcraft, bewitching bracelets and 'sacred mysteries'. He says he would tell us more, but tantalizingly breaks off, since he dares not delay the bearer.

Mary had summoned a parliament, later postponed, for 20 June, although her council now consisted only of the earls of Lennox and Atholl, Lord Ruthven, David Rizzio and, of course, Darnley. Moray and Lethington were noticeably absent. Moray had been expressly summoned but claimed that since armed assassins awaited him in Edinburgh, he would not attend. He was then summoned on pain of being proclaimed traitor, and forty-eight hours later Mary's half-brother and chief counsellor was 'put to the horn' and declared a traitor along with the earl of Argyll.

On 28 July a proclamation was made an hour after sunset at the market cross in Edinburgh.

That forasmuch at the will and pleasure of Almighty God, the Queen has taken to her husband a right excellent and illustrious Prince, Harry, duke of Rothesay, earl of Ross, Lord Darnley. Therefore it is her will that he should be holden and obeyed, and reverenced as King; commanding all letters and proclamations to be made in the names of Henry and Mary in times coming.

Next day, the *Diurnal of Occurents* reports,

'The said Henry, King, and Mary Queen of Scots was married in the chapel of Holyroodhouse, at six in the morning, by John Sinclair, Dean of Restalrig, with great magnificence, accompanied by the whole nobility of the realm.

The groom was destined to be remembered by history, not as King Henry I of Scotland, but merely as 'Darnley'. His entry in *Chambers Biographical Dictionary* reads, 'See Mary, Queen of Scots'. After the marriage ceremony the Queen went to hear Mass, but without her new husband, who went 'to his pastime'. However, for three or four days balls and festivities were held in Holyrood.

The General Assembly of 1565 had sent six articles to the Queen for ratification by parliament. These articles largely reasserted the previous actions of the Kirk towards endorsement of the *Book of Discipline*: the banning of Mass and endorsing of Protestantism; provision of sustenance for ministers; overseeing by the superintendents of all education; the putting in place of proper finance for the support of the poor and town schools; the appointment of judges to prosecute crime of all sorts; and finally, the exemption of poor labourers from tithes. It also took time to concern itself with purely spiritual matters. But they indicate the hardships present. Was it lawful for a minister not receiving a stipend to live else-where than with his flock? It was not, but if hardship forced him to return to previous employment, he might, although his vocation was inviolable.

But there were more pressing matters for Mary. On the 13th she and Darnley had sent a letter to Elizabeth to assure her of their lifelong loyalty, asking for a treaty of friendship, and promising not to interfere with the religion of England should they succeed to its throne. All of this depended, naturally, on Elizabeth acknowledgeing Mary and Darnley as her heirs. The Tudor fury can only be imagined.

Domestically, Knox's old allies, Chatelherault, Moray, Glencairn, Rothes, and so on, had met at Ayr to gather forces. But before they could convene, Mary summoned them all to meet her at Linlithgow on the same date.

To Knox these events must have sounded like the knell of doom for all ideas of reform. He had antagonized his old ally, Moray, although he could be relied on to support the Protestant cause. But Moray was now outlawed and a fugitive. Arran was stark mad – on 24 May Randolph reported he had asked for saws to cut off his legs and hands, as well as ropes and knives to end his own life – and Lethington, an ally in Protestantism if not in democracy, was keeping a diplomatically low profile. Knox's only remaining public outlet was in the pulpit of St Giles and even that was about to be put in jeopardy.

One of Darnley's many shortcomings was a childish desire to please everyone. Although a Catholic, he had not attended the nuptial mass, and had heard Knox preach in St Giles. He was said to be either papist or Protestant as it suited him, and he must have had enough political sensitivity to realize that the Edinburgh bourgeoisie would not be kept in order merely by his wife's cavorting amongst them in masquerade. To this end, he attended St Giles, to hear Knox preach again. This was clearly a very formal situation as a throne had been prepared for him in the Church, and Knox was well warned of his coming. One hopes the throne was especially comfortable, since the service lasted an hour longer than normal. The results of Knox's sermon were so severe that he took the extraordinary step of writing it down 'as far as memory serves' on 30 August and having it published on 19 September. He apologizes by saying that, normally, his 'tongue and lively voice' were moved extempore by God, but since this sermon was heard not only by the faithful, but also by 'rank papists, dissembled hypocrites, and no small number of covetous claw-backs [back scratching sycophants] of the new court', he felt that a record of it should be made. The printed version of the sermon is prefaced with a quotation from Timothy, 'The time is come that men cannot abide the sermon of verity nor wholesome doctrine.'

His text, from the 13th to 23rd verses of Chapter 26 of Isaiah, gave warning of what was to come. 'O Lord, our God, other lords besides thee have ruled us . . . in trouble have they visited thee . . . the Lord cometh out of this place to visit the iniquity of the inhabitants of the earth upon them.' All eyes would have been on Darnley shifting uneasily on his new throne.

Knox explained that Isaiah had foretold that there would be no rest for the whole body until the head had returned to judgement. He went on to assert unsurprisingly that kings have no absolute power to rule as they please, but may only rule according to God's word. Would that Scotland have a king to rule in justice, equity and mercy! He bade his congregation subject themselves to the Lord their God before Scotland and Edinburgh was punished, as had been Judea. If you see impiety in the seat of justice, then, 'accuse thine own ingratitude . . . I will appoint, sayeth the Lord, children to be their princes, and babes shall rule over them. Children are extortioners of my people, and women have rule over them.'

Knox had no need to name names, as the whole church winced in embarrassment and the royal teeth gritted harder and harder. The *Diurnal of Occurrents* says that Darnley was 'crabbit' – a wonderfully expressive and virtually untranslatable Scots word – as sour as a crab-apple, as angry as a trodden-on crab, as dangerous as a beclawed predator: in short, very displeased. But Knox was only warming to his theme. He discoursed fluently on unjust rule in the Old Testament and God's judgement on the peoples and their rulers. 'It is almost incredible that man should be so enraged against God that neither his plagues, nor yet his mercy showed, should move them to repentance.' He inveighed against Ahab for tolerating the heresies of his wife Jezebel – always a favourite subject with Knox – 'but what was the end thereof? The last visitation of God was that dogs licked the blood of one [Ahab], and did eat the flesh of the other [Jezebel].'

This was enough of a warning, but Knox was only two-thirds through. He ended by praying that the people might survive the present yoke of His displeasure, and see what punishment He had created for the cruel tyrants: '. . . in thee may we find comfort till that this thy great indignation, begun amongst us, may pass over . . .' At the conclusion of this sermon Darnley stormed from the church in a white fury. Surrounded by his entourage he arrived back at the palace, refused the meal that had been prepared for him, leapt on to a horse and vented his fury by spending the afternoon hawking.

Once again Knox had managed to make a severe enemy of authority and while we might again note the absence of diplomacy, we cannot but admire the tenacity. Shorn of powerful friends and influence, with a Queen totally opposed to him and the General Assembly his only ally, a lesser man might have despaired. However, as when the Queen Regent's forces were within gunshot of St Andrews, he climbed into his pulpit and let fly with all guns. He found it impossible to dissemble, and although well aware that his 'vehemence of spirit' could well be his undoing, delivered the message that his duty impelled him to deliver.

The *History* states that Knox was 'immediately commanded' to appear before the council, while other authorities claim he was called from his bed later that night. Given the weight of the summons, it must have originated from the palace, and in any case Knox must have anticipated repercussions of some sort after his sermon, so it is difficult to believe that he had quietly gone to bed. Also we are told that he was accompanied to the council chamber by a 'great number of the most apparent men of the Town'.

Waiting for Knox were Atholl, Ruthven, the Justice Clerk, Lord Advocate, and Secretary Lethington. In the manner of one delivering a distasteful message, Lethington declared that, 'the King's Majesty was displeased with some of the words spoken in the sermon, and Knox was to abstain from preaching from fifteen or twenty days'. John Craig was to stand as substitute. A marginal note claims that Darnley had blamed Mary for having him tarred with the papist brush. At this Mary naturally had a fit of weeping and demanded Knox's removal from the pulpit.

The Burgh Council immediately objected to having their minister summarily dismissed, but Mary in turn instructed them to remove the provost. He obediently resigned, and the citizens of Edinburgh were excused from compulsory service in the pursuit of the outlawed Moray. Knox's ban was limited to an abstention while Mary and Darnley were in Edinburgh. Two days later they did leave the capital in pursuit of the rebel lords, 'to daunt the earl of Moray', and took with them six pieces of artillery.

The rebels following Moray now had about 1,000 cavalry, and the leaders included Chatelherault, Moray, Glencairn, Ochiltree and Kirkaldy of Grange. With almost comic synchronicity, as Mary's forces entered Glasgow, the rebels entered Edinburgh on 31 August. There was no welcome for them as the citizens refused to take any part and the governor of the castle issued an ultimatum demanding their removal under pain of being bombarded by his cannon. Erskine, the governor, had recently been created earl of Mar; he received no answer and started his bombardment at four o'clock in the afternoon of the 1st September, thus annoying Knox who was trying to write out his troublesome sermon in his manse, half a mile from the castle. The rebels expected Argyll to join them, but knew they were outnumbered. They wrote to Mary saying that their revolt was not against royal power, but about the maintenance of the Protestant religion. By way of answer she locked up their messenger.

This was the start of what has come down to us as 'the Chaseabout Raid', when Mary's forces pursued the rebels all over the south of Scotland. Mary herself, it was said, rode with a pistolet in her hand, while Darnley stood out in 'a gilt corselet'. Although the opposing forces never met, nobles on both sides took the opportunity of burning and pillaging in payment of old scores, with Morton joining the rebels by the 9th. At the end of the month the royal pair sent a proclamation to the market cross in Edinburgh, declaring that the revolt was not over religious matters, but over the basic right to govern, 'to invert the very order of nature, to make the prince obey, and subjects command'. Her council was now dominated by David Rizzio, and curiously had been joined by one James Balfour, who in 1548, some seventeen years previously, had sat beside Knox on a slave's bench in a French galley. Bothwell arrived from exile in France and was welcomed to the council. Mary, seriously running out of money, rounded up the richest citizens of Edinburgh and sent six of them to the castle under threat of death until the remainder paid up a thousand marks. (The mark or 'merk' was an accounting unit worth two-thirds of a pound.) The revolt ended with Moray and the rebel lords retreating into England at Carlisle after repeated demands to Elizabeth for men and supplies. There the rebels enjoyed the hospitality of the earl of Bedford in Newcastle, while Moray posted south to London. He was publicly rebuffed by Elizabeth: 'How he, being a rebel to her sister of Scotland, durst take the boldness upon him to come within her realm.' He returned north, where Elizabeth did grant the rebels some covert ('not manifest') aid. The public rebuff most probably had the Tudor tongue well in the royal cheek. Knox prayed openly for the rebels, and when questioned by the council, Lethington affirmed that he had heard the sermons and found nothing at which any man could be offended – according to scripture it was lawful to pray for all men.

In November Mary wrote to Paul de Foix, the French ambassador in England, with news to be passed on to Elizabeth that Moray had plotted to murder Darnley and his father Lennox, taking Mary prisoner. Mary and Darnley had managed to alienate nearly everyone of influence in Scotland. The resentment against Rizzio was enormous, as he had ousted Moray and Lethington and closed the royal ear to Scots advice. Atholl and Cassilis alone remained at her side as staunchly Catholic lords.

Lennox was included in the royal circle, although as Darnley's father this was hardly surprising. Knox describes Darnley as 'having in his company gentlemen willing to satisfy his will and affections'. This comment may be innocent enough, but can be read as hiding a suspicion of Darnley's bisexuality. Mary and Darnley had quarrelled over an appointment, with the Queen supporting Bothwell and Darnley proposing his father. But by November the rumour, reported by Randolph as fact, began circulating that Mary was pregnant. A week later it was a false alarm. She was pregnant and the likelihood was that the child would be christened as a Catholic. If male, then the next king of Scotland would be the enemy of the Reformation.

13   A New King

The General Assembly faced one of the bleakest prospects for the Reformed Church. The weather had been unusually hard for two winters, with poultry freezing to death and spectacular displays of the aurora borealis – described by Knox as: 'in the firmament battles arrayed, spears and other weapons' – and there was universal hardship. All previous requests to Mary for payment of the 'thirds' had been rebuffed and the Church was cripplingly short of money. The assembly was attended by Lethington, along with the earls of Morton and Mar; together they appointed a commission to petition the Queen. They were met with her assertion that the omission of payments of the 'thirds' was entirely due to the actions of Wishart of Pittarrow, the comptroller, and that as far as questions concerning religion were concerned she would not debate with the commissioners, since they were so much more learned than herself. This was, 'nothing but delay and driving off in the old manner . . . [while] the Queen was busied with banqueting about.' Supplications to Mary from former friars that they might be allowed to preach were immediately granted. The assembly was being quietly sidelined.

Knox was bidden to write to all the ministers of the Church, stiffening their spirit. In his letter he admits that he knows

> how vehement a dart poverty is, and what troublesome cogitations it is able to raise, yea, even in men of greatest constancy . . . and shall we for poverty leave the flock of Jesus Christ before that it utterly refuse us? God forbid, dear Brethren, for what shall discern us from the mercenaries and hirelings, if our constancy in adversity shall not do it? . . . Let us be frequent in reading . . . earnest in prayer, diligent in watching over the flock committed to our charge, and let our sobriety and temperate life shame the wicked, and be example to the godly.

The assembly also took the extraordinary step of ordering a general fast, and Knox wrote a long *Order and Doctrine for the General Fast*, explaining it to the faithful. The dates were to be the last Sunday in February and the first Sunday in March. Knox justifies what could be seen by some as a papist rite, since they fasted publicly and boasted about it. Knox explained that there were two kinds of fasting described in scripture: the private, which was a personal penitential statement of conscience; and the public which was one decreed by the Church on a particular occasion and for a particular purpose. Scotland was already infected with the Mass, and the Council of Trent had decreed that all of the new religion should be exterminated. 'If we would that our palaces should be so destroyed, that they should remain desolate, and be dens to dragons . . . then we need neither to fast or pray, repent nor turn to God: but if we desire either to find mercy in this life, or joy and comfort in the life to come, we must show ourselves unfeignedly sorry for the abominations that now reign.' The chief among these abominations was self-satisfaction with being law-abiding. In a marginal note he says, 'Christian justice craves more than Civil Laws', and goes on to decry the philosophy of simply doing no worse than any other:

> Thus does every man lean on the iniquity of an other, and thinks himself sufficiently excused when he meets craft with craft, and repels violence either with deceit or else with open injury. Let us be assured, dear Brethren, that these be the sins which have heretofore provoked God, not only to plague, but also to destroy, and utterly overthrow strong realms and commonwealths.

This was completely in line with his belief that universal justice encompassed laws that took precedence over all others, including the man-made laws of magistrates. These were only valid when in accordance with the greater good of the people.

The system of the fast was comparatively severe, with only bread and water between eight o'clock on Saturday night and five o'clock on Sunday night, with no games or 'gorgeous apparel', but with the sick and weak exempted from the exercise. The length of church services was to be extended – but not made tedious – to three hours in the morning and two in the afternoon, and the rest of the day was to be spent by each family in meditation. This, he felt, was truer and less vain than the much vaunted papistical abstention from flesh while filling, 'the belly with fish, wine, spices and other delicacies'. The *Diurnal* hoped that the fast would cause

God to 'inform, mollify and make soft the hearts of our sovereigns towards our nobility which are now in England'. This was a reference to Moray and his supporters Argyll and Glencairn, who were now in open revolt against Mary. These fasts were not in fact held until 3 and 10 of March, and by then matters had changed out of all recognition.

The assembly was not alone in its trouble, for the vexed question of whether Darnley should be invested with the crown matrimonial was a constant irritant. It was solved by Mary allowing him only his arms as duke of Rothesay – 'whereby it was perceived that her love waxed cold towards him.' The royal seals were given to Rizzio, who arranged everything. Darnley's dislike of Rizzio was now so great that there must, 'grow a scab between them'. Knox says that Rizzio's help was provided only if 'his hands were anointed' [a bribe was given] but this accusation seems beyond proof, either way. In February Mary injudiciously proposed that Mass be said in St Giles, but wiser heads prevailed. Lethington felt privately that there was no way out of the now numerous schisms rending Scotland unless 'we chop at the very root'. Mary, ever fearful of English involvement, banished Randolph, the somewhat reluctant English ambassador, on suspicion of his having lent Moray 3,000 crowns. Randolph promptly left for Berwick, and Elizabeth, equally promptly, expelled the Scottish ambassador. Randolph was able to reveal a bond signed by Argyll, Moray, Glencairn, and the others, that at the next parliament after their return from England they would grant the crown matrimonial to Darnley, as well as maintaining the religion established by the Queen after her arrival. In other words, an end to the toleration of the Mass. In return Darnley promised to allow their return, free of forfeiture, and support the reformed religion. Rizzio, however, was moving parliament towards restoring the old religion and imposing heavy forfeitures on the exiles. More important than that, Randolph revealed that Darnley was determined to be 'at the apprehension and execution of him, whom he is able manifestly to charge with the crime, and to have done to him the most dishonour that can be to any man'. Darnley was said to believe any misinformation, 'in the foulest way'.

Those privy to this plot were named as Argyll, Morton, Boyd, Ruthven, Lethington, Moray, Rothes and Kirkaldy of Grange, as well, of course, as Randolph and his host the earl of Bedford. By the 8th the exiled lords were gathering with Morton in Edinburgh and Argyll expected. The deed was to be done 'as time and opportunity will serve', but before Moray's return. James Melville had warned Mary and Rizzio of impending danger, but

Mary defied the rebels. 'What can they do, and what dare they do?' And Rizzio himself 'disdained all danger and despised counsel . . . the Scots would brag but not fight.' In spite of this braggadoccio he surrounded himself with a bodyguard of Italian mercenaries. The temperature of intrigue in Edinburgh was very high and the slightest spark could set off an explosion. It might seem that the only person of note in Scotland who did not know of the impending action was John Knox.

The events of the night of 9 March 1566 are well known. The Queen was in her private supper-room with five others: Lord Robert Stewart, her half-brother; Jane, Countess of Argyll, whose marriage Knox had tried to mend; her equerry Erskine; her page Standen and David Rizzio. The room itself is no more than a closet some twelve feet square, and it must have been quite a crush. The fire was ablaze and the room was candle-lit, so allowing for the press of people and the costume of the time, it would have been hot and stuffy, especially for the six-months-pregnant Mary. The first addition to the company was Darnley, whose arrival was a considerable surprise. He would have been able to enter the Queen's apartments by a private stair from his rooms on the floor below, but since relations had deteriorated between him and the Queen he was rarely seen, spending most of his leisure in the taverns and low-life meeting houses of the town. His function on this evening, however, seems to have been to ensure that the Queen remained in her place, for he took up post leaning on her chair. His other function was to allow the conspirators access to his private stair. They, along with the earl of Morton, had already gained access to the palace, taking keys from the porter, and had left a number in the courtyard to seal off the royal apartments.

The next entrant into the Queen's supper room was Ruthven. He was more than half mad, a meddler in witchcraft, and on this occasion in armour. His complexion was also heavily flushed as a result of a long illness. Mary asked, 'What strange sight is this, my Lord? Are you mad?' Ruthven replied, 'We have been too long mad'. The atmosphere in the tiny room now changed from close discomfort to terror, as Ruthven demanded that Rizzio be given up to him to be hanged. Rizzio, understandably retreated to the furthest spot from the door and the Queen's servants protested. Ruthven drew his sword and five more conspirators, armed with swords and pistols, rushed into the room. There were now thirteen people in the room, and candles and tables went over as one George Douglas seized Darnley's dagger and plunged it into Rizzio. He was clinging to Mary's skirts and screaming for her to help him, but to no avail. Rizzio's hands were prised loose by Ker of Fawdonside, who was holding a pistol to the Queen's pregnant belly, by bending the Italian's fingers to breaking point. Still screaming, Rizzio was dragged through the bedchamber to the audience chamber beyond, where, according to the *History*, he was killed with fifty-three dagger and sword strokes. All of which butchery would have been clearly audible to the terrified company, left wondering if they would be next. Ruthven at this point apparently sat down and sent a servant to fetch him a drink. In a letter to the archbishop of Glasgow, Mary's ambassador in Paris, written nearly a month later, she says that Ruthven told her that he was highly offended with her proceedings and tyranny, and resented being abused by Rizzio, who maintained the ancient religion, turned loyal lords into fugitives, entertained treaties with foreign princes, and put the traitors Bothwell and Huntly on the council. He went on that they had only meant to hang Rizzio – they had brought ropes for the purpose. She was told that she was a prisoner and if she tried to escape she would be 'cut into collops'. Rizzio's body was then thrown down the palace stairs leaving only copious pints of blood to mark his exit. Until quite recently, this bloodstain could be seen on the floor and ghoulish tourists would remove pieces as souvenirs. The palace authorities, tired of continually replacing the bloodstain, now have marked the spot with a brass plate. One of the 'Maries' rushed past the scene of carnage to her mistress with the news that Rizzio was dead. Mary responded, 'No more tears! I will now think upon revenge!'

By now the alarm was sounding and men were rushing about in panic. The earls of Atholl, Bothwell and Huntly, who had quarters in the palace, escaped the confusion by 'leaping down out of a window toward a little garden where the lions were lodged'. Bothwell and Huntley escaped to Crichton, Bothwell's castle, south of Edinburgh. Lethington had fled to Atholl's lands near Dunblane. The assassins' plan was to carry the Queen to Stirling Castle, where she would be kept prisoner until the birth of her child. Its sex would determine their next move, and if there was any attempt to rescue Mary, 'she would be cut into gobbets and thrown from the terrace'. Ruthven appears to have been fond of this threat. The general alarm sounded in the streets and the provost, newly appointed at Mary's insistence, arrived at the now locked palace gates, but was convinced by Darnley that the Queen was quite well, 'and thereafter the Provost came home with his inhabitants of Edinburgh'. The citizens were, however, equipped for a search, with £4.7s.6d worth of wax torches, specially provided at the town council's expense. Darnley attempted to see the Queen but was refused admittance and spent the remainder of the night drawing up orders for the prorogation of Parliament. In effect, Mary was no longer Queen. Next morning, Melville of Halhill was leaving the palace on the pretext of going to hear Knox at St Giles, when Mary appeared at the window of her apartments, where she was still being held prisoner, and shouted to him to summon again the provost and citizens again to rescue her. His rescue attempt was thwarted by the remaining conspirators.

The exiled lords returned to Edinburgh and parliament was suspended. Darnley made a proclamation exiling all papists from Edinburgh, 'which proclamation was indeed observed, for they had, "a flea in their hose." ' The wearing of weapons in the streets was also forbidden. The Queen, with Darnley – 'the uxorious King' – (also, 'the simple king, who was allured by her sugared words') met with Moray, probably in the very room in which Rizzio had bled his last two days previously. She offered the rebels a conditional pardon, which was refused, and called for a midwife, pretending the onset of childbirth. From her private chamber she and Darnley escaped that evening, and they fled to Dunbar, as had her mother. The panic seemed to be over.

> The Church Reformed . . . was delivered and freed from all the apparent dangers which were like to have fallen upon them; for if Parliament had taken effect . . . the true Protestant Religion should have been wrecked, and Popery erected; and for the same purpose, there were certain wooden altars made, to the number of twelve, found ready in the Chapel of the Palace of Holyroodhouse, which should have been erected in St Giles . . .'

Knox's spirits must have lifted by this turn of events, but what previous knowledge of it did he have? And had he endorsed the activities of the conspirators? As we have said, he seemed to have no knowledge of the plot, but this is hard to believe of the man who was the spiritual leader of the Protestants, and had been the personal friend of most of the disaffected. Moreover, and probably most importantly, he was possessed of the best spy network in Edinburgh. Knox must have known that the proposed parliament would have re-established the Catholic religion and that Rizzio was the main proponent of this policy. Things had gone far beyond the possibility of even Lethington having any influence over the outcome while the

Queen and Darnley were being led by Rizzio. This would have caused a real dilemma for Knox. The obvious answer to the problem in a sixteenth-century aristocrat's mind would have been Rizzio's death, and Knox would have condemned that course of action out of hand. His solution, probably one of prayer and an appeal to the people, would have seemed ludicrous to one such as Ruthven, whose natural recourse was to the dagger. From the plotters' point of view, therefore, it would be better for Knox to be kept in ignorance as far as possible, and this might have been made very possible by Knox himself studiously not wanting to know what was being planned. From his pulpit he would have looked into the faces of men he must have suspected were plotting the murder of a high officer of state and very deliberately not enquired any further. A letter from Randolph to Cecil on the 21st has an additional page attached to it, not in Cecil's hand, listing the persons implicated. They are not surprising – Morton, Ruthven, Lyndsay, Lethington and a list of lords, including Ker of Fawdonside. The note goes on, 'All these were at the death of Davy and privy thereunto, and are now in displeasure with the Queen, and their houses taken and spoiled.' Then a little lower down, 'John Knox, John Craig, preachers'. This does sound like a round-up of 'the usual suspects' with Knox and his assistant included as an afterthought. This seems to imply that as a leader of both spiritual and political life he must be included, even if no evidence existed for such an inclusion.

It might seem at this point that the Protestant lords had gained victory, no matter how murderously the means. But by internal squabbling they allowed the victory laurel to fall. Bothwell and Huntly had joined the Queen at Dunbar, as did the master of Maxwell, and together they managed to dissuade her from wholesale revenge but to march on Edinburgh. This she did, entering the town on 18 March with 8,000 men and pitching cannon in the centre of the town – opposite to where the Tron Church stands today. Mary gave amnesty to all who were not directly involved in the plot. The direct perpetrators, having been 'put to the horn', had fled to England, Lethington was hiding in Dunkeld, and only one minor conspirator, Thomas Scott, was taken, hanged, drawn and quartered on 2 April. That seemed to draw a line under the conspiracy for the moment, except for the part played by Darnley.

The *History* takes up the story:

Within five days after their entry, here was a proclamation made at the

Market Cross, for the purgation of the king from the forsaid slaughter; which made all understanding men laugh at the passage of things.

Knox himself left for Kyle in the west of Scotland, having once again seen victory disappear. He prayed, 'Put an end, at thy good pleasure, to this my miserable life: for justice and truth are not to be found among the sons of men.' He did not doubt himself to be elected to eternal salvation, and that he should rise again in glory, but felt that the wicked would for a time tread him under their feet. He asked for his 'now desolate bedfellow, Margaret,' to feel God's merciful providence, as well as his children and his soon-to-be-born daughter.

The state of the Kirk was summed up by Bishop Grindal in a letter to Bullinger in Zurich: no payments to ministers for three years; the Queen doing all in her power to extirpate Protestantism; six or seven Masses daily at court; and John Knox banished with no sign of his possible return. Mary wrote to the new Pope Pius V, thanking him for his (unspecified) aid and for exhorting other Christian monarchs to do the same.

Darnley was now to all intents and purposes an exile in his own country, 'condemned and disteemed, so that scarcely any honour was done to him, and his father likewise'. He was travelling with few attendants and spreading discontent wherever he went. He wrote to Pope Pius as well as the kings of France and Spain, claiming that Mary was being lax in restoring the Catholic faith. These letters were intercepted by the royal intelligence service and read by Mary herself. She 'threatened him sore; and there never was after that any appearance of love between them.'

This was not however true of Mary's feelings towards Bothwell, who had now risen to be her chief counsellor in all things. James Hepburn, Earl of Bothwell, was a bandit from a long line of aristocratic bandits. Knox's family had been their feudal inferiors, and he had interceded in Bothwell's contretemps with the lunatic Arran. Bothwell had seized English gold, which he then delivered to Mary of Guise – how much of this gold stuck to the Hepburn fingers is not known – and had joined the Lords of the Congregation, embracing Protestantism. He had also embraced numerous women in his time. A breach of promise suit by one Anna Throndsen was waiting for him in Scandinavia. He had reputedly been the lover of Janet Beaton, mother of one of the 'Maries', herself possessed of a ferocious sexual appetite and accused of witchcraft. He was married to Jean Gordon, Huntly's sister, who provided much needed wealth. He was, in fact, everything that Darnley was not: short rather than tall, stocky rather than lissome, and forceful rather than effete. His portrait in the Scottish National Portrait Gallery depicts a man ready for a fight in a street brawl. And he was, at the moment anyway, a Protestant, although he was not a church attender.

Chatelherault had withdrawn to his estates in France, and Lethington, having been accepted by Bothwell, had returned to court with much reduced influence. Argyll and Moray, having had no direct hand in Rizzio's murder, were banqueted by the Queen, but under the watchful eyes of Bothwell and Huntly, while she 'graciously' received yet another supplication from the superintendents and ministers of the Kirk. She equally graciously vowed to ease their distress, but only after parliament had so instructed her. Then on 19 June 1566, in a tiny ante-room in Edinburgh Castle, she gave birth to a boy child. Since Mary was in good health and only twenty-three years of age it seemed that on her death an adult king would succeed to the throne of Scotland for the first time since Robert III over 200 years previously. The news was therefore greeted with enthusiasm, and the fervent hope that he would be baptized as a Protestant. Melville was sent at once to take the news to Elizabeth. After a ride of four days, he told Cecil 'at Greenwich, where Her Majesty was in great merriness and dancing after supper'. Cecil whispered the news to the Queen and 'all merriness was laid aside for the night . . . [the Queen] bursting out to some of her ladies that the Queen of Scots was lighter of a fair son, while she was but a barren stock'. Since Elizabeth was still famously a virgin, her reaction seems rather self-indulgent.

On 25 June, as ever, the General Assembly met for its biannual conference. The assembly, having passed judgement on the seducer Paul Methven and sentenced him to formal acts of repentance, passed to the vexed question of payment. Given the non-appearance of money for stipends, the assembly allowed for the mobility of ministers in areas of hardship, but forbade them to abandon their flocks and their vocation. The inevitable petition was sent to the Queen and Alexander Gordon, the superintendent of Galloway, and got 'fair answers'. This was not surprising, since he was Huntly's nephew and now styled himself the bishop of Galloway. Knox was still in his, admittedly self-imposed, exile, but was probably in St Andrews in September to consider a letter that had asked for Scottish endorsement of a new *Helvetic Confession of Faith*. (Calvin having died in 1564, de Beza was now the leader of the Genevan Church). The Scottish Kirk was in complete agreement with the *Confession*, except for the celebration of Christmas, Easter, Ascension, Pentecost, and so on, for which no scriptural authority could be found. However, forty ministers, including Knox, signed the endorsement, which was taken so seriously by de Beza that the Scottish comments were printed as an addendum in the French reprint of the *Helvetic Confession of Faith*.

The Queen was also tying up some loose ends and one Henry Yair, who had deserted from service in the Chapel Royal to serve Ruthven, was arrested, tried for treason and hanged and quartered. She also added to gossip by riding to Hermitage to nurse Bothwell, who had been wounded in a fight with Border brigands. She subsequently fell ill and lay near death in Jedburgh attended by Lethington. Curiously, Darnley attempted to visit her but was rebuffed. She did recover in time for James's baptism in Stirling on 17 December 1566.

Mary had written to Pope Pius V, thanking him for money and vowing that James would be raised as a Catholic. He was certainly baptized as one, in spite of the difficulty of finding torch-bearers, with great pomp by the archbishop of St Andrews; the countess of Argyll, a Protestant, but Mary's half-sister, attended the Queen. The French ambassador, du Croc, reported that he was christened Charles-James, Charles being the name of Mary's brother-in-law, the king of France.

There is a note of cynicism and sourness about the ceremony, which was not attended by Knox or Darnley, although he was in Stirling, and with the bulk of the Scots nobility standing outside the chapel to avoid the taint of papism, along with the English ambassador and the earl of Bedford. They had brought Elizabeth's christening present, a solid gold font worth 3,000 crowns, but after the ceremony, Bedford rejoiced to Mary that out of twelve Earls attending 'only two assist at this baptism to the superstition of Popery'. 'At the which saying the Queen kept good countenance.' Darnley left at once for Glasgow, where, it is alleged, he recovered from a poisoning attempt. His behaviour was now such that du Croc could not put it in writing, and Mary, having hurt one of her breasts in a riding accident en route for Stirling, had taken to her bed with tears of pain.

With Protestantism becoming tolerated again in court circles, and free of all taint from Rizzio's murder, there was now nothing to prevent Knox from returning to Edinburgh. The assembly met on 25 December, and used as it was to sending endless and fruitless petitions to the Queen was amazed to receive payments at last. This hardly resulted in unequivocal gratitude as a marginal note in the *History* shows: 'The Queen intending vengeance upon the poor King, and being in love with the Earl Bothwell, grants to the Protestants their petitions, that they may be quiet and trouble not their plots.'

Written with savage hindsight, this probably has a grain of truth, and Bothwell, as a Protestant, may well have been instrumental in moving Mary's mind towards this. Knox was extremely distrustful of the gift, which was a one-off payment and did not signal the regular payments of the 'thirds'. In a pamphlet to the Protestant community he is puzzled: 'how that any such assignation, or any promise made thereof, can stand in any stable assurance, when that Roman Antichrist (by just laws once banished from this realm) shall be intrused above us, we can in no wise understand'.

This pamphlet was an addendum to a letter from Knox to the nobility, responding to an act of Mary's made two days previously, on the 23rd. This act was a flagrant provocation, with an assembly convening so shortly after, for it reinstated the archbishopric of St Andrews as under the full author-ity of Rome. In his letter Knox regretted the prevalence of Satan and thus the extreme danger faced by Protestantism. He warned that the Queen was not well informed, and might break the laws of this realm. He was justly afraid that, as he had said before, this would represent the thin end of the wedge. 'Weigh this matter as it is, and you shall find it more weighty than it appears to many.' He beseeched the lords to give him an answer quickly, but even the assembly in its justified paranoia could not have guessed that the archbishopric had been restored merely to perform one future function.

Knox was also given the responsibility of writing to the Church of England, where disputes had broken out over the wearing of copes and surplices – the Romish rags – and internecine war seemed to be imminent. It was only just over eleven years since Bishop Hooper had been burnt for declining to follow *The Book of Common Prayer*'s rules on clerical dress. Such seeming trifles could seem of the utmost importance to emergent faiths.

Knox quoted scripture, 'If ye bite and devour one another, take heed ye be not consumed of one another', and in a gentle letter advised the quar-relling pastors to cling to the central core of their faith rather than the peripheral issues. Knox did not sign this letter personally, since another piece of business for the assembly was to grant him a leave of absence, in order that he could visit England. He had previously been granted such a leave, with Goodman to act as his substitute. The steward of Knox's household was instructed by the burgh council to wait on Goodman's table, showing that not only did Knox keep a certain luxury in his domestic arrangements, but that his servants were in all probability paid by the burgh council. Since this leave had been arranged for the start of 1566, Knox had become too embroiled in the general fast, and then the aftermath of the Rizzio affair; this was, then, a second application. It was granted and Knox was supplied with testimonials and endorsements as to his probity within the Church.

His sons, aged nine and eight, were being looked after by their grand-mother Elizabeth, who was living with her brothers in the north-east of England. Like everything in Knox's private life, this is all shrouded in mystery. We do not even know exactly where in Northumbria or Durham they were living, and certainly have no idea why Knox should want to leave his comparatively new wife and infant daughter, Martha, in Edinburgh. The absence of Elizabeth is understandable since at any time in history, new wives have not taken easily to a household dominated by another woman; and in this case that woman would have been the mother of her husband's dead wife. The absence of his sons could simply be explained by Margaret's wish for a clean start, especially when her pregnancy became apparent. Knox, however much he disapproved of passages in the English *Book of Common Prayer*, had nowhere else to send the boys, and for once may have chosen domestic peace over liturgical practice. At any rate, in the early months of 1567, Knox had certainly earned a holiday.

But as soon as Knox left the stage the limelight was occupied by Mary and Bothwell. Darnley was still in Glasgow, recovering from his supposed poisoning, although Mary complained of his continuing bad breath. These symptoms, along with the decomposition of his face that caused him to appear from time to time in a silk mask, were probably a result of the syphilis he had contracted during his various adventures in the dens of Edinburgh's Cowgate. Notwithstanding this, Mary visited him and his father, 'using him kindly, with many gracious and good words'.

She persuaded Darnley to return to Edinburgh, lodging, not with his wife in Holyrood Palace, but at Kirk O'Field, a house belonging to Chatelherault just inside the city boundaries, where he was being bathed and cosseted. He was totally unaware that two months previously, Mary, Bothwell and Lethington, along with Argyll, Huntly, and James Balfour, had decided at Craigmillar Castle that Darnley should be killed. On the night of 9 February, when there were more alibis in Edinburgh than fleas on a dog,

Darnley's lodging was blown apart by a giant explosion of gunpowder. The explosion was probably not as effective as the plotters had wished, since next morning Darnley's corpse was found unmarked in the next-door garden. He had been strangled.

Mary seemed unmoved by her loss and now spent more of her time with Bothwell, even bestowing Darnley's armour and clothes on him. The tailor who was cutting it down to fit the new owner 'acknowledged here the custom of the country, by which the clothes of the dead fall to the hangman'. Obviously, there had to be a scapegoat, even though none of the plotters from Craigmillar were anywhere near Kirk O'Field on the night in question, and eventually Mary gave in to pressure from Lennox as well as 'murmuring from the people' and summoned Bothwell for a trial. He arrived in Edinburgh, where Bothwell's ally Sir James Cockburn now held the castle. The city was crowded with his armed supporters and Bothwell was found not guilty – unsurprisingly, since no one came forward to give any evidence against him. Many of the nobility subscribed to a bond that Bothwell was 'a proper person on several accounts for partaking [of] the honour of the Queen's bed'. Bothwell's arrogance had not yet alienated them.

On 24 April Mary set out for Stirling, but was intercepted by Bothwell with an armed force of 700 or 800 men and she was carried off to his castle at Dunbar '. . . as [if] it had been by force, although everyone knew it was with the Queen's liking'. Lethington, Huntly and Melville were also taken 'prisoner' and after Bothwell had boasted to them that he would marry the Queen, 'whether she would herself or not', all but Melville were allowed to return to Edinburgh. Melville spent that night with Mary and Bothwell in Dunbar, departing for Edinburgh in the morning, saying, 'the Queen could not but marry him, seeing he had ravished her and lain with her against her will'. Clearly the pretended abduction and probably willing 'rape' were face-saving fiction, but the charade was well suited to Bothwell's buccaneering style, as well as pleasing Mary's romantic leanings. The eighteenth-century historian Robert Keith says, 'it were strongly to be wished the Queen had not given too much ground to posterity, to suspect her imprudence at least in this unhappy transaction'.

The political rumours were transmitted by Kirkaldy of Grange to the earl of Bedford. 'She was minded to cause Bothwell to ravish her, to the end that she may the sooner end the marriage, which she promised [to do] before she caused [the] murder [of] her husband.' But there were more focused political minds behind the abduction, as the newly empowered archbishop of St Andrews came to play his part. On 3 May Lady Bothwell was given a judgement against her husband on the grounds of adultery with her maidservant, and on the 7th the good archbishop dutifully annulled the marriage on the grounds of consanguinity, ever available for the aristocracy. The wronged Lady Bothwell subsequently became the countess of Sutherland. On 6 May, accompanied by Lethington, Mary rode up to the castle with Bothwell, 'leading the Queen's Majesty by the bridle as captive'. By the 9th John Craig, deputizing for Knox in St Giles, refused to read the banns and explained to his congregation that the marriage was at best adulterous.

He was forced to repeat his reasons to an uneasy council, and there he openly charged Bothwell with adultery, ravishing, collusion between him and his wife, and suspicion of involvement in the king's death.

'But he answered nothing to my satisfaction.' Craig was recalled on the 13th and reproved for exceeding his calling. Bothwell silenced Craig's defence, threatened to hang him and 'sent him from the Council'. The *History* asks us to 'mark the difference between this worthy minister Craig, and this base bishop.' (Although the final book of the *History* was completed by an unknown hand based on notes, this comment sounds like authentic Knox.) Two days later, Bothwell, who had been created the Duke of Orkney, was married to the Queen according to the Protestant rite. It is curious that Mary's two previous marriages, which were dynastic and purely for reasons of state, were accompanied with the full panoply of royal ceremony, while this one, which was the result of a romantic spirit, was held almost furtively.

Between Darnley's death and the royal marriage, Bothwell and Mary had managed to antagonize all the Protestants, and unite most of the nobility against them. The citizenry of Edinburgh regarded her as a wanton strumpet and the papacy led most of Catholic Europe in denouncing her seeming abandonment of the Catholic faith. Her attempts to improve her situation with the Kirk by distributing greater portions of the 'thirds' were met with sullen gratitude. Mary and Bothwell prepared for war by melting down Elizabeth's gold font to provide 5,000 gold crowns, and on 15 June the two sides met at Carberry Hill, a few miles to the east of Edinburgh for what was, in effect, a non-battle. Mary and Bothwell were outnumbered by Atholl, Glencairn, Mar, Ruthven and the rest of the Protestant lords, who were reluctant to launch an attack on their sovereign, their reasoning being that they had come to deliver her from imprisonment. Mary told them that she was in no way imprisoned by her husband. M. du Croc, the French ambassador, attempted to parley, asking Mary to give up Bothwell as he was the murderer of the late King. Mary, who probably now knew herself to be pregnant by Bothwell, refused point blank. Bothwell, with his medieval mentality to the fore, now challenged all and sundry to single combat. Given his reputation with arms, not many accepted, and those that did were rejected by him as being of insufficient estate to meet him. Then while Mary negotiated, Bothwell rode off to raise more support, having been official royal consort for just over four weeks.

The rest of his story is one of darkest tragedy. Having failed to find any support in Scotland, he eventually took ship for England but was seized by Scandinavian pirates, who delivered him into the hands of the relatives of one Anna Throndsen. She accused him, probably rightly, of past breach of promise. This resulted in his being imprisoned by King Frederick II, who attempted to use him as a pawn for international gain. But Bothwell, thanks to his marriage to Mary, was too hot a potato for anyone to handle and he became an embarrassment to the King, who sent him, in a blood-chilling phrase, 'to a place where men may forget him'. This was the castle of Dragsholm, where the earl, who had spent most of his life on horseback in the Border country of Scotland, was chained to a pillar in the dungeons. In 1578, half blind and totally mad, after eleven years during which time his feet had worn a deep circular trench around the pillar, Mary, Queen of Scots' third husband mercifully died.

Mary herself was taken to Edinburgh, clearly now a prisoner, and held in the house of the provost. She had been deserted by everyone – even the mob that had laughed at her escapades of disguise among them now pelted her with rubbish and called her whore. After a sleepless night spent under the cold eyes of soldiers, she appeared at her window, reputedly naked to her waist and screaming for release. Lethington attempted to persuade her to abandon Bothwell and condemn his actions against Darnley. Mary refused and Lethington left her to her fate. It is said that her apartments in Holyrood were looted, some of her jewellery ending up under the covetous eyes of Elizabeth. Mary was taken, a close prisoner without even a change of clothing, to the island fortress on Loch Leven, where some five weeks later she would miscarry twins.

Glencairn sent men to the abbey of Holyrood to destroy the Catholic altars, and Lethingon, who had been beside Mary at Carberry, joined the rebel lords. He stated that his reverence for the Queen, his mistress, had kept him with her although he had been in mortal danger of assassination by Bothwell, who was jealous of his position. Moray and Chatelherault were in France, and Argyll and Huntly both wanted to see Mary back in Holyrood. The situation was almost that of a few months before her return from France, and Knox's leave of absence was almost at an end – by 21 June he was back in Edinburgh.

He was in time to attend the assembly held on the 25th, whose main business, after commanding another general fast on 13 and 20 July in Edinburgh only, was to postpone itself until 25 July, so that they could meet in sufficient number. To this end a letter was sent to the nobility and envoys were sent to encourage their brothers to attend. Knox was sent to the west of Scotland, where he had previously preached with great success. The proposed meeting would be of the first importance, since, with the Queen a virtual prisoner and calls for her execution for murder and adultery echoing around the streets, the combination of nobility and the assembly would again be responsible for deciding the future government of Scotland. The letter to the nobility spelt out the aspirations of the assembly: 'Whereby a perpetual order may be taken for the liberty of the Kirk of God, sustenation of the ministers, and failzied [deceived] members thereof, that a sure union and conjunction may be had for the liberty of God's Kirk, whereby we may be able to withstand the rage of violence of our foresaid enemies.'

Mary's deposition in one form or another seemed imminent, as the lords started melting down the royal plate and sending for the coronation regalia to be delivered to them. France already had M. du Croc as ambassador in Edinburgh, and Elizabeth, who had serious reservations about deposing a Queen, Catholic or not, sent Nicholas Throckmorton post haste to Edinburgh. Among his instructions was a suggestion, no more, that the infant king might do well in England, where 'many good things may ensue to him'. Throckmorton was met by Lethington and Morton, and sensing the fury of the people against Mary – 'the women be most furious and impudent against the Queen, and yet the men be mad enough' – he encouraged the assembly to be postponed until feelings quietened down. He dreaded the arrival of Knox, 'whose austerity against the Queen I fear as much as any man's'. He was able to put this to the test three days later when he met Knox and Craig, whom he persuaded to preach and persuade 'leniently'. He did find them as austere as he had feared and they clearly amazed him with the depth of their knowledge:

They are furnished with many arguments; some forth of the Scriptures, some forth of histories, some grounded, as they say, upon the laws of this realm, some upon practices used in this realm, and some upon the conditions and oaths made by their prince at her coronation.

Having previously met only the civilized diplomacy of Lethington, Sir Nicholas had been surprised to discover that men he considered to be rough-hewn were possessed of such learning. But their vehemence was still a shock.

Knox was now in the strongest position he had ever found himself in. The unjust magistrate, Mary, had been removed by the nobility with the total endorsement of the people. The Protestantism of the Reformation parliament would be endorsed by the joint assembly, and the chances of all the recommendations of the *Book of Discipline* being made firm law were stronger than ever before. He was in personal discussion with Elizabeth's ambassador, and despite her personal dislike of the author of the *First Blast of the Trumpet* and distrust of the deposer of queens ('We do not think it consonant with nature that the head should be subject to the foot'), there was, at least, unqualified support for his faith from his southern neighbour. Events had moved to this position during his absence – an absence which was entirely coincidental, since he would never have condoned the murder of Darnley, brought about by Mary's headstrong involvement with Bothwell, and thus alienating her own nobility. But it was due to his life-time's work that the Protestant faith lived so strongly in Scotland, and he would now be called on to provide a spiritual lead to what he hoped would be a new form of government.

Knox continued to raise the temperature before the assembly met through his sermons, now being given daily. For example, on 19 June he preached from a text in the book of Kings. To Throckmorton's horror he 'did inveigh vehemently against the Queen and persuaded extremity against her'. Such behaviour would never have been tolerated in Tudor England and Throckmorton told his Queen that he had persuaded the lords to advise the preachers not to meddle in politics until the politicians had made up their own minds. He had a great fear that the people could take the law into their own hands and the politicians would have to give way to popular demands. Knox continued to pray for the continuation of friend-ship between Scotland and England, eschewing the 'auld alliance' with France, 'as they would fly from the pots of Egypt, which brought them nothing but sugared poison'. He also foretold that the great plague of God would fall on the country if Mary was spared her condign punishment. This was overly severe, since the assembly had merely excommunicated Paul Ruthven for his adultery, and after a period of contrition allowed him to return to the Church. But Mary was a flagrant symbol of Catholicism and was now at Knox's mercy. The lords, likewise, were enthusiastically condemning Mary for the murder of Darnley and for committing adultery with Bothwell. These cries were being orchestrated hypocritically by Morton, who himself had murdered Rizzio and fathered several illegitimate sons. Moray was in France to see if there could be any advantage in rekindling the alliance Knox was condemning. For example, Lethington could use Moray's mission to put a brake on Elizabeth's possible intervention, by threatening an alliance with France. He delivered this threat to Throckmorton at the same time as asking for Elizabeth's support, warning that 'they lose the game who leave the table' and stressing the necessity of his cause. When Throckmorton asked how far this 'necessity' extended, Lethington, 'made me none other answer, but, shaking his head, said, "Vous estes ung renard" [(sic) You are a fox]'. Knox knew nothing of these pieces of back-door diplomacy, which would probably have baffled him completely. Meanwhile Lethington prevaricated with all the skill of the practised politician.

However, all this diffuse activity came into sharp focus when the postponed assembly finally met with several of the lords sending letters of apology. The assembly confirmed the actions of the Reformation parliament of 1560, including acceptance of the *Book of Discipline*. The lords agreed to carry these decisions forward to the next meeting of parliament, in the form of eight clauses, with special regard to the application of poor relief and the payment of stipends.

Clauses that took the current situation into account were added: 'That all kings, princes, and magistrates, which hereafter in any time to come shall happen to reign and bear rule over this realm, their first interest before they be crowned and inaugurated, shall [be to] make their faithful league and promise to the true Kirk of God, that they shall maintain and defend.'

Politically events were also moving at speed. While the assembly was meeting in Edinburgh, Mary in Lochleven was being beset by embassies from her nobility. The Lords Ruthven and Lindsay brought her a document renouncing the crown in favour of the infant James – amounting to an act of abdication. There was also a sterner mission by Robert Melville, acting on Lethington's instructions, to tell her to sign or to face 'that present death which was prepared for her highness, if she refused the same'. Throckmorton managed to advise her that any agreement signed under such duress was invalid, and so inevitably, 'with many tears never liking what was contained in the writings', she signed. A second document appointed Moray as regent during James's minority.

On 29 July 1568 in the parish church of Stirling James was crowned as James VI of Scotland by the bishop of Orkney – who was recognized by Catholics as a bishop but also regarded as a minister by the Church of Scotland. Various political positions were demonstrated as Throckmorton obeyed his mistress's orders and failed to attend, Morton and Erskine of Dun took the oath for the infant King, Ruthven and Lindsay affirmed Mary's abdication and Knox delivered the sermon from a text in the Book of Kings. This text seems to have been from 2nd Kings, 22, verses 1 and 2, where Josiah is crowned at eight years of age and 'did what was right in the sight of the Lord'. There is no record of the sermon, although one contemporary called it an 'excellent discourse'. The party then processed to the castle, with Atholl carrying the crown, Morton the sceptre, Glencairn the sword, and Mar bringing up the rear carrying the infant King. What had not been popular was that the year-old boy was anointed, although, according to Calderwood in his *History of the Kirk*, 'Mr Knox and other preachers repined at the ceremony of anointing.' Knox willingly agreed 'ask instruments', that is to say, to be officially recorded with the Justice Clerk and Campbell of Kinzeancleugh, as official witnesses that James Stewart was King of Scotland and had been crowned as such. As the regency and coronation were proclaimed in Edinburgh with 'joy, dancing and acclamations, throughout Scotland there were widespread bonfires, shooting off of cannons and ringing of church bells'. Mary, now a prisoner on Loch Leven, heard them and wept. She was no longer Queen of Scotland. Elizabeth vowed, as a prince, 'if they continue to keep her in prison or touch her life or person, she will not fail to revenge it to the uttermost on such as shall be in any wise guilty thereof'. Throckmorton was bidden 'to declare this message as roundly and sharply as he can'.

Moray impressed Throckmorton as, 'some which have led the people of Israel, rather than captains of our age', but he reassured Cecil that Moray seemed unlikely to execute Mary or keep her in prison for ever. Moray was proclaimed regent in the Tolbooth on 22 August amid great joy, and then proclaimed again at the high cross with heralds and trumpets.

Knox had made up his differences with Moray and could look forward to the coming parliament as the summation of all his efforts. He was included, with Craig and Lindsay, on the drafting committee of the Lords of the Articles which met on 3 December. The result was that ninety-five articles were presented to the parliament twelve days later. The reason for the unusually high number was that this parliament was free of the taint of illegitimacy that applied to its predecessor in 1560. This parliament was legally summoned by Moray, acting as Regent, and therefore had the full authority of the crown, and it set about legitimizing the previous acts. Knox preached the opening sermon, exhorting the parliament to start their deliberations by righting the wrongs that had been done to the Kirk. His exhortation was successful since the parliament set about, first, the abolition of the authority of the Pope; secondly, the abolition of idolatry; and thirdly, the abolition of the Mass. The next nineteen acts ratified various aspects of the *Book of Discipline*, and the remainder concerned the secular business of the realm. The *Confession of Faith* was adopted as the only doctrine of Scotland, and, at last, all the 'thirds', since their granting in 1561, would be awarded to the Kirk. More importantly, they would be calculated and gathered by collectors appointed by the Kirk. The banning of women from public office was 'found good' but did not become law, while the export of horses for profit was referred for further consideration. Throughout the parliament Mary was referred to as 'our sovereign Lord's mother'. Inasmuch as the events of 1567 constituted a revolution, endorsed by this parliament, the Scottish Reformation could now draw a line and consider its work done. The Protestant religion was nationally established, future kings would swear to uphold it in their coronation oath, the structure of parishes with ministers and superintendents was not only in place but now financially viable, as was the enactment of the poor laws as set out in the *Book of Discipline*. The final dream of a democratically based education system was being realized, and the Kirk was represented on the key committee of the Lords of the Articles. Knox had achieved everything he had set out to do: the Mass was outlawed; church sessions sat as courts on minor civil offences and major spiritual ones; and the preaching was assured of conformity thanks to commissioners appointed by parliament. Knox, obviously, was one of them.

14   Full of Years and Honours

The assembly met in December, this time with very little to do. It confirmed that Knox should travel between Stirling and Berwick, and heard John Craig vehemently answer the slander that he had pronounced the banns for Bothwell's marriage. Its triumphal statement summed up the victory:

> Our enemies, praise be to God, are dashed; religion established, sufficient provision made for ministers; order taken, and penalty approved for all sorts of transgressors; and, above all, a godly magistrate, whom God, of his eternal and heavenly providence, hath reserved to this age, to put in execution whatsoever he by his law commandeth.

Slight cracks were appearing in this otherwise glittering façade, since one of the other acts of the assembly was to ask Willock, who had gone to England in 1566, to return, 'to reap in blitheness that which by you was before sown in tears'. He did briefly, but left again to be rector of Loughborough. Goodman had left in 1565 never to return, and Knox's sons would study at St. John's College, Cambridge. Knox wrote to a friend, John Wood, secretary to Moray, that he hoped his days might not be long, and that God should put an end to the miseries of France, where civil war had restarted and which, he feared, could easily spread to England or Scotland. Wood was in England and presumably in touch with some of those who had been exiles with Knox in Geneva. Knox addressed them thus:

> God comfort that distressed little flock, amongst whom I once lived with quietness of conscience and contentment of heart; and amongst whom I would be content to end my days, if so it might stand with God's good pleasure.

Knox had known despair before, during his exile and during the war with the Queen Regent, so this is not surprising. Nor is it surprising that after the victories of the parliament there should be a feeling of anti-climax, as the revolutionaries at last became the establishment. But the divisions within that establishment were bitter and deep. The old duke of Chatelherault did not attend James's coronation, but sent another member of the Hamilton family, Arthur, to declare that if James died without heirs – always a strong possibility in Scotland – then the Hamiltons stood next to inherit the crown. Throckmorton told Cecil,

> As for the Hamiltons and their faction, there conditions be such, their behaviour so inordinate, the most of them so unable, their living so vicious, their fidelity so fickle, their party so weak, as I count it lost whatsoever is bestowed upon them.

The hatred between the Hamiltons and the Stewarts, now headed by Moray, was long-lasting and still very much alive. Therefore, when in May Mary escaped from Loch Leven it was to the town of Hamilton in the west that she fled. From there she poured vitriol on all who had been party to her deposition. Oddly enough, with the exception of Knox and the ministers, since this was not a religious, but a dynastic matter with the support of 'our dearest father adoptive, the good duke of Chatelherault'. It was now a straight fight between Mary and her half-brother, Moray, while the aristocracy responded to its atavistic loyalties and flocked to their Queen. Kirkaldy of Grange held Edinburgh Castle for the Regent at present, but clung to the idea that his loyalty should be to the lawful government. Mary shortly had an army of 5,000 to 6,000 men as opposed to Moray's 4,000 to 5,000 and the two sides met at Langside, to the south of Glasgow.

Moray had a great advantage, however, in having Morton, supported by Kirkaldy of Grange, as his generals, and they supplied experience far in excess of anything offered by Mary's commander Argyll. When Mary's cavalry fought their way forward, Argyll totally failed to follow up the advance and Mary's horsemen were cut down by fierce musket fire from Kirkaldy's men. Why Argyll displayed such ineptitude is a mystery usually attributed to illness 'he swooned as they were joining for fault of courage' – although Antonia Fraser in her *Mary, Queen of Scots* points out that since Argyll was Moray's brother-in-law and recent ally, treachery cannot be ruled out. In any case, the result was that Mary's army turned into a leaderless mêlée and she had no option but flight. On 16 May 1568, accompanied by fifteen of her personal servants and escorted only by Lord Herries, who had welcomed her at Leith seven years and five months previously, she fled to England, leaving behind her a Protestant nation dominated secularly by her half-brother, Moray, and guided spiritually by Knox.

As a Catholic sovereign fleeing the Protestant powers that had forced her abdication it does seem that a flight to France would have been her most rational plan. Charles IX, her brother-in-law, for whom she had named her son, was still King, although Catherine de Medici still held the reins of power. Mary's pension had included huge land holdings and a promise of, if not royal wealth, at least considerable comfort. Instead of which Mary chose to throw herself on the mercy of the leading Protestant monarch in Europe, one whose throne she had claimed. Elizabeth had protested violently at Mary's ill-treatment as a sovereign queen – she could hardly do anything else – but Elizabeth was unlikely to look fondly on a woman who still declared her a bastard and asserted her own rights to the kingdom. Mary Stuart had made many impetuous and headstrong decisions, and this was one of her worst.

At first she was treated as a refugee of the highest rank, but as she was passed from damp house to damp house it became clear that she was in fact a prisoner. After nineteen years, crippled with arthritis, she fell into a trap, carefully prepared by Elizabeth's master spy, Francis Walsingham, agreeing to occupy Elizabeth's throne after she had been assassinated. This was her last bad decision, and she went to her execution with great dignity at Fotheringhay Castle on February 1587. She was forty-four years old and had outlived both her now forgotten husband Bothwell by nine years, and her old adversary Knox by fifteen.

At present, Knox was in his mid fifties and would see his second daughter, Margaret, born in this year. He now held only the ministership of St Giles, where he preached three times a week and twice on Sundays. He was, however, regarded as the elder statesman of the Reformation, and the final arbiter of orthodoxy, travelling widely at the behest of the assembly. Although holding no secular position, he was well abreast of affairs and knew that Moray's regency was still fragile, with the Queen's supporters poised to raise an army for her return. Argyll issued a call to arms and wrote to Elizabeth asking for help. Two days later he was in contact with the duke of Alva, the Spanish governor of the Netherlands, asking him to use his influence with his master, Philip II. However, within the week Mary assured Elizabeth that her forces would stand down. Knox, rightly, was not convinced that the threat had gone away and on 10 September he told his friend John Wood,

> I am informed both by letter and by tongue . . . that the Duke and his friends are inflamed against me . . . we look daily for the arrival of the Duke and his Frenchmen, sent to restore Satan to his kingdom, in the person of his dearest lieutenant, sent, I say, to repress religion, not from the King of France, but from the Cardinal of Lorraine in favour of his dearest niece. Let England take heed, for assuredly, their neighbour's house is on fire. Without support we are not able to resist the force of our domestic enemies (unless God work miraculously) much less are we able to stand against the puissance of France, the substance of the Pope and the malice of the house of Guise, unless we be comforted by others than ourselves . . . The whole comfort of the enemies is this, that by treason or other means they may cut off the Regent and then cut the throat of the innocent King . . . As their malice is not quenched, so ceases not the practice of the wicked, to put in execution the cruelty devised. I live as a man already dead from all affairs civil, and therefore I praise my God; for so I have some quietness of spirit, and time to meditate upon death, and upon the troubles I have long feared and foresee.

Knox had gone from the pinnacle of achievement to the pit of despair. Despite the genuineness of Knox's distress, he also knew full well that Wood was a regular correspondent of both Leicester and Cecil and that his summary of the state of affairs in Scotland might well reach royal ears. So much for a man 'dead from all affairs civil'.

Moray continued to keep his hold on power, while Elizabeth did what she and Cecil did best. They prevaricated, negotiated with everybody and agreed to nothing. Petitions flew and conferences were held, with Moray visiting York and London. On 2 February, avoiding confrontation and possible capture by Norfolk and his Catholic faction in England, he returned to an Edinburgh struck by a plague in which 2,500 died. It had been so severe that the General Assembly of December 1568 was postponed until February. It met as Chatelherault arrived back in Scotland and promptly declared himself the supreme authority. Moray called for his forces to report to Glasgow on 10 March and prepare for civil war. But Chatelherault had written to the assembly, offering to set up an inquiry into Darnley's death and asking for its support. Knox was instructed to reply in the name of the assembly.

His answer grew into a letter to all Protestants in which he spelt out the troubles of the land: 'We see a wicked woman, whose iniquity [is] known, and lawfully convicted, deserves more than ten deaths, escaped from prison.' He goes on to declare that if she had been executed the plague would not have arrived, how the faithful had survived the nine years of her reign, only now 'to see brethren seek with all cruelty the blood of their brethren'. He begs everyone to cling to the reformed faith or 'will we (albeit with grief of heart) be compelled to draw the sword committed to us by God, and to cut them off from all society of the body of Jesus Christ', in other words, the unreformed will be excommunicated. The letter, which for its time is short, reads like the exhortation of a tired man, its prose lacking the vigour of the past and giving flat condemnation without the careful arguments of the scholar. Knox seems to feel that the stone is rolling down the hill yet again and he is being called to play Sisyphus long after he should have been safely freed from his labours.

Moray managed to neutralize the threat from Chatelherault and Herries by inviting them to a convention in Edinburgh and promptly locking them up in the castle. But Lethington, who was now suspected of changing sides and supporting Mary's proposed marriage to the duke of Norfolk, had 'drawn the laird of Grange, Captain of the Castle, to the Queen's faction'.

Moray summoned Lethington and had him arrested, only for Grange, by use of forged authority, to get the secretary transferred to his care in the castle. From here Lethington wrote to Mary on 20 September, 'I have of late dealt with divers ministers here, who will not be repugnant to a good accord, howsoever I think Knox be inflexible.' Not only would he be inflexible, he would be aware of Lethington's manoeuvres, even though Lethington claimed that no one would find any incriminating document written or signed by him. On the day of Lethington's trial, Edinburgh was so packed with the secretary's supporters that Moray had to let him temporarily go free.

He joined the long list of noblemen whose trials had been completely ineffectual. The failure of a Catholic rising in England by the earls of Northumberland and Westmoreland resulted in Westmoreland's flight to Holland. But Northumberland's capture by Moray put the seal on Elizabeth's friendship with the Regent. The forces of England were his to command and it seemed that Knox's fears of a Counter-Reformation in Scotland were groundless, with the nation being held steady by Moray. Knox wrote to Cecil to congratulate him on Elizabeth's deliverance, but advised him that

If you strike not at the root, the branches that appear to be broken will bud
again (and that more quickly than men can believe) with greater force than we
would wish . . . albeit I have been fremmedly [harshly] handled, yet was I
never the enemy of England.

He signs this letter as 'John Knox, with one foot in his grave' and was
clearly feeling tired and depressed, although the situation seemed to be
stable again.

As commonly happens in Scottish politics, the situation changed
violently later in the month when the earl of Moray was assassinated. James
Hamilton of Bothwellhaugh had stalked the regent for some time and
Moray had been well warned of the risk. He was advised in Linlithgow that
he was in great danger, but insisted on riding openly past the house of the
Bishop of St Andrews, where Bothwellhaugh held a sniper's position behind
drying sheets, which would hide the smoke from his hackbut. The bullet
caught the regent 'a little under the navel' and at first he seemed only
slightly hurt as he walked back to his lodging. There he was able to declare
that he in no way repented of his leniency towards the Hamiltons. He died
about eleven o'clock that night, as Bothwellhaugh was being received with
praise by his supporters in Hamilton. Knox had foreseen that an attempt
would be made on the regent's life a few days earlier, and had warned that
it would result in the destruction of the house of Hamilton. This was not a
prophecy in the Old Testament sense, but merely a demonstration that
Knox's intelligence service was as good as ever.

For all that had passed between them, which had led to a breach of eighteen years, Knox and Moray were the firmest of friends, and as Knox was
the spiritual leader of the Reformation, so Moray had been the firmest of
the leading secular protagonists. He had been the Reformation's steadiest
champion among the often vacillating aristocracy, and Knox must have felt
that the foundation stone had now been knocked away. He wrote a special
prayer which he used after dinner and supper, 'when the thanksgiving for
bodily sustenance was ended'. He praises God for freeing Scotland from the
bondage of idolatry and the yoke of Mary. He thanks God for the life and
actions of Moray, and notes that, as a punishment for ingratitude, he had
been allowed to fall into the hands of murderers. Then he encapsulates the
situation as he saw it: 'Seeing that we are now left as a flock without a
pastor, in civil policy, and as a ship without a rudder in the midst of the
storm, let thy providence watch, Lord, and defend us in these dangerous

days.' He also calls upon God to confound Mary's faction and her subtle enterprises. This prayer lasts some five minutes, so with grace before and thanksgiving after, Knox's mealtimes would have been bracketed by ten minutes of prayers.

However devout Knox had been in his personal life, he was always liable to attack from all and sundry for a deviousness he did not possess. A pamphlet circulated in which the anonymous author told of how Moray had held a meeting with six others, Lindsay, Pittarrow, John Wood, James McGill, the unnamed tutor of Pitcure and Knox. To give credibility, the author claimed that the meeting was held in a privy chamber and he was sleeping in a cabinet in the room. He wakened and overheard all that was said. Moray asked each of them in turn what he should do, and Knox was reported to say that Moray should continue as regent long after James's majority, that he had a book ready for the printers demanding that the system of royal succession by birth be abandoned in favour of a system of appointment by the people. It would be put to the next assembly, which would approve the policy. This pamphlet also contains the first reference to Maitland of Lethington as Machiavelli. It does, however, go totally against Knox's loyalty to King James and his speech is missing the scriptural quotations invariably adduced in support of his arguments. Nevertheless, the pamphlet was in popular circulation and came to the attention of the wife of the laird of Ormiston. She took it to Knox, who read it and said, 'You shall know my answer afterwards.' The pamphlet had been written by Thomas Maitland, Lethington's younger brother, with whom Knox had had another confrontation a day or so previously. Knox had been given a note in the pulpit of St Giles saying, 'Take up the man you accounted another God, and consider the end whereto his ambition has brought him.' Knox, realizing that this referred to Moray, warned against rejoicing over what was a matter for sorrow and prophesied that this wicked man (the author of the pamphlet) should not die unpunished and 'shall die where none shall be to lament him'. He finally responded to the pamphlet from the pulpit, saying it was inspired by the Devil, the Father of Lies, and was as false as God was true. What was also true was Knox's prophecy, since Thomas Maitland did die alone, two years later, in Italy. Nau claimed that Knox, 'the calamity of Scotland', began to preach publicly from the pulpits that the monarch should be elected, and that the people ought to elect the person who seemed best adapted for the preservation and extension of religion. While the central argument of the magistrate's responsibility to the people is true, Knox never quite advocated the appointment of sovereigns by simple election. Nau's claim is pure Marian propaganda.

On 14 February Knox preached a funeral sermon over his friend, before Moray was buried in the south aisle of St Giles. His text was, 'Blessed are they that die in the Lord.' All of this was in direct contravention of the strictures laid down for unadorned funerals by Knox himself in the *Book of Discipline*, but Moray had been a particular friend of Knox, and, more importantly, a steadfast hero of the Reformation.

With Moray's assassination one of the lamps of progress had been extinguished and Knox duly moved the congregation of St Giles to tears. Once they had dried them, the powers of Scotland yet again drew up the battle lines of what could turn into another civil war. Lethington was brought from the castle and duly swore his innocence before the lords. 'So he was set at liberty', in fact to rejoin the Hamilton faction. A figure from the past reappeared in the person of the earl of Lennox, Darnley's father and so grandfather of the King. After some debate as to whether his loyalties lay with Scotland or with Elizabeth, he was appointed regent with the support of Morton and the Douglas faction.

He also had the support of Knox and the boroughs, including Edinburgh. The castle, however, was still held by Grange who stood for Mary, as did the Hamiltons and Gordons. The Marian leader was Argyll, with Hume and Herries, all of the Queen's support being orchestrated by Lethington.

The orchestra played discordantly, though, with the Marians writing to Elizabeth for support at least in principle, to avoid the intervention of strangers in Scotland, but with Elizabeth sending English troops to support Lennox and burning Hawick as well as various Border castles. In fact there never was a civil war in the sense of armies fighting formal battles, but rather there was widespread destruction by independent armed bands claiming loyalty to one side or another. Houses were destroyed, farms burnt, animals and goods were seized and many old scores were settled without achieving anything concrete in a political sense. There were Catholics and Protestants on each side and Spottiswoode in his *History of the Church of Scotland* says,

> You should have seen fathers against their sons, sons against their fathers, brother fighting against brother, nigh kinsman and others allied together as enemies seeking one the destruction of the other. Every man, as his affection led him, joined to the one or other party; one professing to be the King's men

the other the Queen's. The very young ones scarce taught to speak had these words in their mouths, and were sometimes observed to divide and have their childish conflicts in that quarrel. But the condition of Edinburgh was of all parts of the country most distressed, they that were of a quiet disposition and greatest substance being forced to forsake their houses; which were partly by the soldiers, partly by other necessitous people (who made profit of the recent calamities), rifled and abused.

Spottiswoode's description would have held good for the Wars of the Roses, and is sadly just as true for the Balkans, Indonesia, or many other conflict zones in the contemporary world. Perhaps the severest lesson of history is that we learn nothing from it except possibly to adapt more advanced technology for further destructive use. The lords loyal to the King ranked the rebels as the authors of the cruel murders of Darnley and the Regent, as those who had sworn to defend the King and now impugned that oath – finally, 'such as had servile minds and without regard to conscience or honour did follow those to whom they had addicted them-selves'. Nature took a hand in all this anarchy by visiting an earthquake on Glasgow at ten o'clock on the night of 3 July, which put the inhabitants 'in great terror and fear'. Meanwhile in Loch Fyne a monstrous huge-eyed fish appeared, 'as high as the mast of a ship', with two crowns on its gigantic head, a clear sign of 'a sudden alteration in the realm'.

By August 1570 Lethington had been replaced as secretary by Robert Pitcairn, commendator of Dunfermline and on 17 September he was declared outlaw as a rebel to the King, as shortly after were Chatelherault and Lord Hamilton, the earl of Arran.

More pertinent to Knox, however, was that 'In the mean time John Knox was stricken by a kind of apoplexy, called by the physicians "resolu-tion", whereby the perfect use of his tongue was stopped.' As is usual we get no further information but can deduce that Knox suffered a transient ischaemic attack, or TIA, often called a 'stroke'. In this event a thrombus, or clot, temporarily blocks one of the blood vessels serving the brain, or, more often, there is a cerebral haemorrhage in which a vessel bursts, inter-rupting the blood supply. He would have had little or no warning, apart from sudden blurring of vision and the loss of use of his legs. The attack would have lasted a few minutes but he would have been left with a loss of spatial perception on his right side – he would have bumped into doors and dropped objects – as well as aphasia, or loss of speech. This would have been restored in time as would most of his faculties. But TIAs are prone to recurrence if the sufferer's lifestyle is not altered. The cause of the attack is unknown, but at his age of fifty-seven, hypertension, or high blood-pressure, is the most likely, given the vigorous lifestyle of the reformer.

However, the *History* reports,

> Hereof did the wicked not a little rejoice. The rumour passed, not only through Scotland, but also to England, that he was become the most deformed creature that ever was seen; that his face was turned into his neck; that he was dead; that he would never preach nor yet speak! Wherein Good, [Knox's correspondent in England], within few days declared them liars; for he [Knox] convalesced, and so returned to his exercise of preaching, at least on the Sunday.

Margaret now had the problem of caring for an ailing husband, who cannot have made the easiest of patients, as well as looking after their family of the four-year-old Martha, the two-year-old Margaret, and the recently arrived Elizabeth. This last born was Knox's final child and it is tempting to think that her name was chosen, not only in memory of Zachary's wife and John the Baptist's mother, but also of his own mother-in-law, Elizabeth Bowes. Even with servants to help, the plight of a young wife with an aged husband is not easy.

Even though Knox now was limiting his preaching to Sundays, this still left him ample scope for controversy when it occurred, and occur it did on 21 December. Kirkaldy of Grange controlled Edinburgh Castle, and although a Protestant – he had been a regular attendant at Knox's sermons in St Giles – acted for the Queen's party. A kinsman of his, one John Kirkaldy, was beaten up in Dunfermline, and when Henry Seton, one of his assailants, was about to board ship in Leith, Grange sent along six of his servants to repay the injury. Seton obviously put up a spirited defence and injured one of Grange's men, who put aside their clubs and batons, drawing their swords. The unfortunate Seton fell over an anchor rope on the quayside, and once he was down Grange's men killed him. The town guard arrived and all but one Fleming made it back to the safety of the castle. Fleming was imprisoned in the Tolbooth. Grange then mounted a carefully planned rescue operation, including battering rams and masked and heavily armed men, which shattered the door of the jail and released the inmates. The entire party then retuned uphill to the castle, slammed its gates and launched a volley of nine cannons as a mark of defiance to the regent. This was not only an insult to Lennox, it was a reminder to the citizenry of Edinburgh as to where the real power lay. The minister of Edinburgh's High Kirk could not let the insult lie.

On the 24th Knox climbed into his pulpit and displayed his old talent for over-vehement condemnation of wrongs done. What had taken place was no more than a nobleman using his personal muscle to avenge a perceived slight, which had unwisely offended the pride of Edinburgh, but this was not how Knox saw it. Grange, heavily attended by burly supporters, came to St Giles, where he sat through a violent condemnation of his actions by his old friend. Knox claimed that in all his days he had never seen so slanderous, so malapert, so fearful, and so tyrannous a fact. By way of qualification he went on,

> If the committer had been a man without God, a throat-cutter, one that had never known the works of God, it would have moved me no more than the other riots and enormities which my eyes have seen the prince of this world, Satan, to raise by his instruments. But to see the stars fall from heaven, and a man of knowledge commit so manifest a treason, what godly heart cannot lament, tremble and fear? . . . within these few years, men would have looked for other fruits than have budded out of that man.

The bitterness is justified to the extent that Grange had been a loyal supporter of the Protestant cause and was now a committed supporter of Mary, and thus in Knox's eyes, Catholicism. Knox never understood that noble blood gave their loyalty to their queen first and to the Church second. The civil war of 1560 had been possible only because the Queen was an exiled child in a foreign country. Mary of Guise was a foreign female regent and her removal became linked with the reforming of religion, inspired by the unifying voice of Knox. Grange was now simply following his instincts to serve the monarch and Knox saw this as treason. Grange was so furious at this that he in his turn misunderstood and immediately wrote to Craig, Knox's deputy, with a denial to be read from the pulpit. He denied that he was a throat-cutter – an act of which Knox had not accused him – and asked who, between himself and Knox, had been responsible for shedding more innocent blood. Craig, with great wisdom, claimed that he could read nothing without the consent of the Kirk. And 'the dart being shot, the force of it vanished'. But the 'force of it' did not

vanish and on the 28th Grange complained formally to the kirk-session of
St Giles about Knox's slanders, which now included murder and a long
reputation of bloodthirstiness. Knox, now walking with the aid of a stick,
came to the session, claiming that he had done no more than a good pastor
should do in advertising sin where he found it. Grange's temper seemed to
have cooled and embassies went back and forth from the session to the
castle. Knox preached repentance, which infuriated Grange again and he
again appeared at St Giles with his original bully-boys and there, 'most
proudly maintained their transgression'. The Protestants in the west sent a
letter from Ayr, stating that they could not believe that Grange, a defender
of reform, now was planning to kill the man who had been 'the first planter
and also the chief waterer of his kirk among us'. But as is so often the
outcome in such cases, both sides calmed down, although still breathing
hard, and the episode passed.

The result was that irreparable harm was done to Mary's cause, for any
attempt on Knox's life would have caused the country to explode and
Grange had simply antagonized Edinburgh, embarrassed the Marians and
hardened English attitudes against restoration. Knox and the Reformation
had survived unscathed and strengthened, since, as a way of gauging public
support, Grange's actions had proved very valuable. The effects of Knox's
stroke had clearly left him with some incapacity of the legs, but any other
advice to moderate his vehemence had gone unheeded.

There would be a further opportunity to vent his righteous anger when,
on 1 March the twenty-second General Assembly met, at which it seemed
certain Grange would try once again to attack Knox. On the night of the
second day there was an act of considerable provocation by Grange. He
staged a mock attack on the castle, with half the garrison acting as English
troops. The soldiers, as soldiers will, seemed to enjoy this exercise greatly,
with salvoes of cannon being fired. Meanwhile the citizens had little idea of
what was happening. 'At divers tables there were divers communications',
and those living near the castle must have suffered it as much as the contemporary residents of the castle crag suffer the annual Edinburgh military
tattoo. Knox, who was hosting a small dinner-party, sourly commented, 'I
also saw great bravery in the castle of St Andrews, and yet [a] few days
brought a miserable desolation.'

On the next day, at the assembly, an anonymous letter was received,
which was also fixed to the assembly door in good Lutheran style that night.
According to the *Diurnal of Occurents*, 'there were certain reprehensions

set up in divers places in Edinburgh,' reminding Knox that it was his duty to pray for all the fallen and especially for the Queen his sovereign, whom he had called idolatress, murderer and adulteress. If he failed in this duty, the next assembly should reprimand him. Knox's rebuttal from the pulpit was that Mary was never and never would be his sovereign or that of Scotland; therefore, he had no obligation to pray for her and the accusers were traitors. For this uncharitable attitude the people, quite rightly, 'grudged'. The battle of the pamphlets went on until 10 March, when the bell-man (town-crier) delivered yet another to Knox as he was dressing. Knox read it, and dismissively gave it to his servant Richard to take to the assembly. Richard did this, and on his own account asked the assembly to endorse Knox's preaching against Mary. The assembly had changed from the avid reformers of the past and were now learning politics, so they refused 'the said Richard, being not a little in choler that his just desire was refused'.

The last pamphlet of the campaign attempted to accuse Knox of hypocrisy. How could the author of *The First Blast of the Trumpet* support the authority of Elizabeth? On the Sunday, after his sermon, he read the pamphlet to his congregation and asked for 'a little audience' to answer it. His answer, while not in the great tradition of past invective, shows that he had lost none of his debating skills. He refers, without using his name, to Sir James Balfour, the president of the council, as the author. 'The indictment seems to smell of some crafty lawless man of law's brain.' He goes on to point out that he has never acted against the interests of Scotland and has only sought foreign support in maintaining those interests against foreign incursions. At any rate, seeking help from the wicked does not prove that the godly justify the wicked. Seeking aid from Elizabeth does not justify her authority, and the debating skill of the old Schoolman is again backed up by scriptural precedents. And he does promise 'to give him a lie in his throat, that either dare or will say that ever I sought support against my native country'. He ends, complaining about the cowardice of the anonymous in magnificent style: 'For to me it seems a thing unreasonable, that in this my decrepit age, I shall be compelled to fight against shadows and howlets [owls] that dare not abide the light.' Bannatyne, Knox's secretary, reports, 'This answer [was] given to that horned [deceived] public, with greater vehemence than it is written, [and] accusation by writing against John Knox ceased for a time; for men had other things to think upon'.

313

Knox, however, continued to preach with his usual stridency against the exiled Queen and to pray for the King and regent as the properly authorized government. It was becoming harder for the citizenry of Edinburgh to follow his lead, as the Hamilton faction packed the town during April, and by the 18th, 'This night some brethren fearing for John Knox, their minister, came and watched all night in his house.' On an unspecified night, probably previous to this guard being mounted on Knox's house, an unsuccessful attempt was made on Knox's life. When Knox dined he usually sat at the head of the table, but with his back to the window and in view of the street below – a reassuring sight for his passing congregation. For no particular reason, on the night in question, Knox had chosen to sit at the side of the table and the assassin, who must have been in a hurry and shooting without taking careful aim, fired through the window at an empty chair and merely made a hole in the ceiling at the point from where the chandelier hung. After this Knox was persuaded to take more care and was even, astonishingly, offered protection by Grange, who suggested that Knox move into the castle. He would then be given a guard, under the command of Captain Melville, 'an old Protestant', to convey him to and from St Giles. Grange, his temper cooled, was clearly concerned as to the safety of his old colleague, and was trying to maintain his independence as master of the castle. Bannatyne says, 'he would give the wolf the wether [a castrated ram] to keep' and Knox unsurprisingly refused the offer.

On 13 April, at the market cross, Grange had also defended himself against calumnies of disloyalty spread by Lennox, whose regency Grange denied, declaring that any who denied he was a true Scottish man lied in their throat. Inevitably he challenged Lennox to single combat on horseback or on foot. The middle ages cast a long shadow over sixteenth-century Scotland.

Lennox attempted to lure the garrison out of the castle on the 29th, and on the next day Grange gave the regent's supporters six hours to quit the city. He fortified the gates of the city, which Knox still had not left in spite of the now overt danger. Melville was beseeched not to harm him and replied that he would still have safe conduct to the castle, although worryingly he 'could not be answerable for the rascal multitude'. By the 4th Chatelherault and his son Claud Hamilton entered the city at the head of over 100 men, and Grange, with little option, made a formal alliance with the Hamiltons. Knox was now completely beset with enemies and could no longer safely preach in his church, since holes had been made in the roof so that snipers could take aim at whoever was inside. A delegation from his congregation, led by John Craig, visited Knox and begged him to leave town. In spite of Grange's continued assurances, he was still in danger but refused to abandon his flock.

The delegation argued that, if he stayed, there would be bloodshed as they defended him against the rebels and that their blood would be on his head – so for their sakes, would he please leave. Knox agreed and on the morning of 8 May 1570 he left for Abbotshall, near Kirkaldy in Fife, before passing to St Andrews in July where he remained for over a year.

Two days later Chatelherault, Claud Hamilton and the rest of the Castilians attended St Giles but swept out after Craig's sermon, in which he lamented that there was no neutral man to make agreement between the opposing parties. Craig was replaced by the bishop of Galloway, who, although a Protestant, supported the Queen's party and the Hamiltons.

In his old haunt of St Andrews Knox, his wife Margaret and his three daughters, Martha, Margaret and Elizabeth, took up residence in the Novum Hospitalum of the Priory, probably where he had lodged eleven years previously. From here he wrote to Goodman, and others in England, that,

> From the castle of Edinburgh have sprung all the murders first and last committed in this realm . . . God confound the wicked devisers, with their cruel vices. So long as it pleased God to continue me in any strength, I ceased not to forewarn these days publicly, as Edinburgh can witness, and secretly, as Mr Randolph, and others of that nation with whom I secretly conferred can testify.

He also wrote to his brethren of the Church in Edinburgh:

> 'I would write a long letter; but being in that estate that I may not write with my own hand two lines, I must abide the leisure of God . . . Of one thing I must put you in mind . . . that the word of God preached by the mouth of man is not a vain sound.

The assembly met in Stirling, and Knox wrote from St Andrews apologizing for his absence:

> If ability of body would have suffered, I should not have troubled you with this rude letter . . . the daily decay of natural strength threatens unto me

315

certain and sudden departure from the miseries of this life . . . Remember the Judge before whom you must make account, and resist that tyranny as you would hell's fire. The battle, I grant, will be hard . . . God give you wisdom and stout courage in so just a cause, and me a happy end.

This letter was read to and approved by the assembly, but a picture is emerging of a John Knox whose course was now run. He was certainly very tired, with increasing physical disabilities – difficulty in walking, loss of full control of his hands – but there was still fire enough when he was in the pulpit, as James Melville records in his *Diary*:

I had my pen and my little book, and took away such things as I could comprehend. In the opening up of his text [on the prophecy of Daniel] he was moderate the space of half an hour; but when he entered to application he made me so to grue [fear] and tremble that I could not hold a pen to write.

Melville gives us a charming picture of the old reformer taking his rest in St Leonard's College yard among the young scholars, whom he exhorted to 'stand by the good cause'. Melville saw him going about slowly with a 'furring of martriks' (pine-marten?) at his neck, leaning on a stick, with Richard Bannatyne holding his other armpit. Another servant then lifted him into the pulpit, where 'he was so active and vigorous that he was like to beat that pulpit into pieces and fly out of it'. The fire might have been flickering but it was a long way from going out.

Both rebels and the regent's men held parliaments, with the five-year-old King James personally confirming the regency of his grandfather, Lennox. Then with the startling percipience of youth, he sighted a hole in the roof of the Tolbooth and said, 'There is a hole in this Parliament.' Seven days later Regent Lennox was shot.

The earl of Mar was appointed regent in Lennox's place, although the real power lay with the energetic earl of Morton. George Bell and Captain Calder, who had killed Lennox, were taken and accorded the fearful privilege of being the first Scotsmen ever to be 'broken on the wheel'. This form of execution, popular in France, involved the victim being spread-eagled on a cartwheel with the projecting hub in the small of his back. His arms and legs were then smashed with hammers or lead flails and the wheel was hoisted to the top of a pole, where he was left to die in agony. As Knox withdrew more and more from political life – although his correspondents

in England kept him well informed of national and international affairs –
the rumour-mongers were finding it more difficult to spread slander about
him. A desperate example of this became current about the end of 1571,
when Knox was said to have been expelled from St Andrews, since 'in his
yard he had raised some saints, among whom came up the devil, with
horns; which, when his servant Richard Bannatyne, saw, he ran mad and so
died'. This was weak stuff, believed by only the most gullible. Bannatyne
says he would scarcely have blackened paper to report it.

On 12 January 1572 a 'Convention of Superintendents, commissioners,
ministers, and commissioners from towns and kirks' met in Leith. It was,
for some reason, very keen not to be called a General Assembly but to give
itself the powers of a General Assembly. This may have been because it had
foreknowledge that the hierarchical changes it would ratify were at vari-
ance with the *Book of Discipline* and would kindle the wrath of Knox.

At some point during this convention a request for a meeting came from
the rebels in the castle, and 'Certain Commissioners [were] sent to the
castle, by the general Kirk convened in Leith, to pacify the troubles of this
country.' The rebels were represented by Chatelherault, Grange, James
Balfour (lord president) and Lethington, but the identity of the Church's
representatives poses more of a problem. Named are John Winram, the
superintendent of Fife; along with John Craig, commissioner for
Edinburgh; and Andrew Hay, commissioner for Renfrew; and Clydesdale
and Lennox. But the author of the document given in Bannatyne's
Memorials was also present, and he names himself simply as 'Mr John'. His
identity has been the subject of much debate. Some authorities are certain
that the 'Mr John' was Knox himself, but this seems problematic on several
counts. Given the gulf between Knox and Lethington and the sterility of
their past encounters it is unlikely that, taking his bodily fragility into
account, Knox would have travelled from St Andrews for such a meeting,
even allowing for Grange's offers of safe conduct. Moreover, the style of
writing is gentler than we have come to expect from the old warrior, and
his reported exchanges with Lethington are even affable. Knox never softened his reporting. The most likely candidate would have been John Row,
superintendent of Lothian, but why the partial anonymity is observed is an
unresolved puzzle.

The meeting took place in a bedroom occupied by Lethington just off
the Great Hall, on the south side of Crown Square at the heart of the
citadel of the castle. Lethington was sat in a chair by his bed, with a pet dog

on his lap, and Grange had organized chairs for everyone. The main agenda of the meeting was to get the Kirk to agree to the legality of the rebel party and to accept Mary as the rightful sovereign. The debate was conducted almost entirely between Lethington and 'Mr John'. Lethington argued that the setting-up of the King's authority was 'a fetch, or shift' to allow continuity of rule until Bothwell was gotten rid of. He then went on to confess that his support for this was 'very evil and ungodly' and that the parliament that enacted the transfer of power 'cannot be judged a lawful Parliament'.

'See ye not what the men in the Canongate [the Regent's forces] pretend? Nought else, I warrant you, but to rug and reive [steal] other men's livings, and to enrich themselves with other man's gear . . .'

Craig countered, 'Such as is spoken of them that be yonder, much worse is spoken of them that are here!'

The arguments went back and forth in more or less good humour. 'Here we began to mow [joke], and as it were every one to laugh upon another, and to raise [jest]'.

It is inconceivable that Knox would have joined in the general merriment over the fate of the nation.

Lethington concluded, 'We are joined in loyalty and amity with France, but England has been over old [for a long time] enemies.'

'Mr John' concludes, ' "My Lord, that argument appears now nothing, for we have peace and amity with England, presently, as we have with France" . . . and with this we took our leave and came our way.'

All of this seems to have been a half-hearted attempt to keep the Kirk on the side of the rebels, and Lethington may well have known what was about to be enacted at the convention in Leith. This body had agreed that whatever it enacted would be presented to an assembly on 6 March in St Andrews. This convention was about to propose action totally contrary to the reform of the Kirk and probably wished to take its decision before a full assembly met.

It decided to establish bishops and archbishops, answerable spirtually to the assembly and temporally to the King, in all the vacant sees. These bishops would supplement the work of the superintendents, but were never intended to replace them. They would have to be acceptable to the Kirk, although nominated by the lords. From now on, joked one preacher, Patrick Adamson, instead of 'My Lord Bishop' one would now say, 'My Lord's Bishop'. These new bishops, who would act alongside the existing superintendents, were nicknamed 'tulchan' bishops. A tulchan being a stuffed calf-skin placed under a cow to ensure the flow of milk.

This was bringing the Church much further under state control, and more importantly, was giving the income of the bishoprics to the lords for distribution to the Kirk. It would now receive less than it had under the agreement of the 'thirds', but the new bishops would now be paid as officials of the Crown, albeit with a tenth of their income going to support the poor. However, monastic property was to provide stipends for ministers as well as supporting students at the universities.

This was the Agreement of Leith. Knox could never have been in complete accord with this. He would have seen it as another step in the dismantling of the *Book of Discipline*. His chance to make his opinion clear came immediately, since the see of St Andrews was vacant and Regent Mar allowed Morton to nominate the rector of St. Andrews University, John Douglas, to the bishopric. Douglas had wisely agreed to allot his tithes to Morton. On 6 February he preached 'specimen doctrine' in the pulpit at St Andrews in front of his sponsor, twenty-eight ministers, two priors and John Winram, the superintendent of Fife. Unsurprisingly, two days later, the thirty-one clerics elected John Douglas bishop of St Andrews. On the 10th Knox preached in front of Morton but refused to inaugurate the bishop and declared anathema on Morton and Douglas. Winram then carried out the exhortation, after which John Spottiswood, and David Lindsay laid hands on Douglas and embraced him as the new archbishop. Morton, untroubled by the declaration of anathema, and well satisfied with affairs, left for Edinburgh.

However, he left behind a St Andrews torn apart by the divisions of the country. Only St Leonard's College backed the King's supporters, and even there a certain vacillation was seen. In St Salvator's, one William Ramsay had supported the regent, but now was in the party of the Hamiltons. The students asked for him to answer to the assembly, but when he died suddenly, they accused St Leonard's of his murder. Knox determined to answer the slander but was forestalled. John Rutherford, provost of St Salvator's, publicly alleged that Knox resented the choice of John Douglas because he had wanted the archbishopric for himself. He refuted this from the pulpit. 'I have refused a greater bishopric nor ever it was, which I might have had with the favour of greater men nor he hath his. I did, and do repine, for discharge of my conscience, that the Kirk of Scotland be not subject to that order.'

Knox had also prophesied that Edinburgh Castle should collapse and 'run like a sand-glass; that it would spew out the captain [Grange] with shame; that he would not come out not at the gate but over the walls'. Robert Hamilton, a minister in St Andrews, was to witness these very events himself during a later parley at the castle and 'was compelled to glorify God', but he remained a bitter opponent of Knox.

In Geneva, on 12 April, Theodore de Beza wrote to Knox, 'his very dear brother and fellow minister'. The letter is affectionate and congratulates the Scot for a life spent in constant struggle. It reads almost like an obituary.

Although, my Knox, we are in body separated by so great a distance of both land and sea, yet I have not the least doubt that there has always existed, and that there will exist to the last between us, that complete union of mind which is confirmed by the bond of one and the same spirit and faith . . . For the surest proofs, I infer that the Scottish churches are such, that the numerous and severe and continued attacks of Satan, the like of which I believe no nation has hitherto borne within so few years, have not succeeded in corrupting among them the purity of doctrine, or in changing the rule of strict discipline neglected by so many nations. Blessed be the Lord our God, who has gifted thee, my brother, as placed at the helm, and others as rowers and under-rowers, with such constancy and courage. It is a great gift of God, that you carried together into Scotland both pure religion and good order, the bond by which doctrine is secured . . . I would remind yourself and the other brethren that as Bishops brought forth the Papacy, so will false Bishops (the relics of Popery) shall bring in Epicurism [devotion to earthly pleasure] into the world. Let those who devise the safety of the Church avoid this pestilence, and when in process of time you have subdued that plague in Scotland, do not, I pray you, admit it again . . . Farewell, excellent man, and brother much to be esteemed.

This letter must have caused Knox to look back almost with pleasure to the days when his battle was simply against papacy, as opposed to battling with Lethington, Grange, and the entire Hamilton clan; Protestants committed to restoring a Catholic queen; as well as resisting Morton and the creeping threat of episcopacy on his own Protestant side. He wrote his doubts to his friend Sir James Douglas of Drumlanrig. 'Lying in St Andrews, half dead on 26th May,'

. . . Dead Scotland, waken! Who before would not be admonished of troubles to come! But now in the midst of troubles it seeks a wrong remedy; for it is neither England, France, nor Spain, in whom God has placed any comfort to poor Scotland, but only it rests in Himself, and only of Him must we receive it. I say that the traffic with that Babylon, the Castle of Edinburgh, shall [at] once bring Scotland into that misery that we and our posterity must mourn for a time.

By August the General Assembly met in Perth and Knox wrote, almost apologetically, with a reminder:

Albeit I have taken leave not only of you, dear Brethren, but also of the whole world and worldly affairs; yet remaining in the flesh I could not nor cannot cease to admonish you of things which I know to be most prejudicial to the Kirk of Christ Jesus within this realm. Above all things preserve the Kirk from the bondage of the Universities. [Clearly his recent experiences with the Colleges of St Andrews had had some effect.] Persuade them to rule themselves peaceably, and order their schools in Christ; but subject never the pulpit to their judgement, nor yet exempt them from your jurisdiction.

Accompanying this letter were ten articles and three questions for the assembly, putting limitations, especially financial limitations, on the Agreement of Leith.

Curiously the assembly raised no objection to the appointment of bishops, but wished to dispense with the remaining titles (abbot, prior, and so on) in the hierarchy. Knox had tacitly endorsed, with qualifications, the appointment of bishops in his submission to the assembly. The assembly replied politely, finding his exhortations both reasonable and godly. They promised to promote their furtherance but did not wish to bother him with a long letter. They clearly believed that Knox had in fact retired from public life. They were wrong.

Robert Leprevik, who was printer to the assembly, had also moved to St Andrews, and in July 1572 he published *An Answer to a Letter of a Jesuit named Tyrie* by John Knox. The letter itself had been given to Knox seven years previously, having been sent by James Tyrie to his brother David and then passed on to Knox for refutation after Rizzo's murder, and Knox had wished to give them no publicity. But the comparatively new Society of the Order of Jesus was flexing its considerable intellectual muscle, and so he now published Tyrie's letter with a detailed refutation. Tyrie claimed that without the consent of the Holy Catholic Church there could be no salvation. Knox, after sweeping aside the papists' 'rabble of ceremonies', points out that the word 'Catholic' means 'Universal – the congregation of the wicked as well as the congregation of the godly.' Tyrie infers that the Church of Rome is the Holy Church and that the Protestants have declined from it. Knox demands that Tyrie prove that the Church of Rome is holy. 'This we think shall be very hard to Master Tyrie and all the Jesuits in Europe to prove.' Tyrie calls the Kirk of Scotland 'invisible and therefore no Kirk', but Knox points out that its sacraments are totally public and shared. One by one Knox meets Tyrie's arguments: the divisions in Protestantism are no greater than those among the early Christians; the preaching ministers 'within the Realm of Scotland are oxen, ever labouring under the yoke, and that into the husbandry of the Lord', Aventinus' histories are brought out to display the errors of Rome; and finally, Knox fears not to affirm that the doctrine of the papistical Church is altogether corrupt and hopes for Tyrie's conversion. The writing had all the old vigour and the conviction never wavers, although while he was preparing it for publication he only rose from his bed once a week, 'and yet without corporal pain'. He wrote to his old friend Goodman that they would never meet again since he was too frail to endure the journey to England.

Included in the pamphlet was a letter Knox had written in 1554 to Elizabeth Bowes. This was the only one of these personal letters that Knox published, and his intention was so that 'they, whom Satan has not blinded by envy, may see and understand what a troubled conscience craves in the day of battle'. He obviously meant this to be his final publication, as he finishes,

I heartily salute and take my good-night of all the faithful in both the realms; earnestly desiring the assistance of their prayers, that without any notable slander to the Evangel of Jesus Christ I may end my battle: for as the world is weary of me, so am I of it.

Of St Andrews, the 12th July 1572.

Knox was fifty-nine years old and almost totally exhausted.

On 31 July, a truce was brokered by France and England that allowed a period of normality to return to Edinburgh. The returning citizens sent a commission to the General Assembly in Perth asking for Knox's return, since John Craig had, according to one commissioner, 'swayed over much to the sword hand. I will say no more of that man, but I pray God continue with him his Holy Spirit, and that he be not drawn aside by Lethington.' A letter making the formal request was passed to Knox.

He agreed to return with the proviso 'that he should not be desired or pressed in any way to temper his tongue, or cease to speak against the treasonable doings of the Castle of Edinburgh'. The commissioners agreed and Knox gathered what strength he had left for a last journey. He left St Andrews on 17 August, arriving in Leith on the 23rd, six days later, for a journey of twenty-five miles to the ferry at Kinghorn and the crossing of the Forth to Leith. He rested in Leith for a few more days before arriving at his final lodging. The length of time for this journey can be explained by Knox's infirmity, the unreliability of ferries across the estuary, and the difficulties for the burgh authorities in finding a suitable lodging for Knox. Much of the western end of the high street, where his manse had stood, had been destroyed in the skirmishing from the castle, but there was a very desirable vacant property beside the eastern gate, the Netherbow. It belonged to James Mossman, who had been Mary's goldsmith and had been responsible for the minting of coins. But in the recent troubles he had moved to the Castle, so, by tradition, it was into this house that Knox and his family moved. It is still known as 'John Knox's House'.

Knox was back in his old pulpit in St Giles, but his voice, which once had thundered, was now so feeble and weak that he could hardly be heard. He did confess that, in spite of his reputation as a 'thunderer', the acoustics of St Giles were so bad that he had never been heard by the entire church. It was decided that henceforth he should preach only on Sundays in the smaller Tolbooth Church, which held about a hundred. This meant that the pulpit of St Giles was now vacant, Craig being unacceptable to the congregation, having gone over to the castle faction. To this end Knox wrote to James Lawson, sub-principal of the university of Aberdeen, begging him to come with 'haste, lest you come too late'. Lawson preached in St Giles on the 14th and was liked by all, leaving Knox free to start preaching in the Tolbooth on 21 September. Henry Killigrew, a 'good and godly protestant' and Elizabeth's ambassador, reported that Knox was carried to the church – the distance is about half a mile – but preached with the same vehemence and zeal as ever, 'abhorring the fact in France'. Knox also advised Killigrew and Cecil not to trust 'them of the Castle' and bade a formal farewell to Cecil, now Lord Burghley.

The 'fact in France' had occurred on the day of Knox's arrival in Leith, when French Protestantism was dealt the severest blow it ever suffered. On the eve of the feast of St Bartholomew, 24 August, 20,000 Huguenots were butchered, along with their leader the Admiral Coligny, in the streets of Paris with the connivance of Charles IX and Catherine de Medici. The Pope greeted the news with a celebratory *Te Deum* and Philip II of Spain laughed uproariously. Knox, we are told, was almost 'exanimated' at the enormity of the slaughter, and with the other ministers in Edinburgh inveighed against the murders, calling Charles IX a traitor and murderer of his own subjects. The French ambassador, du Croc, took particular exception to Knox's accusations. Knox had bidden du Croc tell his king,

> that sentence is pronounced in Scotland against that murderer, the King of France, that God's vengeance shall never depart from him nor his house, but that his name shall remain in execration unto the posterity to come; and that none that shall come from his loins shall enjoy that kingdom in peace and quietness, unless repentance prevent God's judgement!

Unaccustomed to receiving such criticism from an ailing old cleric, du Croc complained to the council, which told him that they had no powers to 'stop the mouths of ministers', and du Croc left Scotland. The ailing old cleric could still wield a big stick.

The assembly of August 1572 was certainly aware of his opinion as they accepted the Agreement of Leith reluctantly and only on a temporary basis. They also found 'certain names, such as Archbishop, Dean, Archdean, Chancellor, Chapter . . . slanderous and offensive to the ears of many of the brethren . . . appearing to sound of papistry'. They refused to use these names.

The government of Scotland was becoming more and more ineffective as winter came on, and the death of Regent Mar on 29 October made little difference. The earl of Mar had been an ineffectual regent, the real power having lain with Morton, but his death had two singularities for the time. First, he died of natural causes, the only one of James's regents to do so, and, secondly, there was no talk of foul play. A convention was called to meet in Edinburgh on 15 November to appoint a new regent.

James Lawson was inducted as minister of St Giles by Knox who declared to the congregation the duty of a minister and the congregation's duty towards him. So Knox, according to Bannatyne,

> made the marriage, in a manner, between Mr James Lawson, then made minister, and the folk; and so prayed God, that had given them one in place

of himself, that was now unable to teach, and desired God to augment him a thousandfold above that that he had, if it were his pleasure, and so with the common blessing ended.

This was Knox's last public appearance since, enfeebled by the stroke which had most probably recurred, he now seems to have fallen sick with pneumonia. He developed a severe cough that left him so weak that he had to abandon his reading the Bible aloud. He was persuaded to summon Dr Preston, his physician, saying that 'he was unwilling to despise or neglect ordinary means, although he knew that the Lord would soon put an end to his warfare', and he asked Margaret, his wife, to take over the task of paying the servant's wages. He personally paid his servant, James Campbell, saying, 'You will never get no more of me in this life!' He then gave Campbell twenty shillings in addition as a final gift. Margaret and Richard Bannatyne were now reading to him from John 17, some of the Epistle to the Ephesians, and Isaiah 53.

Knox's political chickens were coming home to roost, as Lethington wrote a peevish letter to the kirk session of St Giles denying Knox's slanderous accusations that he was an atheist, and had declared 'There is neither heaven nor hell', and that these things were devised to 'frighten bairns'. He offered to defend himself in debate with Knox and then 'ye may use him accordingly'. The session showed Knox the letter which he gladly would have disputed had he been given time. By Friday the 14th he was found half into his hose, having tried, to the consternation of those around him, to get up from his bed. He had mistaken the day for Sunday, and wished to preach. But next day he was back in control of his mental faculties as he kept a prearranged social engagement, when John Dury and Archibald Stewart came to dinner. Knox insisted on broaching a hogshead of wine from his cellar and told Stewart to continue drinking it after his death. (A hogshead held over 50 gallons.) His confusion over the days of the week continued, however, but at Knox's request on Monday the 17th the kirk session came, probably with Lethington's letter. He made to them what under another form of Christianity could have been called a last confession, and bade them, especially Lawson, continue the good fight, 'but as I breathe with difficulty, I must here have done'. He then asked Lawson and David Lindsay privately to go to Grange at the castle and make a last attempt to bring him to the King's party, since he had previously been constant and courageous in the cause of the Lord. Otherwise, 'he shall be dragged disgracefully from his nest to punishment and hung on a gallows in the face of the sun, unless he speedily amend his life, and flee to the mercy of God. The man's soul is dear to me, and I would not have it perish if I could save it.' The two friends did try to reach Grange's conscience, but to no avail.

By now all Edinburgh knew that the author of the Scottish Reformation was dying and crowds had gathered outside his house to take their leave. When a gentlewoman, who had been admitted, started to praise him, he upbraided her. 'Tongue! Tongue! Lady, flesh of itself is over proud and needs no means to esteem the self.' The nobility, one by one, came to pay their respects, including Morton, now the regent presumptive, whom Knox questioned closely over his part in Darnley's death. Morton denied all knowledge of it but clearly failed to allay Knox's doubts. On Friday 21 November he ordered Bannatyne to have his coffin made and by the Sunday he declared that he had been in heaven and tasted of heavenly joy. On Monday the 24th 'a pious man', Robert Campbell of Kinzancleuch, asked if he was in much pain and Knox replied that he did not think it to be pain that put an end to so many distresses and heralded eternal joy. He bade Campbell take care of his wife and children. He asked Margaret to read Chapter 17 of John's Gospel, 'where I cast my first anchor' to him; this she did and he said, 'I hear, and understand far better, I praise God!'

Between seven and ten that evening he lay still, with his friends occasionally wetting his mouth with weak oil. The company said their evening prayers and Dr Preston asked him if he had heard them. He answered, 'I would to God that you and all men heard them as I have heard them; I praise God for that heavenly sound.' He then raised his hand, gave two sighs and died at about eleven o'clock.

Two days later, on 26 November 1572 Knox was buried in the churchyard of St Giles. The burial was attended by most of the nobility who were in Edinburgh for the confirmation of Morton's regency. Morton, who was a man of few words, declared, 'Here lies a man who neither flattered nor feared any flesh.'

As we might expect, Knox left a detailed will, starting with a warning to the papists, that since God has preserved him from their 'cruel enterprises', and he had been, to all intents and purposes, a dead man for two years, they were now under the undivided scrutiny of a God who knew all, and so his death might bode ill for them. To the congregation he gave assurances that he had always preached adherence to the scriptures and bade them do the same, pointing out that he had never acted for earthly gain: 'None have I corrupted, none have I defrauded, merchandise have I not made.'

The merchandise he did have to bequeath was some £1,526 (Scots) or a total worth of about £90,000 in modern terms. He gave £500 (Scots) to his brother-in-law Robert Bowes in trust for his sons Nathaniel and Eleazar aged fifteen and fourteen respectively. They were also left two silver cups, saltcellars, and spoons weighing 56 ounces, also £30 worth of his books, to be kept by Margaret until the boys' twenty-first birthdays. Both boys matriculated in the University of Cambridge eight days after Knox's death and studied at St John's College. Nathaniel died of the 'tertian ague' [probably malaria] in 1580 after achieving the degree of BA. Eleazar became vicar of Clacton Magna in the archdeaconry of Colchester on 17 May 1587, but died in 1591 and is buried in the chapel of St John's College. Neither son married and so the male line of John Knox died out nineteen years after his death.

He left £100 (Scots) to his nephew, Paul Knox, and the remainder of the estate was divided amongst Margaret and his daughters. Martha, the eldest, was seven years old and lived until she was twenty-seven, having married Alexander Fairlie and borne him three sons and a daughter. Martha, the second daughter was four or five at Knox's death, and she eventually married Zachary Pont, brother of Timothy, the distinguished cartographer. She bore Zachary at least two sons. Elizabeth married in 1594 one John Welsh, a minister in the thick of controversies over James VI's episcopal reforms. Welsh died in London in 1622, but Elizabeth returned to Scotland to die at Ayr in 1625. Margaret Knox, however, was only twenty-five and a vigorous young widow. She remarried, choosing an equally vigorous Andrew Ker of Fawdonside, the man who had held a pistol to Mary's pregnant belly during Rizzio's murder. She outlived him by fourteen years to die in 1612, aged sixty-five. As well as the portion of Knox's estate, Margaret also benefited by the petition of Regent Morton to the assembly of March 1572 for Knox's pension of that year to be paid to her. This amounted to 500 merks (Scots) (£330), and quantities of wheat, barley and oats and were granted.

Secular affairs came to a head in February 1573, when a peace treaty was signed at Perth, leaving only Grange, Lethington and others in Edinburgh Castle as the last remaining opposition to James's rule. Elizabeth sent 1,500 men to Leith, and Grange was called on to surrender at risk of his life. He refused and the artillery assaults began, blocking the wells with debris and destroying St David's tower. Grange, Pittarow, Robert Melville and William Drury were lowered by rope over the fallen masonry and asked terms of surrender. These were refused, but the soldiers of the now starving garrison ('victuals were scant enough') did surrender and on 16 June the entire garrison entered imprisonment. There were 164 men, thirty-four women and ten boys. After a summary trial the ringleaders were hanged, including James Mossman, in whose house Knox had died. Grange told David Lindsay, the minister of Leith, that he now knew 'that Mr Knox was the true servant of God, and his threatenings to be accomplished'. He also said that Knox had assured him there would be mercy for his soul. He was executed at four o'clock: 'the sun being west ... he was thrust off the ladder. As he was hanging his face was set towards the east; but within a pretty space, turned about to the west, against the sun, and so remained.' If Knox had ever uttered his prophecy of Grange 'dying in the face of the sun', it was now fulfilled and his old friend was dead.

Knox's other old adversary, Lethington, was imprisoned in Leith and on 9 July he died of poison, reportedly self-administered. Calderwood writes a grim and unpleasantly biased obituary on this Renaissance man, 'Michael Wylie':

> He lay so long unburied, that the vermin came from his corpse, creeping out under the door of the house where he was lying. This man was of a rare wit, but set upon wrong courses, which were contrived and followed out with falsehood. He could conform himself to the times, and therefore was compared by one, who was not ignorant of his courses, to the chameleon.

The March 1573 General Assembly allowed £40 to Richard Bannatyne to finish Knox's *History of the Reformation* and 'to put the said scrolls and papers in good form'.

The cemetery in which Knox was buried extended from the south side of St Giles down the steep hill to the Cowgate. This cemetery was completely destroyed in 1633 and the site levelled to allow for the building of Parliament Hall. So where Knox's bones now lie is entirely a matter for speculation. Until recently the supposed site was marked with a stone simply marked 'I.K.1572'. However the square has now been resurfaced and the stone is hidden below the tarmac. Only a square of yellow paint now marks the spot where the founder of the Kirk of Scotland was buried.

There are no plans to retrieve the stone and since the square is a car park reserved for members of the Scottish Bar, even the square of yellow paint is usually obscured by a lawyer's car.

15   Knox's Legacy

Knox's will disposed of his worldly assets with admirable thoroughness but he also left his achievements, both the reformed Church of Scotland itself and his aspirations for a democratic Scotland in the form of the *Book of Discipline*. Below his statue in the courtyard of New College, Edinburgh – also the north entrance to the temporary residence of the parliament of Scotland – is inscribed, 'Erected by Scotsmen who are mindful of the benefits conferred by John Knox on their native land.'

It has already been said that the Scottish Reformation would have taken place without John Knox, but without doubt it would have been longer in its birth pangs and may well have finally appeared in a different form. Knox was at once the Reformation's creator and spiritual leader and he was instrumental, not simply in banishing Catholicism, but in creating the new Church which took its place. This Church and its doctrines he created and refined from the *Helvetic Confession* preached by Wishart, the *Justification by Faith* of Balnaves and his own experiences in Frankfurt and Geneva. His first precept throughout all his arguments was a simple one, that the truth was the word of God as found in scripture, and that all of humanity relied on Christ's intercession for salvation, as laid out in the Gospel of St John, chapter 17, his 'anchor'.

This meant that his Church was a communion of individuals guided, but not ruled, by a minister whose principal task was teaching. Each individual, through Christ, could thus attain salvation without the intervention of a priesthood. There was no need for an elaborate hierarchy, and all prayer should be directed to God, not to a multitude of saints. The obscurantism of Latin should be replaced by the clarity of the vernacular. The church service, while adhering to a formula, should not have the rigid formality of the Mass. It was a Church of the people.

His support among the nobility came partly from their opposition to the Queen Regent and partly from a desire to hold their salvation in their own hands. The Reformation meant that all Christian power, secular or spititual, arose in Scotland, without any dogmatic qualifications from Rome. The local parishes had the power to select their own ministers. Knox also tapped the feeling of disillusion with the established Church that had spread from Europe and which the Counter-Reformation, in the shape of the Council of Trent, sitting intermittently from 1545 to 1563, was too late to correct. The riches of the Church should be directed towards support for the ministry, providing help for the incapable poor and ensuring education for all. With all education in the hands of the Church, it might seem that not very much had changed, but with the elaborate devolution of power downwards to the parishes, the Church was technically in the hands of the people. It was a delicate balance.

Knox knew his preaching had the power to command attention from no matter who heard it, but he also knew that one of his flaws was his vehemence. It was a flaw he took few pains to correct. He took no pleasure in moving Mary to tears, hardly a difficult task, but could find no way to soften his arguments. This vehemence without subtlety is often found in the autodidact, and although Knox was thoroughly educated at school and university, he came to his apostasy alone, before having his conversion confirmed by meeting Wishart. It was during his gentle employment in the Lothians, in the ten years after his ordination, and before accepting the task of Wishart's sword carrier, that he had moved away from Rome. He found no outlet for his new-found convictions until called to preach in St Andrews, when his mouth was summarily stopped. It is therefore more than likely that these years of frustration led to the vehemence complained of as much by his supporters as by his opponents.

The world had already had a taste of Knox's thought in the *Letters* of 1558, especially as far as obedience to an unjust magistrate was concerned. His return to Scotland placed him in the forefront of a civil insurrection, during which he was able to put this theory into action. At the conclusion of the rising he was able to codify his thought in the *First Book of Discipline* and the speed with which this and the *Confession of Faith* were produced makes it clear that they encapsulated already existing thought. This religious and political manifesto was his first great legacy to Scotland.

He had left a Scotland in which the *Confession of Faith* formed the basis for a reformed Church, with a structure of ministers, elders, and superintendents as laid down in the *Book of Discipline*. Existing Catholic benefice holders would keep their privileges but the benefices would die with the holders. Appointments to Church office were in the gift of the assembly, but this would pass to election by parishes as suitable candidates became available. The payment of stipends to these office-holders still depended on the collection of tithes and this, while it had been agreed in principle, was still sporadic. It was a Church wholly outside the control of the state, and given the structure of Knox's education system, that state would become increasingly theocentric.

But as Knox had feared, the appointment of bishops by the state meant that independence of control was becoming more and more vulnerable. Especially so since Regent Morton was keen to see Scottish acceptance of the English *Book of Common Prayer* with the concomitant passing of power from the assembly to the sovereign. It is highly likely that he supported the uniting of the two kingdoms, seeing the control of spiritual power as a first step. He might have had his way were it not for the return to Scotland of Andrew Melville.

Melville was a 29-year-old theologian, educated at St Andrews and Paris before going on to teach in Poitiers. He became professor of humanities in Geneva at the age of twenty-three. He returned as principal of Glasgow University, where he taught Latin and Greek, philosophy, mathematics, geography, physics, history, Hebrew, Aramaic and theology. His arrival caused such a rush of students that 'the rooms were scarce able to receive them'. Although the two men had never met Melville was a committed Knoxian, adding some even tighter strictures of his own. Regent Morton's first clumsy attempt to woo him by offering him the rich living of Govan, provided he endorsed the appointment of bishops, failed as Melville refused the offer absolutely. He was, however, taken into the councils of the assembly, whereupon, in 1576, Morton demanded that the assembly either commit themselves wholeheartedly to the Agreement of Leith or define exactly what their policy would be. The assembly, with Melville, took this opportunity to produce the *Second Book of Discipline*.

In this work the separation of Church and state is clearly defined: the state is a kingdom with the power of the sword, while the Church is a kingdom with the power of the keys (that is a God-given licence to preach and administer the sacraments) and the head of the Church is Jesus Christ and only Him.

Under the new arrangements, all office-bearers have a vocation and are elected, with the additional exercise of ordination to include the laying-on of hands by the eldership. The titles of minister, pastor, bishop and presbyter are defined, and bishops are simply pastors of a particular flock without 'superiority and lordship'.

There would be assemblies for the parish – the kirk session, composed of minister and elders; the province with representatives from the parishes; and an assembly for the nation made up of provincial representatives. There was even provision for an international assembly of all Protestant nations, but the General Assembly of the Kirk of Scotland would be the supreme arbiter in the spiritual affairs of Scotland. The *Second Book of Discipline* defined the Reformed Church with great clarity, and set Knox's beliefs in a practical form, without denying the spiritual proposals of what we must now call the *'First' Book of Discipline*. The ceremony of laying-on of hands, which had been recently used during the ordination of John Douglas as bishop of St Andrews, however, caused some vivid dissent.

The *Book* was considered by various delaying committees and ratified by the General Assembly of April 1581. This assembly also confirmed the existence of a new layer of administration, the presbytery. This was a convocation of sessions and elderships and came before the 'synods'. The synods were to be another filter overseeing the presbyteries before the ultimate authority of the General Assembly. This assembly of 1581 also set out to reduce the existing 924 kirks to 600, divided into fifty presbyteries, with a 'certain number of presbyteries' making a synod. This concentration of power in the presbyteries led to the Kirk of Scotland being known as the Presbyterian Church, as distinct from the other branches of Protestantism.

In 1584 James VI felt that total power was being withheld from him and passed the 'Black Acts'. They made the meeting of presbyteries illegal, and invested bishops with royal power and a mandate to rule over the Kirk. These Acts threw the Reformation into reverse, and in 1592 James wisely passed the Golden Act, enshrining the principles of the *Second Book of Discipline*. This left the bishops as a kind of phantom Church, waiting in the wings for a recall to the stage. Melville himself spelled out the position to James. 'There is Christ Jesus the King and His Kingdom the Kirk, whose subject James VI is, and in whose kingdom he is not a king, nor a lord, nor a head, but a member.' There are echoes here of Knox and Mary.

This 'member' of the Kirk further attempted to assert himself by proposing Five Articles to the assembly. They reintroduced the holy days of

Christmas, Easter, Whitsun, and Ascension; allowed, in case of need, baptism to be given outside a church and Communion to be taken at home by the sick; ruled that only bishops could confirm children; and, as a final nail in the *Book of Common Order*'s coffin, insisted that the congregation must kneel when they receive the sacrament. In other words, a unified kingdom must have a unified prayer book. The introduction of the Five Articles caused wide displeasure and matters came to a head when James's son, Charles I, introduced the *Scottish Book of Common Prayer*, calling the bishops in from the wings. The result of this folly was disaster and riot.

Seven months later, on 28 February 1638, the National Covenant was presented in Greyfriars Kirk, Edinburgh. This document, eventually signed by thousands, confirmed the people's loyalty to the sovereign, but declared that the various agreements by past sovereigns to uphold the Presbyterian faith must be observed, and the signatories resolved to defend the 'true Religion . . . and to labour by all means lawful to recover the purity and liberty of the Gospel'. The Covenant was endorsed throughout Scotland, barring parts of the Western Highlands and Islands, and this only really for reasons of geography. It would, however, leave these regions susceptible in later days to Catholic proselytization. The Covenanters demanded General Assemblies (they had not met for twenty years) and the removal of the bishops. Had Knox been alive, he would almost certainly have signed the Covenant. Indeed it would have been surprising if he had not had a major role in its drafting.

An assembly was held in Glasgow Cathedral in November 1638 which condemned the new prayer book, the Five Articles, and declared episcopacy unlawful. The effect of this on Charles I's Stewart brain was to provoke further folly and he raised an army to invade Scotland. The Covenanters' army was much smaller but had actual battlefield experience as mercenaries in Europe, as had its general Alexander Leslie. Thus in two campaigns – the 'Bishops' Wars' – the royal armies were swept aside and Charles had to agree to the re-establishment of the Presbyterian Kirk. By 1641 royal influence in Scotland was at a very low ebb and the country was virtually free to govern itself. The people had risen against an unjust magistrate and replaced him. Knox and Goodman's principles had been applied effectively to Mary, Queen of Scots' grandson.

But Covenanting Scots were not Charles's only worry for in 1642 the English Civil War broke out, with the King opposed by parliamentary forces. In August 1643 the General Assembly approved a treaty by which

Scotland would provide military support for parliament – paid for by England, since the Bishops' Wars had all but bankrupted Scotland – in return for English acceptance of Presbyterianism. This was the Solemn League and Covenant, and while it ensured the continuance of the Reformed Church, it also ensured that Scotland was now the very junior partner in English affairs. At the same time a party of Scottish divines joined an assembly at Westminster and produced the all-embracing Westminster Confession. Although the Scottish delegation at Westminster was heavily outnumbered, this document became the bedrock of the Church of Scotland. It consisted of larger and shorter catechisms, a directory of public worship, a form of Church government, and a confession of faith. This was much narrower in view than normal practice, and acceptance of its doctrines was ensured by the rote-learning of the catechisms. Soon most Scots could quote them fully, without understanding a single word. At the same time all formal prayers, including the Lord's Prayer and the Apostle's Creed, were banned, Bible reading during the service ceased in favour of expositional lectures and church music all but disappeared. This betrayal of Knox's ideas of debate and worship in communion was brought about by expediency, creating a coercive spiritual union with a more powerful senior partner. The Church had become authoritarian to a degree that ran counter to the precepts of the *First Book of Discipline*.

For the moment, however, the military campaign was in a state of confusion. The marquis of Montrose led a brilliant guerrilla campaign – his tactics were studied by Che Guevara – but he achieved no more than a lasting glamorous reputation. Charles tried to take refuge with the Scottish Army but was handed over to parliament in exchange for English payment for its part in the campaign, as laid down in the Solemn League and Covenant. He then found himself in the hands of Cromwell and the New Model Army and on 29 January 1649, after a trial of dubious legality, he was executed. The Scots, true to their Covenant, declared Charles II King while Cromwell famously begged the Covenanting leaders, 'I beseech you, in the bowels of Christ, think it possible you may be mistaken.'

His appeal fell on deaf ears and by 1653 Scotland's committee of estates – the last vestige of government – was suspended and the General Assembly was broken up by Cromwell's officers, to start an absence of almost forty years.

The Solemn League and Covenant had attempted to join Melville's Two Kingdoms of the Sword and the Keys with disastrous results. Apart from some still-resisting Covenanters in the West, nothing remained of Knox's Kirk. Within twelve years total victory had turned to total annihilation.

The Restoration of Charles II in 1660 lifted the burden of Puritanism, and the situation returned to more or less that pertaining before the two Covenants. Attempts to give bishops the power to appoint ministers failed after an attempt by an undisciplined privy council to impose it, and the Covenanters of the West attempted to impose Presbyterian strictures on a yet-to-be-restored parliament. Holding fast to their beliefs they held 'conventicles' in the open air, but were suppressed with total savagery. Their suppression led to their militancy increasing from a need for survival, which, naturally, led to more torture and destruction. Finally their army met the duke of Monmouth in 1679 at Bothwell Bridge and it was convincingly defeated. Monmouth, in an attempt to be merciful, sent 200 Covenanters into exile to Barbados. Their ship foundered off Orkney in a storm and they all drowned.

But the movement remained alive, when in the next year Richard Cameron caused a declaration to be made in the village of Sanquhar in the Border hills some thirty miles east of Ayr. It disowned Charles II as King. This brave act of defiance was treated with more savagery than necessary and resulted in 'Cameronian' becoming an adjective for Presbyterian anti-Stewart revolt. Political events in England provided the impetus for change and by 1688 a Protestant Dutchman, William III, sat on the throne. The Presbyterian Church was re-established by law in 1690 as it had been after the National Covenant, free from state control. The Covenanters may have been misguided in endorsing military intervention in English affairs, but their tenacity kept the ideals of Knox's reforms alive.

There was a remainder of worshippers in Scotland who supported the authority of bishops, and they formed the Episcopalian Church. With the fashion for education in England increasing, mainly by the upper classes at the great public schools, this Church took on the appearance of Anglicanism, although remaining separate from the Church of England.

In the Church of Scotland a procedure that would have gladdened Knox was introduced in 1697. All proposals coming to the assembly as 'overtures', and then being approved by the assembly, had to be passed back to the presbyteries for final approval. Only with a two-thirds majority of the presbyteries would the 'overture' become Church law. This was the Barrier Act, which, with modifications, is still in force today. It provides a brake on the absolute power of the assembly and upholds the democratic principle at the root of the Church. Ten years later, in 1707, the Act of Security became a vital part of the Act of Union negotiations and guaranteed the future independent survival of the Church. With this guarantee in place the Church reluctantly decided not to oppose the Act of Union and Britain became one country, with Anglicanism and Presbyterianism fiercely guarding their independence. Toleration Acts protected the Scottish Episcopalians, and, although they stretched this tolerance dangerously by supporting the Jacobite risings, their existence continued.

The tenacity which had maintained the Church encouraged it to strengthen its hold on the behaviour of its parishioners, and it pursued those who offended against its precepts with a vigour that would have dismayed Knox. The services were still largely devoid of music, with lectures by the ministers and the elders behaving with unnecessary severity. This rigidity stood in contrast to the Age of Enlightenment which was emerging in Scotland through people like Adam Smith and David Hume. Liberality of thought always makes religious doctrine a comfortable haven for the confused.

There had been confusions enough inside the Church with dissenting sects forming and dissolving throughout the century, but the start of the nineteenth century saw the whole society of Scotland changing as urban industrialization took root. One result of this, as we shall see later, was to put an enormous strain on poor relief, and the other concomitant was the Church's difficulty in reaching the urban poor. No one was more aware of this than Thomas Chalmers, who had filled the Tron Church in Glasgow to overflowing with a return to evangelical preaching. His appeal was to everyone, rich and poor alike, although his parishioners came mainly from the educated middle class. But at the same time an age-old problem was coming to a head. Knox's precept that ministers should be elected was being ignored widely and local landowners were using their patronage to place their own candidates in pulpits. These landowners made up the bulk of the electorate prior to the Great Reform Bill of 1832 and often they could depend on an income from tithes still unpaid to the Church. In some respects, the objections to the redistribution of wealth and influence that had been raised in 1560 were still valid. The courts made a series of judgements favouring patronage against the legality of General Assembly decisions vis-à-vis court orders, and the Church's power to create new parishes was condemned. These decisions, which were unsuccessfully challenged, dismantled the independence of the Church and placed it firmly under government control. Lethington would have cheered.

The Church's response was for the assembly to draw up the Claim of Right. The Church claimed 'as of right, that she shall freely possess and enjoy her liberties, government, discipline, rights and privileges, according to the law, especially for the defence of the spiritual liberties of her people.' When the assembly met on 18 May 1843, the Moderator, Professor David Welsh, declared that it could not be properly constituted while the Claim of Right was still being debated. Accompanied by Chalmers and 200 commissioners, as well as other delegates, he left the chamber, and these dissenters declared themselves the Free Church of Scotland. In other words, free of governmental control. This 'Disruption' as it came to be known, split the Kirk of Scotland in two. The astonished government hastily remedied the powers of patronage and the rights of the Church to create parishes, but too late.

Four years later, another movement created the United Presbyterian Church, which financed itself purely by voluntary contributions from its 518 congregations. But the energy of Chalmers drove the Free Church forward, not only in collecting money and building churches – nearly 700 at his death – but also in founding theological colleges to train new ministers: New College in Edinburgh, where Chalmers was principal and professor of divinity, and Aberdeen and Glasgow soon having equivalent establishments. At his death in 1847 the Free Church was flourishing, with nearly half the worshippers in Scotland. At first it took over the Established Church's foreign missions, before a resurgence of energy in the Established Church brought back the work, which culminated in David Livingstone's missions.

By the end of the century it seemed as if the three Churches were vying with each other in contests of piety, with a ban on almost all activities on the Sabbath. However, at the same time the rigidities of the Westminster Confession were being relaxed, as Dr Robert Lee of Greyfriars Church in Edinburgh returned the services to conform with Knox's *Book of Common Order*. Stained glass started to appear, as did organs, and congregations remained in their pews to receive Communion. In 1888 women became deaconesses, and it seemed inevitable that there should be a reunion of the three Churches.

The first move came in October 1900 when the United Presbyterians and the Free Church joined to form the United Free Church, although remnants of the Free Church, mainly in Highland parishes, clung to the

Westminster Confession and the extreme rigidity of Sabbath observance. They exist today as the Free Kirk, or, more commonly, the 'Wee Frees'.

It was now obviously only a matter of time before the Established Church joined this alliance. The movement was led by John White, of the Barony Church in Glasgow, an Established Church, and by 1914 the 'articles declaratory' had been accepted by the General Assembly. However, before the presbyteries or sessions could agree, preparatory to parliament giving its consent, war intervened. The articles declaratory were finally approved by Parliament in 1921 and enacted by the General Assembly in 1926. They stated,

1. The Church of Scotland is part of the Holy Catholic, or universal Church; worshipping one God . . .

2. The principal subordinate standard of the Church of Scotland is the Westminster Confession of faith approved by the General Assembly in 1647 . . ..

3. This Church is in historical continuity with the Church of Scotland which was reformed in 1560, whose liberties were ratified in 1592, and for whose security provision was made in the Act of Union of 1707 . . .

4. This Church, as part of the Universal Church wherein the Lord Jesus Christ has appointed a government in the hands of Church office-bearers, receives from him, its Divine King and Head, and from Him alone, the right and power, subject to no civil authority, to legislate, and to adjudicate finally, in all matters of doctrine, worship, government, and discipline within the Church . . .

5. This Church has the inherent right, free from interference by civil authority . . . to declare the sense in which it understands the Confession of Faith . . .

6. This Church acknowledges the divine appointment and authority of the civil magistrate within his own sphere . . .

7. The Church of Scotland . . . recognizes the obligation to seek and promote union with other Churches in which it finds the Word to be purely preached . . .

8. The Church has the right to interpret these Articles, and . . . to modify or add to them . . .

9. Subject to the provisions of the foregoing Articles, and the powers of amendment therein contained, the Constitution of the Church of Scotland in matters spiritual is herby anew ratified and confirmed by the Church.

This was at last, after nearly 400 years, a guarantee of complete independence, beyond anything Knox could have hoped for. The question of income was agreed, as tithes combined with the large voluntary contribution of the United Free Church. As the reliance on tithes ceased, the national Church was now totally free, with a membership of 1.3 million.

Episcopalians, Free Presbyterians, Roman Catholics, Jews, Methodists, Baptists and many other sects were tolerated. Scotland now had one self-financing Church, whose laws were codified by J.T. Cox in 1934.

The membership remained steady for a time – in 1961 it was 1,292,617 – but has now fallen to 626,665, with 1,143 minsters serving 1,280 parishes. The parishes still have power of acceptance over their ministers and will elect their own elders. These elders – who must be over twenty-one and may be of either sex – have a pastoral role to play, as well as being part of the kirk session.

In a few parishes the office of 'reader' as lay preacher still continues. The session consists of the minister and elders and operates as a board of management for the church, even occasionally having a 'deacons court' to manage purely temporal affairs. The session will elect elders to attend, with the minister, and the local presbytery (the area executive council of the Church), holding the power of veto – under the Barrier Act – over matters proposed by the General Assembly.

The presbyteries, forty-six in Scotland, appoint representatives – commissioners – to attend the General Assembly. At one time the synods, as proposed in the *Second Book of Discipline*, were an intermediary court between the presbyteries and the assembly but they were dissolved in 1992. Knox would have recognized this structure and endorsed its democratic establishment.

There have been many debates recently as to whether the Westminster Confession should be modified or even rewritten, but as one commissioner to the assembly of 1974 remarked to Andrew Herron – quoted in his *Kirk Lore* – 'the old battleship may bear the scars of many wars and be a bit dated, but we daren't scuttle her to set sail in a coracle.' It is interesting to reflect that setting sail in a coracle is probably exactly what Saints Ninian and Columba did to bring Christianity to Scotland.

It is too simplistic to say that today's Church of Scotland is the Church Knox founded, but it still adheres to his principles. These are the principles he first heard declared by George Wishart and refined by himself during his years of exile. Its doctrine is codified by the General Assembly, consisting

of commissioners from parishes and depending on ratification by the presbyteries. At every stage the parishioners can, and do, exercise control.
Knox's Church is probably the most democratic organization of its size
anywhere.

In the late sixteenth century it was the only organization with a democratic membership, and in the *First Book of Discipline* Knox intended to use
it as an administrative organ for the treatment of the poor and for the
education of all. This could never work in practice, although most people
would agree that there is a moral imperative on civilized society to take care
of the poor and indigent. Fewer people would attempt a structure for this
care and fewer still would willingly administer this structure. Knox had
stressed its importance in the *First Book of Discipline* and sought care for
'the widow and the fatherless, the aged, impotent, or lamed, who neither
may travail for their sustenation', and had suggested that individual Kirks
keep a roll of the needy in their parish to be paid a stipend according to the
'wisdom of the Kirk'. Much more would be needed before these good
intentions were carried forward into action.

Up to Knox's death the Poor Laws that existed were largely punitive,
defining those who were allowed to beg, and describing the mutilation,
banishment or death to be meted out to those who were able-bodied but
idle. He planted the seed of the idea that help might be preferable to
suppression. The first sign that this idea had taken root was in the Poor Law
Act of 20 October 1579. The genesis of this Act was probably a reaction to
Regent Morton's attempts to introduce English legislation throughout
Scotland, but it contained much of Knox's recommendations. Needless to
say, it starts with punishing 'masterful and idle beggars' by nailing their ears
to trees, committing them to the stocks, burning holes in their ears with hot
irons, or finally by executing them. The list of such at risk was long and
specific: jugglers, fortune-tellers, 'Egyptians', minstrels (not already in
service), vagabond scholars, and sailors, claiming without proof to be the
victim of shipwreck. The 'vagabond scholars' referred to were students who
begged for their fees between terms. Some were excluded from the exigen-
cies of the Act by being licensed to beg by their university.

Hospitals should be built to house the truly indigent. The indigent would
be registered on a roll and examined to establish their need. All of this
would be paid for by estimating the expense and then levying it as a tax on
the inhabitants of the parish. The administration would be in the hands of
the provost and bailies of the towns and of the judges in the countryside.

A chilling proviso in the Act concerned 'beggars' bairns'. 'If any beggars' bairns being above the age of five years and within fourteen, male or female, should be liked of by any subject of the realm of honest estate, the said person shall have the bairn . . .' The chosen children could not then leave their masters until the age of twenty-four, so that having raised the unfortunate child recompense could be had by way of some years of slave labour. There is, however, no evidence whatsoever of any application of this proviso and it seems, like ear burning and execution, to have existed merely to frighten.

As we have seen already, passing an Act was easy enough, but putting it into effect was much more difficult, and by 1597 the authority to adminis-ter the Act passed to kirk sessions under the control of the now professional session clerk. He could call on the 'heritors' for a large portion of the funding. They were property owners who had the responsibility for upkeep of the church and school in their parish. After all, the only form of what we would recognize as local government was in the hands of the kirk.

In his *The Kirk's Care of the Poor* Dr McPherson sums up

> the brave way in which, for three centuries, she [the Kirk] fulfilled her ministry. With no resources but the men of goodwill, she cared for the poor with unceasing devotion. She nursed them, fed them, clothed them, physicked them and kept them in being. When they drew their last breath she buried them.

The heritors supplied meal at lower than market prices and often made substantial quantities available free. The cessation of the American War of Independence 'liberated' large amounts of white peas destined for the Navy and these were distributed in the north-east. In 1783 the Bank of Scotland made the town council of Elgin an interest-free loan of £500 to purchase corn.

As we have seen, in 1597 the care of the poor was entrusted to the kirk session of the parish, and by 1695 heritors and sessions were formally made joint administrators, but in practice the poor were cared for by the kirk. Even in the burghs the work was happily left to the kirk. In 1651 a presbytery asked whether a minister cared for the poor and was told, 'He had a care for them at such times as were most needful.'

The weekly collections taken either in the church or throughout the parish provided the bulk of the funds, augmented in many varied ways. The 'mortifications', in other words the lending-out at interest of the funds – especially legacies from heritors – was immediately attractive. But it was tempting for session clerks or 'masters of mortifications' to invest funds to alleviate future hardship while ignoring present poverty. In 1812 one session in the north-east increased its £497 to £616 in twelve years while the parishioners went hungry. Many sessions tragically lost all their funds thanks to unwise investments or the failure of banks.

But the kirk could levy various fees to swell the poor box. Because coffins were unornamented, by the seventeenth century the church would provide a mortcloth of varying richness to cover the box and receive a fee for its use. A handbell and ringer were also supplied for a fee. With the introduction of permanent seating it became possible to rent out pews or even construct special pews whose rents were specifically dedicated to poor relief.

There were also special collections for dedicated projects, and Communion and harvest times were regarded as propitious moments for particular pleading. Often admission to the poor roll meant agreeing that one's possessions were pledged to the kirk after death. The sales of these few belongings also went to augment the contents of the poor box, but many felt that agreeing to these terms incurred an unacceptable loss of dignity. The less one has, the more precious it becomes. Collection boxes were placed strategically about the parish. Individual songs were composed and sung for deserving cases.

Churchyard trees were sold, raffles were disapproved of, but their proceeds accepted, as were discretionary awards by sheriff courts from the prosecution of illicit distilling. Often a 'stent' or tax was raised on the heritors. None of the funds so raised could be used for stipends, neither for the minister or schoolmaster, nor supporting the fabric of manses, churches or schools, although creative accountancy often led to disputes. The presbytery made rigorous annual inspections and imposed penalties where misapplications had taken place.

The original Act made provision for overall assessment and 'stenting', but by 1700 only three parishes had adopted this practice, most of Scotland preferring to make local arrangements. Knox had suggested the application of charity according to the 'wisdom of the Kirk'. The principle was general but the application was particular.

The poor came in many shapes and forms, but the Session's first duty was to its own parish poor. Then there were the travelling poor, the deaf, dumb, blind, mad and lame. The session was bound to see to the provision of food, clothing and fuel as well as providing assistance to carry on one's ordinary vocation. Help to buy a horse or a cow was available, as was help to move to another parish or even emigrate. The kirk would provide for abandoned children, but at one time carried out the bizarre and distasteful practice, when a foundling was discovered, of having all unmarried women between twelve and fifty, as well as widows, inspected by midwives for signs of lactation. Mercifully, this practice had ceased by the early nineteenth century. The kirk also provided an early form of national health service for the poor, paying for the nursing of foundlings, surgery of all forms, as well as the physician's treatments. When all of these failed the burial would be provided free, even occasionally with a provision of whisky and beer for the mourners. Paupers' houses were maintained, and repairs after the all-too-frequent fires were undertaken. Collections were made for fishermen's bereaved families, as well as support for families whose menfolk had been genuinely taken by pirates. The General Assembly allowed special collections to be made for specific capital projects, such as the building of churches in especially remote areas or the erection of almshouses, or 'bedehouses'. Remembering the arrogant independence of the Gordon lords, it is hardly surprising that in the early eighteenth century they allowed a 'popish bedehouse', complete with an altar, for the celebration of Mass on their lands. Hospitals and children's homes were being funded by the kirk. In short, all functions of what we today would expect to be provided by the ministries of health, education, employment and social services were eventually being provided by the kirk.

Direct contributions were made either to the regular poor, that is, those on the church's roll, or to those who received occasional support. Open begging in the churchyards, in most cases, was forbidden. The relief was either in kind or in money, although money distribution was unpopular since the recipients often spent it immediately on luxuries such as tobacco and drink. Distribution in kind was usually of meal or corn and went to supplement the existing feeble diet of vegetables. Even with this help, deficiency diseases of all sorts abounded and an existence was maintained that aimed to prevent death by starvation but no more.

Also times of distribution varied from annually to monthly or daily, and all depended on the contemporary prosperity of the parish. In times of famine, which were frequent, everyone suffered.

The local poor were often supplied with badges permitting them to beg inside their home parish. Less mobile indigents were often provided with 'barrows' or litters in which they might be carried to beg from door to door, but still inside their home parishes – a variety of laws attempted to define qualifications for residence.

Travelling beggars were a constant problem for the parishes. The 'gentle beggar' was a traveller who came from the upper classes but had fallen on hard times – some had 'a grand manner and no morals, [so] were a danger to the country'. But 'gentle' beggars also included former ministers and indigent schoolmasters. All parishes, however, had the problem of coping with the 'sturdy beggar' who usually demanded, sometimes with threat of violence, charity, rather than appealing for it in a more humble way. About the middle of the sixteenth century bands of 'Egyptians' had appeared, often armed with broadsword and matchlock, who with the sturdy beggars continued, despite repeated proscription, to form roving bands of robbers. Attempts to certificate the bona fide travelling poor simply led to certificates being stolen or forged and the parishes had to make difficult individual judgements. The idea of support remaining with the parishes is a direct continuation of what Knox proposed in the *First Book of Discipline*.

In 1817 the select committee on English poor laws reported on 'the admirable practice of Scotland . . . where the local management and maintenance of the poor has been best conducted'. We are told that by 1835 the problem of the sturdy beggar had more or less disappeared, thanks to increases in employment and general prosperity. In 1840 David Moneypenny stressed that voluntary contributions made with the imperatives of conscience – such as Dr Guthrie had received at the parish of St John's in Glasgow – were still more effective than the imposed assessments recommended as occasional alterations to the Poor Law. But W.P. Alison pointed out in his *Illustrations of the Operation of the Scottish System of Management of the Poor*, 'The higher ranks in Scotland do much less (and what they do, less systematically, and therefore less effectually) for the relief of poverty and sufferings resulting from it, than those of any other country of Europe.' In practical terms the old system of parochial relief was breaking down, and by the 1920s the situation had been reversed, with only four parishes rejecting assessment. This change can also be explained by the fact of the toleration by the Established Church of varying creeds and of the Disruption in 1843 within the Established Church itself. Also populations had grown faster in relation to the number of parishes.

In 1844 a special commission examined the working of the Poor Law, and its recommendations were enshrined in the Poor Law Amendment Act of 1845. The basic principles of the 1579 Act were restated, with the additional proviso of allowing assessment where it was needed, and giving overall control to a national board of supervision that devolved decision-making down to local parochial boards. Their membership varied, with elected members coming from the heritors, kirk session and directly from ratepayers. They would compile the poor roll and appoint an inspector of the poor. In certain cases poorhouses could be erected, although they had existed in Scotland, starting with Glasgow Town's Hospital in 1733. They would be inspected, as could the poor, by the inspector. The administration was passing from the kirk into the hands of the civil power.

An Unemployed Workmen's Act in 1904 was overtaken by the Liberal Government of 1911 introducing unemployment benefit for the able-bodied out-of-work, although, as Professor T.C. Smout points out in his *Century of the Scottish People*, 'The rewards of unemployment have always been designed to be more unpleasant than the reward of even the nastiest labour.'

Public assistance committees gave way to unemployed assistance boards, in turn to national assistance boards, and so on down to the present day. Application of a means test in one form or another is still resented and still applied, even to old-age pensioners' investments, but the principle of charitable help to those who cannot help themselves continues, as had been set out in the 1579 Act. Knox had categorized their need in 1560. There was no possibility that with the increases in population and the growth of towns-based industry, the parish structure as set out by Knox could be effective. But his impetus was crucial and in the seventeenth and eighteenth centuries when the kirk sessions were the most active forms of local government their activities were essential. Even into the twentieth century the long-term poor were referred to as having 'gone on the parish'.

The third great topic to be dealt in the *First Book of Discipline* was education. Up to the Reformation the educational system of Scotland was almost entirely Church-based, either directly as in the 'song' schools attached to clerical establishments or indirectly in the 'grammar' schools, where the teachers were inevitably ordained clerics. Although the poor could attend the schools free of charge there was little incentive to do so, since it meant that the child's labour became unavailable to the family. We have heard already that James IV's Act of 1496, commanding barons and freeholders to send their eight- or nine-year-old sons to school until they had perfect Latin was more often seen in the breach than in the observance. Also the entire system was designed primarily to produce an educated clergy. Before the Reformation, at least according to John Mair, it had failed to do even that.

In the *First Book of Discipline* of 1560 Knox and the other five 'Johns' had set out a far-reaching plan for universal education, which, if put into practice, would have set up an educational system beyond the dreams of the most radical minds of the twenty-first century. Control of education ultimately meant control of the minds of the people, and so, after spirituality, the subject was perhaps the most crucial. To exercise control over education has always been the ambition of totalitarian regimes and Knox's idea that it should be in the hands of the parishes was liberal in the extreme. Although the *First Book of Discipline* allowed only for choice of teachers and laid down rigid strictures on choice of syllabus Professor H.M. Knox in his *250 years of Scottish Education* states, 'nearly all the progress achieved since then has been a gradual approximation to the ideals expressed in that document'.

Knox had called for schools in all cities and chief towns to be overseen by the magistrates and with the preservation of religion as their first aim; but now the obligation was extended to every parish. The appointment of the schoolmaster, (*magister* or *dominus* in Latin, hence 'dominie' in Scots) was the task of the parish, who had already appointed and approved the minister, so that either the minister took over the work of teaching, or in larger towns, a qualified teacher would be appointed. This meant that the religious atmosphere of the parish was extended to the preaching and teaching within it and would rise upwards through the universities, eventually to influence the entire state. The subjects to be taught did not vary greatly from those Knox himself had experienced – Greek and Hebrew were included in divinity courses, perhaps reflecting Knox's own feelings of deficiency.

All children would attend the schools and would progress upwards according to their 'docility' (that is, their aptitude for further instruction). Knox fully appreciated that the numbers would decrease during this upward journey, but made certain by the application of bursaries that neither money nor rank would be a bar to higher education, indeed laying down a tariff of charges for the nobility at university.

This ensured an equality of opportunity, but also made certain that the state gained the greatest rewards possible from those of greatest 'docility'.

This is a direct echo of the strictures that the able-bodied unemployed should not be recompensed for idleness but helped to work.

Everyone who could contribute to the state should be directed to put their skills at the disposal of all. Education would be available from the age of five to the age of approximately twenty-four and, although there was no precise stipulation that religious conformity was essential, it was unlikely that teachers could be found who were not acceptable to the reformed ministry. Since the basis of the system was the parish, and the parish was the basis of the reformed Church, the educational system was still as Church-based as had been the system under the Catholic Church. The difference was that the parish could decide on the appointment of the personnel who would operate the system. It was not to be hierarchical, it was to be democratic.

The traditional Scots reverence for education of all classes dates from the *First Book of Discipline* as does the belief, now less strongly held, that anyone can achieve anything, given the opportunity of education. This is despite the fact that any recommendations costing money were never accepted by Parliament in spite of repeated attempts by the General Assembly to gain their enactment. Education Acts were passed with great regularity from 1567 onwards, always with Knox's ideas behind them, but without any firm structure for finance, which still largely fell on the heritors of the parishes. The Privy Council, in December 1616, declared, 'the King's Majesty [as] having a special care and regard that the true religion be advanced and established in all parts of the Kingdom' to which end a school should be established in every parish and a 'fit person' appointed to teach in it, 'upon the expense of the parishioners'. This would not be overseen by the presbyteries, but by the bishops. In the same act the Gaelic language was forbidden, 'as a cause of barbarity and incivility among the inhabitants of the Isles and Highlands', and the chief men of the Highlands were instructed to send their children to the Lowlands to be educated in English by the age of nine. This was designed largely to spread Presbyterianism throughout the still predominantly Catholic Highlands.

The Act for the Founding of Schools, of February 1646, passed the supervisory power back to the presbyteries. While the parishes lacked the funds to move further, in most burghs schools they were already in existence, although, as might be expected, where the burgh councils provided funds they also took greater control. This control was more often than not shared with the local presbytery, who supervised the suitability of the teacher as well as the syllabus. Parents were encouraged to send their children to the schools, and by the mid-seventeenth century local truancy acts were in force, as were acts forbidding the opening of private or 'adventure' schools and discouraging attendance at the existing private schools. Hours were long, the work unremitting and discipline severe. In 1674, in Dundee, the penalty for swearing, breaking the Sabbath or rebelling against the master was a public whipping for the first offence, a flogging for the second and expulsion for the third. Children were struck on the hand with the 'taws' – a thick leather strap split at the end into two or three branches, described as 'the national instrument of flagellation'. Although the Council of Dunbar in 1679 declared that the master who uses the rod least uses it best, the taws was still in enthusiastic use fifty years ago.

Holidays were a matter of privilege, not of right, frequently leading to revolts by the scholars of which the most extreme was at the Royal High School of Edinburgh in 1594. The school was barricaded by the pupils under arms and the town guard called out. The leader of the 'barring-out' was one William Sinclair who shot and killed Bailie John McMoran before the revolt calmed down and holidays were granted as a right. Since Sinclair's father was chancellor of Caithness he was merely admonished, although the headmaster, Hercules Rollock, was dismissed.

However lacking in the general execution of Knox's aspirations, the Act for Settling of Schools passed in 1696 caused Macaulay to state:

> By this memorable law it was, in the Scotch phase, statuted and ordained that every parish in the realm should provide a commodious schoolhouse, and should pay a moderate stipend to a school master . . . Before one generation had passed away it began to be evident that the common people of Scotland were superior in intelligence to the common people of any other country in Europe . . . This wonderful change is to be attributed, not indeed solely, but principally, to the national system of education.

The situation was indeed improving by the start of the eighteenth century. Most of Lowland parishes by then possessed a school – in Lothian only one parish lacked a school and in Fife, of sixty parishes there were fifty-seven parish schools and fifty grammar schools. The kirk session undertook to pay for poor children; 'such as are poor shall be furnished upon the common expenses'. In extreme cases there were dukes' sons and cobblers' children attending the same school and the tradition of the 'lad o'pairts' had begun. This was the poor child who could rise to the highest station through education, and the history of the seventeenth and eighteenth centuries is crowded with examples of them. The Act provided for the appointment of the schoolmaster on the advice of the minister and heritors. The master had to be examined by the presbytery and not all were found capable. The Kirkaldy presbytery, 'appointed to try Mr Andrew Walker, his qualification and 'hability' for teaching the grammar, reported that in their judgment he was unqualified'. The heritor was to supply the house and salary for the schoolmaster, but was now allowed in some cases to split the cost with his tenants. Like the Reformation, all of this would probably have happened in time without Knox, but his ideas were driving the consciences of many of the intelligentsia, if not opening the purses of the heritors.

Under the 1707 Act of Union the Education Law remained intact, as did other laws, and the Act of Security guaranteed the continuance of Presbyterian control over all teachers from University to parish school. With this in mind, and the problem of continuing Catholicism in the north-west, the Society in Scotland for Promoting Christian Knowledge (SSPCK) was founded in 1709 to drive out error, idolatry, superstition and igno-rance. But while English-speaking teachers taught Gaelic-speaking children their catechism from the Westminster Confession, by 1758 there were still 175 Highland parishes without a school.

At the parish level the schoolmaster was still poorly paid, extracting fees from pupils where he could and the teaching was largely in the three 'Rs' of reading, writing and arithmetic – Latin was extra. In most cases he was also employed as the session clerk and would receive a small salary for those considerable duties. He would also be expected to act as precentor in the church and thus to lead the singing of Psalms.

The burgh schoolmasters had wider catchment areas on which to draw and their fees could provide greater comfort. Two radical changes took place when Francis Hutcheson began to teach in English (as opposed to Scots or Latin) in Glasgow in 1729, and the SSPCK set up spinning schools, soon to be converted into sewing schools. These were mainly for girls and were designed to answer the needs of the industrial revolution.

The curriculum in general was widening with the emergence of commer-cial schools, and, thanks to public petitions, in Perth in 1761 a new school teaching the sciences, history, drawing and painting was established. To differentiate it from the other schools this establishment was named an 'academy' and others of the same type followed, mainly paid for by public subscription. By the start of the nineteenth century education had become much more general and with the huge increase of population more legislation was needed.

Total control was slipping from the Kirk as minimum and maximum salaries for a parochial schoolmaster were fixed by the Education Act of 1803 from £16.3s.4d. to £22.4s.5d. per annum; the provision of 'side' schools was established where the parish had become too large for a single school. However, the heritors were still responsible for fabric and upkeep, while the presbytery oversaw the appointment and examination of schoolmasters.

The Kirk was founding elementary schools in the rapidly swelling burghs, and setting up a permanent education committee to increase the availability of schools generally. By 1829 Roman Catholic children were admitted and throughout the 1830s government grants were made, with a committee of council overseeing education nationally. The permanent secretary to the new committee was Dr James Kay-Shuttleworth, a graduate of Edinburgh University. His committee appointed the first HM inspectors of schools, in Scotland under the management of the Church of Scotland.

The Disruption in the Church of 1843 raised an unforeseen problem in that the sole HM inspector in Scotland was from the new Free Church and so another had to be appointed, bringing greater expansion to the system. The Disruption also led to an Act in 1861 excusing schoolmasters from signing the confession of faith and gave the powers of examining them to the universities, although ministers and heritors still oversaw negligence or incompetence. The Act authorized the employment of women teachers, although they had in practice taught for some time. It marked the start of control passing from the clerical to the secular powers, as had control of the Poor Law in 1845.

When the Westminster government's department of education introduced formal standards to be achieved, with concomitant payments for performance, the impossibility of imposing one set of regulations on both countries became clear. The imposed English system took no account of the broad classless base striven for in Scotland, or of the idea of a 'general' education superseding the rigidly subject-based English model, with its grants to promote the education 'of children belonging to the classes who support themselves by manual labour'. This would never have done for Knox and it would not do for nineteenth-century Scotland. The answer was a royal commission.

It became known as the Argyll Commission and deliberated from 1864 until 1868, finding a wide variation in standards. There was large-scale elementary absenteeism in the cities, and while secondary pupils were well catered for the variations in standards of facilities and in teacher qualifications were too wide to be satisfactory. What had evolved locally was unable to cater for the size of population and to this end a board of education was proposed, culminating in the Education Act of 1872.

This divided Scotland into nearly a thousand districts, roughly equivalent to the old parishes and burghs. The management of the schools was vested in elected school boards, the elections themselves to be overseen by the heritors and ministers, with finance distributed and standards maintained by a central department of eductaion. All children between five and thirteen years would attend, with attendance guaranteed by 'attendance officers' and with the school boards having the power to waive all fees in the case of poverty.

Religious instruction would be kept separate from secular subjects and there would be no further ecclesiastical control of the syllabus. The election of the school boards was still in line with Knox's original principles, as, probably more importantly, was the provision of free education, even though it was secular, and for all, regardless of class or sex. When in 1944 an Education Act was passed in England guaranteeing free secondary education for all, it merely followed the example already active in Scotland.

The current system is based on the Education (Scotland) Act 1980 (which has been amended several times) as well as the School Boards (Scotland) Act 1988, providing a formal structure for School Boards, and the Self-governing Schools etc. (Scotland) Act 1989, which allows schools to opt out of education authority control and to be funded directly by government. Universities, teacher training, examination criteria, and so on are likewise regulated by legislation. No doubt all of this will change from time to time according to circumstances, but the basic credo exists that it is the duty of all parents to see that their children are educated and the duty of all local authorities to provide free education. Religious education is compulsory unless the children are withdrawn by parental instruction. The phrasing of the government policy documents replaces Knox's 'docility' with 'age, ability and aptitude'.

Given the massive increase in population since Knox's day and the current complexity in social structures and communications it would be surprising if his recommendations had survived intact. But much of his dream is in place. 'A school in every parish' there certainly is, with 1,280 parishes served by 2,291 primary schools, but the number of parishes has declined seriously over the years. However, even allowing for the continuing controversy over the financing of university students, the principle of free education for all is irreversibly established.

The increased specialization necessary for progress in the complex world of the twenty-first century, has made the generality of Scottish education that was so admired in the first half of the twentieth century disadvantageous, but the idea that a 'lad o' pairts' can succeed regardless of class is as strong as ever. The structure has had to change but the principles remain. These principles were laid out by Knox and his colleagues in 1560.

Knox had in the *First Book of Discipline* laid the foundations for these three structures. He had also demonstrated that, if the will was strong enough, unjust rulers might be removed. The Reformed Church had been established. Through the strength of the General Assembly popular opinion was being voiced. In all of these movements the crucial element was the elective voice of the individual, even although Knox gave no definition of the breadth of the franchise. In faith, he believed that each individual was responsible for his own salvation; in lay affairs, the voice of the individual was the driving force of the parish. In every aspect of his thought, worship in its purest scriptural form by individuals was of paramount importance. The reformed Church was a democratic Church. Knox's ideal state was democratic. John Knox was a democrat.

The ideal he gave Scotland as a legacy was of a democratic state, caring for its weakest members, with free education available to all, fiercely independent and with its own voice in Europe. Time will tell what we have done with that legacy.

Bibliography

This is intended to be a guide for readers who wish to follow the individual paths that have led to the writing of this book. The principal work to be consulted is, of course: *The Works of John Knox*, edited by D. Laing, Edinburgh, 1845

Biographies and articles relevant to Knox

Adamson, M.R., 'A Symposium on the Ordination of John Knox'; *Innes Review* vol VI(2) (Edinburgh, 1955)

de Beze, Theodore (trans. Simon Goulart), *Les Vrais Portraits des Hommes Illustres* (John of Laon, 1581)

de Beze, Theodore, *Icones* (Laon, 1580)

Book of the Old Edinburgh Club, Vols 5, 12, 14

Burns, J.H., 'John Knox and Revolution', *History Today*, Vol. 8, 1958

Carlyle, Thomas, *Portraits of John Knox* (Chapman and Hall, 1875)

Hume Brown, P., *John Knox* (London, 1895)

Lorimer, Peter, *John Knox and the Church of England* (London, 1875)

McCrie, Thomas, *John Knox* (Belfast, 1874)

Mason, Roger A., *John Knox on Rebellion* (Cambridge, 1994)

Miller, R., *John Knox and the Town Council* (Edinburgh, 1898)

Percy, Eustace, *John Knox* (Hodder & Stoughton, 1939)

Ridley, Jasper, *John Knox* (Oxford, 1968)

Shearman, P.J., 'Father Alexander McQuhirrie', *Innes Review* vol VI(1) (Edinburgh, 1955)

Stanford Reid, W., *The Trumpeter of God* (Scribner's, New York, 1974)

Stevenson, R.L., *Familiar Studies in Men and Books* (Nelson, 1924)

Other relevant biographies

Ackroyd, Peter, *The Life of Thomas More* (Vintage, 1999)

Bainton, R.H., *Here I Stand, A Life of Martin Luther* (Abingdon, 1950)

Baumgartner, Frederic. J., *Henry II* (Duke University, 1988)

Bouwsma, William J., *John Calvin* (Oxford, 1989)

Brandi, Karl, *Charles V* (Cape, London, 1939)

Brantôme, Pierre, *Vie de Dames Illustres*, Oeuvres Complet, vol. 5 (Paris, 1833)

Broadie, Alexander, *The Circle of John Mair* (Oxford, 1985)

Fraser, Antonia, *Mary, Queen of Scots* (Weidenfeld & Nicolson, London, 1969)

Hay Fleming, D., *Mary, Queen of Scots* (London, 1897)

Hudson, W.S., *John Ponet* (Chicago, 1942)

MacCulloch, Dairaid, *Thomas Cranmer* (Yale, 1996)

MacKay, A.J.G., *A Memoir of John Major* (Edinburgh, 1892)

Marshall, Rosalind, *Mary of Guise* (Collins, 1977)

Nau, Claude (ed. J. Stevenson), *History of Mary, Queen of Scots* (Edinburgh, 1883)

Rogers, Revd Charles, *The Life of George Wishart* (W. Paterson, 1876)

Russell, E., *Maitland of Lethington* (London, 1912)

Seward, Desmond, *Francis I, Prince of the Renaissance* (Constable, 1973)

Memoirs and State papers

Acts of the Parliament of Scotland, vols II & III

Bain, J. (ed.) *Calendar of State Papers* (Scotland/Mary), vols 1 & 2 (Edinburgh, 1900)

Bannatyne, Richard, *Memorials of transactions in Scotland* (Edinburgh, 1836)

Burton, J.H. (ed.), *Register of the Privy Council of Scotland*, vols I-X (Edinburgh, 1877)

Clifford, A. (ed.), *State Papers of Ralph Sadler* (Edinburgh, 1809)

Diurnal of Occurents in Scotland 1513/1575 (Bannatyne Club, Edinburgh, 1833)

Hannay, R.K. (ed.), *Extracts from the Burgh Records of Edinburgh* (Edinburgh, 1875)

Herries, Lord, *Historical Memoirs of the Reign of Mary, Queen of Scots* (Abbotsford Club, Edinburgh, 1836)

Labanoff, A. (ed.), *Lettres, instructions et memoires de Marie Stuart*, vols I,II,III (London, 1844)

Melville, Sir James of Halhill, *The memoirs of Sir James Melville of Halhill*, (Bannatyne Club, Edinburgh 1827)

Peterkin (ed.), *The Buke of the Universal Kirk* (Edinburgh, 1839)

Pitcairn, R. (ed.), *Criminal Trials in Scotland* (Edinburgh, 1833)

Pollen, J. H. (ed.), *Papal negotiations with Mary Queen of Scots* (Scottish Historical Society, 1901)

Stevenson, J. (ed.), *Selection from unpublished manuscripts illustrating the reign of Mary, Queen of Scots* (London, 1836)

Teulet, A. (ed.), *Inventaire des documents relatif à L'Histoire d'Ecosse* (Abbotsford Club, Edinburgh, 1839)

Teulet, A., *Documents relatif à l'Histoire d'Écosse* (Paris, 1851)

Histories of Scotland

Broadie, Alexander, *The Tradition of Scottish Philosophy* (Polygon, 1990)

Buchanan, George (trans. Aikman), *History of Scotland* (Edinburgh, 1827)

Burns, James, 'The Scotland of John Mair'; *Innes Review*, vol. II (Edinburgh 1951)

Cant, R.G., *The University of St Andrews* (St Andrews University Library, 1992)

Devine, T.M., *The Scottish Nation 1700–2000* (Penguin, 1999)

Harvie, C., *No Gods and Precious Few Heroes, Scotland since 1914* (Edinburgh University Press, 1981)

Lamont-Brown, Raymond, *The Life and Times of St Andrews* (John Donald, 1989)

Lindsay of Pitscottie, R., *The Chronicles of Scotland* (Edinburgh, 1814)

Lynch, Michael, *Scotland* (Pimlico, 1992)

Rait, R.S., *The Parliaments of Scotland* (Glasgow, 1924)

Slezer, J., *Theatrum Scotiae* (London, 1693)

Smout, T.C., *History of the Scottish People, 1560–1860* (London, 1969)

Smout, T.C., *A Century of the Scottish People 1830–1950* (London, 1986)

Society of Antiquaries of Scotland (vol. 3) [Proceedings of the], (ed. J. Stevenson) 1857

Scottish Historical Review, vols 1 & 27

Tytler, P.F., *History of Scotland* (Edinburgh, 1845)

Wodrow Miscellany, *Historie of the Estate of Scotland*, vol 1 (Edinburgh, 1844)

Wormald, Jenny, *Court Kirk and Community, Scotland 1470–1625* (Edinburgh, 1981)

Scottish Church History

Calderwood, David (ed. Thomson), *History of the Kirk of Scotland* (Edinburgh, 1842)

Cameron, J.K., *The First Book of Discipline* (Edinburgh, 1972)

Donaldson, Gordon, *The Scottish Reformation* (Cambridge, 1960)

Heron, Alasdair, I.C. (ed.) *The Westminster Confession in the Church today* (St Andrews Press, Edinburgh, 1982)

Herron, Andrew, *Kirk Lore* (St Andrews Press, Edinburgh, 1999)

Kernohan, Revd. R.D., *Our Church* (The Saint Andrew Press, Edinburgh, 1985)

Keith, R., *History of the affairs of Church and State in Scotland* (Edinburgh, 1734)

Kirk, J., *The Second Book of Discipline* (Edinburgh, 1980)

Knox, John (ed. Dickinson), *History of the Reformation in Scotland* (Edinburgh, 1949)

McEwen, A.R., *A History of the Church in Scotland* (Hodder and Stoughton, 1913)

McGillivray, Revd A.G. (ed.), *The Church of Scotland* (The Saint Andrew Press, Edinburgh, 1996)

Reid, J.M., *Kirk and Nation* (London, 1960)

Row, John, *History of the Kirk of Scotland*, (Edinburgh,1842)

Scottish Church History Society Records, vol. 1 (1926)

Spottiswood, J., *The History of the Church of Scotland* (Edinburgh, 1850)

Strype, J., *Ecclesiastical Memorials* (Oxford, 1822)

British and European History
Allen, J.W., *A History of Political Thought in the 16th Century* (Methuen, 1928)

Batiffol, Louis, *The Century of the Renaissance* (London, 1916)

Baudrillat, H., *Jean Bodin et son temps* (Paris, 1853)

Belfort-Bax, E., *The Rise and Fall of the Anabaptists* (London, 1903)

Bindoff, S.T., *Tudor England* (Penguin, 1969)

Black, J.B., *The Reign of Elizabeth* (Oxford, 1969)

Bodin, Jean (trans. Tooley), *Six books of the Commonwealth* (Oxford, 1955)

Bonney, Richard, *The European Dynastic States, 1494-1660* (Oxford, 1992)

Cameron, Euan, *The European Refomation,* (Oxford, 1991)

Clasen, Claus-Peter, *Anabaptism – A Social History* (Cornell, 1972)

Davies, Norman, *Europe* (Oxford, 1997)

Davie, George, *The Democratic Intellect* (EUP, 1961)

Durkan, J., *The Scots College, Paris* (*Innes Review*, 2/1951)

Encyclopaedia Britannica, 14th Edition

Feiling, Keith, *History of Britain* (Macmillan, 1950)

Fisher, H.A.L., *History of Europe* (London, 1937)

Garrett, C.H., *The Marian Exiles* (Cambridge, 1938)

Garrisson, Janine, *A History of 16th Century France* (Macmillan, 1995)

Goodman, Christopher, *How Superior Powers Ought to be Obeyed* (The English Experience, Amsterdam, 1972)

Grimm, E.J., *The Reformation Era* (New York, 1973)

Guilmartin, J.F., *Galleys and Gunpowder* (Cambridge 1974)

Jal, Augustin, *Nouveau glossaire nautique* (Editions du Centre National de la Recherche Scientifique 1989)

Kautsky, Karl, *Communism in Central Europe in the time of the Reformation* (London, 1897)

Klooster, Fred H., *Calvin's Doctrine of Predestination* (Baker Book House, 1977)

Knappen, M.M., *Tudor Puritanism* (Chicago, 1939)

MacKie, J.D., *The Earlier Tudors* (Oxford, 1978)

MacKinnon, J., *A History of Modern Liberty* (London, 1906)

McNalty, *British Medical Dictionary* (Caxton, 1961)

Major John, *A History of Greater Britain* (Scottish Historical Society, Edinburgh, 1892)

Martin, Charles, *Les Protestants Anglais refugiés a Genève* (Geneva, 1915)

Mezeray, *Extrait de l'Histoire de France*, vols 5 and 6 (Paris, 1672)

Monter, E. William, *Historical Demography in 16th Century Geneva* (Variorum, London, 1987)

Neale, J.E., *The Age of Catherine de Medici and essays in Elizabethan History* (Cape, 1970)

Oechsli, Wilhelm, *History of Switzerland* (Cambridge, 1922)

Ponet, John, *A Short Treatise of Politic Power* (The English Experience, Amsterdam, 1972)

The Poor Law

Alison, W.P., *Observations on the Management of the Poor in Scotland* (Edinburgh, 1840)

Cage, R.A., *The Scottish Poor Law 1745–1845* (Scottish Academic Press, 1981)

Graham, J.E., *The History of the Poor Law of Scotland previous to 1845* (St Andrews, 1924)

McPherson, J.M., *The Kirk's Care of the Poor,* (Aberdeen, 1941)

Mitchison, R., *The Poor Law, Essay in People and Society in Scotland* (John Donald, Edinburgh, 1988)

Mitchison, R., *The Old Poor Law in Scotland* (Edinburgh University Press, 2000)

Mitchison, R. and Cage R.A., Articles in *Past and Present*, May 1974 and November 1975

Moneypenny, D., *Proposed Alteration of the Scottish Poor Laws* (Edinburgh, 1840)

Education

Beale, J.M. (ed. D.J. Withrington), *A History of the Burgh and Parochial Schools in Fife* (Edinburgh, 1983)

Education and Training in Scotland, National Dossier 99 (Scottish Executive, 2000)

Education and Training in Scotland, Summary (Scottish Executive, February, 2000)

Grant, James, *History of the Burgh Schools of Scotland*, vols 1 & 2 (Glasgow, 1876)

Knox, H.M., *250 Years of Scottish Education* (Edinburgh, 1953)

Scotland, J., *History of Scottish Education*, 2 vols (University of London, 1969)

Index